The *Sams Teach Yourself in 24 Ho*

Sams Teach Yourself in 24 Hours books provide quick and easy a
step-by-step approach that works for you. In just 24 sessions of c
will tackle every task you need to get the results you want. Let c
authors present the most accurate information to get you reliab.

Common Tasks

At www.SourceDNA.com, we field literally hundreds of requests for help a week from both beginner and advanced Web developers alike. These are some of the most commonly asked-for tasks from these developers.

Submitting a Form to the Server

After you learn how easy it is to code Active Server Pages, you will no doubt find countless situations in which you want a form running on the client workstation to be submitted to the server ASP for processing. This can be done with the following steps. For more information on forms processing, refer to Hour 7, "Document and Form Processing with Client Scripts."

1. Write the client-side form.
2. On that form, add a <FORM> tag to the page (in the <BODY> section) that specifies the ACTION and METHOD attributes.
3. Add a Submit button to the form.
4. Write the server-side ASP referenced in the <FORM> tag's ACTION attribute.
5. Here's an example of a client form that is submitted to Test.asp when the user clicks the Submit button:

```
<BODY>
<FORM name=myForm method=post action=Test.asp>
<!-- rest of HTML that makes up form -->
<P><INPUT id=submit1 name=submit1 type=submit value=Submit></P>

</FORM>
```

Creating a Database Query

How to create a database query is definitely one of the most-asked questions from beginner-level Visual InterDev developers discovering for the first time that they can now do almost anything with their databases that they normally had to have a DBA perform. For more information on working with the Database Designer and the Query Designer, refer to Hour 15, "Using the Database Designer," and Hour 16, "Using the Query Designer."

1. Either create a Database project or add a data connection to an existing Web or Database project.
2. Open the Project Explorer and right-click on the data connection.
3. Select the Add Query menu option.
4. Name the query.
5. When the Query Designer appears, you can either graphically create your query or type the SQL into the SQL pane.

Passing Variables from One Page to Another

There are several ways to share data across multiple pages. One way is with session variables, which are discussed in Hour 12, "Using the Active Server Page Object Model." However, session variables can be overkill in a lot of situations, especially when the scope of the problem is to simply pass a value (or set of values) from one page to another page. Here are the steps and a sample code snippet to illustrate how you would do this:

1. From the first page, create a link to the second page with the following format:

```
<target page>?<variable1=value>&<variable2=value>...
```

2. On the second page, retrieve the value via the Request object's QueryString method:

```
LocalVariable = Request.QueryString("variableName")
```

3. This code snippet displays several hyperlinks that all result in the TeamInfo.asp page being loaded. As you can see, each hyperlink passes a different value to the page.

Client page

```
<BODY>
H1 align=left>NL Central Teams</H1>
<P>
<A href="TeamInfo.asp?team=Houston Astros">Houston</A><BR>
<A href="TeamInfo.asp?team=Cincinnati Reds">Cincinnati</A><BR>
<A href="TeamInfo.asp?team=Pittsburgh Pirates">Pittsburgh</A><BR>
<A href="TeamInfo.asp?team=Chicago Cubs">Chicago</A><BR>
<A href="TeamInfo.asp?team=St. Louis Cardinals">St. Louis</A><BR>
<A href="TeamInfo.asp?team=Milwaukee Brewers">Milwaukee</A><BR>
</BODY>
```

Server page (TeamInfo.asp)

```
<P align=center><FONT face="Comic Sans MS" size=6>
➥<%=Request.QueryString("team")%></FONT></P>
```

Retrieving Data with ADO

ActiveX Data Objects (ADO) provide an incredibly powerful and quick means of developing your database applications. Use the following steps to submit an SQL statement to a database and process the returned rows:

1. Use the Server CreateObject method to create an ADO Connection object.
2. Call the ADO Connection object's Open method (passing it the name of the ODBC DSN, user ID, and password) to open the connection to the database.
3. Use the Server CreateObject method to create an instance of an ADO Recordset object.
4. Call the Recordset object's Open method, passing it the SQL you want to execute and the Connection object.
5. Iterate through the returned Recordse+ object using the MoveXXX methods to retrieve your data.
6. Close both the Connection object and the Recordset object via calls to their Close methods.
7. Here's a very simple example that lists all the authors in the Pubs SQL Server 7 sample database. Note that this example assumes that you have an ODBC DSN named Pubs that references the Pubs database.

```
<%
 dim conn
 Set conn = Server.CreateObject("ADODB.Connection")
 conn.Open "DSN=Pubs", "sa", ""

 dim rs 'recordset
 dim sql 'sql statement

 set rs=Server.CreateObject("ADODB.Recordset")
 sql = "select * from authors"
 rs.Open sql, conn
%>
<H1>Listing of all Authors</H1><BR>
<%
 do while not rs.EOF
  Response.Write("<p>" & rs("au_fname") & " " &
  ➥s("au_lname") & "</p>")
  Response.Write vbcrlf
  rs.MoveNext
 loop

 rs.Close
 conn.Close
%>
```

SAMS

Tom Archer

SAMS
Teach Yourself
Visual InterDev™ 6
in 24 Hours

SAMS

A Division of Macmillan Computer Publishing
201 West 103rd St., Indianapolis, Indiana, 46290 USA

Sams Teach Yourself Visual InterDev™ 6 in 24 Hours

Copyright © 2000 by Sams Publishing

International Standard Book Number: 0-672-31642-0

Library of Congress Catalog Card Number: 99-60356

Printed in the United States of America

First Printing: September 1999

02   01   00   4   3

Trademarks

Warning and Disclaimer

ASSOCIATE PUBLISHER
Bradley L. Jones

ACQUISITIONS EDITOR
Chris Webb

DEVELOPMENT EDITOR
Matt Purcell

MANAGING EDITOR
Jodi Jensen

PROJECT EDITOR
Dana Rhodes Lesh

COPY EDITORS
Rhonda Tinch-Mize
Bart Reed
Amanda Nases

INDEXER
Johnna VanHoose

PROOFREADERS
Megan Wade
Betsy Smith
Amanda Nases

TECHNICAL EDITOR
Ken Cox

MEDIA DEVELOPER
Todd Pfeffer

TEAM COORDINATOR
Meggo Barthlow

INTERIOR DESIGNER
Gary Adair

COVER DESIGNER
Aren Howell

COPY WRITER
Eric Borgert

LAYOUT TECHNICIAN
Liz Johnston

Overview

Contents

About the Author

TOM ARCHER is a consultant specializing in distributed, event-driven, Windows NT–based solutions. He is also an accomplished Webmaster and maintains the popular Visual C++/Visual Basic Web site, CodeGuru (`www.CodeGuru.com`). In addition to that site, Tom has spun off an additional Web site (`www.SourceDNA.com`) that is dedicated to the emerging DNA technologies such as MTS, MSMQ, and ASP, as well as Web-based development technologies such as DHTML, design-time controls (DTCs), XML, and Enterprise JavaBeans.

Dedication

This book is dedicated to my very best friend/supportive fiancée, Krista! You've been so supportive throughout this process, and I can't thank you enough. This book definitely would never have been completed without you. In addition, a very special, warm thank-you to my very good friend Maria. You really took a load off me with Peter and Chris, and I also can't thank you enough. I swear one day I'm going to get you both up to speed on the CodeGuru and SourceDNA stuff. Then you'll see firsthand why it is I never get a chance to sleep!

Acknowledgments

I would like to start by thanking my acquisitions editor, Chris Webb. Without his constant support and open-mindedness, I never would have even received the opportunity to write the book you are now holding. I certainly hope that the fruits of our labor justify his belief in me. I would also like to personally thank the editors (Matt Purcell and Dana Lesh) who realized early on that I am no writer. What I am is a good programmer who writes. There's a big difference between the two. Luckily for me, I had great editors who recognized this and very patiently helped me to turn my gibberish into something that I hope will help other developers as they face the same challenges I did when I started with Visual InterDev. Thanks also to Ken Cox (my tech editor), who understood that a lot of this book was written between the hours of midnight and 6 a.m. Thanks for not busting my chops too badly on some of that code that never should have escaped my box!

I also don't want to forget the efforts of the great guys at www.DynamicDrive.com and www.ASPToolbox.com. I learned many cool tricks from both of these sites, and they were kind enough to donate not only their code, but also their time to this project. Neither the DHTML or the ASP chapters would have been nearly as good without their help. While on that subject, I also want to recognize Rick Leinecker for his contribution of the ImageObject library. For those who are interested in this incredibly flexible, lightweight imaging toolkit, it can be found at www.InfiniteVision.net.

I want to thank my fellow coders (Rick, Steve Woods, and Chris Maunder) at SourceDNA (www.SourceDNA.com). Thank you so much, guys, for covering for me while I finished up this book. I guess I'm on the hook now for the next 50 or so articles!

Last, but certainly not least, I want to thank you, the reader, for taking a chance on this book. I certainly hope that this book helps you in some small way avoid many of the pitfalls and problems that I encountered while learning how to use this wonderful development tool. For those of you who are interested, I will continue to enhance and add the same types of demo applications that can be found on this book's CD-ROM on our SourceDNA Web site. As always, if you have any questions related to this book or to DNA/Internet development in general, please drop by and leave us an email. We'd love to hear from you!

Tell Us What You Think!

As the reader of this book, *you* are our most important critic and commentator. We value your opinion and want to know what we're doing right, what we could do better, what areas you'd like to see us publish in, and any other words of wisdom you're willing to pass our way.

As an associate publisher for Sams Publishing, I welcome your comments. You can fax, email, or write me directly to let me know what you did or didn't like about this book— as well as what we can do to make our books stronger.

Please note that I cannot help you with technical problems related to the topic of this book, and that due to the high volume of mail I receive, I might not be able to reply to every message.

When you write, please be sure to include this book's title and author, as well as your name and phone or fax number. I will carefully review your comments and share them with the author and editors who worked on the book.

Fax: (317)581-4770
Email: adv_prog@mcp.com
Mail: Bradley L. Jones
          Associate Publisher
          Sams Publishing
          201 West 103rd Street
          Indianapolis, IN 46290 USA

Introduction

As the tag line on the cover indicates, you picked up this book because you "only have time for the answers." However, it would be prudent to take just a few moments to read through this introduction. That way, you can better acquaint yourself with the target audience and the overall layout and design of the book in order to make absolutely sure that this book is for you.

Like any other book, this has a target audience, and I want to make sure that you realize exactly what this book is intended to do and what you can get out of it.

Who Should Read This Book?

This book is targeted at the developer who is new to Visual InterDev 6 and wants to learn it from the ground up. I make two assumptions here: The first is that you are at least a beginning-level developer and understand some of the basic concepts of software development, such as variables and debugging. The second assumption is that, although you aren't an expert with Web-based development, you are at least comfortable with basic Web terms such as *hyperlink*, *HTML*, and *Web server*. Aside from that, I'm going on the assumption that you have little-to-no Visual InterDev experience.

Please be cognizant of one very important fact: Visual InterDev is not a standalone tool for writing Web applications. Instead, it is a tool that can be used to integrate many other very rich, complex technologies that are used to create professional Web sites. As an example, this book has an hour (Hour 9) dedicated to using Dynamic HTML (DHTML) within a Visual InterDev project. DHTML is an Internet Explorer (IE) feature that allows for the creation of dynamic content on the client's browser even after the Web page has been downloaded. However, it would take a complete book to fully teach something as powerful and robust as DHTML. Therefore, when you see that an hour is dedicated to the teaching of a particular technology (such as DHTML), realize that the hour is used to introduce the feature and to illustrate how to use it with Visual InterDev. In other words, the focal point of this book is always Visual InterDev. If after discovering a new topic of interest, you want to learn more, you will need to purchase a book that is dedicated specifically to that technology.

What You'll Learn in the Next 24 Hours

After the indicated target audience, I had two main goals as I wrote this book. First, I wanted to design the book so that a logical progression of learning can be achieved as you work your way from the first hour to the twenty-fourth hour. To that extent, the first hours deal exclusively with creating your first HTML-based Web pages and adding features such as hyperlinks, tables, and multimedia. After you've mastered creating basic HTML pages, you then learn how to write client script so that your pages actually do something. You then learn about the exciting possibilities achieved with DHTML, scriptlets, and Active Server Pages (ASPs). After you've mastered the concepts of scripting both the client and server side of your Web application, you move into the area of database development in Part III, "Creating Database-Driven Web Sites." In this part, I've tried to cover all the newest and most productive ways to write database applications using ADO, data-bound design-time controls (DTCs), and the new Data Environment (DE). Finally, the book finishes with a part that is devoted to the tasks of securing your Web site, deploying or copying your Web site into production, and then maintaining your Web site when it's in production. The book's appendixes contain the answers to the quiz and exercise questions and instructions for installing and configuring SQL Server.

The second goal I had for this book was to have "real content" throughout. I absolutely cannot stand purchasing a book and finding it to be made of mostly "fluff." Too many books today fill the first three or four chapters with text that can best be described as nothing more than marketing material. You can recognize these books very quickly because as you flip through them in the bookstore, you can see that you don't do any actual coding until well into the book. To that end, as I said, I have tried to create real content in every chapter. That's why this book has you creating your first Web page in the very first hour and continues that theme throughout.

What You Need

In terms of the operating system needed to develop the examples in this book, you will need to run Microsoft Windows 95/98 or Windows NT on the development workstation. You will also need to install Visual InterDev 6 and a relational database that ships with an ODBC driver or OLE DB provider. One thing to note is that most of the database examples are done using the sample databases that ship with SQL Server 7 (Pubs and Northwind). For more information on the different versions of SQL Server available (including a version that runs on Windows 95), refer to Appendix B, "Installing and Configuring SQL Server."

Now let's talk about the Web server. You can run a Web server directly on your development workstation, or you can designate another workstation on your network as the Web server. In either case, that workstation needs to be running the Microsoft Personal Web Server (PWS) if you are using Windows 95/98 or Windows NT Workstation or Microsoft Internet Information Server (IIS) if you are running Windows NT. Both of these products are available as part of the Windows NT Option Pack, which can be downloaded from the Microsoft site.

As always with Microsoft products, I strongly recommend being up-to-date with all the latest service packs.

Downloading the Examples

The examples presented throughout the book are located on the CD-ROM, along with an installation utility to make it easier to find just what you're looking for.

For some reason, although many developers have no problem telling their managers that bugs in software are just a fact of life, these same developers find it incomprehensible that the software found in a book can be anything less than perfect. Although the editors of this book have done a tremendous job in testing the examples, unfortunately, as with any other software project, bugs do in fact exist in everyone's code. Therefore, I would strongly recommend always checking the MCP Web site at `ftp://www.mcp.com/product_support` for the latest versions of the source code.

Contacting the Author

One of my primary motivating factors in writing books and contributing my personal time to newsgroups and developer Web sites is that I enjoy helping my fellow developers. To that extent and also as my way of saying "Thank you" for purchasing this book, please don't hesitate to contact me with any questions regarding this book or DNA/Web development in general. I can be reached at a Web site that I've created specifically for Web developers like yourself at `www.SourceDNA.com`.

Conventions Used in This Book

This book uses different typefaces to differentiate between code and regular English and to help you identify important concepts.

Text that you type and text that should appear on your screen is presented in a `mono-spaced` type:

```
It will look like this to mimic the way text looks on your screen.
```

Line numbers are used to reference the lines of the code during explanation of the script. Do not type any line numbers that appear at the beginning of lines in listings! Type

```
Output:<BR>
```

instead of

```
1: Output:<BR>
```

Placeholders for variables and expressions appear in *`monospace italic`*. You should replace the placeholder with the specific value it represents.

The arrow ➥ at the beginning of a line of code means that a single line of code is too long to fit on the printed page. Continue typing all characters after the ➥ as though they were part of the preceding line.

A Note presents interesting pieces of information related to the surrounding discussion.

A Tip offers advice or teaches an easier way to do something.

A Caution advises you about potential problems and helps you steer clear of disaster.

PART I

Designing Web Sites

Hour

HOUR 1

Creating Your First Web Page with Visual InterDev

Welcome to the world of Internet development using Visual InterDev 6! In this first hour, you will jump right into learning the Visual InterDev development environment and creating your first Web page. Although this Web page will be very simple, the things learned in this hour will be used over and over again when creating *any* Web page regardless of the complexity or size of the page.

The highlights of this hour include

- How to create a Visual InterDev project
- How to find out what files get created (and where) when you create a new project
- How to add an HTML page to your solution
- How to add an Active Server page to your solution
- How to test your first Web page

Creating a Visual InterDev Project

The very first thing you will learn is how to create a Visual InterDev project. Start by opening the Visual InterDev application. As you can see in Figure 1.1, the Visual InterDev Integrated Development Environment (IDE) shows quite a bit of information about a given project using a tabbed metaphor and several different windows.

The Visual InterDev 6 development environment.

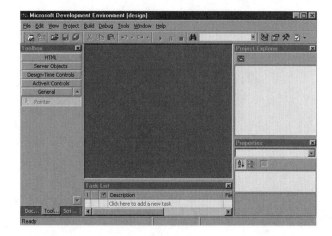

In time, you will certainly begin to learn what each of these windows is used for. However, without any content to actually view yet, this part of the hour will stay focused on the task at hand: creating a new project. After a project has been created, you will see what these different windows are used for.

Using the Web Project Wizard

The first project you will create is a Web-based address book application. This serves as a good teaching example because it not only involves database I/O, but also a good amount of scripting. This application won't be fully implemented until you get to the hours on server-side scripting and database development, but it does give us a good starting point for your first project.

The first step to creating a Web site using Visual InterDev is creating a project. The steps needed to create a new Visual InterDev project depend on whether you are currently running the Visual InterDev application. If you aren't, then start the application. By default, the first thing you will see is the New Project dialog. If you are already in Visual InterDev, choose File, New Project from the main menu.

Instead of the more common File Open dialog you are probably accustomed to, the New Project dialog is a tabbed dialog that enables you to create new projects and open existing projects from the same dialog (see Figure 1.2).

FIGURE 1.2

The New Project dialog box.

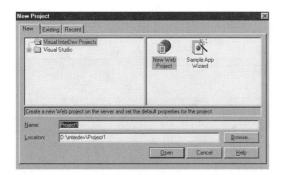

At this point, make sure that the New Web Project icon is selected on the New tab. Enter AddrBook in the Name edit control. Notice that the Location edit control is updated to include the fully qualified name of your project as you type. After typing in the project name, click the Open button.

You now see the Web Project Wizard shown in Figure 1.3. The Web Project Wizard is a series of dialogs that will allow you to finish specifying the initial settings for your new project.

FIGURE 1.3

The Web Project Wizard - Step 1: Specifying a Web server and mode.

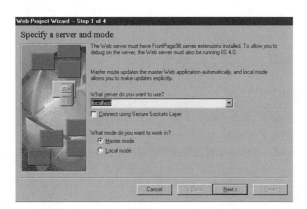

Below the question What Server Do You Want to Use?, you need to specify the name of an active Web server. If you are currently developing on a machine that is also the Web server, you can specify the value localhost. Note that you don't specify the http or `https` prefix. The next option you should take note of is the option for Secure Sockets Layer (SSL). SSL is a security protocol from Netscape that is used to encrypt and decrypt HTTP traffic being sent to and from a Web server. For now, leave this option unchecked. Finally, you need to select the mode in which you want to work. Basically, Local mode means that you want to work in an isolated environment such that any changes you make to your project are not replicated on the Web server. For this project, select the Master Mode option and click the Next button, which will bring you to the dialog shown in Figure 1.4.

FIGURE 1.4

Web Project Wizard - Step 2: Specifying a Web.

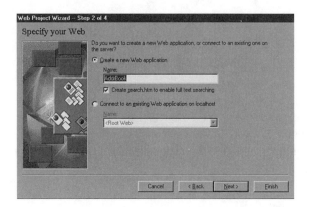

Step 2 enables you to specify whether the project you are creating is for a brand new Web application or if it is to be added to an existing application. Notice that the wizard defaults to a new application and gives it the same name as the project. For now, leave this value as it is. This dialog also gives you the option of specifying whether you want the search.htm file created for you automatically. This file enables the user of your Web application to perform text searches on all pages defined within the application. Leave this option checked at this time.

The next two steps of the Web Project Wizard deal with selecting a layout and theme for your application. Because these topics will be covered in Hour 3, "Creating Professional Sites with Themes and Style Sheets," skip over them (they will default to No Layout and No Theme) by clicking the Finish button at this point.

After you have clicked the Finish button, Visual InterDev will go about the process of creating the new files for your project. When this process is finished, Visual InterDev should look very similar to what you see in Figure 1.5.

FIGURE 1.5

The Visual InterDev 6 development environment after creating the AddrBook project.

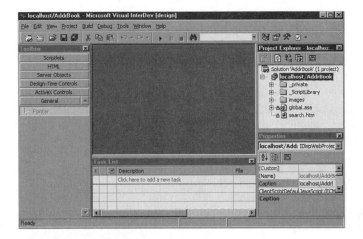

Examining the Client Files

Now that Visual InterDev has created the files for your new project, take a peek at what exactly was created on your behalf. It is very important to realize that two distinct sets of files have been created: one local set (residing on the client) and one set that resides on the server. The reason for this is simple. Having a local copy of the files enables you to work "offline" in an isolated environment without touching the server files until you have tested your code and are ready to move your work into production.

Because you specified a location on the New Project dialog, you already know what directory the local files are in, but what files were created and what function do they serve? To answer the first part of that question, open a copy of Explorer and browse to the location in which you want to create the project. Figure 1.6 shows my local copy of the AddrBook project using Explorer (after selecting File, Save All).

FIGURE 1.6

Viewing the local copy of a project's files using Explorer.

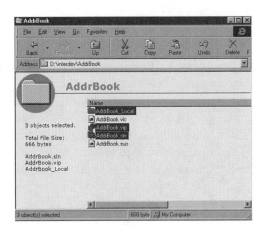

In Figure 1.6, I've highlighted three files/folders. The first is the AddrBook.vip file. This file is the Visual InterDev project file that you just created.

The second file is the AddrBook.sln file, which is a Visual InterDev solution file. A solution is a grouping of one or more projects that make up a Web application. A solution simply enables you to group a set of logically related projects into one entity so that you can manage the development on them together.

Solutions and Workspaces

If you have used other Microsoft Visual Studio products such as Visual C++, you are familiar with the term *workspace*. In that case, you can think of a *solution* as serving the exact same purpose. Microsoft has simply changed the name, so it has more of a marketing flair.

Along with those two files, you will also see a folder named AddrBook_Local. This folder is always created with the format of *xxx*_Local where *xxx* is the project name and contains all the scripts, HTML pages, images, and so on, associated with the project.

Both the solution file (.SLN) and project file (.VIP) are ASCII text files and contain information such as the projects contained within a given solution, the Web server being used, and the different UUIDs for the solution and its project(s). However, as tempting as it might seem, I would recommend manually changing these files only if you are absolutely sure that you know what you are doing.

Using Explorer, double-click the AddrBook_Local folder. You can see my version in Figure 1.7. The global.asa file will be covered in more detail in Hour 12, "Developing with the Scripting Object Model." For now, realize that its purpose is to contain server-side script for initialization and termination of a session or application. On the Web Project wizard, you were presented with a choice of whether you wanted a search page. The search.htm file is created if you selected that option. This is a great addition to Visual InterDev because it gives your Web site a complete text-based search engine without any work on your part! The other folders that can be found in AddrBook_Local— such as _ScriptLibrary and Images—are used to hold the different elements of your application. Those files will be covered later on as you start to make use of them.

FIGURE 1.7

The AddrBook_Local files structure.

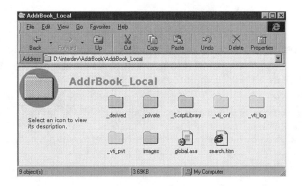

Examining the Server Files

Now that you've seen the local files, where do the files on the Web Server get placed? Actually, it's very easy to know exactly where these files will be created for any Visual InterDev project that you create. If you are using Microsoft Internet Information Server (IIS) or Microsoft Personal Web Server (PWS), a folder with the same name as the project will be created in the folder defined as the root directory for the Web Server. For example, when I installed IIS 4 on my box, I specified that I wanted my WWW root to be d:\inetpub\wwwroot. Therefore, in my situation, Visual InterDev created the new files for this project in d:\InetPub\Wwwroot\AddrBook on my Web server PC. If you take a look at my server files in Figure 1.8, you will see a very similar file structure to that of the local file structure.

FIGURE 1.8

The project file structure on the Web server.

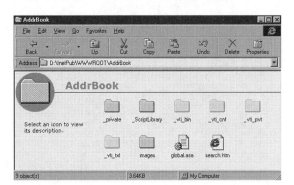

> **Virtual Root Directory**
>
> The AddrBook folder on your Web server is sometimes referred to as the *virtual root directory*. This is nothing more than a directory that contains all the files for a given project. The benefit of this directory is that your users can access your project through a Uniform Resource Locator (URL) just like they would any Web page on the World Wide Web (WWW). As an example, if you create a default.htm file for this project, anyone using a browser would be able to type `http://Web server/AddrBook` and they would automatically see the contents specified by your default.htm file. You will see this in the next section.

But hold on! If you already have a valid set of files (including HTML) on the server machine, doesn't it mean that you can have someone view your work across the Internet now? The answer is yes. If you are familiar with such programming environments as Visual C++ or Visual Basic, you are also accustomed to having to build an application first before you can actually run it. Then, of course, you need to distribute it to the server where everyone else can execute it. However, with a completely interpretive environment such as HTML and ASP pages, after the files are on the host, you're set. Therefore, if you launch your browser and type in `http://Web server/AddrBook/search.htm`, you will see results similar to those shown in Figure 1.9. You are only part way through the first hour, and you've already created your very first Web page!

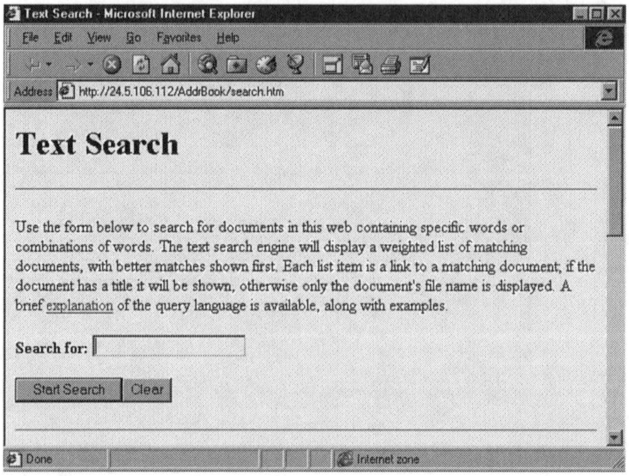

FIGURE 1.9

The Web Project Wizard–generated search page.

Exploring the Visual InterDev Interface for a Project

Now that you've created a Visual InterDev project, the next thing you will need to start exploring is the Visual InterDev User Interface.

The Title Bar

When you look at Visual InterDev after creating a new project, the first thing you might notice is that the title bar of the Visual InterDev application has changed to include the fully qualified name of your solution. This qualified name is in the format *Web server/ solution name* and is based on the values you entered when you created the solution/ project. Because I used the value localhost as my Web server and AddrBook as the name of the solution, my title bar now reads localhost/AddrBook.

The Project Explorer

Like the structure of a Web site, the Project Explorer displays the solution's files in a hierarchical manner. The files listed include all the HTML pages, Active Server Pages (ASP), images, applets, and so on that have been defined for each project.

This window is called the Project Explorer because it does in fact, support all the same Explorer-like functions you're accustomed to seeing such as drag and drop, creating new folders for organization, renaming items, and context menus. At this point, click around on the different folders to get a feel for what the different folders contain and what functions are supported for each of the different item types. One thing to keep in mind is that, like most 32-bit Windows applications, if you wonder what you can do with a particular element, simply right-click to display a context menu that will list all the options specific to that element.

If you look at the second element in the Project Explorer, you'll see the entry *Web server*/AddrBook. This entry represents your project's virtual root (as discussed earlier) and is the starting point for your application. If a solution contains multiple projects, each of those projects will have its own virtual root listed under the fully qualified solution name.

For some reason, when you create a Visual InterDev project, each folder in the Project Explorer is preceded with a +. Normally, this indicates a tree view item that can be expanded. However, you will find that when you do click on a number of these, the plus sign will simply disappear. Therefore, if you do this, don't despair. As a colleague of mine is fond of saying, "There's always one more bug." Even in Microsoft products.

At the top of the Project Explorer, you will see a toolbar containing one to five buttons, depending on the element that is currently selected. If the solution name is selected, the only toolbar button will be one that enables you to display the properties of that solution. If, however, any other item is selected, you will see the following buttons:

- Open—This button is used to open a file such as an HTML page or ASP for editing.

- Refresh Project View—Clicking this button will refresh the Project Explorer to reflect any external changes to the project's files.

- Synchronize Files—This option enables you to synchronize the local files with those on the server and vice versa. This is most useful in situations in which you're working offline and want to update the server or if your local copy of the files is out of synch with the server.

- Copy Web Server—You will see the full benefits of this in Hour 24, "Maintaining Your Web Site." However, for now it's sufficient to know that this option is used to either copy a project to another Web server or to duplicate a project on the same Web server using a different project name.

- Properties—This option is used to display an object's property page. Depending on the object type, this page typically shows things such as the local filename for the object, the server filename for the object, and other file-level information. If you have installed a version control system such as Visual SourceSafe, the property page will show information related to that as well.

Another thing to notice here is the icon to the left of each item in the Project Explorer. A small, pencil-shaped icon indicates that you have a local read/write version of the file. A small lock means that you have a local copy of the file, but it is read-only.

Because you do have a valid project at this time, invoke the context menu for the search.htm file. Among the myriad options, you will see four options for opening the search.htm file: Open, Open With, Get Latest Version, and Get Working Copy.

- Open—This option is used to open the file for editing. If the local file is read-only, Visual InterDev displays a message asking whether you want to retrieve the current version of the file from the server or open the file in read-only mode.

- Open With—This option enables you to open the file using another application that supports the type of file being opened. In the event the local file is read-only, Visual InterDev displays the same options that appear when you choose the Open option on a read-only file.

- Get Latest Version—This option is used to synchronize a local copy of a file with the copy on the Web server. For example, say you know that a more recent version of a file or group of files exists on the Web server. Selecting the desired file(s), and then choosing the Get Latest Version can be more efficient than synchronizing the entire project or solution.

- Get Working Copy—This option explicitly tells Visual InterDev that you want to retrieve a read/write version of the file from the Web server.

The Properties Window

Another window to take a look at is the Properties window. By default, this window is located directly below the Project Explorer. The Properties window is used to display design-time settings for the element currently selected in the Project Explorer. That element's name can be seen in a combo box at the top of the Properties window.

The Properties window also has a toolbar that contains three buttons which are used to more easily view the selected element's properties:

- Alphabetic—This option enables you to order the properties by the property name. This might not seem like much when you're looking at an element with 3 properties, but believe me, when you start working with elements with 20 or 30 properties, you will definitely see the value of having this option.

- Categorized—As opposed to the Alphabetic listing that shows all properties at the same level, this option enables you to categorize the properties. For example, say you're looking at the properties for an element that has ten Appearance properties and ten Misc. properties. Using the Alphabetic button, you would see all these properties mixed because they would be listed in alphabetic order without regard to their logical meaning. However, with the categorized setting, each of these ten properties would be listed under the heading of its category.

- Property Pages—This button functions the same as clicking the Properties toolbar button on the Project Explorer.

The Standard Toolbar Load/Save UI Button

Another incredibly nice feature of the Visual InterDev UI is the last combo box on the right side of the Standard toolbar. If you drop down through the options available, you will see that you can completely change the look-and-feel of Visual InterDev, depending on your particular taste or background. For example, Visual C++ developers might like to change this option to DevStudio because it more closely resembles the Visual Studio UI. Visual Basic programmers, on the other hand, might want to change the view to Visual Basic look-and-feel. To return to the original setting, simply select the Design entry.

You'll also notice that you can type into the edit control part of the combo box. This enables you to open the Windows and toolbars you want, size them to your needs, and then save this view with a name that is meaningful to you. That way, regardless of the project being worked on, you will always have a UI that you are comfortable with.

Adding Pages to Your Project

Now that you've created your first Visual InterDev project and seen it run across the WWW, it's time to see just how incredibly easy it is to design and create new pages for your project. You will start out by creating a simple page that will serve as a main menu of sorts. Then you'll add a link from that page to an ASP that will contain a table of names and phone numbers.

Adding an HTML Page

If a user attempts to surf to a page on your Web server, he can explicitly type in the full URL, or he can type in just the Web server name and the virtual directory if you have created a file named default.htm. Therefore, the first page you will create will be the default page for your project.

With Visual InterDev being touted as such a highly regarded Web application development environment, you would expect creating HTML pages to be a breeze. Well, as you're about to see, that would be a good assumption to make. Creating an HTML page is as simple as right-clicking the project root and selecting the Add, HTML Page menu option. Doing so at this point should result in the Add Item dialog shown in Figure 1.10. Simply verify that the HTML Page item is selected on the New tab, type default in the Name edit control and click Open. After you click Open, Visual InterDev will create the source code for your default.htm file. Notice, by the way, that you do not have to specify the extension for an HTML page because it will default to htm.

FIGURE 1.10
The Add Item dialog.

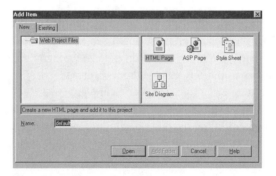

Most Web servers, including Microsoft Internet Information Server and Microsoft Personal Web Server, use default.htm as the default document name for a Web application. Therefore, if you want to use a different file-name (such as default.html), you will need to configure your Web server accordingly.

1

When completed, Visual InterDev will automatically open the new file. Notice how the file has three tabs running horizontally along the bottom: Design, Source, and Quick View. These views are an example of how much forethought Microsoft put into the design of Visual InterDev.

The Design view enables you to visually edit your page by doing such things as dragging and dropping elements onto the page or by selecting text and changing its font, pitch, and other attributes. The great thing about the Design View is that it enables you to construct an HTML page without knowing any HTML. Although I would certainly recommend learning at least a small amount of HTML to anyone developing a Web application, the Design view does at least allow you to perform the basic routines of adding texts and links in a manner much faster than manually typing in HTML code.

The Source view enables you to view the HTML source code for a given page. This can come in very handy when you want to manually type your HTML into a page. An example of when you would want to do that is in the incorporation of CGI scripts for such tasks as adding page counters to your Web site so that you can track how many people are visiting your site each day. A number of free counters are available on the Internet where the provider of this service simply tells you the HTML you need to place in your page in order to call their CGI script. The CGI script is then responsible for keeping track of how many hits your Web page has for a given period of time.

The last view is the Quick view, and it enables you to view the page as though you were looking at it with a browser. The benefit of this view is that you don't have to continually switch over to another application in order to test your page.

At this point, click the Design tab, and then click into the client area of the default.htm file. Now type in the text Main Menu. After you've typed that in, highlight the entry and—using the HTML toolbar—change the font from the default of Times New Roman to Comic Sans MS. You can change the size of the font by simply selecting a new size from the combo box located on the same toolbar. At this point, change the font size for your new text to a value of 6. Finally, center the text by selecting the Center button from the same toolbar.

If you are having trouble locating these buttons, there might be one of two different reasons why. The first is that the toolbar might not be visible. The HTML toolbar includes two large combo boxes that make it easy to spot: one for the style of the text (Normal, Heading 1, and so on) and another for the font to be used. If you do not see a toolbar with these combo boxes on it, right-click the Visual InterDev menu bar and click the HTML menu option. This will cause the HTML toolbar to become visible. If the HTML toolbar is present, but you just can't locate the buttons, you can see the name of a toolbar button by holding the mouse over the button for about 3 seconds. Doing this over each button is a good way to find out what each button is responsible for.

Now that you've entered a title for this page, move the caret to the end of the line and press the Enter key twice to move down a couple of lines in the editor. When there, click the Align Left toolbar button, change the font size to 3, and type the words Address Book (remember to save your work often). Now, to make these words a hyperlink to another page, simply select the entire line of text and click Link on the HTML toolbar. (It is the last button on the far right side and resembles a linked chain.) Figure 1.11 shows the Hyperlink dialog that will appear.

FIGURE 1.11

Hyperlinks can be added to a page with a single mouse click.

In the URL edit control, simply type in the name of the page that will be responsible for displaying the Address Book information. For now, that will be http://Web server/ AddrBook/AddrBook.asp. At this point, just for grins, you might want to click the Source tab to see how much Visual InterDev has done for you based on nothing more than a couple of mouse clicks. Another thing that you should take note of is how much the Visual InterDev changes when you switch between the different views in the editor. This is because Visual InterDev is smart enough to only enable the options that are applicable for a given view. Thankfully, Microsoft realizes that there's nothing more irritating than a system that enables you to click a menu option or toolbar button only to let you know that the selected option is an invalid choice.

Adding an Active Server Page

Now that you have a default page created for your project, create one more page before
testing it with a browser. In this section, you'll create a very simple ASP.

You really won't be doing much with your first ASP here, but because this first hour is about
creating a Web page, I did want to show you how easy it is to add an ASP to a project.

Active Server Pages are a combination of HTML and scripting code. As the name suggests,
Active Server Pages reside on the server and provide an ability to display active, or dynamic,
content. A great example of an ASP is the Microsoft Web site. When you browse around the
Microsoft Web site you'll notice that many times you are viewing an ASP. That is because
Microsoft makes extensive use of the Active Server Page's capability to dynamically create
content for the user depending on such dynamic factors as the date and the user's profile.

The issues of server-side scripting and ASP are so important to Internet development that
several hours in this book are dedicated to those topics. For now, however, you will create a very simple ASP with some static "dummy" data to test your Address Book project.

To create a new ASP, right-click the project root in the Project Explorer and select Add,
Active Server Page. This results in the Add Item dialog being displayed and the ASP
Page item being selected by default. Simply type AddrBook.asp into the Name edit
control and click the Open button.

Just as you did in the last section, after clicking the Design view tab, click the Align Center
toolbar button and select the Comic Sans MS font and a font size of 6. Then type in the
words Address Book. After that, press Enter twice. At this point, you would normally have
to make a decision regarding how the data will be retrieved. However, because accessing
data from a database won't be covered until later on, you'll just create a table and manually
type in some static text data so that the page shows something useful when displayed.

To add a table to a page, simply click Table, Insert Table from the Visual InterDev main
menu. Visual InterDev will then display the Insert Table dialog shown in Figure 1.12.

As you can see, this dialog enables you to specify many different options for the new
table. At this point, just accept the defaults and click the OK button.

You should now see a small 3×3 table. Change the font size to 3 and in the top row, type
the following column headings: Name, Email Address, and Company. When finished,
highlight the first row of information and click the Bold button on the HTML toolbar.

FIGURE 1.12
The Insert Table dialog makes it a breeze to add a table to any Web page.

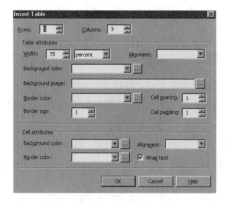

After you have finished with the column headings, type the following data into the two rows:

| Tom Archer | tarcher@codeguru.com | Infinite Vision Technologies |
| Krista Crawley | kristalinksi@yahoo.com | Data General |

If the data doesn't fit nicely into the different cells, you might need to resize the table. This can be accomplished by clicking the border of the table, and then positioning your mouse cursor so that the cursor becomes the two-headed sizing cursor. At this point, size the table and columns so that each cell's data fits onto a single line.

Viewing Active Server Pages

If you attempt to view an Active Server Page from the Quick View in Visual InterDev, you will receive a warning that Visual InterDev cannot process server-side scripts or server-based controls. This is because those scripts and controls must run on the server and not on the local machine. However, you can still view the results of the HTML because that part of the ASP is meant to be executed on the client side. If you do want to view the page and have its script run, you can select View, View in Browser.

Testing the Sample Web Application

At this point, you're ready to test your page. Simply type `http://Web server/AddrBook` into the Address or URL field in your browser or in the Windows Start, Run dialog. The results should be similar to what you see in Figures 1.13 and 1.14.

FIGURE 1.13

Your Visual InterDev–generated Web page.

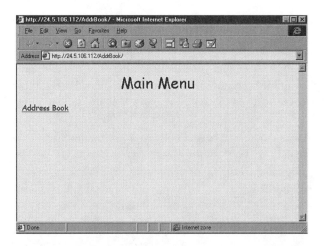

FIGURE 1.14

Your Visual InterDev–generated Active Server Page.

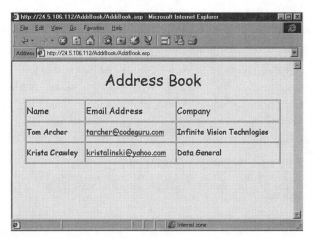

Notice how the email addresses show up as hyperlinks and when clicked on, automatically display your default email program with the "To Field" initialized. If you go back to Visual InterDev and click the Source view for the AddrBook.asp file, you'll see that Visual InterDev was smart enough to realize that the values you typed into the second column of the table were actually email addresses. Therefore, Visual InterDev automatically created the HTML necessary to display the addresses as hyperlinks and to start your email program when they're clicked. Yet another example of the time and energy saved by the Visual InterDev visual editor.

Summary

This hour introduces you to the world of Internet development via the Visual InterDev tool. You learned about some of the slick features of the IDE and created a brand new Web application from scratch. From there, you moved on and learned about some of the unique characteristics of the IDE that make Visual InterDev a very robust and flexible development environment. You finished up the hour by taking what the Web Project wizard gave you and adding a new HTML page with a link to an Active Server Page that you also created. If you're starting to get excited about the possibilities that lay ahead, you have only touched the tip of the iceberg regarding the incredible things you can do with Visual InterDev.

Q&A

Q Using Quick View, how difficult is it to customize Visual InterDev so that it uses a different browser than Microsoft's Internet Explorer (IE)?

A Actually, you can't use the Quick View feature with Netscape. However, you can specify that you want to view your pages from within the Netscape browser. To do so, simply select View, Browse With from the Visual InterDev main menu. You will then be presented with the Browse With dialog, which will allow you to select the browser of your choice. Now, when you want to view your page in Netscape, just open that file and select the View, View in Browser menu option.

Q How proficient at programming—in languages such as Visual C++ or Visual Basic—do I have to be in order to create a great Web site for my own small company?

A You can create a fully functional commercial Web site using the Visual InterDev WYSIWYG editor without knowing any other programming languages besides a very small amount of HTML. As you will see later, many companies and individuals have made ActiveX controls and CGI scripts freely available that carry out the majority of tasks that a commercial Web site needs to perform (for example, page counters, site registration, logging in/out of a system, shopping carts, and so on).

Workshop

The Workshop is designed to help you anticipate possible questions, review what you've learned, and begin thinking ahead to put your knowledge into practice. The answers to the quiz and exercises are in Appendix A, "Answers."

Quiz

1. What is the difference between a Visual InterDev solution and a Visual InterDev project?

2. Why are two sets of files created when you create a Visual InterDev project?

3. Where do the files for a Visual InterDev project get created on the server?

4. What is the Project Explorer used for?

5. What is the difference between a pencil icon and a lock icon when shown next to an element in the Project Explorer?

6. What is a virtual root directory and what is it used for?

7. What is the filename of the Web page that you must create in order to allow a user to browse to a project by specifying just `http://Web server/project name`?

8. How do you create a hyperlink on a Web page in Visual InterDev?

9. What is an Active Server Page?

10. When viewing an Active Server Page in Quick View, why will Visual InterDev not run any of its embedded server-side scripts?

Exercises

1. Try adding a new link to the default.htm file to point to an existing Web page such as `http://www.microsoft.com`.

2. Try adding more rows and columns to the table in the AddrBook.asp Active Server Page.

HOUR 2

Enhancing Your Web Pages

In the previous hour, you learned how easy it is to use Visual InterDev to create a simple Web page. In addition to creating the page, you added static text and a hyperlink that allowed the user to jump to another page. That was a great start. However, in order to maximize your site's attractiveness for your users, you need to go beyond simple static text. Therefore, in this hour, you will learn how to add the HTML elements to your pages that will dramatically increase the usability of your Web pages.

The highlights of this hour include

- How to set styles
- How to define links to other pages
- How to define bookmarks to a page
- How to partition your content with dividers
- How to add graphics to a page
- How to define a background image
- How to share HTML across several pages
- How to add video clips to a page
- How to define background sound for a page

Using Styles to Format Your Web Pages

With regards to Web pages and HTML, a style is used to define the appearance of the various text elements in a given document. No page is going to look very good if the entire text of the page is presented with the same style. Therefore, styles are used to visually differentiate between elements such as headings, footers, image captions, and body text. That way, users can easily scan through the page and find what they are looking for. You can apply a style to an entire document, a paragraph, or even a single word or grouping of words.

Why Use Styles on a Web Page?

As a Web administrator of the popular developer Web site www.CodeGuru.com, one of my responsibilities is ensuring that the content we provide is presented in a manner that is both pleasing to the eye and useful. For an illustration of this, take a look at Figure 2.1. This is a portion of an unformatted article that details a C++ class I wrote for accessing ODBC data sources in a dynamic fashion. As you can see, this formatting has several problems. First, the lack of styles makes it almost impossible for the user to browse around the document in search of specific information. Additionally, reading through long documents of this type can be very tiring on the eyes and generally results in the user not having very nice things to say about your site.

FIGURE 2.1

An unformatted Web page.

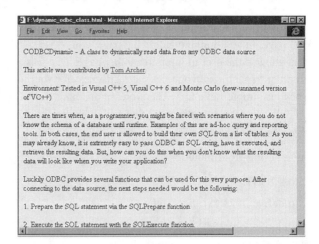

Now take a look at the formatted version of this same Web page in Figure 2.2. As you can see, the addition of a few very simple styles has dramatically improved this Web page. Notice how the heading stands out from the rest of the document, how the underlining of key text helps to draw attention to it, and how a bulleted list makes a series of directions much easier to follow. The consistent use of styles across all the pages in a Web site creates a much more uniform and professional look and feel to the site.

Figure 2.2

A formatted Web page using HTML styles.

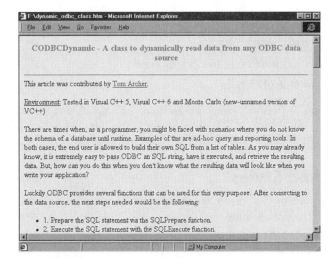

Creating Web Page Captions

As you might guess, applying something as central to the design of a good Web page as styles is incredibly easy with Visual InterDev. As impressive as the Web page in Figure 2.2 is, you are about to see just how quickly you can do the exact same thing on any of your pages using the Visual InterDev WYSIWYG editor.

At this point, use what you've learned in the first hour and create a new Visual InterDev project named AddingElements. After you have finished creating the project, add an HTML page to it called Styles.

At the top of the page, enter the caption Things I've Learned About Visual InterDev. When you've done that, select the text and click the Center Text button on the HTML toolbar. Next, experiment with the Foreground Color and Background Color buttons from the same toolbar to achieve the desired result. You might want to also change the font because this text will serve as the caption to the page.

Creating Bulleted Lists

Bulleted lists can be used to display an ordered set of instructions. For example, in documenting a software module, you might list the steps required to install the system. You could also use a bulleted list to enumerate a list of items such as the ingredients needed in a recipe or the items that make up a bill of lading.

At this point, click the Align Left button and type in the following list of items:

- How to create a Web page
- How to create an Active Server Page
- How to apply Styles

When you've finished, select the lines you've entered, and then click the Bulleted List button on the HTML toolbar. Notice that to the right of the button is a Numbered List button you can also use, depending on whether the list should be numbered.

Heading Styles

Headings are used to organize the content on a given page. Visual InterDev provides six different levels of heading styles that can be accessed via the Styles combo box on the HTML toolbar. As with the other styles you've already seen, all you need to do is simply enter the text into your page, select the text, and select the desired style. Visual InterDev automatically inserts the appropriate HTML.

As a test, type in the same items you used for the preceding bulleted list. As you will see later, those bullets will serve as hyperlinks to these sections. Now, using the Styles combo box on the HTML toolbar, select a line of text and experiment with some of the different styles such as Formatting, Address, and Normal. When you're finished experimenting, set the style for all three lines of text to Heading 2. That way, your final result will match the sample project on the companion CD-ROM. Figure 2.3 shows what your current project should now look like.

FIGURE 2.3

Text with Normal and Heading 2 styles specified.

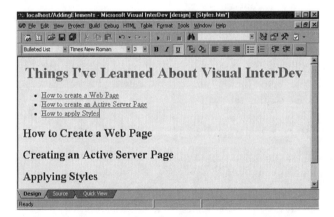

At this point, it's obvious that the main benefit of styles is that they enable you to define the visual characteristics for text at the touch of a button. Additionally, as previously mentioned, another huge benefit derived from styles is the ability to have a consistent look and feel across your pages. In Hour 3, "Creating Professional Sites with Themes and Style Sheets," you will take what you've learned here to the next level and see how to modify the existing Visual InterDev styles and how to define new styles to meet your own unique requirements.

One of the nicest features regarding the Visual InterDev development environment is that it can be a great teaching tool. Say that you are interested in learning more about the HTML language and want to know what specific HTML tag was used in order to create a given effect. To do this, simply click the appropriate toolbar button and then switch over to the Source tab to view the resulting HTML. This will enable you to easily see the HTML tags that were created on your behalf. For most of the basic page formatting that you'll need, the editor does a great job of isolating you from the HTML, but it's always nice to know that you can get to the source code this quickly and easily.

Defining Links to Other Pages

You will recall from the first hour that adding a hyperlink to a page is as simple as selecting the text and choosing the HTML, Links menu option (or pressing Ctrl+L) whereupon Visual InterDev presents you with a dialog that is used to define the hyperlink. However, what wasn't covered then and does bear mentioning is that you can use the Hyperlink dialog to define a link to *any* Internet resource. As you can see in Figure 2.4, the Hyperlink dialog includes a combo box that allows you to specify the hyperlink type. This list includes the obvious Internet server types such as http, ftp, and mailto, but also included in this list are such types as gopher, telnet, and news. After you've selected a type, the dialog automatically prepends the hyperlink URL with the appropriate Internet server type prefix.

FIGURE 2.4

You can create a URL that links to any Internet resource via the Hyperlink dialog.

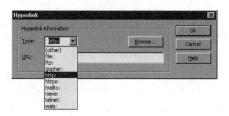

Specifying Pages in Other Visual InterDev Projects

In addition to having the ability to explicitly enter a URL, you can also use the Hyperlink dialog to browse to any defined page on any of your Visual InterDev projects. To do this, simply click the Browse button. The ensuing Create URL dialog (shown in Figure 2.5) displays all the Visual InterDev projects defined within the current Visual InterDev solution. You can then browse through these projects to find the exact resource you want to link to.

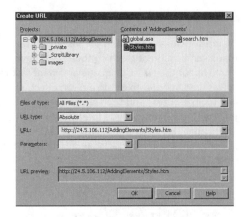

Advanced Hyperlink Properties

If you right-click the text for your hyperlink, you'll see a menu option entitled Properties. Click that option to display the <A> Properties dialog shown in Figure 2.6. This dialog enables you to set some of the more advanced hyperlink attributes.

In the previous hour, when you tested your link from the HTML page to the Active Server Page, you saw that browser displaced the HTML page with the Active Server Page. In most cases, this is fine. However, say that within a given page on your Web site, you have a hyperlink to another site. For example, some companies will give away free services such as Web page counters if you place a hyperlink to their page somewhere on each page you want to keep track of. Although you might not mind your users being able to jump to another company's page, you certainly don't want them to lose their place on your site or forget about your site entirely.

To prevent this, simply select the Frame Target of blank. Now when the user clicks the hyperlink, the associated page will be shown in its own instance of the browser. That way, even if the user does go to the other page and browses around a bit, when she closes the browser, your page will still be up, yelling, "Hey! Don't forget me!"

Another thing to notice on <A> Properties dialog is the Popup Text edit control. Any text entered here will be displayed as a ToolTip when the user pauses the cursor over the hyperlink. Most users are accustomed to moving the cursor over a hyperlink and finding out the target URL from the status bar. However, the status bar only shows the actual URL, which can sometimes be somewhat less than descriptive. By using the pop-up text, you can be as descriptive as you please in informing the user the results of clicking the hyperlink.

The last thing you'll look at regarding hyperlinks is the Bookmark. Bookmarks are pretty much the same things as hyperlinks except that they are used to navigate within a given document. Say that you have a very large document that contains many sections. You might display a table of contents at the top of the page with hyperlinks to specific sections of the page. In fact, using that very example, you will update the Styles.htm page to include bookmarks.

At this point, perform the following tasks for your current project.

- Open the Styles.htm page in Source view.
- Select the Heading 2 text, Creating a Web Page.
- To define it as a bookmark, choose the HTML, Bookmark menu option (or press Ctrl+Shift+L).
- When the Bookmark dialog appears, type the name of the bookmark. In the demo, I named the bookmark after the text, HowToCreateAWebPage. Press Enter to create the bookmark.
- Now select the text that will serve as the hyperlink. In this case, that will be the How to Create a Web Page text near the top of the page in the Normal style.
- Choose the HTML, Link menu option.
- Type a pound sign (#) followed by the name of the bookmark that you want to jump to when this hyperlink is clicked. Therefore, the entry should be #HowToCreateAWebPage.

That's it! Obviously, you would normally only create bookmarks with a much greater volume of information than you've entered here, but now that you know how to create bookmarks, you can provide your users with the ability to easily navigate around a Web page of any size.

At this point, go ahead and create the bookmarks for the remaining items on the page. When finished, your Web page should resemble Figure 2.7.

FIGURE 2.7
Bookmarks can make navigating within a page much easier.

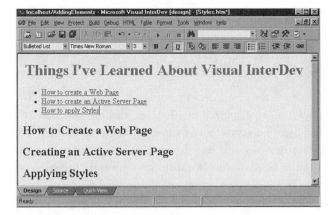

Partitioning Web Page Content with Dividers

The next thing to look at is dividers. Dividers help to visually segment a Web page. As you saw back in Figure 2.2, CodeGuru uses dividers to separate the article heading from the article text. That way, the user can quickly see the name of an article and proceed from there.

To add a divider after the Style page's caption, simply complete the following in the Styles.htm page:

- Open the Styles.htm page in Design view.
- Move the cursor to the end of the caption and press Enter.
- Now, select the HTML, Div menu option.
- When the Insert Div dialog appears, press OK.
- To change the divider's color, simply select the divider and change its background color property in the Properties window.
- Use the mouse to size the divider horizontally to your specifications.

Adding Graphics to Your Web Page

Now that you've seen how to present the text of your Web pages in a visually attractive manner, take a look at what it takes to incorporate graphics into your Web page content as well.

Absolutely nothing conveys a message better than the combination of an articulate article and a supporting graphic or set of graphics. In this hurry-up world where everyone seems to have more and more to do in less time, people are just not inclined to read through page after page of documentation to find out what your product does. This is why companies spend massive amounts of money in the development of catchy phrases and visuals that will grab the prospective client's attention. The hope is that if they can grab your attention with a nice visual, the product will do the rest.

Images are inserted into a page by selecting the location in the page where you want the image to appear and then choosing the HTML, Image menu option. Doing so will invoke the Insert Image dialog shown in Figure 2.8.

FIGURE 2.8

The Insert Image dialog is used to define a graphic for a Web page.

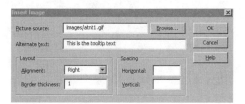

The Insert Image dialog gives you a considerable amount of control over how graphics are displayed on your Web page. Here's a quick rundown of the options available to you and how they can be used to produce the desired effect:

- Picture Source—Simply type in the fully qualified path to the desired image or click the Browse button to search for the image within the current Visual InterDev project. To see how to make images available for selection, refer to the following sidebar, Adding Images to a Visual InterDev Project.

- Alternate Text—This text will display xe "Alternate Text, images"in a ToolTip when the user pauses the cursor over the image.

- Alignment— Quite a few options here give you the ability to position the image anywhere you need. For example, if you want the image to appear on the right side of the Web page with the text on the left and below the image, you would specify the alignment to be Right. Figure 2.9 shows an example of how that would appear. Take a few minutes to experiment with the different alignment choices so that you can decide for yourself which option is best for your needs.

- Border Thickness—This option is really helpful if there is no delimiting characteristic between your image and the background of the Web page. For example, if you have an image of a blue sky on a white or light blue background, it might be difficult to visually discern the boundaries of the image. Therefore, in a case like this, setting a border might be helpful.

FIGURE 2.9
*Using the Alignment
keyword on the* IMG
HTML *tag, you can
define how the image
should be aligned in
relation to the text on
the page.*

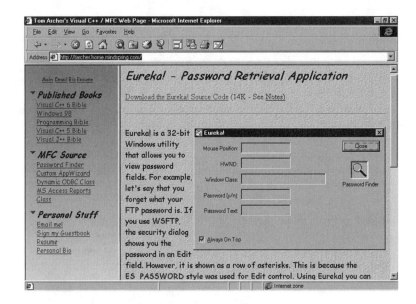

- Horizontal and Vertical Spacing—These options allow you to define how many pixels you want to have between the image and the surrounding text. This helps to avoid an unprofessional, cluttered look of having the image butted up against the text.

Adding Images to a Visual InterDev Project

In order to insert an image into a Web page, that image needs to be defined as belonging to the project. This can be done very easily via the Project Explorer. Simply right-click the Images folder of the project and select the Add, Add Item option from the context menu. When the Add Item dialog appears, click the Existing tab to indicate that you are searching for an already existing file (as opposed to creating one). Then select the Images entry in the Files of Type combo box. At this point, you can browse to the location of your image and select it. When you click the Open button, the image will then be copied into the project's Images directory, and you will see that reflected in the Project Explorer.

Setting a Background

This is an area that many beginner-level Web developers overlook. Choosing a pleasing, unobtrusive background can greatly ease your user's eyestrain caused by the default Web page combination of black text on a bed of stark white. Additionally, the defining of a background gives you the opportunity to subliminally sell your product or company without taking up any valuable screen real estate. Almost all professionally developed Web pages have a background.

To set the background of a Web page, open the Web page in Design view. Then, open the Properties window. Locate the `.backgroundImage` style and select it. This will cause a button with an ellipsis to appear on the right side. Clicking this button will result in the display of the Create URL dialog. Just as you did when inserting an image into a Web page, simply select the desired image and click the Open button. One common technique in Web development is to create a "water mark" image that has your company's name or product drawn in a very elegant, yet light color. Remember the idea here is to display an image that keeps your name in front of the user while at the same time, not interfering with the content on the page itself.

Sharing HTML Across Several Pages

As you learned earlier, one of the most important aspects of any professionally designed and developed Web site is consistency. If, while the user navigates through your Web site, each Web page is presented with a completely different look and feel, the user isn't going to have as good a feeling about your company as you would probably like him to.

As an example, if you want to have the company logo and copyright information in the footer of each page, it should appear exactly the same on each and every page. Although this might seem obvious, it does cause some problems. First, it takes a lot of work to copy and paste the HTML to each Web page on even a small Web site. Second, what if after setting the HTML for a dozen or so pages, you decide to make a change to some of the footer information? Now you have to go back and make that change to every single page. Luckily, there's a much easier way to handle scenarios in which you have a snippet of HTML that you want to use across multiple pages—and that is with the use of the `include` directive.

The `include` directive is used to insert the content of another file into the current file. The syntax for this directive is as follows:

```
<!-- #include virtual | file = "filename"-->
```

In order to insert this directive into a page, simply open the page in Source view and manually insert the directive that indicates where you want the included file's contents to be displayed.

The usage of the virtual and file keywords with the `include` directive is mutually exclusive.

Using the Virtual Keyword with the `include` Directive

The use of the virtual keyword dictates that the following filename will be relative to the specified virtual directory. Therefore, the following line of code would insert the footer.inc found in the virtual directory MyProject.

```
<!--#include virtual = "/MyProject/footer.inc"-->
```

Using the File Keyword with the `include` Directive

If you specify the file keyword, the specified filename indicates a relative path from the current Web page. For example, say that your current page is located in a directory on your Web server named invoicing. You might then have the include file for footer information in a directory named global because it is to be included by all your pages. The `include` directive would look as follows:

```
<!-- #include file "global/footer.inc"-->
```

You can also use the notation `../` syntax in order to specify the root directory. That way, using the previous example, if you were to move your entire Web site's directory structure, your code would still work. Here's an example. Say that you have four directories (order_entry, invoicing, receiving, and global), located in the virtual root of a given project. If the order-entry, invoicing, and receiving pages had an `include` directive like the following, the code would break if all the directories were moved into a parent directory called distribution.

```
<!-- #include file "global/footer.inc"-->
```

However, if the `include` directive used the `../` syntax, the code would still work because the global directory would not be assumed to be in the current directory. Instead, the global directory would be relative to the current directory. Therefore, the following example lends itself to being more maintainable in terms of being more resilient.

```
<!-- #include file "../global/footer.inc"-->
```

Note that the use of the extension .inc for filenames specified in the `include` directive is simply a convention that many Web developers choose to follow. Your choice of file extension should be based on the type of file being included and whether you want that information to be viewable from the client workstation. For example, if you are including code that's not sensitive, you can store it in an .inc file and include it where necessary. However, if the code you are including should not be viewed on the client workstation, name the file with an .asp extension. That way, if the user attempts to view the file, the code will execute because of the .asp extension.

This `include` directive is called a *server-side include* because the inclusion of the other file occurs on the server side. As an example, say that you place an `include` directive in your HTML to include the code that will display the information for your page's header. If the user uses his browser's "view source" function, he would not see the `include` directive. Rather, he would see the actual code that was inserted from the file that specified by the `include` directive. In the hours on scripting, I'll get into why this is sometimes a very undesirable thing and how scriptlets solve that problem.

2

Adding Multimedia to Your Page

A few years ago, adding multimedia such as full motion video and sound to a Web site was almost a giveaway that you were "playing around" and not a serious company. This is no longer the case as more and more companies are realizing the importance of multimedia in attracting prospective clients to their Web sites. Therefore, in this section you'll see how easy it is to incorporate multimedia into your Web pages.

Video

Inserting a video clip such as an AVI file is almost the same as inserting an image in that they both are done via the `IMG` tag. The difference is that although the SRC keyword is specified for an image, the DYNSRC keyword needs to be indicated for a video clip.

At this point, open the Project Explorer and right-click the project's root. When the Project Explorer context menu is displayed, select the New Folder menu option and type in `Video`. This creates a new folder beneath the root directory into which you can place all the video files for this project.

Next, locate an AVI file on your local system to copy into the project. If you are using either Microsoft Internet Information Server (IIS) or Microsoft Personal Web Server (PWS), free sample video clips will have been provided for you in the InetPub directory. Right-click on the newly created Video folder. When the Video folder's context menu appears, select Add, Add Item. From the Add Item dialog, select the Existing tab, change the Files of Type combo box to Video Files and browse to the desired video clip. When you've located the video you want to play from your Web page, click the Open button to insert it into the project's Video folder.

You can also use Windows Explorer when adding files to a Visual InterDev project. To do this, simply open an Explorer window and browse to the desired file. Then drag the file and drop it onto the Visual InterDev Project Explorer window.

At this point, open up any Web page in Design view, place the cursor where you want the video to appear on the page and choose the HTML, Image menu option. Click the browse button to display the familiar Create URL dialog. From the Projects tree view, select the Video folder and select the All Files entry from the Files of Type combo box. You will now see the video file you added to your project in the list view titled Contents of Video. Select the desired file and click OK. When you return to the Add Item dialog, click OK.

The video clip has now been inserted into your Web page. However, because you specified that the file was going to be an image, Visual InterDev has inserted the keywords for an image into the HTML IMG tag. Therefore, click the Source tab for the Web page and locate the newly added IMG tag. It will look similar to the following (depending on the file you selected).

```
<IMG alt="" src="Video/CUP.AVI">
```

To make the browser realize that this is a video, simply change the SRC keyword to DYNSRC. Your HTML line should now look like the following:

```
<IMG alt="" dynsrc="Video/CUP.AVI" LOOP=Infinite>
```

The START and LOOP keywords provide you with the capability to customize when the video starts and how many times it is to be run. The defaults are to start the video when the page is displayed and to run the video only once.

Here are some examples of how to use the START and LOOP keywords.

By using the following code, the video plays each time the user moves the cursor over the video.

```
<IMG alt="" dynsrc="Video/CUP.AVI" START=MouseOver>
```

With the following, the video will not play until the user has moved the cursor over the video. However, when the video does start playing, it will loop indefinitely.

```
<IMG alt="" dynsrc="Video/CUP.AVI" START=MouseOver LOOP=Infinite>
```

You might have noticed that if you have the Properties window open while you are typing HTML directly into the Source view, the Properties window dynamically changes. For example, when you type <IMG, the Properties window automatically shows you the available properties for the IMG tag. Therefore, instead of having to remember all the keywords for each HTML tag, you can simply type the tag and then fill out the properties in the Properties window.

Adding Sound to a Page

Adding sound to a Web page is even easier than adding video. It simply involves adding the HTML BGSOUND tag to your Web page.

Once again, add the desired sound file to your project in the same manner that you added the video file. You might want to also create a folder specifically for the project's sound files. Open a Web page in Source view and add the following HTML tag to the source code:

```
<BGSOUND>
```

At this point, move back into the <BGSOUND> tag and press F4 to display the Properties window to see the available properties for this tag. To select a sound file, simply click the SRC property and then click the ellipsis button. When the Create URL dialog is displayed, browse to the location of the project in which you inserted the sound file and select it. Next, click the Loop property and set it in units of milliseconds. As with the video LOOP keyword, you can also specify the value Infinite.

Summary

Wow! Two hours into your Visual InterDev learning experience and you've already added the following elements to your Web pages: hyperlinks, bookmarks, dividers, images, video, and sound. In addition, you've had the chance to learn some HTML by manually coding the IMG and BGSOUND tags and discovered the server-side include directive.

Q&A

Q When looking at another Web site, I know I can view their source, but is there an easy way to copy some of the elements of their site so that I can learn?

A Absolutely. Actually, once again Visual InterDev has an incredibly cool feature that allows you to do just this. Simply browse to the desired page, press the Ctrl+A combination to select the entire page's contents, and then press Ctrl+C to copy those contents to the clipboard. Then, return to the Visual InterDev application, select the Design view for a page, and press Ctrl+V to paste the contents into your page. Voilà! You can now use this technique as a learning tool by clicking the Source view and examining the HTML code, and you can use the copied Web page as the starting point for your own creations.

Q Where can I learn more about the different HTML tags and keywords?

A Visual InterDev comes with a copy of the MSDN Library. The best way to search for InterDev-specific topics is to start the MSDN Library, set the Active Subset to Visual InterDev Documentation, and then search for the desired topics.

Workshop

The Workshop is designed to help you anticipate possible questions, review what you've learned, and begin thinking ahead to put your knowledge into practice. The answers to the quiz and exercises are in Appendix A, "Answers."

Quiz

1. Why is the use of styles so important in presenting a professional Web site?
2. When creating a hyperlink, how do you specify that the page being linked to should be opened in its own instance of the browser?
3. What is the difference between a hyperlink and bookmark?
4. How are dividers added to a Web page?
5. What must you do before you can insert an image onto a Web page using Visual InterDev?
6. Which HTML tag is needed to define a background image for a Web page?
7. What benefits are derived from using the `include` directive?
8. What is the difference between the virtual and file keywords on the `include` directive?
9. What are the keywords used to control when a video clip plays and how many times it plays?
10. When manually typing HTML tags into a Web page's Source view, how does Visual InterDev make remembering the different keywords unnecessary?

Exercises

1. Take a look at one of the articles on www.codeguru.com and see how closely you can make one of your Web pages match it.
2. Now that you've seen most of the basic elements to a Web page, start thinking about how you want to lay out your Web site.

HOUR 3

Creating Professional Sites with Themes and Style Sheets

In the previous hour, you learned how to make your Web site more consistent through the use of the Visual InterDev built-in styles. In this hour, you will take that a step further and discover how to not only redefine these styles per your own unique requirements, but you'll also learn how to create brand new styles. Finally, you will learn how to define these styles in such a way that they can be used globally across your entire Web site or only within a specified context such as a Web page or paragraph. All of which, when finished, will help you build much more professional looking Web pages with less effort.

In this hour you will discover

- Templates and how to define them
- Cascading Style Sheets and what they are
- Cascading Style Sheets and how to use them
- The Cascading Style Sheet Editor
- Themes and their impact on a Web site

Templates

Templates are another means of promoting consistency within a given Web site. A template is basically a generic master file from which other files can be created. The new files are then modified as needed to handle the unique characteristics of the given task. As an example, at SourceDNA we wanted all the articles to have the same consistent look and feel. Therefore, we published an article HTML template from which each article of a given type is created. This template defines things such as how the article heading is to appear, the location of the author's name and email address, the format of the IMG tag(s), the style used for code snippets, and so on. Obviously, not all these things are needed for each article, and some articles even have unique characteristics that aren't covered by the template. However, the template gives the author of an article something to start with and ensures that common elements are handled in a uniform fashion across the entire Web site.

Templates can be created in Visual InterDev for HTML documents, Active Server Pages, Cascading Style Sheets (more on these later in this hour), or any text file. I can tell you from experience that although it might take a lot of time up front to create a template, it can be an invaluable source as your Web site gets larger and more complex.

Creating Visual InterDev Template Files

There are two ways to create and add files to a Visual InterDev Web project. One way is to right-click the project in the Project Explorer and select the desired Add menu option. As you've seen, this displays the Add Item dialog (see Figure 3.1), which enables you to create a file based on any of the following templates: HTML Page, ASP Page, Style Sheet, or Site Diagram. These templates are simple text files that are stored in the C:\program files\Microsoft Visual Studio\VIntDev98\Templates\Web Project Items folder (assuming that you accepted the default installation folder when you installed Visual InterDev).

FIGURE 3.1

The Add Item dialog uses templates stored in the Visual InterDev Templates\Web Project Items folder.

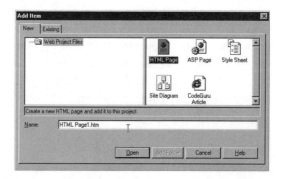

The second way to create and add a new file to a Visual InterDev project is to use the File, New File menu option. When you choose this option, the New File dialog is displayed (see Figure 3.2), which enables you to create either General files (Text File or HTML Page) or Visual InterDev files (HTML Page or Style Sheet). The Visual InterDev files are based on two templates stored by default in the C:\program files\Microsoft Visual Studio\VIntDev98\Templates\NewFileItems folder.

FIGURE 3.2

The New File dialog uses templates stored in the Visual InterDev Templates\NewFileItems folder.

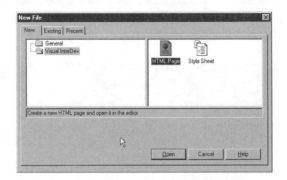

As a very simple test, say that your boss asks you to centralize all the documentation for your company's internal software. Right off the bat, you might be thinking this is the perfect chance to learn a little bit of Visual InterDev. After all, you could easily convince your boss that if the documentation were placed on the company's Web server, everyone in the company would have access to the documentation from any machine whether at home, at work, or even on the road. After she agrees to that, then you convince her that the only logical choice for developing these HTML pages is Visual InterDev!

Using this software documentation example, each project might have its own table of contents, and each table of contents would contain hyperlinks to the different Web pages that define a particular project. In this example, you would probably want to have a template defined for each table of contents so that you present your boss with a nice, professional-looking series of linked documents. Sounds pretty easy, and in fact, using Visual InterDev, it is.

At this point, let's walk through the process of creating a template. To accomplish this, select the File, New File menu option. From the New File dialog, select the New tab and click on the Visual InterDev folder. On the right side of the dialog, you will see the templates that ship with Visual InterDev. For this example, select the HTML Page item and click the Open button. Visual InterDev will then create a new HTML page and place it in the Miscellaneous folder of the Project Explorer.

By default, Visual InterDev will name the file New HTML Page1.htm. Because this isn't a very descriptive name, you'll change it to something more meaningful. Because you need to store your custom templates in your own folder, let's see how to create that new folder and change the template filename in one step. Both tasks can be accomplished via the Save File As dialog, so select the File, Save New HTML Page1 As menu option. When the Save File As dialog appears, navigate to the Visual InterDev Templates folder. After you've located that folder, right-click the folders list view and select the New Folder menu option. Because all your templates can be located in one folder, the task of creating a custom template folder will have to be performed only one time. At this point, name the folder My Templates. Then save the template file in the My Templates folder and name it Table of Contents.htm. After you've saved the template, click the Design tab and define the page like the one shown in Figure 3.3.

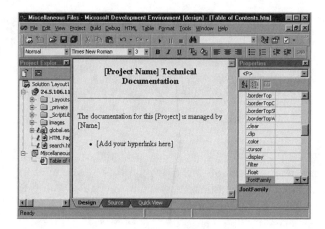

Now that you've created the template file, you need to let Visual InterDev know about it. First, exit Visual InterDev. Then open an Explorer window and browse to the Visual InterDev Web Projects Items folder. Now, open a text editor and create a new file called My Templates.vsz.

VSZ files are used to represent the items that appear in the Add Item dialog and the New Project dialog. The VSZ file contains information that identifies a wizard and provides custom information for it. The information that can be specified in this file is illustrated in Table 3.1.

TABLE 3.1 VSZ File Information

Record	Description
VSVersion	Specifies the Visual InterDev wizard interface that the wizard (specified by ProgID) will implement
Classname	The ProgID of the wizard
Param	Custom parameters that will be passed to the wizard

For the purposes of this example, update your My Templates.vsz file so that, when finished, it looks like Listing 3.1. Note that line 3 might have to be changed, depending on where you installed Visual InterDev.

LISTING 3.1   The My Templates.vsz File

```
1: VSWIZARD 6.0
2: Wizard=VIWizard.CTemplatePageWizard
3: Param=c:\program files\microsoft visual studio\vintdev98\
   ➥templates\my templates
```

Now that you've created the .vsz file, you need to update one last file—the .vsdir file. To do that, open the NewWebItems.vsdir file located in the Visual InterDev Web Project Items folder. When you open that file, you will see the information that defines the HTML Page, ASP Page, Style Sheet, and Site Diagram files. Each of these templates is described on a different row in the file, with each field in that row being separated by a vertical bar character (|). Table 3.2 shows what each of these fields is used for.

TABLE 3.2   Field Information

Field	Description
RelPathName	The fully qualified filename of your .vsz file.
{clsidPackage}	GUID representing the DLL that contains the resources for the template.
LocalizedName	The name that will appear in the Add Item dialog or the string resource ID for that name.
SortPriority	A number that represents how the item is sorted in the dialog.
Description	Once again, this can be either text or a string resource ID. The resulting string is also displayed in the Add Item dialog.
DLLPath or {clsidPackage}	Either the fully qualified DLL that contains the wizard icon or its GUID.
IconResourceID	Icon resource ID.
Flags	A flag that specifies whether the item is disabled. A blank means that the item is enabled. A value of 8192 means disabled.
SuggestedBaseName	The name that will automatically be displayed as the new file's name when a user creates a file. Visual InterDev automatically appends a number to this filename in order to keep the name unique in its folder.

3

Now that you know more than you ever wanted to know about the structure of a Visual InterDev .vsdir file, append the following line to the end of the NewWebItems.vsdir file. Note that because the GUIDs aren't different than the other entries in this file and because they can be difficult to type in, you can simply copy one of the other entries and change all the fields except for the two GUID fields.

```
My Templates.vsz¦{164B10B9-B200-11D0-8C61-00A0C91E29D5}¦
➥Table of Contents¦50¦
Create a Table of Contents and add it to this project¦
➥{164B10B9-B200-11D0-8C61-00A0C91E29D5}¦296¦ ¦TOC
```

Now, to test your new template, open the Project Explorer and right-click the project to display its context menu. Then select the Add, Add Item menu option. You will now see that in addition to the standard icons for the Visual InterDev templates, you will also see an icon for your newly created Table of Contents file. Selecting this file and clicking the Open button will cause Visual InterDev to generate a new HTML file based on your template. Now all you need to do is inform others that when creating a table of contents for a new project, they should use your template.

Prompting the User for Input

Creating templates is great. However, one problem that hasn't been addressed yet is that with a large enough document, there's always the chance the user could forget to enter some mandatory data. It would be nice if Visual InterDev provided some way of prompting the user for the necessary information needed to fill out a template. Well, luckily for us, it does, and it's as simple as a single tag of code.

To specify that the user is to be prompted for input, simply open the template page in Source view and use the <%# and #%> delimiters to define the variable. As an example of how to use prompts from a template file, let's look at the documentation example. Say that every table of contents page is going to have a heading that will look like the following:

```
<H2>[Project Name] Technical Documentation</H2>
```

Using template prompts, you can have Visual InterDev automatically prompt the developer for the project name so that you know it isn't forgotten. To test this, open the Table of Contents.htm template and insert the following line of HTML:

```
<H2><%#Enter the project name#%> Technical Documentation</H2>
```

Now when a file is created from this template, the user will be prompted with a dialog asking her to enter the project name. When the project name has been entered, the file is created with the specified project name in the title.

A Visual InterDev template variable can be up to 100 characters in length and are case sensitive. Other than that, the only restriction placed on these types of variables is that the following are reserved by Visual InterDev and cannot be used:

```
<%#DataConnection#%>
<%#FileNameWithExtension#%>
<%#FileNameWithoutExtension#%>
<%#ThemeName#%>
```

Cascading Style Sheets

At its simplest, a Cascading Style Sheet is simply a file containing the definition of HTML elements. For example, say that you wanted to redefine the <H1> style (Heading 1) to use a different font and point size. If you wanted this change to be global to all pages on your Web site, you would redefine that style in a Cascading Style Sheet.

You will sometimes hear the terms *style sheets* and *Cascading Style Sheets* used inter-changeably. The term *Cascading Style Sheets* comes from the fact that the scope of a given style sheet has a nested, or cascaded, effect and that multiple sheets can affect the same Web page. For example, you can define a global Cascading Style Sheet for all the pages within a given Web site. Then you can override that Cascading Style Sheet at any level from a group of specific pages down to a single paragraph.

The ability to redefine HTML elements is certainly a very powerful tool. However, it would be a mistake to assume that that is the only thing you can do with Cascading Style Sheets. With a Cascading Style Sheet, you can go way beyond what HTML can do. In HTML, elements are generally defined in very broad strokes. For example, in plain vanilla HTML, you cannot do something as simple as defining a given text string as being a specific point size. With Cascading Style Sheets, the control over defining your Web page is at a much more granular level. The following example of an excerpt from a Cascading Style Sheet file redefines the <H1> tag so that it uses the Comic Sans MS font with a 12-pt. size:

```
<STYLE>
H1
{
 COLOR:navy;
 FONT-FAMILY:'Comic Sans MS';
 FONT-SIZE-12pt
}
...
</STYLE>
```

Creating Cascading Style Sheets

To create a new Cascading Style Sheet for a project, simply right-click the project root and select the Add, Add Style Sheet menu option. Leave the filename default Style Sheet1.css for now and click the Open button. You will then be presented with a view similar to Figure 3.4.

FIGURE 3.4

The Cascading Style Sheet editor enables you to redefine existing HTML elements.

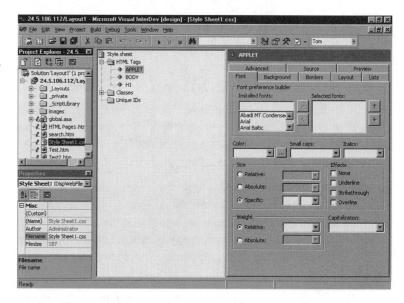

Redefining HTML Elements

Now that you have a Cascading Style Sheet open, you can see just how easy it is to redefine HTML elements. At this point, simply right-click the HTML Tags folder and select the Insert HTML Tag menu option. When the Insert New HTML Tag dialog appears, select the desired HTML tag from the combo box and click the OK button. For purposes of this example, select the <H1> tag. When the dialog is dismissed, the H1 style will be added to the Cascading Style Sheet's HTML Tags folder.

At this point, you can use the tabs on the right side to do just about anything you could possibly imagine to this style. For now, set the font to Comic Sans MS, the color to Navy, and the size to 12 pt.

Previewing Your Changes

When you have made a change to a given HTML element, clicking the Preview tab will show you exactly how that element will be interpreted when displayed.

If you want to quickly see the difference between the default implementation of a tag and your new version, use the Cascading Style Sheet Applied check box. This check box will not only toggle the current preview, but it will also maintain the correct position within the document.

Another feature of this editor that I like is the ability to specify which HTML page will be used in the Preview tab. Simply click the Preview tab and then click the ellipsis alongside the HTML page to preview the Cascading Style Sheet with the edit control. From there, you can specify any Web page in your current project. If you change your mind later, you can always revert back to previewing with the original HTML page by clicking the Use Default Page button.

Looking at the Source Code

To see the resulting HTML code for a given HTML style, click the Source tab. Although you can't change the code manually, you can learn quite a bit by changing the styles through the different tabs and switching over to the Source tab to see the results. One nice feature of this tab is that when you select an HTML tag, that tag's source code is scrolled into view and is shown in bold text.

Creating New Classes

Below the HTML Tags folder, you should see a folder titled Classes. Classes give you the ability to define a given HTML tag in different ways. For example, say that in the documentation of your company's software projects, you want the Visual Basic code to be formatted differently than the Visual C++ code.

This can easily be done by right-clicking the Classes folder and selecting the Insert Class menu option. When the Insert New Class dialog is presented, specify the name of the class as VB, check the Apply Only to the Following Tag check box, select the CODE style from the combo box, and click OK. An entry titled CODE.VB will be inserted under the Classes folder. Now, you can select that class and set that style's characteristics to your liking. Doing the same thing for a class named CODE.VC gives you two distinct CODE styles to use in your Web pages.

To use the new class in an HTML file, simply start the specification of the style as you normally would and then add the CLASS keyword. Listing 3.2 is an example of how you would format a snippet of Visual Basic code and Visual C++ code using the two classes you defined previously.

LISTING 3.2   Setting the CODE Class with Visual Basic and Visual C++ in the Same Code

```
 1: <LINK rel="stylesheet" type="text/css" href="Style Sheet1.css">
 2:
 3: <PRE>
 4: <CODE CLASS=VB>
 5: Private Sub Command1_Click()
 6:  Set app = CreateObject("MSDev.Application")
 7:
 8:  app.Visible = True
 9:
10:  Dim docs As Documents
11:  Set docs = app.Documents
12:  docs.Open ("d:\program source\testapp\testapp.dsw")
13:  app.ExecuteCommand ("BuildRebuildAll")
14: End Sub
15: </CODE>
16: </PRE>
17:
18: <PRE>
19: <CODE CLASS=VC>
20: void CCodeguruView::OnFileSave()
21: {
22:  CCodeguruDoc* pDoc = GetDocument();
23:  ASSERT(pDoc);
24:  if (pDoc)
25:  {
26:   CString strNewShtmlDocument;
27:   GetWindowText(strNewShtmlDocument);
28:
29:   pDoc->UpdateShtmlDocument(strNewShtmlDocument);
30:   pDoc->DoFileSave();
31:  }
32: }
33: </CODE>
34: </PRE>
```

Applying Styles to a Web Page

As you have seen, styles are used to format text according to a set of predefined instructions. A number of ways to specify styles for a Web page are as follows:

- By linking a Web page to an external Cascading Style Sheet file. This technique is typically used when the defined styles will be used for multiple pages.

- By defining document-level styles in which the defined styles are applicable only to a specific Web page.

- By applying styles to specific regions of a Web page such as a paragraph or to collections of elements in divisions or spans.

As mentioned earlier, the term *Cascading Style Sheets* comes from the fact that styles can be nested. With the preceding list, each subsequent manner of specifying a style will override an existing style. For example, if an external Cascading Style Sheet file is being used for a given page and that sheet has redefined the <H1> style, any subsequent redefinition at the document level or lower will override it.

Linking a Web Page to an External Cascading Style Sheet

Now that you've defined your Cascading Style Sheet, it's time to link it to a Web page. To do this, simply open any Web page in Source view and drag the desired Cascading Style Sheet from the Project Explorer between the <HEAD> and </HEAD> tags. Here's what the resulting line of HTML will look like:

```
<LINK rel="stylesheet" type="text/css" href="Style Sheet1.css">
```

> For a Cascading Style Sheet to work correctly, you *must* drag and drop it between the <HEAD> and </HEAD> tags. Otherwise, not only will the Cascading Style Sheet not be linked to properly, but also you will not receive an error indicating your mistake.

Defining Document-Level Styles

As opposed to defining a set of styles and saving them in a file that can be used by multiple Web pages, you can also define styles at the document level. This is generally done only if you know that the current document is the only document that will use a given style.

To illustrate how this is done, perform the following steps:

1. Open a Web page in the Source view.
2. Insert a new line between the <HEAD> tag and the </HEAD> tag.
3. On the newly created blank line, enter a style block that begins with a <STYLE> tag and ends with a </STYLE> tag.
4. Now enter redefine a style (for example, H1) in which the syntax is

   ```
   tag { style1: attribute; style2: attribute;...;}
   ```

   or

   ```
   tag.classname { style1: attribute; style2: attribute;...;}
   ```

The syntax might seem a bit crude at first, but it's really very easy to adapt to when you understand it. Here's an example of a style that would redefine the H1 style with a color of red.

```
H1 { color:red;}
```

Now, let's see why Cascading Style Sheets are called *cascading*. If you created the Cascading Style Sheet introduced earlier and then inserted the following HTML into a page, any <H1> elements would be rendered with the Comic Sans MS font (along with a color of navy and a point size of 12):

```
<LINK rel="stylesheet" type="text/css" href="Style Sheet1.css">
```

Then, if you followed the preceding line of HTML with the following line, you would override the Style Sheet1.css file's definition of the <H1> tag:

```
<style>H1 {color:red;}</style>
```

The important thing to realize here is that *both* styles would be used. In other words, the second definition didn't completely wipe out the first one. It only changed those parts of the style that it referenced. Therefore, you end up with a combination of the two styles; any <H1> elements in this document will now be rendered with the Comic Sans MS font, along with a color of red and a point size of 12.

As you saw earlier, the Cascading Style Sheet editor is used to create external Cascading Style Sheet files that are generally used for a group of pages or an entire Web application. However, even if you are creating the style(s) for one specific document, you will probably find it much easier to create a style using the editor and then copy the code into the Source view of the current page rather than manually key in each style tag.

Themes

Themes are a collection of Cascading Style Sheets that compose a coordinated group of elements. Each theme is a set of graphics, fonts, bullets, background images, and other page elements that combine to form a consistent visual design for the Web pages of a given Web site.

To illustrate this, select the New, New Project menu option. When the New Project dialog is displayed, name the new project Theme1 and click Open. After selecting the appropriate Web server, proceed to step 4 of the Web Project Wizard, and you will be prompted to specify a theme for the new project.

As you can see in Figure 3.5, this dialog is very similar to the dialog used to specify a project's layout. Notice that once again, you have the ability to preview the element before creating the project. In addition, you can specify a path to the themes that are installed on your system. The default path for a Visual InterDev installation is C:\Program Files\Microsoft Visual Studio\VIntDev98\Themes. If you take a quick peek at the directory, you'll see that there is a directory for each theme listed on the dialog.

Additionally, if you look into one of the Theme directories, you'll see that just two files make up a theme: an information file (.inf) with the same name as its parent directory, and an .elm file that is used to define the actual Theme and its elements.

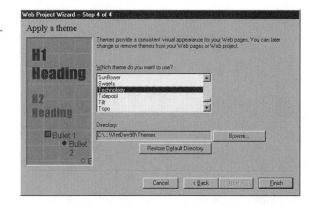

At this point, select the Technology Theme and click the Finish button. When Visual InterDev has finished creating the project, open the search.htm file in Design view. Figure 3.6 shows what you will see at this point and illustrates just how big a difference a color-coordinated theme can make to a Web page.

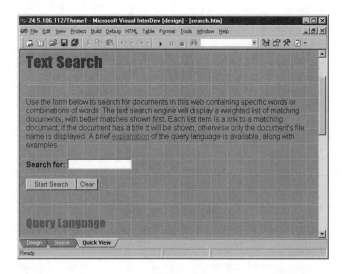

One last thing to consider is how to apply or change a theme for a project that already exists. To do this, right-click a project in Project Explorer and select the Apply Theme and Layout menu option. The Apply Theme and Layout dialog (see Figure 3.7) displays the themes and layouts on two different tabs (similar to the way they are displayed in the New Project Wizard). To change the project's current theme or its layout, click the appropriate tab, click the Apply Theme (or Layout) radio button, and select the desired theme or layout.

FIGURE 3.7

Visual InterDev enables you to apply a theme or layout even after you've already created the application.

Summary

Over the past hour, you've gone from creating only very simple Web pages to using layouts and themes to produce a consistent visual interface for your users. In addition, you took what you learned in the previous hour about styles and built on that by discovering how to create Cascading Style Sheets and apply them at several different levels of your Web pages.

Q&A

Q If I create my own layouts, how can I incorporate them into Visual InterDev?

A Create a directory for each individual layout in the Visual InterDev Layouts directory. Then for each layout, copy the necessary information, preview, and definition files into that layout's corresponding directory.

Q When I create a theme, any new Web pages that I create automatically have their own definitions for some main HTML elements. Are those definitions housed in an external Cascading Style Sheet file and if so, can I modify them?

A The answer to the first question is yes: Each theme includes a Cascading Style Sheet file. The answer to the second question is yes, you can. However, I would highly recommend against it because you can easily destroy a Visual InterDev theme that way.

Workshop

The Workshop is designed to help you anticipate possible questions, review what you've learned, and begin thinking ahead to put your knowledge into practice. The answers to the quiz and exercises are in Appendix A, "Answers."

Quiz

1. How are layouts and navigation bars related?
2. How do you create a new template file?
3. How can you create a file from a template?
4. What are Cascading Style Sheets?
5. Why are they called *cascading*?
6. How do you link a Web page to an external Cascading Style Sheet file?
7. How do you define document-level styles?
8. How do you apply styles to an element of a Web page such as a division or span?
9. What is the order of precedence regarding Cascading Style Sheets?
10. What are style classes and how are they defined?

Exercises

1. Create a template for a very simple bug-tracking Web site in which each bug is listed on one page that contains a link to another page detailing the nature of the bug. Remember to allow for input of information from the user as he creates his pages.
2. Give the users the ability to create either a Visual Basic page or a Visual C++ page in which the CODE styles of each page are completely different.

HOUR 4

Designing Your Web Site with the Site Designer

Now that you know how to design and create individual Web pages, it's time to turn to the all-important task of site design. After all, it doesn't really matter how many HTML tricks you know or how fancy your graphics are if your users can't navigate around the site in an efficient manner. To that extent, you will spend this hour learning how to use a Visual InterDev tool called the Site Designer.

The highlights of this hour include

- Creating a site diagram for your Web site
- Adding Web pages to a site diagram
- Creating links to hyperlinks in other applications
- Attaching and detaching child pages
- Using the PageNavBar DTC
- Creating navigational links to Web pages

Site Designer Overview

The design of any application takes research, analysis, and thorough testing of all ideas that relate to the proposed finished product. This is even more the case with a Web site. Whereas users are accustomed to a typical Windows application being somewhat restrictive regarding how it allows the user to perform his work, Web users have become accustomed to more of a free-form atmosphere in which they can browse from page to page without restriction and easily return to any given point with a click of the mouse. Therefore, before you start writing the HTML and script that will constitute your site, you need to decide how the information on your site is going to be organized so that users can easily navigate through it without getting that "I can't get there from here" feeling.

Site Diagrams

Site diagrams are graphical representations of the Web pages in a Web application that show how navigation between these pages is defined. Within a site diagram, logically related pages can be connected into hierarchical groupings called trees. Each tree is then used to define the navigation bar links in a site. The hierarchical relationships between pages can easily be modified by simply moving the images that represent the different Web pages around on the site diagram. If this sounds a bit abstract, don't worry. You'll see how to do this shortly.

Benefits of Using the Site Designer

One of the main benefits of using the Site Designer is that it allows for the quick and easy prototyping of a Web site without each HTML page and Active Server Page having to be coded first. Additionally, the Site Designer is used to define the overall site navigation that defines how the users will interact with the Web site.

Site diagrams provide a way for you to rapidly design and populate a Web application. You can create new pages with a click of the mouse and you can even open other applications such as Internet Explorer and drag hyperlinks onto the diagram. Doing this has the effect of adding that page to your Web site. When you save the site diagram, any pages not already existing in the project are automatically created and added to the project.

If you created the project using a theme or a layout, any newly created pages will be created just as if you had created them via the Project Explorer. Also, if you have a navigational structure defined for the site, it will be automatically updated for each page.

Besides allowing you to simply lay out the Web pages of your Web site in a nice graphical environment, the Site Designer also provides a means for you to define the way in which the user can navigate from page to page.

Creating a Site Diagram

At this point, I will create an example project, so you can see some of this in action:

1. Create a new Web project called SiteDesign.

2. After the project has been created, open the Project Explorer.

3. Now, right-click on the project name and select the Add, Site Diagram menu option.

4. When the Add Item dialog is displayed, name the site file SiteDesign.wdm (see Figure 4.1). This file is called a site structure file. Although you can define multiple site diagrams for a given project, there is only one site structure file per project. Therefore, this file is normally given the same name as the project to which it is being added.

FIGURE 4.1

Site diagrams enable you to quickly create large, visually consistent Web sites.

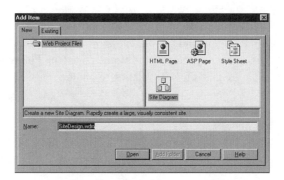

4

5. After Visual InterDev has created the new site diagram, you will see results similar to those shown in Figure 4.2.

FIGURE 4.2

Notice that a newly created site diagram starts you off with a Home Page icon.

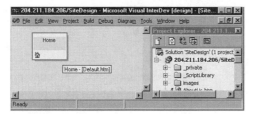

Adding Pages to a Site Diagram

When you have the site diagram created, there are several ways in which to add other HTML pages and Active Server Pages:

- Create new pages to the site diagram
- Add pages to the site diagram from a project
- Add pages from other applications to the site diagram

Creating New Pages in the Site Diagram

To create a new page and add it to the site diagram, simply select the Diagram, New HTML Page or Diagram, New ASP Page menu option depending on the type of page you want to create. A rectangle representing the page will be displayed. Notice that when you create a page, Visual InterDev assigns it a unique name. Because this name will be used as the actual filename of the page, when the site diagram is saved, you'll see how to change this value in the next section.

When adding a page to a site diagram, it will be created as a child page of the currently selected page. In other words, if the Home Web page is selected and you click on the Diagram, New HTML Page menu option, a new window representing a new page will be created and automatically connected to the Home page (see Figure 4.3). This is how you can quickly create a page and show its relation to another page at the same time.

FIGURE 4.3

Creating a child page.

When adding a new page to a site diagram, realize that the page will not appear in the Project Explorer until you have saved the site diagram.

If you want to create a page that has no parent page, click the background of the site diagram first. Then select the Diagram, New HTML Page menu option. Now, the page will be created, but it will not have the line drawn that connects it to another page. An example of this type of page is shown in Figure 4.4.

FIGURE 4.4

Creating a page without a parent page.

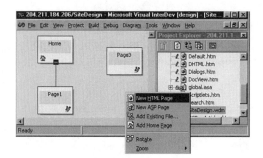

Adding Pages to the Site Diagram from a Project

Another option in adding pages to a site diagram is to add them from the current project. This is especially useful when the page existed before you created the site diagram. In order to add an existing page to the site diagram, complete the following steps:

1. Create or open the site diagram.

2. Right-click the page that will be the parent of the page you are going to add. If you don't want the new page to have a parent, right-click the background.

3. From the ensuing context menu, select the Add Existing File menu option. This causes the Choose URL dialog to be displayed (see Figure 4.5).

FIGURE 4.5

Existing pages can easily be added to the site diagram.

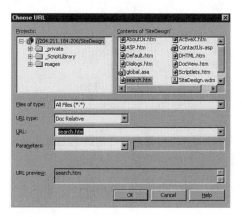

4

4. From the Choose URL dialog, select the desired page, specify any needed parameters, and click the OK button.

Adding Pages from Other Applications to the Site Diagram

One of the coolest features of the Site Designer is the ability to drag and drop hyperlinks from other applications onto the site diagram and have that page defined within the Web project. To do so, implement the following steps:

1. Open or create a site diagram.
2. Open the application (for example, a browser such as Internet Explorer) that contains the hyperlink you want to add to the site.
3. Align the applications visually so that you can see both the source application (the one that contains the desired link) and Visual InterDev.
4. Select the link in the source application.
5. Drag the link over to the site diagram.
6. Drop the link onto the site diagram.

Site Diagram Legend

Before doing any more work with site diagrams, take a look at what those funny looking icons mean that are displayed in the pages of a site diagram. Table 4.1 illustrates the different icons that can appear in these site diagram pages and what they represent.

TABLE 4.1 Site Diagram Icons

Icon	Meaning
	Home Page.
	Modified Page—This icon means that the page has been changed and not saved (that is, the page is "dirty").
	External Page—This icon is used to represent a link to a page that was dragged and dropped from another application.
	Global Navigation Bar—This icon means that the page is a default navigational link for all other pages.

Changing the Page Names

As you add pages to the site diagram, you will certainly want to add more meaningful names than what Visual InterDev creates for you. In order to change the name of a page, simply click the part of the page on the site diagram where the name is. When the name has been highlighted, make the necessary changes to create the name of your choice, and then click somewhere outside of the text area.

Remember that with the exception of the Home page, the name you see in the site diagram directly correlates to the name of the actual file. Figure 4.6 shows the process of changing the name of a page.

FIGURE 4.6

To rename a page, simply highlight the old name and type in the desired name.

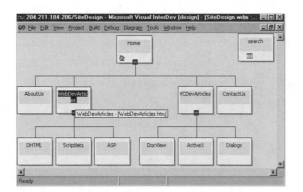

Removing Pages from the Site Diagram

In order to remove a page from a diagram, simply select the desired pages (you can select multiple pages or even all pages with Ctrl+A) and press the Delete key. When you do this, the Delete Pages confirmation dialog is presented (see Figure 4.7). Read this dialog carefully because it is not your normal Are you sure? type dialog. This dialog gives you the ability to not only remove the page from the site diagram, but to also remove it from the project and delete the underlying physical file. So, again, make sure that you read this dialog carefully!

In Figure 4.7, you can see that the selected page (DocView) had no children pages. If you click on a parent page and press the Delete key, you will see the Delete Pages and Children dialog (see Figure 4.8), which lets you know that your action will not only remove the currently selected page(s), but also their children as well.

FIGURE 4.7

*The Delete Page func-
tion lets you just
remove the page from
the diagram, or you
can also remove it
from the project at the
same time.*

FIGURE 4.7

*The Delete Page func-
tion lets you just
remove the page from
the diagram, or you
can also remove it
from the project at the
same time.*

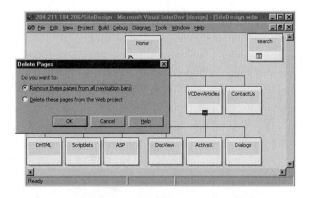

FIGURE 4.8

*You can remove whole
branches and trees of
pages from the site
diagram with a single
mouse click.*

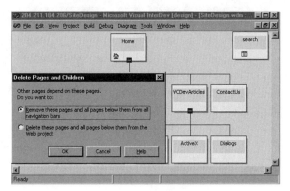

Attaching and Detaching Pages

There will be times when, through the design stage of your Web site, you will change
your mind as to how your pages are associated. As you saw earlier, the parent of a page
is defined when the page is added to the site diagram. However, this is very easy to
change after the page has been added.

To attach a child page to a parent page, simply drag the child page to the parent page. As
you drag the child page, you will see that you are dragging a dotted outline of the page.
When the page is moved within a close proximity of another page, a dotted line connecting the child page to the other page will be displayed. Releasing the mouse button at this
point will connect the child page to the other page, thereby creating the child/parent relationship between the two pages. As you can see in Figure 4.9, you can drag to attach a
single page or an entire branch of a tree.

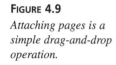

FIGURE 4.9

Attaching pages is a simple drag-and-drop operation.

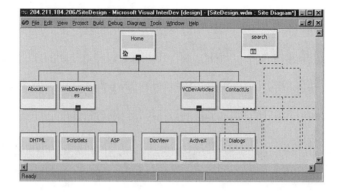

Detaching a child page from a parent page is just as easy. Simply drag the child page away from the parent page and drop it in an open area of the site diagram.

Working with the Navigation Bar

So far, you've seen how easy it is to create a site diagram that shows the relationships between the different pages of a site. However, this relationship doesn't actually do anything. In other words, just because you defined PageA as being the parent of PageB in the site diagram, nothing automatically creates a link from one page to another. At least not that you've seen yet. In this section, you'll learn how to use something called the navigation bar and how it, in combination with the site diagram, helps you to define the site's navigational characteristics.

Adding a Navigation Bar to a Web Site

As you saw in the last hour, the navigation bar is used to add navigational ability to your Web site by placing buttons to key pages on each page of the site. As an example, you would almost certainly want the user to always get back to the home page, so you would have a button for that on each page. To create a navigation bar, use the PageNavBar design-time control (DTC):

1. Create or open a site diagram.
2. Double-click the Home page icon to open it in the editor.
3. Switch to the Source view.
4. Place the caret immediately after the <BODY> tag.
5. Open the Toolbox window and click the Design-Time Controls tab.
6. Double-click PageNavBar DTC to insert it into the source code (see Figure 4.10).

4

FIGURE **4.10**
The PageNavBar DTC needs to be inserted directly into the HTML code of the page.

7. After the PageNavBar DTC has been inserted into the page's HTML code, right-click the DTC and select the Properties menu option. The Properties dialog enables you to define exactly what type of navigational bar you want (see Figure 4.11). For example, you can specify that you want the page to contain links to all children pages or all first level pages. These options are a little involved, so they are discussed in more detail in the next section.

FIGURE **4.11**
The PageNavBar Properties dialog.

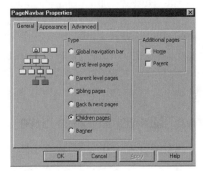

Setting the PageNavBar Properties

As you saw in Figure 14.4, after you insert a PageNavBar DTC into a page, you can set quite a few options in order to configure how the navigation bar will appear at runtime. Here are the three different tabs to that dialog and what they do. They are the General tab, Appearance tab, and Advanced tab.

The General Tab

The General tab enables you to specify which type of navigation bar you want. For example, the default type is Children pages. This means that all child pages (as defined on the site diagram) for the page containing this PageNavBar DTC will appear as links.

The icon on the left side of the dialog updated automatically to give you an idea of which pages in a site diagram would be available for each type as you click the different types. Notice also that there are two check box controls that allow you to add the Home page and the parent page to any navigation type.

The Appearance Tab

The Appearance tab enables you to define what will appear as the link. For example, you can choose to have buttons or text appear as the links, and you can choose where you want the navigation bar to appear (running vertically along the side of the page or horizontally across the top).

The Advanced Tab

The Advanced tab only has one option: Alternate Page. This option enables you to specify an alternate page that will contain the navigational structure for the page. Say that your default.htm (the Home page) doesn't have the main menu, but the main menu is on a completely different page. In that case, you would probably want to name the menu page as the alternate page because it contains the links to all the main pages on the site.

Adding Links

At this point, you finally get to discover how the PageNavBar DTC and the site diagram work together. To see how this works, create a page hierarchy like the one you saw earlier in Figure 4.6, and then follow these steps:

1. Open the site diagram.
2. Right-click the WebDevArticles page and select the Diagram, Add to Global Navigation Bar menu option.
3. Click OK to the warning that the child page will be disconnected from the parent page. In order for a page to be placed on a global navigation bar, it cannot have a parent page, so this dialog is completely expected in this situation.
4. Right-click the VCArticles page and select the Add To Global Navigation Bar menu option.
5. Once again, click the OK button when the disconnect warning appears.
6. Select the File, Save All menu option from the main menu.
7. Right-click the Home page and select the View In Browser menu option because you cannot view navigational bars in Quick View. You should now see the two links to the WebDevArticles and VCArticles Web pages.

4

Summary

No matter what kind of fancy ideas you have for whiz bang graphics and dynamic HTML, if you don't take the time to thoughtfully lay out your Web site, the chances of creating a site that is easy for you to maintain and the user to navigate will not be good. Therefore, this hour focuses on using the Site Designer tool. Using this tool, you learned how to create a site diagram, add and remove pages, rename pages, and attach and detach pages.

Q&A

Q Why does the PageNavBar DTC not display correctly when I display my Web pages?

A One reason might be that in order to work with PageNavBar DTC, you must have FrontPage98 Extensions installed on your Web server.

Q When I create a site diagram, Visual InterDev automatically selects one of my application's pages as the "home page." How does it know which is the home page?

A That depends on the Web server being used. If the Web server is Microsoft Internet Information Server (IIS), Visual InterDev will use default.asp file as the home page. If the Web server is Microsoft Personal Web Server (PWS), default.htm is used. In either case, if the home page doesn't exist, it is created for you when the site diagram is created.

Workshop

The Workshop is designed to help you anticipate possible questions, review what you've learned, and begin thinking ahead to put your knowledge into practice. The answers to the quiz are in Appendix A, "Answers."

Quiz

1. What is a site diagram used for?
2. What are the different options for adding pages to a site diagram?
3. How do you add a link from another application to the site diagram?
4. Can a project have multiple site diagrams?
5. How is the site diagram stored?
6. Can a project have multiple site structure files?
7. What are the options when you attempt to remove a page from a site diagram?

8. How do you attach and detach a page that already exists on a site diagram to another page?

9. What DTC is used to create a navigation bar?

10. What is the limitation Visual InterDev imposes when stipulating that a page is to be added to the global navigation bar?

Exercise

Design a Web site that has several layers of Web pages to it and play around with the different layouts and PageNavBar properties. Once you learn how to integrate these tools into your design of a Web site, you'll find that they are indispensable tools for getting a prototype of a Web site up quickly.

4

Hour 5

Protecting Your Investment with Version Control

In the past few hours, you've learned quite a bit about developing your Web pages. However, most of what you've accomplished has been done using the Visual InterDev WYSIWYG editor and hasn't involved writing much actual code (besides a little HTML). Therefore, now would be a perfect time to introduce the concept of version control and the version control system (Microsoft's Visual SourceSafe) that Visual InterDev supports.

In this hour, you will discover

- Configuring SourceSafe
- Using Visual InterDev and Visual SourceSafe
- Visually merging files
- Applying labels
- Viewing history
- Reports and searches

What Is Version Control and Why Do I Need It?

With today's RAD (rapid application development) environments, even the simplest of applications can easily grow into a large set of files, which can become quite unmanageable over time. Whether you are working on a team or by yourself, version control is an indispensable tool for any size development effort. Among other things, version control helps with the following tasks:

- Team Coordination
- Versioning
- Reusability of sharable code

Team Coordination

Version control is used to coordinate a team approach to software development. It does this by maintaining a central storage place (typically in some sort of proprietary database format) for all the source code that makes up a development effort and presenting the concept of locking and unlocking files.

In order for a programmer to make a change to a file that has been defined to the version control system, that programmer must first check the file out, thereby locking it. By default, no other programmer would be able to check that file out until the lock has been relinquished. After the changes have been made, the programmer can then check the file back into version control, thereby unlocking the file and freeing it for other developers to work on.

Anyone who has ever worked on a software development team that didn't have version control in place knows only too well the many lost evenings and weekends that can be attributed to trying to recover from not having this capability. Therefore, the ability to coordinate a team's efforts by not allowing developers to accidentally overwrite the work of others is the principal justification for using version control on any team, regardless of size.

Versioning

As the name implies, versioning is another incredibly important benefit of using a version control system. Versioning gives you the ability to define that on a specific date and time, a specified grouping of files were in a known state. For example, say that on November 1, 1999, you implement a new receiving module into your company's distribution system. The day you introduce the updated modules into production, you would want to create a label defining the current state of the files in version control. You might name that label something like "Receiving module inserted," or if your product has a version number associated with it, you might just name the label the same as the new version number of your product. What you've just done with versioning is given yourself a tremendous amount of latitude to handle several problems.

If, after another month of development, you install a new version of the receiving module and find out that the new version doesn't work, you can easily go back to version control and pull out the exact source required to build the version that did function.

Why Use Visual SourceSafe?

Now that you know what version control is and realize its role in the development of any size project, the next question might be, "Why use Visual SourceSafe?" Actually, without getting into a feature-by-feature comparison of each version control system on the market, I'll just list a few of the reasons why you might want to choose Visual SourceSafe as your version control tool of choice.

- File level tasks such as checking files into and out of version control can be done directly from Visual InterDev. This, obviously, is much easier and more convenient than having to continually switch between your development environment and your version control system every time you want to perform a given task.

- Project level information can be viewed from Visual InterDev. Once again, almost any version control system is going to enable you to maintain and view project-level information. However, being able to view this information from within your development environment is a definite plus.

As you can see, the overriding theme here is the integration between Visual InterDev and Visual SourceSafe. After all, unlike Visual Basic or Visual C++, Visual InterDev isn't a compiler or language. Rather, the biggest advantage of using Visual InterDev in your development efforts is that it enables you to integrate all the tools necessary to build a complex, robust Web application from a single development environment. Therefore, it only makes sense to use a version control system that is also integrated with Visual InterDev.

5

Configuring SourceSafe

I won't get into all the different options regarding the installation of Visual SourceSafe because the documentation that is provided with Visual SourceSafe does a pretty good job of that. However, after you've installed Visual SourceSafe, you will need to understand how to configure the following before being able to use Visual SourceSafe from the Visual InterDev environment.

Creating Users

Assuming that you've installed Visual SourceSafe on a server, or the local box if you're doing all your development on a single machine, you will need to define the developers (users) who will have access to the source code. The process of creating and removing users is done via the Visual SourceSafe Admin application. Figure 5.1 shows an example of the Visual SourceSafe Admin application with a couple of users already defined.

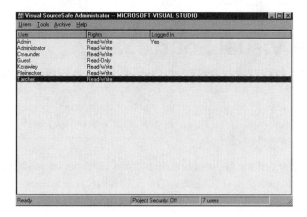

At this point, start the Visual SourceSafe Admin application and select the Users, Add User menu option. The Add User dialog will then be displayed and enables you to define the username, password, and whether the user has read/write or read-only access to version control. In the next section, you'll learn how to specify this on a project-by-project basis.

After you have entered the user's information and clicked the OK button, the user will be created and added to the application's list view. Notice that Visual SourceSafe always capitalizes the first letter of the username despite what you type into the Add User dialog. However, when you log in, the username is not case sensitive.

Establishing Rights

After you have created the desired user(s), you will probably want to set up each user's rights at the project level. The first thing you will need to do is to turn on Project Level Security. To do that, simply select the Tools, Options menu option. You will then be presented with the SourceSafe Options dialog. Click the Project Security tab (as shown in Figure 5.2).

As you can see, the Project Security tab also enables you to specify the default project rights. That way, if most users you create will have all rights except the ability to destroy, you can simply leave it as the only check box turned off.

You might have noticed that there's an option for defining a user's ability to delete and another option for defining a user's ability to destroy. The difference is that when a file or project is deleted, it can still be recovered. *However*, if a file or project is destroyed, it cannot be recovered.

FIGURE 5.2

To define project-level rights for a given user, you must first enable project security.

After the project level security has been enabled, you need to define the user rights for each project. To do that, click the Tools, Rights by Project menu option. This will result in the Project Rights dialog being displayed as you see in Figure 5.3.

FIGURE 5.3

Visual SourceSafe enables you to define a user's rights at the project level.

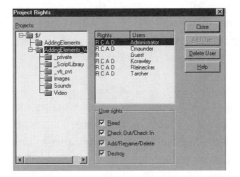

Defining a specific user's rights is as simple as selecting the desired project, selecting the user, and finally, clicking on the appropriate check boxes that define that user's capabilities. One thing of note here is that the rights do cascade down the project tree unless overridden. For example, in Figure 5.3 you can see two top-level projects: AddingElements and AddingElements_Web. Several folders under the AddingElements_Web project help to organize that project's files. If I select the AddingElements_Web project and specify that Tarcher has all rights, Tarcher will also have all rights to any folder within the AddingElements_Web project. However, I can always override that, by selecting a specific folder and changing Tarcher's rights for that single folder irrespective of the other folders in the AddingElements_Web project.

Establishing Version Control Standards for Your Team

One thing that almost all chapters on version control leave out is a section that warns new users of the choices they'll need to make when installing and configuring version control. It has been my experience that knowing these issues and establishing a set of version control guidelines will go a long way in helping to make version control work for you instead of against you. Although this is far from an exhaustive list, this list can get you started with regards to deciding how to manage your version control system:

- When to check in
- Multiple file check out
- Checking binaries into version control
- Specifying comments when checking in files

When to Check In

One debate that I hear constantly is this one. Some people believe that each programmer should check her work on a daily basis. Others believe that code should only be checked into version control if it doesn't "break" anything. It basically revolves around whether you think version control should be used as a backup system. Personally, I don't think code should ever be checked into version control if it compromises the integrity of the state of the code in version control. In other words, you should know that at any time, you could download the source code from version control and build a working version of the product. Therefore, I believe that code should only be checked into version control if it doesn't break anything.

Multi–Check Out

The multi–check out issue basically revolves around whether you are going to allow multiple users to check out the same file at the same time. This used to be a bigger issue than it is today because previous version control systems either had no capability to merge files or a very poor and kludgy way of doing it. Visual SourceSafe has such a powerful merging capability that almost all shops turn this feature on. After all, the idea of version control is to enhance productivity, not hamper it. My take on this is if the version control solves the problem of having one programmer's code wipe out another programmer's code (which it does with the merge feature), that feature should be used.

Checking Binaries into Version Control

There's really two parts to this issue. The first is whether to store the output of your source (binary executables) in version control. The second is whether to store the binaries of third-party vendors in version control.

Once again, my basic philosophy is that I want to know that at any point in time, I can download the files for a given project and build it. With versioning, I don't need to store the binaries in version control because I can build them. However, I do need the third-party binaries in order to run the project. Therefore, I don't store my project's binaries in version control, but I do store any binaries in version control that I can't build.

Specifying Comments When Checking In Files

Because by its very definition, version control is used to help in the management of multiple versions of software, you would think that adding comments to files when checking them into version control would be obvious. However, it has been my experience that left to their own devices, most developers will not add a descriptive comment detailing exactly what they've changed when they check a file back into version control.

The problem this causes is when you want to revert back to a given version of a file. Say that your invoicing application all of a sudden starts printing the wrong date. If comments are being entered when code is checked in, you can easily look at the history for the appropriate source modules and see which change is most likely the culprit. However, without the aid of comments, you will probably need to resort to manually opening and comparing each checked in version of the file(s) until you figure out where the code was broken. Therefore, it is always a good idea to explicitly state in your version control guidelines that a descriptive comment must be entered when code is checked in.

Adding Projects to Visual SourceSafe

Adding a Visual InterDev project to Visual SourceSafe is done after the project has been created. Therefore, the process is the same whether or not the project currently exists. If you have installed Visual SourceSafe, use the Web Project Wizard to create a project called VSSTest.

After it has finished creating the project, select the project root in the Project Explorer, and then select the Project, Source Control, Add To Source Control menu option. You will see a message box asking whether you want to add the entire solution to the Visual SourceSafe or just the selected project. Click the Solution button.

If your Windows user ID is different from your Visual SourceSafe username, you will be presented with the Visual SourceSafe Login dialog. Enter a username and password that you have defined using the Visual SourceSafe Admin application.

At this point, Visual SourceSafe will present you with the Add to SourceSafe Project dialog shown in Figure 5.4.

5

FIGURE 5.4

Use the Add to SourceSafe Project dialog to name the folder and select its location in the Visual SourceSafe hierarchy.

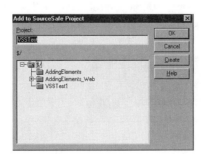

This dialog enables you to specify the name of the folder that will contain your Visual InterDev project's files. In addition, you can specify whether you want to create the new Visual SourceSafe folder at the root or beneath an existing folder. This can be extremely important if you are going to be working on several projects at the same time and need the ability to check them all out at once. Say that you have a distribution system whose source code is in version control. You might want to create a folder in the root called Distribution, and then create each project (for example, Inventory, Receiving, OrderEntry, and so on) in a folder under the Distribution folder. That way, you can check out all the files at once by telling Visual SourceSafe to check out the Distribution folder and to recursively check out all nested folders. At this point, accept the defaults and click OK.

Visual SourceSafe will confirm the creation of the new folder. Click Yes to have the new folder created. Visual SourceSafe will present the Add to Source Control dialog (shown in Figure 5.5) that enables you to specify a comment or description of the new project and whether you want to keep the current project checked out. Accept the defaults and click OK.

FIGURE 5.5

You can specify a comment for your new project via the Add to Source Control dialog.

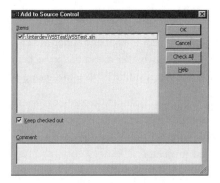

The last dialog you will see is the Enable Source Control dialog (see Figure 5.6) displayed by Visual InterDev, which confirms the creation of the new project and warns that it might take several minutes to complete this task. This warning is simply given because Visual InterDev is not making any assumptions on the speed of the communications between your box and your version control server. Clicking OK at this time will finally cause the creation of the Visual SourceSafe project.

FIGURE 5.6

Depending on how you are connected to the version control server, the step of actually creating the files on the server might take a few minutes.

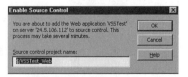

Using Visual SourceSafe from Visual InterDev

Now that you've added a project to Visual SourceSafe, it's time to see how easy it is to use from the Visual InterDev development environment by taking a look at the different options that are available to you depending on the type of file being worked with. As you will see, there are quite a few things you can do with Visual SourceSafe without ever leaving the comfort of your development environment.

Removing a Visual InterDev Solution from Version Control

If for some reason, you decide that you do not want a given Visual InterDev solution to participate in version control, Visual InterDev does provide this capability. You can do so by following these steps:

1. Display the Project Explorer.
2. Select the solution name.
3. Select the Project, Source Control, Remove [solution name] from Source Control menu option.
4. Click OK to confirm the removal of the solution from Visual SourceSafe.

Enabling and Disabling Version Control

If, instead of removing the Visual InterDev solution from version control, you simply want to disable it. You can do so by following these steps:

1. Display the Project Explorer.
2. Select the solution or project name.
3. Select the Project, Source Control, Change Connection menu option.
4. When the Set Source Control Connection dialog appears, specify whether you are connecting (enabling) or disconnecting (disabling) to version control.

Adding Files to Source Control

This option, as previously explained, can be used to add the selected project to version control. However, it can also be used to add a specific folder or file to version control. Generally, you will not have to perform this task as you do when version control has

5

been enabled for a project; any new files are automatically added to version control and checked out under your username. However, if you add a file to the project while you are disconnected from version control, you will need to follow these steps in order to add the file to version control for the current project:

1. Display the Project Explorer.
2. Select the files or folders you want to add to version control. (You can select more than one entry at a time.)
3. Select the Project, Source Control, Add to Source Control menu option.
4. Specify the target Visual SourceSafe folder and click OK.

Checking Files Out of Version Control

You can only check a file out of version control if you don't already have the file checked out and no other user has the file checked out (unless the Allow Multiple Checkouts is turned on). To check out a file, follow these steps:

1. Display the Project Explorer.
2. Select the files you want to check out.
3. Select the Project, Source Control, Check Out menu option from the main menu or the Check Out menu option from the items context menu.
4. Click OK to confirm the check out.

When the file has been checked out to you, a small red check mark will be placed next to the file in the Project Explorer.

Undoing a File Check Out

This option is only available for files that you have checked out and want to release your lock on. For example, you might have thought you were going to make changes to the file and didn't, or you want to revert back to the version of the file that is in version control. To do so, follow these steps:

1. Display the Project Explorer.
2. Select the files that you no longer want to have checked out.
3. Select the Project, Source Control, Undo Check Out menu option from the main menu or the Undo Check Out menu option from the file's context menu.
4. If you have changed the local version of the file, Visual SourceSafe will ask you to confirm whether you are sure that you want to undo the check out and lose your changes.

Checking Files Back into Version Control

When you have completed your changes and you want to make them available for everyone else, you can check the file in by completing the following:

1. Display the Project Explorer.

2. Select the files that you want to check in.

3. Select the Project, Source Control, Check In menu option from the main menu or the Check In menu option from the file's context menu.

4. Visual SourceSafe will then present you with a dialog that enables you to enter a descriptive comment detailing exactly what changes you made to the file while you had it checked out. This is extremely useful when comparing version of files.

Get the Latest Version of a File or Project

Many times you don't want to check a file or group of files out, but you just need to synchronize with version control in order to get the "latest and greatest" version of the file (referred to as the *tip revision* in version control lingo). This is typically done at the project level, but can also be done on a file-by-file basis as well, as shown in the following:

1. Display the Project Explorer.

2. Select the files that you want to synch on.

3. Select the Project, Source Control, Get Latest Version menu option from the main menu or the Get Latest Version menu option from the file's context menu.

4. If the local version of the file is more recent than the version in version control, Visual SourceSafe will ask you to confirm if you want to lose the changes made to the local file.

Compare Local Files to Files on the Server

This option allows you to compare the local copy with what is on the version control server. This can be extremely helpful in determining things such as why one person can't build the project while another person can when they supposedly have the same versions of the source code files.

Allowing Multiple Simultaneous Checkouts

As mentioned previously, Visual SourceSafe does provide the ability to allow for multiple simultaneous checkouts of the same file. However, in order for you take advantage of that, you must enable that feature.

5

Setting the Allow Multiple Checkout Option

To enable the multiple checkout option, perform the following steps:

1. Run the Visual SourceSafe Admin application.

2. Select the Tools, Options menu option.

3. Check the Allow Multiple Checkout check box and click OK to save your changes.

Visually Merging Files

If programmer A and programmer B check out the same file and programmer A checks the file back in before programmer B does, then Visual SourceSafe will automatically attempt to merge the files when programmer B attempts to check in his file. If there are conflicts, such as the same exact line(s) of code being modified by both programmers, Visual SourceSafe will display the dialog shown in Figure 5.7. This dialog can take some playing around with to get accustomed to, but basically allows you to specify if you want to keep the first version of the code (the SourceSafe version), the second version of the code (the local copy), or if you want to manually merge the code yourself.

FIGURE 5.7

One of the nicest features of Visual SourceSafe is its merge capabilities. However, there are times when you will have to perform a manual merge.

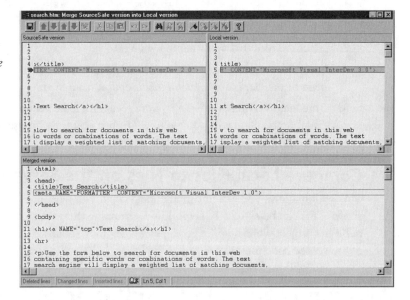

Applying Labels

As mentioned previously, the importance of being able to label a release cannot be overstated. After all, one of the biggest selling points of version control is that you can quickly and easily get any version of your code out of version control.

However, in order to accomplish this, you must first understand the labeling process. Labeling is nothing more than applying a textual description to a grouping of files. That way, when you want to pull down a specific group of files, you need only specify the label name and the rest is up to Visual SourceSafe.

Here's a real life example. Say that you just got your company's brand new product to the point that it's working well enough for a demo. However, the demo isn't for another month. You want to add a few more features, but you do have a working version right now. So, you label the current source code as Version 1.0 and continue working. Now when your boss comes to you two weeks ahead of schedule and says that another client wants to see the product tomorrow afternoon, instead of staring at your shoes and stammering something like you can't because the code is "in pieces on the floor," you smile and say "No problem." You check your current work into version control, start up Visual SourceSafe and do a Get on that particular label. After building the demo from the code you labeled two weeks ago, you check your code back out of version control and continue working. This is exactly why labels are so important to version control.

Applying a Label

To apply a label at any point in the lifecycle of a project, all you need to do is follow these steps:

1. Run the Visual SourceSafe application.
2. Right-click on the desired folder to display its context menu.
3. Select the Label menu option.
4. Type the name of the Label that you want to use and a comment. Labels are pretty terse (you'll see why in a moment), whereas the comments tend to be much longer and descriptive.

Getting a Specific Version of the Code

Now how do you get a specific version of the code? Selecting the Check Out or Get Latest Version options will only retrieve the tip revision of the specified files. In order to retrieve a specific version of a file (either by label or by date), you must do the following:

1. Right-click on the desired folder or file to display the folder's context menu.
2. Select the Show History menu option.
3. You will then see the Project History Options dialog, as shown in Figure 5.8.

5

FIGURE 5.8

The Project History Options dialog gives you a lot of flexibility in how you can search through the history of your source code.

4. As you can see, the Project History Options dialog enables you to search the history of a project using such qualifiers as data ranges, usernames, and whether you only want to see label history. For this exercise, check the Labels Only check box and click OK.

    Figure 5.9 shows you an example of the resulting History dialog.

FIGURE 5.9

From the History of Project dialog, you can do everything from running reports to retrieving a specific version of the project.

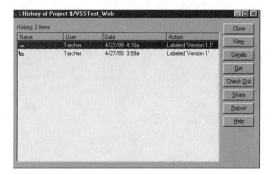

5. From this dialog, clicking the View button would result in a dialog listing all the files that were included in this label. Clicking the Details button would display the date and time of the label as well as the more descriptive comment. However, for the purposes of this exercise, the button you need to notice is the Get button. Clicking this button is how you would retrieve a specific version of a project based on a label.

Retrieving Code to a Different Directory

In the example I gave about your boss coming to you and requesting the demo two weeks early, one of the steps I listed was checking your code into version control and then getting the desired version of the code to build for the demo. However, if you'll recall from earlier in the chapter, I also recommended against checking anything into version control that wasn't functioning or would not build. Therefore, we seem to have a contradiction here.

Actually, there are a couple of ways to circumvent this problem. You could retrieve the label on someone else's box. But what if there is no one else or your machine has been designated as the build machine? In that case, you can simply do the following: While holding down the Shift key, click the Get button from the History dialog. Visual SourceSafe will then display the Get dialog that will allow you to specify to which directory you want to retrieve the source code. Now, you can download the source code for the demo without causing a conflict with the files you've already got checked out.

Reports and Searches

Because one of a version control system's main functions is to keep track of files and who has what checked out, you would think that Visual SourceSafe would provide a reporting or searching mechanism for your projects. Well, they do, and it's as simple as selecting a menu option.

Searching for Specific Files

If you've never worked on a large project, you might wonder how files can be misplaced in a project's hierarchy. Believe me—in even a moderately complex project, this can happen more often than you think. To search for a given file or set of files, simply complete the following:

1. Run the Visual SourceSafe application.

2. Select the folder in which you want to search. If you want the search to be performed on all the folders, select the root folder.

3. Click the View, Search, Wildcard Search menu option (or press Ctrl+W) to display the Search for Wildcard dialog (see Figure 5.10).

FIGURE 5.10

Visual SourceSafe provides a very flexible search ability to locate files by wildcard across all defined projects.

As you can see in Figure 5.10, the Search for Wildcard dialog enables you to search through not only the current project for a given file or set of files, but also through all subprojects or even all the projects defined in your SourceSafe database.

4. Clicking OK will cause Visual SourceSafe to perform the search and display the found files in the application's list view.

If after performing a search, you click on another project and don't see any files: It is because Visual SourceSafe is still performing the search. In other words, whereas Visual SourceSafe refers to this as a search, it is more accurately called a filter because Visual SourceSafe will perform the same search on every folder you click on. Therefore, in order to quit this search and be able to view all the files again, you will need to select the View, Cancel Search menu option or press Ctrl+Q.

Searching on File Status

If you need to search on the status of a given file or set of files such as which files are currently checked out, you can do so very easily by pressing Ctrl+S. In addition, you can also do such things as displaying which files a specific user has checked out. However, when you're finished, don't forget to press Ctrl+Q to cancel the search.

Summary

In this hour, you learned how to use the Visual SourceSafe version control system. At the beginning of the hour, you learned the basics of configuring SourceSafe: creating users, setting their project rights, defining options such as enabling project security, and allowing multiple checkout. You then discovered how to use Visual SourceSafe from within the Visual InterDev environment so that you can have all the benefits of a full-featured version control system without having to leave the comfort of your development environment. Finally, you finished the hour by learning how to perform such tasks as applying revision labels, viewing a change history, and visually merging files when a conflict occurs.

Q&A

Q What is the difference between version control and change control, or change management?

A Version control is software that is used to manage the different versions of files. Examples of version control packages are Visual SourceSafe and PVCS. A change management system is used to track changes to a system at a higher, more logical level. Intersolv's Tracker is an example of a change management system.

Q Can other version control packages, such as PVCS, be used with Visual InterDev?

A Visual SourceSafe is the only version control package that Visual InterDev natively supports.

Workshop

The Workshop is designed to help you anticipate possible questions, review what you've learned, and begin thinking ahead to put your knowledge into practice. The answers to the quiz are in Appendix A, "Answers."

Quiz

1. Name some of the advantages of version control.
2. What is the biggest advantage of using Visual SourceSafe with your Visual InterDev applications?
3. What must you do first before you can define project-level rights for each user?
4. How do you specify that a given Visual InterDev project is to be added to version control?
5. How do you remove a Visual InterDev project from version control?
6. How do you enable/disable version control for a Visual InterDev solution?
7. How do you add files to version control if they've been added to a Visual InterDev project while the project was disconnected from version control?
8. How do you enable the multiple file checkout feature of Visual SourceSafe?
9. How do you create a label in Visual SourceSafe?
10. How do you download from Visual SourceSafe the files that are specific to a given label?

Exercises

1. Test the automatic and manual merge capabilities of Visual SourceSafe.
2. Test the ability to label multiple versions of a project in Visual Source and retrieve only the desired versions.

5

PART II

Empowering Your Web Sites

Hour

Hour 6

Empowering Your Site with Client Scripting

Up until this point, you've discovered how Visual InterDev enables you to create Web pages, add content to those Web pages, and design your Web site all from a single integrated development environment. Now that the prerequisite basics have been covered, it's finally time to dive into the fun stuff: scripting.

The highlights of this hour include the following:

- Learning the benefits of scripting
- Combining script with HTML
- Differentiating between the different script language choices
- Writing Hello World in JavaScript
- Adding HTML controls to Web pages
- Handling control-level events with JavaScript

Benefits of Scripting

When the World Wide Web was first introduced, it represented a means of sharing information between disparate systems and networks. This worked wonderfully for a long
time because the majority of people using the Web in its infancy were simply searching
for static documentation on a given subject matter. However, this all changed when the
world outside of academia discovered the Web and its enormous potential.

At first, companies were thrilled with the fact that they could advertise their services and
products on the Web. After all, the Web provided an extremely inexpensive means of getting
the word out to an absolutely infinite number of potential customers, each of whom could
find these companies' Web sites through search engines that were available free of charge to
everyone. Upon this discovery, companies started developing Web pages that ranged from
very small pages that simply detailed the company's services to very large and elaborate
Web sites that contained complete online versions of the company's entire inventory.

Although this was a tremendous boon for companies attempting to find new advertising
venues, there was still another major obstacle to overcome. When the user was ready to
purchase a service or item or had a question, he or she had to call a telephone number
displayed on the Web page or send an email to someone at the company. This, in turn,
necessitated a return phone call or email to finalize the sale or answer the user's query.
Needless to say, this meant that the Web was being used as nothing more than an elec-
tronic catalog and, as such, was being vastly underutilized.

The problem was that Web pages were developed entirely in HTML, which, while being a
tremendous tool for displaying information, was never intended to be a language for writing
Web pages that would interact with users. What was needed at this point was some means of
allowing users to peruse a company's inventory, query the system, place orders online, and
check order status. The obvious advantage this provides is one of convenience for the customer. As anyone who's ever purchased anything knows, greater convenience equals happier
customers, and happier customers equates to repeat business. Therefore, scripting languages
were invented to augment HTML, and the concept of scripting was born.

Combining Script and HTML

Writing script, or *scripting*, within HTML is very easy. Actually, there's an HTML tag
that informs the browser that a given block of text within an HTML file is actually script
and therefore, needs to be treated accordingly. The HTML tags used for this purpose are
the <SCRIPT> and </SCRIPT> tags, which mark the beginning and end of a block script,
respectively (see Listing 6.1).

LISTING 6.1 An Example of the `<SCRIPT>` and `</SCRIPT>` HTML Tags with VBScript

```
 1: <HTML>
 2: <HEAD>
 3: <META name="VI60_DefaultClientScript" Content="VBScript">
 4:
 5: <META NAME="GENERATOR" Content="Microsoft Visual Studio 6.0">
 6: <TITLE></TITLE>
 7: </HEAD>
 8: <BODY>
 9:
10: <P><FONT size=6>Example page with VBScript</FONT></P>
11:
12: <SCRIPT LANGUAGE=VBScript>
13: <!--
14: this is where you would insert your functions
15: -->
16: </SCRIPT>
17:
18: </BODY>
19: </HTML>
```

Notice that the `<SCRIPT>` tag in the Listing 6.1 also contains a keyword (`LANGUAGE`) that's used to specify which scripting language will be used. The following are valid entries for the `LANGUAGE` keyword:

- `JavaScript`
- `JScript`
- `VBS`
- `VBScript`

As you can see in line 12, the code snippet is informing the browser that VBScript is to follow. The differences between these languages is outlined in the next section; however, one important point you should note now is that Internet Explorer 4 and above ships with the JScript (JavaScript-compatible) and VBScript engines.

Now look at line 13, which follows the `<SCRIPT>` tag. This is the very familiar HTML comment tag. If you've programmed in other languages, this might seem strange at first. After all, in most development environments, comments are not executed and serve only as documentation within the source code. However, the designers of the HTML language faced a dilemma when trying to decide how to allow developers to incorporate scripting into their Web pages for use with the newer browsers while not causing a problem when displaying these pages in older browsers that aren't "script aware." That's where the idea of using the comment tag came about. Using this technique, older browsers will simply see the script as comments and ignore it while newer browser with built-in script engines will interpret everything between the `<SCRIPT>` and `</SCRIPT>` tags as executable code.

6

Scripting Options

You would think that with the standardization of HTML that there would be a standard for scripting as well. Unfortunately, as the expression goes, "The great thing about standards is that there are so many to pick from." Therefore, despite the best intentions of creating a standard scripting language for all uses, several languages do exist, each with its own inherit set of advantages and disadvantages. The currently supported scripting languages are the following:

- VBScript
- JavaScript
- JScript

What Is VBScript?

It's a well-known fact that Bill Gates's vision of a single language that will be used to automate all tasks on a computer is a BASIC derivative. That's why when Microsoft first introduced a means of automating its Office products (Word for Windows, Excel, and so on), it did so by defining a subset of Visual Basic called *Visual Basic for Applications*, or VBA. Therefore, it came as no surprise to anyone that when Microsoft unveiled its version of a scripting language for the Internet, it turned out to be yet another subset of Visual Basic. This scripting language is called *VBScript*.

VBScript is actually a very powerful and robust scripting language and does have many advantages over other scripting languages:

- It's easy to learn and use.
- It's based on Visual Basic.
- It's natively supported by Internet Explorer.

Because VBScript is Visual Basic code, it's a language that's very easy to learn. In fact, the relatively low learning curve has been, for many years, the main reason learning institutions have chosen BASIC as the first language taught to beginner-level computer science students.

By far, the most widely used personal computer operating system is Microsoft Windows. In addition, the most popular programming language of choice for Windows development is Visual Basic. Therefore, the obvious choice as to which language to use as a starting point for a new scripting language had to a very easy one for Microsoft. VBScript enables current Visual Basic programmers to leverage their skill set as they transition into writing Internet-based applications.

With Internet Explorer containing a built-in VBScript engine, there's no need to locate and install an add-in to the browser in order to code VBScript. Additionally, anyone programming in VBScript can do so knowing that his or her code will run without incident on one of the most popular browsers in existence, without any intervention needed on the part of the user.

JavaScript and JScript

Many people believe that JavaScript is from Sun and is a subset of the Java language. Actually, JavaScript is a cross-platform scripting language that was created by Netscape and was first named *LiveScript*. In addition, although both JavaScript and Java have a simplified C-like syntax, JavaScript only vaguely resembles the more robust, full-featured Java language.

For a while, Netscape products were the only ones that supported JavaScript. Then, when the JavaScript language started becoming popular, Microsoft agreed to support it. Unfortunately, Microsoft did so by supporting its own version of it called JScript, and although these two languages were supposed to be compatible, developing JavaScript that executed consistently in both the Netscape and Internet Explorer browsers proved difficult.

Therefore, in 1995, Microsoft and Netscape came together and agreed on defining a single specification that's governed by the European Computer Manufacturer's Association (ECMA). This language is called *ECMAScript* and is supported by Visual InterDev. So when you see the term *JavaScript* used in this book, you should understand that this is the ECMAScript version.

Listing 6.2 shows a snippet of JavaScript code. Notice that the main difference between the VBScript code in Listing 6.1 and the JavaScript code in Listing 6.2 involves the LANGUAGE keyword in the <SCRIPT> tag and the // characters that immediately preceded the HTML tag for terminating a comment in the JavaScript snippet.

LISTING 6.2 An Example of JavaScript

```
 1: <HTML>
 2: <HEAD>
 3: <META NAME="GENERATOR" Content="Microsoft Visual Studio 6.0">
 4: <TITLE></TITLE>
 5: </HEAD>
 6: <BODY>
 7:
 8: <P><FONT face="" size=6>Example page with
 9: JScript</FONT></P>
10:
11: <SCRIPT LANGUAGE=JavaScript>
12: <!--
13:
14: //-->
15: </SCRIPT>
16:
17:
18: </BODY>
19: </HTML>
```

6

Advantages of JavaScript

Just as VBScript has many advantages, so does JavaScript. However, the main advantage to using JavaScript can be summed up very simply. It has a much wider level of acceptance in the Web application development community than VBScript. In a recent journey to my favorite technical book store, I found literally dozens of books on the subject of programming in JavaScript, but it took me almost 10 minutes to find the one and only book the store had on VBScript. In addition, a technical resource with which any developer should become intimately familiar, `www.experts-exchange.com`, has a complete section on JavaScript, with literally thousands of questions and answers dealing with using this very powerful and robust language. Even Visual InterDev, itself, defaults the client-side scripting language to JavaScript. For these reasons, I strongly recommend that new Web application developers concentrate on JavaScript. Therefore, all the examples on client-side scripting in this hour use JavaScript.

Implementing "Hello World" in JavaScript

Now that you've seen some sample code and had a brief rundown of the scripting language options, it's time to write some script!

Any time you write about a technology such as Visual InterDev that incorporates other technologies, there's always the question of how much of the secondary technologies should be covered. Because a language such as VBScript or JavaScript would take an entire book to fully explain, the following sections are not meant for that purpose. Rather, the remainder of this hour is intended to teach you how to incorporate script into your Web pages using the Visual InterDev development environment. For a more thorough coverage of either language, refer to a book whose main focus is the teaching of the desired language.

Unfortunately, once again, Microsoft and Netscape can't agree on a standard when it comes to the presentation of Web pages. In this particular case, Netscape mandates the definitions of a <FORM> tag in order for controls to appear when viewed in the browser. However, forms are not presented until the next hour. So if you are using the Netscape browser, you will need to either view the page in Visual InterDev's QuickView or perform the following steps for any examples that are in this hour:

1. Open the page in Source view.

2. Insert a <FORM> tag immediately after the <BODY> tag.

3. Insert a </FORM> tag immediately before the closing </BODY> tag.

It's customary when learning a new programming language to develop a version of the famous "Hello World" example. Therefore, that's where we'll start. At this point, perform the following steps:

1. Create a new Visual InterDev project called ClientScripts and add an HTML page to it called HelloWorld.

2. When the page is opened up in Design view, click the Center Text button on the HTML toolbar, enter the text This page contains my first script!, and then press the Enter key two times.

3. Now, create an HTML Button control by double-clicking the Button entry in the Toolbox. If the Toolbox window is not visible, select the View, Toolbox menu option and then click the Toolbox tab at the bottom of the window.

4. Now you should have a button in the middle of your page. At this point, change the Name and ID properties to btnSayHello. Although it's strictly not necessary for this simple application, you should get into the habit of giving your controls meaningful names from the beginning.

5. Next, change the text on the button to read Say Hello. There are two ways to accomplish this: If you click the Button control itself, you'll see a caret that indicates you can type text directly into the control. You can also accomplish the same thing by changing the Button control's Value property. Figure 6.1 illustrates what you should now see in your version of Visual InterDev.

FIGURE 6.1

You can add controls to a Web page by simply dragging them to the page from the Toolbox window.

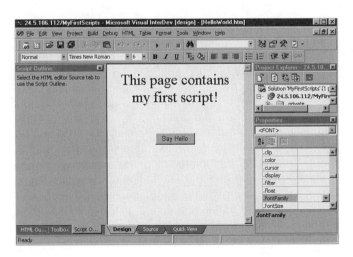

6

6. Now for the fun stuff! Open the Script Outline window. If it's not already open, simply select the View, Other Windows, Script Outline menu option.

7. You won't see much on this window at this point. Therefore, click the HTML editor's Source tab. Now you'll see quite a few options at your disposal. You can see that the Script Outline window shows you the client-side objects, events, and scripts as well as the server-side objects, events, and scripts. If it's not already expanded, open the Client Objects & Events folder to display all the objects currently defined for this Web page.

8. Expand the `btnSayHello` object. This will show you a wealth of options as well as how much control over your objects you have. Note that the lightning bolt icon to the left indicates that the entry is an event for which you can write a handler. At this point, locate the `onclick` event and double-click it. Visual InterDev will respond by automatically creating a JavaScript function in your Web page for this event. Notice also that in the Script Outline window, the `onclick` event has been bolded. Double-clicking on this item will take you straight to its event handler. This is a quick way to navigate around your code.

9. Visual InterDev will automatically place your caret at the beginning of the function. Type in the following:

```
alert ("Hello World");
```

10. The results of running your application and clicking the Say Hello button are shown in Figure 6.2.

FIGURE 6.2

Event handlers for controls can be written with JavaScript or VBScript.

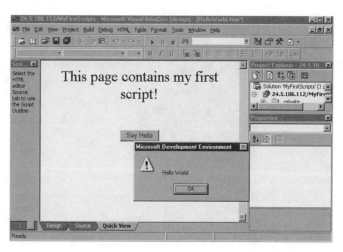

Congratulations! That's how easy it is to add a control to a Web page and then add event handlers with JavaScript. However, as you learned earlier, one of the main advantages of using scripting over HTML is the ability to *interface* with the user. Therefore, in the next example, you'll learn how to retrieve user input and display that information back to the user.

Retrieving Input from the User with JavaScript

In this example, you'll build on the already completed HelloWorld.htm page by adding a TextBox control that will allow the user to indicate his or her name. Then, you'll change the Button control's onclick handler to use the value from the TextBox control in the message that's displayed to the user. In the process of these modifications to your first project, you'll be learning how to retrieve simple input from a user, how to access attributes and methods of an object, and how to use IntelliSense. Here are the steps to follow:

1. Click the HTML editor's Design tab.

2. Insert a blank line before the Button control by clicking the line above the control and pressing the Enter key.

3. From the Toolbox window, double-click the TextBox control. This will add a textbox at the current position within the Design view. Modify the control's Name and ID properties to read txtName.

4. Once you've added the new control, click the Source tab. You'll see that your new txtName control has been added to the Client Objects and Events tab of the Script Outline window. Expand the btnSayHello object and double-click the onclick event.

5. Now change the alert function to the following:

```
alert("Hello " + txtName.value + "!");
```

> Just as Visual InterDev is smart enough to automatically show you the parameters of a function after you type the name of the function, it also shows you the methods and properties of an object once you typed the name of the object. Therefore, you only need to type the first few letters of the desired method or property. Once that item is highlighted in the list box, you can press the Tab key and the appropriate item will be typed in automatically.

6. At this point, save your work and click the HTML editor's QuickView tab. Type any value you want in the TextBox control and then click the SayHello button. The results should be similar to those shown in Figure 6.3.

Writing a Feedback Web Page

In this next example, you'll learn how to write a Web page used to get feedback from a user. As you work your way through this example, you'll learn how to incorporate many other HTML controls on your page as well as how to handle their events and, in some cases, override their default behaviors.

FIGURE 6.3

A script can be written in minutes that will accept user input and provide feedback.

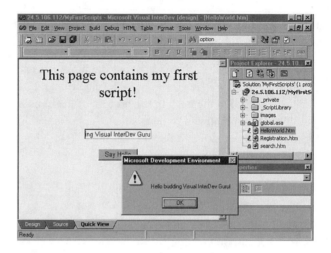

The first thing you'll need to do is to create the Web page and add the necessary controls. Follow these steps:

1. Add a new HTML page called Registration.htm to your ClientScripts project.

2. Add the header and instructional text you see in Figure 6.4.

FIGURE 6.4

The beginnings of a simple registration page.

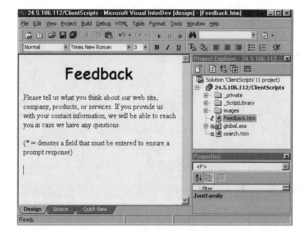

3. After you've added the header and instructional text, add TextBox controls for the user's name and email address, as shown in Figure 6.5. Make sure that you precede each prompt with an asterisk character. (This has become a standard for denoting an input control that must be filled out.) Name these two controls `txtName` and `txtEmail`, respectively.

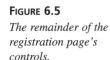

Figure 6.5

The remainder of the registration page's controls.

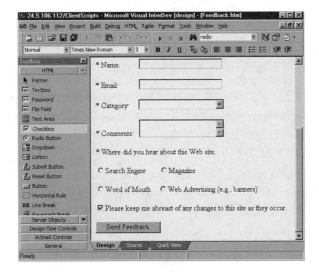

4. Next, add a Dropdown control for the category and name it `cboCategory`. For those of you more familiar with the Windows term *combo box*, that's exactly what a Dropdown control is. You'll see how to initialize this control shortly.

5. Now add the Comments TextArea control, as shown previously in Figure 6.5, and name it `txtComments`.

6. Once you've added the Comments TextArea control, add the radio buttons that will allow the user to specify how he or she found your Web site.

7. Add the CheckBox control that will allow the user to indicate whether he or she wants to be informed of future changes to your Web site. Name this control `chkInform`.

8. Finally, add a Button control so that when the user has completed the form, he or she can click the button to send an email to you. (This functionality won't be added until the next hour, but go ahead and add the button now to finish the page layout.)

Working with HTML Controls from JavaScript

In the first example, Hello World, you learned just enough about the TextBox and Button controls to make your first script work. In this section, you'll learn a bit more about those controls as well as how to incorporate the controls shown in Figure 6.5 into your Web application.

6

Using the TextBox Control in JavaScript

Because the TextBox control is probably the control you'll use most often on your Web pages, we'll start with it. The TextBox control is used to capture a single line of information that's to be manually entered by the user. For example, it's perfect for entering name, address, city, and zip code information. For information that spans multiple lines, use the TextArea control (described later). As you saw in the Hello World example earlier in the hour, the TextBox control can be treated in JavaScript as an object. By that, I mean that it has properties and methods like any other object, which makes using it easier.

To illustrate how to manually add a TextBox control in your code, take a look at the following snippet. This should be similar to the code that Visual InterDev created for you when you dropped a TextBox control onto your Feedback page.

```
<INPUT id=txtName name=txtName style="HEIGHT: 22px; WIDTH: 178px"></P>
```

As you can see, the first thing you must specify is the `<INPUT>` tag. This is true of all the HTML controls that you'll work with in this example. The `<INPUT>` tag simply defines an input-capable control on your document or page.

At this point, click the QuickView tab on the HTML editor. Now type some data into the Name and Email TextBox controls and then tab around the form. If you're accustomed to developing in Windows, you'll be surprised to see that when you tab into a TextBox control, the text in that control is not automatically highlighted. Instead, the control remembers the exact position within the text where you were at when you last vacated the field. Luckily for those who prefer that the text be selected automatically upon entering the TextBox control, there's a very easy way to implement this functionality.

Click the Source tab and locate the `txtName` TextBox definition. Once you've done that, add the following code to the end of the definition (just before the ending right angle bracket):

```
onFocus="this.select()"
```

Do the same thing for the `txtEmail` control. Now whenever the user tabs into either of these controls, any existing text will be highlighted.

Using the Dropdown Control in JavaScript

If you're already familiar with Windows development, you might recognize the Dropdown control as a combo box. Actually, this control has yet another name in JavaScript parlance: a `Select` object. The `Select` object allows you to provide the user with a list of choices, but it doesn't take up as much screen real estate as a list box does.

In order to add items to a `Select` object, you can define an `OPTION` object for each item, like this:

```
<option value="VALUE">ENTRY</option>
```

As you can see, each `OPTION` object has two main parts: the value and the prompt. The prompt is what the user will see in the Dropdown control, and the value is what your script will see when the user selects the associated entry from the control.

To illustrate this, let's add some entries into the Categories Dropdown control. In the Feedback page, the Categories Dropdown control is used to provide the user with a list of categories from which to choose. These categories are meant to describe what the user is providing feedback on. At this point, click the Source tab and locate the `cboCategories` object. When you've located it, add the following lines of code right before the `</SELECT>` tag. Notice that the `Selected` keyword is used to define the default item.

```
<option value="1">Web Site</option>
<option selected value="2">One of our Products</option>
<option value="3">One of our Services </option>
```

Using the TextArea Control in JavaScript

As mentioned earlier, the TextArea control is used when you need to allow the user to enter multiple lines of information. The Feedback page provides a perfect example of this with the Comments field. Here's the script that's created as a result of dragging a TextArea control on the Feedback page:

```
<TEXTAREA id=txtComments name=txtComments></TEXTAREA>
```

Once again, aside from the ability to select the control's contents automatically upon focus, there's really not too much that's exciting about the TextArea control.

Using the Radio Button Control in JavaScript

Radio buttons are used to select one choice from a group of choices. To illustrate this, let's say you have a group of radio buttons that represent the days of the week and you want the user to select the current day. Obviously, only one choice is valid. Therefore, you could represent this using radio buttons.

The great thing about radio buttons is that you basically get this functionality for free. All you have to do is give each radio button that will participate in the same group the same name. That way, when one radio button within that group of radio buttons is selected, the currently selected radio button will be deselected automatically. Here's an example:

```
<INPUT TYPE=radio Name="btnWeekDays" VALUE="0">Sunday
<INPUT TYPE=radio Name="btnWeekDays" VALUE="1">Monday
<INPUT TYPE=radio Name="btnWeekDays" VALUE="2">Tuesday
<INPUT TYPE=radio Name="btnWeekDays" VALUE="3">Wednesday
<INPUT TYPE=radio Name="btnWeekDays" VALUE="4">Thursday
<INPUT TYPE=radio Name="btnWeekDays" VALUE="5">Friday
<INPUT TYPE=radio Name="btnWeekDays" VALUE="6">Saturday
```

6

As you can see, when you're defining the <INPUT> tag, the value that is displayed can be different than the value your script will see as a result of a particular selection.

At this point, switch to the Source view and upon locating the definition of the radio buttons, modify the <INPUT> tag so that entries look as follows (note that the space characters and <P> tags have been purposely omitted for clarity):

```
<INPUT type="radio" name=btnSource Value="SearchEngine" >Search Engine
<INPUT type=radio name=btnSource Value=Magazine>Magazine
<INPUT type="radio" name=btnSource Value="WordOfMouth" >Word of Mouth
<INPUT type=radio name=btnSource Value="WebAdvertising">
➥Web Advertising (e.g., banners)
```

Note that like the Select object, the Selected keyword can be used to define a default selection. It wasn't used here because you want to make sure the user has made an explicit choice.

Retrieving the radio button that's selected is a bit tricky because you have to iterate through all the radio buttons of the group, checking each one's Checked property and using the checked control's Value property. Therefore, I wrote a very simple JavaScript function that simplifies this process (see Listing 6.3). Note that this will work with any group of Radio Button controls because it dynamically iterates through each radio button in the group.

LISTING 6.3 A Simple JavaScript Function to Determine the Value of the Currently Selected Radio Button Control

```
<SCRIPT LANGUAGE=javascript>
<!--
function getRadioValue(radioButtons)
{
    bFoundValue = false
    i=0;
    while (!bFoundValue && i < radioButtons.length)
    {
        bFoundValue = radioButtons[i++].checked;
    }

    return (bFoundValue ? radioButtons[i-1].value : null);
}
//-->
</SCRIPT>
```

In order to insert this code, open the Source Code view of the Feedback page, right-click the HTML editor, select the Script Block, Client menu option, and then enter the function exactly as shown in Listing 6.3.

In order to use this function, simply call it, passing the name of the Radio Button control(s), like this:

```
alert (getRadioValue(btnSource));
```

Using the CheckBox Control in JavaScript

The CheckBox control allows a user to answer a yes or no question, such as "Would you like one of our sales people to call you?"

Here's the JavaScript code that Visual InterDev created for the Feedback Web page example:

```
<P><INPUT CHECKED id=chkInfom name=chkInform type=checkbox>
Please keep me abreast of any changes to this site as they occur.</P>
```

Take a look at the first line of script. This is where the CheckBox control is actually defined. Notice that like the other controls you've added to your Web page, INPUT indicates an input-capable field, and the ID and Name keywords indicate the values you assigned in the Properties window for this control.

However, unlike the other controls, to retrieve a CheckBox's current state (checked or unchecked), you have to query the Checked property. For example, you can easily test this by adding a CheckBox control and a Button control to a page and adding the following code to the Button control's onclick event handler:

```
alert (chkInform.checked);
```

This will cause either a value of "false" or "true" to be displayed for the unchecked and checked status, respectively. In order to default to a specific state, simply check or uncheck the CheckBox control in the Design view of the HTML editor.

Summary

Once again, you've made a tremendous amount of progress on your way to proficiency using Visual InterDev. Not only did you write a very simple Hello World example using JavaScript, you created a Feedback page as well. Along the way, you learned several client-side scripting techniques that you'll find incredibly useful as you continue to enhance your abilities to develop Web applications with Visual InterDev.

6

Q&A

Q I have several banners I want to show on my Web page. I know how to add an image to a Web page, but how do I randomly load a banner ad using JavaScript?

A The first thing you need is a function that generates a random number. To do that, enter the following code:

```
<SCRIPT LANGUAGE="JavaScript">
<!--
function rand(number)
{
 return Math.ceil(Math.random()*number);
};
-->
</SCRIPT>
```

The rand function takes a single argument that defines the largest value that will be generated. As you can see, the function first calls the JavaScript Math object's random function to retrieve a number between zero and one. This number is then multiplied by the passed argument. Finally, the result is rounded off to the nearest integer value. Therefore, the result of calling this function is a random number between one and the number that is passed to it.

The last thing you need to do is add the following code block:

```
<SCRIPT LANGUAGE="JavaScript">
<!--
 document.write('<IMG SRC="banner' + rand(10)
 + '.gif" WIDTH=100% HEIGHT="40">');
//-->
</SCRIPT>
```

The only line of code here uses the document object, which you will learn more about in the next hour and Hour 9, "Using Dynamic HTML." For now, it's enough for you to know that the document.write function writes HTML code to the Web page.

As you can see, this line of code writes an <IMG> tag to the page with a value of bannerx (where x = 1 to 10).

In order to modify this code for your use, simply change the number being passed to the rand function and the literals (banner and gif) that are being used to format the image filename.

Q How can I call an EXE on the local machine from client JavaScript?

A The short answer is that you can't. Browsers are built with a security model that will not allow the Web developer to simply run an application on the local machine from the Web page's script. This is obviously meant to protect the user from irresponsible Web applications.

Workshop

The Workshop is designed to help you anticipate possible questions, review what you've learned, and begin thinking ahead to put your knowledge into practice. The answers to the quiz and exercise are in Appendix A, "Answers."

Quiz

1. Why is scripting needed when you have HTML?

2. Why is script written as though it were a comment or series of comments?

3. How do you add a JavaScript event handler for an HTML control?

4. How can you change the default behavior of a TextBox or TextArea control to automatically select its contents upon receiving focus?

5. How do you add items to a `Select` object using JavaScript?

6. How do you make one of the entries in a `Select` object the default entry?

7. How do you retrieve the value of the currently selected Radio Button control?

8. How is a CheckBox control's state retrieved?

9. How do you insert a new JavaScript function into the source code of a Web page?

10. What JavaScript function is used to display information to the user?

Exercise

Create a new Web page that has multiple groups of mutually exclusive Radio Button controls and figure out how to have them work correctly.

6

Hour 7

Document and Form Processing with Client Scripts

In this hour, you'll learn about the Document and Form objects and how they make life for the Web application developer much easier. Once you've learned the basics of these objects, you'll put what you've learned into practice by developing a Registration Web page that allows your users to register their usage of your product.

The highlights of this hour include the following:

- Learning the basics of the Document object
- Determining a user's browser
- Dynamically changing a page's color properties
- Learning the basics of the Form object
- Developing a Registration Web page
- Emailing a form's data using JavaScript
- Using the onBeforeUnload event handler

The Document Object

Create a new Visual InterDev project called FormsProcessing and add to it an HTML
page named DynamicContent.htm. When that's done, switch the DynamicContent page
to Source view and then open the Script Outline window. As you can see in Figure 7.1,
two objects are defined automatically for every HTML page you create: a Document
object and a Window object. In this section, you'll learn about the Document object.

FIGURE 7.1

Window *and* Document
*objects are always
present in the Script
Outline window for
every Web page created
in Visual InterDev.*

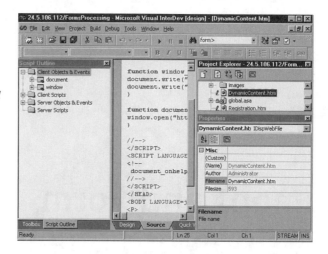

Although the Window object represents the highest-level object for built-in JavaScript objects,
it doesn't actually contain any data. In other words, it serves as little more than a container
for the entire application. The Document object, however, is much more interesting. You can
think of the Document object as you would the actual HTML document that's displayed in
the Web browser. Therefore, it's the Document object that actually contains the HTML that's
interpreted by the browser to produce what the user ends up viewing when your Web page is
presented.

Dynamically Creating Document Content

Up until now, the HTML you've entered for any given Web page has been done via the
Visual InterDev HTML editor. However, using the Document object, you can dynamically
code the content of a Web page using JavaScript. Of course, you might ask the question,
"When would I do this?" Well, one example is a feedback Web page in which you want
to give your users the opportunity to provide opinions and information concerning their
experience with the site. Typically, after the user has filled out the Feedback form and
submitted her information to the server, the Web application displays a page that says
something like, "Thank you, Ms. Smith, your comments are appreciated...." Obviously,
because the Web application doesn't have a Web page defined with each person's name

specified in static HTML, the application needs a means of dynamically generating that output to the user.

Another good example is a Web site that enables you to create greeting cards. After you've finished entering the information that will appear on the card, you are typically allowed to preview how the card will appear to the reader. This is also accomplished by means of the application dynamically generating the HTML that represents the information on the card. As you will see here, although the task of dynamically creating HTML content might seem daunting at first, it is actually very easy using the Document object.

At this point, expand the Window object entry in the Script Outline window and add a handler for the Window object's onload event. Assuming that you haven't changed the default client-scripting language from JavaScript, insert the following script into the window_onload function:

```
document.write("This is a link to ");
document.write("<A HREF=http://www.CodeGuru.com>CodeGuru</A>");
```

Figure 7.2 illustrates what you'll see when you enter this code and click the QuickView tab.

FIGURE 7.2

The ability to dynamically manipulate the HTML of a Web page has exciting possibilities.

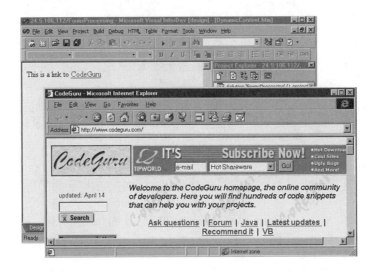

Using the Document object's write method, you simply specify the actual HTML code just as you would type it into the HTML editor. You can use the Document object's write method to literally specify any valid HTML. Here's a list of the Document object's methods that aid you in dynamically creating HTML content:

- open—This method is used to open a stream for writing purposes.
- write—As you saw from the previous example, this method is used to write HTML to the document.

7

- writeln—As its name suggests, this method works like the write method. The difference is that the writeln method appends a carriage return/line feed at the end of the specified expression.

- close—This method is used to close a stream that was opened via the open method.

- clear—As you might guess, this method is used to clear the contents of a given document.

Determining the Browser Type

As mentioned earlier, one reason for needing to dynamically create HTML content is application need (for example, a feedback page or greeting card application). Another major reason is the issue of incompatibility between the different competing browsers. In other words, depending on the capabilities of the browsers you decide to support, your application might have to present completely different content for each browser.

Luckily, not only can you generate your own HTML at runtime via the Document object, but as you will see, you can also determine the exact browser being used to view your application using a special object, Navigator.

To test the capability to determine a user's browser at runtime, complete the following:

1. Add a new HTML page named ShowBrowserName.htm to the FormsProcessing project.

2. Open the ShowBrowserName page in Design view and enter the following text:
   ```
   You should see the browser information in a message box before
   this message appears!
   ```

3. Now, switch the HTML editor to the Source view.

4. Right-click the first blank line immediately below <BODY> and select the Script Block, Client menu option.

5. Modify the newly added script block so that when finished your code looks like Listing 7.1.

LISTING 7.1 A Simple JavaScript Function to Determine the User's Browser and Display a Message

```
1: <SCRIPT LANGUAGE=javascript>
2: <!--
3:
4: var browser=navigator.appName;
5: if ("Netscape" == browser)
```

```
 6: {
 7:     alert ("I can't believe you're running Netscape!");
 8: }
 9: else if ("Microsoft Internet Explorer" == browser)
10: {
11:     alert ("Good job! You're running IE! Bill's plan for total
        ➥assimilation is working.");
12: }
13: else
14: {
15:     alert("I have no idea what you're running :)");
16: }
17:
18: //-->
19: </SCRIPT>
20:
```

6. After you've typed in the JavaScript to determine the current browser, running it will (depending on your browser) yield results similar to what you see in Figure 7.3.

FIGURE 7.3

The Navigator *object allows you to determine the browser that's currently being used to view your Web page.*

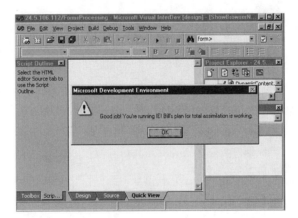

Controlling Document Colors

One very popular question on the different JavaScript and Web development newsgroups and Web sites is how to control the Document object's colors.

The user is typically in control of setting the different configurable Web page colors via the browser. However, there are times when, as a developer, you might find the need to override the browser color settings and programmatically impose your own application-specific colors. For this purpose, the Document object defines the following five different properties:

7

- aLink—This property defines the color of the link after it has been click (but before the mouse button has been released).
- bgColor—This property represents the background color of the document.
- fgColor—This property defines the foreground color of the document.
- linkColor—This property defines the color of an unvisited link on the Web page.
- vlinkColor—This property defines the color of a visited link.

You can set all these properties statically via the Properties window after clicking the Document object in the Script Outline window. Additionally, you can set them dynamically from script by prepending the property names with the document name.

What's more, there are two ways to specify a color for each of these properties from JavaScript. The first way is to specify a predefined literal value for the desired color. Here's an example:

```
<SCRIPT ID=clientEventHandlersJS LANGUAGE=javascript>
<!--

function window_onload() {
 document.bgColor="lightcyan";
}

//-->
</SCRIPT>
```

You can also specify the RGB value of the color as follows:

```
<SCRIPT ID=clientEventHandlersJS LANGUAGE=javascript>
<!--

function window_onload() {
 'change background color to light cyan
 document.bgColor="EOFFFF";
}

//-->
</SCRIPT>
```

In Windows development, the RGB macro represents three comma-delimited numbers that are the values for the red, green, and blue components of a color. Likewise, in JavaScript, when you need to specify an RGB value, you do so by specifying the amount of red, green, and blue. However, the difference is that in JavaScript, the numbers are not comma delimited and they're in hexadecimal form.

Using the preceding example, you would specify light cyan using the standard Windows RGB macro like this:

RGB(224, 255, 255)

However, in JavaScript, this same value would be written as either of the following.

EOFFFF

#EOFFFF

The Form Object

Whereas the Document object serves as the container for the HTML that makes up a Web page, the Form object is used as the container for HTML controls such as the ones you added in the previous hour. The Form object is used most often in situations where the data on a Web page is going to be sent to a Web server for processing. By having a higher-level container, the programmer doesn't have to individually send each element of the form and can instead think of all the elements as a collection and can treat them as a logical unit.

Defining a Form Object for a Web Page

A form is defined in HTML with the <FORM> and </FORM> tags and has the following syntax:

```
<FORM
        ACTION=url
        CLASS=classname
        ENCTYPE=encoding
        ID=value
        LANG=language
        LANGUAGE=JAVASCRIPT ¦ JSCRIPT ¦ VBSCRIPT ¦ VBS
        METHOD=GET ¦ POST
        NAME=name
        STYLE=css1-properties
        TARGET=window_name ¦ _blank ¦ _parent ¦ _self ¦ _top
        TITLE=text
        event = script
>
```

The simplest way to define a Form object is to add the following line of code:

```
<FORM Name=MyForm>
```

7

To see this in action, create a new page called FormTest.htm and insert the preceding <FORM> tag just after the FormTest page's <BODY> tag. Now insert a closing </FORM> tag just before the </BODY> tag. When you've finished, take a look at the Script Outline window. You'll see a new object type that you haven't see before. You've just defined a Form object for your Web page.

However, to clearly see what's going on here and the ramifications of what you've done, click the Design view and add a TextBox control to the page between the two graphics that indicate the beginning and ending of the Form definition. Now click back to the Source view and look at the Script Outline window again. Where's the new TextBox control? Before when you created an HTML control on a page, it showed up in the script outline. Not to worry. It's there. However, because you've now defined a Form object for your Web page, the HTML controls you create "belong" to that Form object (if you create them between the two form graphics). Therefore, if you expand the MyForm object in the Script Outline window and scroll past all the MyForm events, you'll find your newly created text1 TextBox control. Additionally, if you look at the Source view, you'll see that the text1 TextBox control was defined via the standard INPUT tag between the <FORM> and </FORM> tags. This is how incredibly easy it is to define a parent Form object for your HTML controls in Visual InterDev.

Sending Data to the Server

You've probably seen Web sites that have Submit buttons which allow you to send a form's data to the Web server for processing. Submitting a Form object (and its data) to a server involves a simple two-step technique from the client page's perspective. Obviously, what the server then does with that data is completely defined on the server side.

The first step is to define a Form object, as you saw in the previous section. However, if you're going to submit the form to the server for processing, you'll need to also specify the Action and Method values (and optionally, the ENCTYPE value):

- Action—This property allows you to specify the URL to which the form is being sent. Although this is typically a CGI script or a LiveWire application, it can also be a mailto: address, as you'll see later on.

- Method—This property is used to define how the form data will be sent to the host. The only valid values for this property are GET and POST. For more information on the GET and POST methods, refer to the following note.

- ENCTYPE—The ENCTYPE value is used to specify the format of the data being sent. By default, this is set to "text/plain".

When you're specifying the <FORM> tag, the Method property has only two valid values: GET and POST.

Let's take a look at a simple example (a Web search) to explain the differences between them:

```
<form action="mysearch.cgi" method="get">
<input type="text" name="search_string">
<input type="submit" value="Search">
</form>
```

Let's say you enter "my home page" in the search field and then click the Submit button. The browser then adds the query string to the URL of the search CGI and issues a GET request to the server. The new URL then becomes this:

```
"mysearch.cgi?search_string=my+home+page"
```

As you can see, the GET method adds to the current URL because a GET request to the server is a regular page request. However, if you choose to change the method to POST, the browser instead issues a POST request to the server and sends the content of the form in the request, and the URL stays unchanged.

The GET method is practical when you want to give the user a link that can be bookmarked from the browser. That way, the search (or the running of the CGI) can be automated. The POST method should instead be used when you want to hide the content. An example of that would be a login procedure. In this situation, the GET request would leave the user's username and password in the history list as well as the Web server's log. Therefore, a fair amount of care must be taken when deciding on the best way of submitting your form's data to a server.

Once the Form object is defined, you simply need to either explicitly call its Submit method somewhere in your code or add a Button control of type "Submit" to the page.

Writing a Registration Form with JavaScript

Now that you've seen learned the basics of the Window, Document, and Form objects, it's time to put what you've learned into practice by creating a sample Web page. Probably the most common form everyone is accustomed to filling out on the Web is the registration form. Therefore, that will be the focus of this example.

7

Creating the Web Page

The first thing you'll need to do is to create the Web page and add the necessary controls. Follow these steps:

1. Add a new HTML page named Registration.htm to your FormsProcessing project.

2. Open the Registration Web page in Source view and insert a `<FORM Name=MyForm>` tag just after the `<BODY>` tag.

3. Insert a `</FORM>` tag just before the `</BODY>` tag.

4. Next, add the header and instructional text you see in Figure 7.4.

FIGURE 7.4

Standard instructions on filling out a registration form.

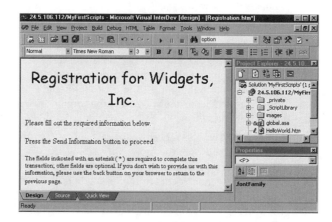

5. After you've added the header and instructional text, add TextBox controls for the First Name, Last Name, Phone, and Email entries (shown in Figure 7.5). Make sure to precede each prompt with the asterisk character—this has become a standard for denoting an input control that must be filled out. Name these controls, `txtFirstName`, `txtLastName`, `txtPhone`, and `txtEmail`, respectively.

6. Next, create a ListBox control that will allow the user to select a country. You'll see how to fill a list box with its text entries shortly. Name this control `lbxCountries`.

7. Now, add a TextArea control that will enable the user to specify remarks. The main difference between the TextBox control that you used earlier and the TextArea control is that the TextArea control allows for multiple lines of input. Name this control `txtRemarks`.

8. Add a Password control to the form and name it `txtPassword`. This control acts just like the TextBox control, except that any data that's entered in the Password control is displayed as asterisks. That way, the user can enter his or her password without worrying about someone trying to steal it.

FIGURE 7.5

The ability to drag and drop HTML controls from the Toolbox makes designing Web pages a breeze with Visual InterDev.

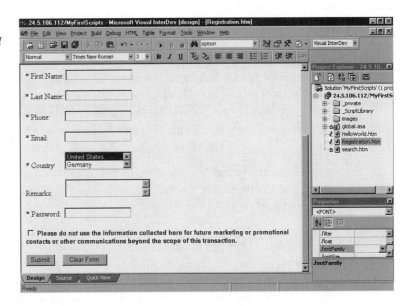

9. After adding the Password control, add a CheckBox control and the text you saw earlier in Figure 7.4. Name this control `chkDoNotUseInfo`.

10. Finally, add a Submit Button control and a Reset Button control and name them `btnSubmit` and `btnReset`, respectively.

11. At this point, your page is complete. Now, it's time to add the script that will make this thing go.

Adding Items to a ListBox Control

At this point, you need to add the defined countries to your Countries ListBox control. Follow these steps:

1. Open the Registration.htm file in Source view.

2. Search for the definition of the ListBox control by pressing Ctrl+F, entering the text `lbxCountries`, and clicking the Find button.

3. Once you've located the `lbxCountries` ListBox definition, add the following code just before the `</SELECT>` tag:

```
<option selected value="1 ">United States
<option value="2">Germany
<option value="3">India
<option value="4">China
<option value="5">Taiwan
<option value="6">Canada
<option value="0">None of the above
```

7

As you can see from this code snippet, you can add values to a ListBox control by using the OPTION tag along with the value keyword. The text that follows the equal sign is the value that will be returned to the script when the object is queried for its value. The text that follows the right angle bracket is what will be displayed in the list box. Therefore, when the page is processed, the lbxCountries object will reflect a value of 3 if the user has selected the "India" entry. You can have both values be the same thing. However, I wanted to make them distinct to illustrate what's displayed in the list box versus what value is returned from the list box upon request for its Value property after a selection has been made.

Finally, notice that the preceding code above includes the Selected keyword. This keyword allows you to set a default value for the ListBox control. That way, you can determine which entry will be selected when the page is initialized.

Form-Level Processing

At the beginning of the hour, you learned about the concept of sending a Form object to a server for processing. Now it's time to put what you read into practice. You've no doubt seen Web pages with buttons for submitting the information on a page or resetting the page's controls to their initial values. This is where you finally get to see how the Submit and Reset buttons you added to the page come into play.

Emailing from JavaScript

Because you haven't learned how to write server-side script yet, you don't have anything on the server to process this form with. However, you can still perform the same steps required for posting a form to a server by emailing the form to yourself!

As you already know, defining a Form object is simply a matter of inserting the <FORM> and </FORM> tags into the source code for the Web page. When you added the HTML controls for this page, you also defined a Form object named MyForm. However, you're going to need to make a couple modifications in order to submit your form.

If you recall from earlier, you added a very special type of Button control called a Submit button to the Registration page. If you search for that control's definition in your source code, you'll find something similar to the following:

```
<INPUT id=btnSubmit name=btnSubmit type=submit value=Submit>
```

You already know about the ID, Name, and Value keywords, but check out the Type keyword. This keyword designates this button as being very special. Because this button is defined as being of the type Submit, now when you click on it, the Form object's Submit method will be called.

At this point, find the <FORM> tag that you entered earlier and modify it so that, when you're finished, your code looks like this:

```
<FORM NAME="MyForm" ACTION="mailto:tarcher@codeguru.com" method=Get>
```

This alone is enough to have the default email program loaded and initialized to send an email to the specified address. However, an email with a blank subject line doesn't tell you much, so let's take a look at how this is filled in from JavaScript:

```
<input name=subject type=hidden value="New%20Registration">
```

Note that now if you were to test your page, the subject would correctly be initialized to New Registration. The %20 is used to denote a space character because some older applications do not handle the inclusion of spaces in literals very well. This way, you're explicitly stating via the hexadecimal representation of the space character what you want the subject field to be set to.

At this point, your email message looks pretty good. However, there's only one thing missing: no message body. Therefore, locate the txtEmail control in your code and change the control's Name keyword to Body. When finished, it should look like this:

```
<INPUT id=txtEmail name=body>
```

You saw that the form knew to automatically use the value of the control named Subject in the email message's Subject line. The same principle applies here in that because the name of this control is now Body, its value will be used as the body text of the email message being sent. At this point, running your registration application, entering a value of tarcher@codeguru.com, and clicking the Submit button should result in the what you see in Figure 7.6.

FIGURE 7.6

An example of using a Submit button to send email via JavaScript.

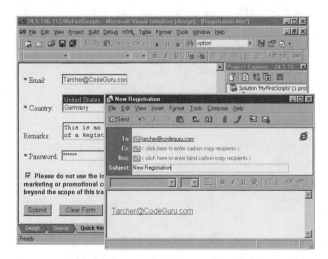

7

Adding a Reset button

The last thing you'll add to your form is the ability for the user to clear, or *reinitialize*, the form's values. Once again, because you have a Form object, this is incredibly easy. Actually, you've already done it and don't realize it! When you added the Reset button, a control of the type Reset was created in your code. Because you didn't write an explicit handler for this control's onclick event, the Reset event "bubbled up" to the form. Because the form knows about all its controls and their initial values, the form automatically initializes everything for you!

Adding an onBeforeUnload Event Handler

The last thing you'll look at this hour deals with both the Window object and forms processing in general. Say that a user of your application spends five minutes filling out a form and then hits the browser's Back button. In most Windows applications, the user would see a confirmation message warning her that her action is going to result in the loss of work and asking her if that is acceptable. You can create something like this with an onBeforeUnload event handler. However, one thing I will point out before continuing is that this nifty little feature exists only with Internet Explorer 4 and higher.

The intent of this event is to allow applications to do any needed pre-unload processing and to give the user the opportunity to cancel the unload event. Unfortunately, some sites have taken advantage of this feature to "grab hold of the user" and not let him leave the site. Trust me—be careful to use this feature in only the way that it was originally intended to be used. One way or another, the user is going to end the session, and stunts such as this do nothing to win over customers.

Now that you know basically what the onBeforeUnload event does and when it should be used, let's see how to implement it. Using the same registration example you've been building, simply add the following code to the Registration.htm page:

```
<SCRIPT LANGUAGE=javascript>
<!--
window.onBeforeUnload = preUnload;

function preUnload ()
{
 msg  = " If you click the OK button all work will be lost.
 ➥Click Cancel to continue editing the form.";
 return msg
}
//-->
</SCRIPT>
```

As you can see, the only thing you need to do is assign a function name as the window.onBeforeUnload event handler and code the specified function. In this case, I used a function name of preUnload. (It can be any name you choose.)

The last thing to mention regarding this event handler is that you cannot programmatically stop the page from being unloaded. By returning a message from the event handler, you are simply asking that Internet Explorer present the specified message to the user. The user can then decide to ignore the message and continue unloading the page or cancel the unload process. Figure 7.7 shows the dialog the user will see when the preceding code snippet is added to a page and the user attempts to the leave that page.

FIGURE 7.7

The onBeforeUnload *event handler enables you to do pre-unload processing as well as confirm that the user wants to leave the page.*

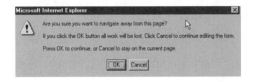

Summary

In this hour, you learned about the basics of one of the most important tasks of Web-based development: form processing. You started out by discovering the existence of several key objects (Window, Document, and Form) that can be used in form processing. You learned about the Navigator object and how it can be used to query the client's browser. You then finished up the hour by coding a simple registration Web page to put what you learned into practice.

Up until now, everything you've done with your Web pages has been done in HTML. In the next hour, you will learn how to leverage the work of others and apply the concept of code reuse by incorporating ActiveX controls into your Web application.

Q&A

Q If I can dynamically create content for a Web page, can I also dynamically create the document itself?

A Yes. First, use the Window object's Open method to open a new page in a separate browser window. This method will return the Window object representing the newly created HTML document. At this point, you can call that Document object's write or writeln methods to create the HTML content for the page. Here's an example of doing just that:

```
winMyWindow = window.open("", "", "height=300, width=500");
winMyWindow.document.write("This is the first line on my
➥new window!!!");
```

7

Q From this hour I've learned that I can send a form to a server application or CGI script, and I've learned how to send a form via email. How can I FTP the contents of my form?

A Unfortunately, at this time, JavaScript does not support the FTP protocol. However, you can submit the form to a server-side Active Server Page that can FTP for you. This wasn't covered here simply because Active Server Pages aren't discussed until Hour 11, "Developing Active Server Pages." The accompanying CD-ROM includes an example of how to perform this very thing!

Workshop

The Workshop is designed to help you anticipate possible questions, review what you've learned, and begin thinking ahead to put your knowledge into practice. The answers to the quiz and exercise are in Appendix A, "Answers."

Quiz

1. What is the top-level object in the JavaScript object hierarchy?

2. What two `Window` object events are typically the only ones you would use from JavaScript?

3. What `Document` object methods are used to write HTML to a Web page?

4. How can you determine the current browser being used to view your Web page?

5. How do you specify RGB values when setting any of the `Document` object's color properties?

6. What is the difference between the `aLink` and `vlinkColor` properties of the `Document` object?

7. What is the `ENCTYPE` property used for in the `<FORM>` tag?

8. How do you submit a form from a Web page?

9. How do you send email using JavaScript?

10. How do you add the capability for the user to reinitialize a Web page?

Exercise

Open the ClientScripts project you created in the last hour and modify the Feedback page so that it emails you the information from the form when the user clicks the Send Feedback button.

HOUR 8

Adding ActiveX Controls to Your Web Site

In the last two hours, you've learned how to add HTML controls to a Web page and write JavaScript to handle events and manipulate those controls. However, wouldn't it be nice if you didn't have to write everything from scratch? After all, someone out there must have faced the same technical challenges and written what you need. Wouldn't it be great if there was some way to just plug that directly into your Web application and be done? Well, there is, and the technology that allows for this "plug 'n play" functionality is called ActiveX. In this hour, you will learn about this exciting technology and how it allows you to incorporate already-programmed, packaged functionality into your Web application, thereby saving you countless development hours and enabling you to get your product to market that much faster.

In this hour, you will learn

- The difference between ActiveX and ActiveX controls
- How ActiveX controls promote code reuse
- The HTML needed to add an ActiveX control to a Web page

- How Visual InterDev makes using ActiveX controls a breeze
- How to set the properties and call methods of an ActiveX control
- Where you can find other ActiveX resources on the Internet

An Introduction to ActiveX

Because you've no doubt seen the many books whose entireties are devoted to ActiveX, it's obvious that fully teaching this subject matter in a single chapter is not feasible. However, a little information detailing the basics of ActiveX and its pros and cons with a demo or two thrown in should help you in deciding whether ActiveX is right for you and your projects.

The actual technology that is at the core of ActiveX has been around for several years now. It all started when Microsoft announced something called COM (Component Object Model). COM defines a binary standard for describing software components so that they can be used from any language, regardless of which language was used to write the component itself. The first product Microsoft built that was based on COM is OLE. At the time, OLE stood for Object Linking and Embedding, and it allowed for the creation of compound documents. A *compound* document is a document that can contain objects created and maintained by other applications. For example, a Microsoft Word application can contain a link to an Excel spreadsheet and a PowerPoint slide.

A couple of years later, Microsoft released OLE 2. OLE 2 added things like OLE Automation, in-place activation, and OLE controls. Obviously, OLE had become much more than just compound documents, so Microsoft did two things regarding the name. First, they dropped the version number and second, they announced that OLE no longer was an acronym for anything. The public was just to accept it as a class of COM-based technologies meant to enhance interoperability between applications.

When Microsoft finally accepted the reality that the community at large had embraced the Internet as a viable resource, Microsoft's marketing types huddled up once again and emerged with another buzzword: ActiveX. Microsoft currently defines ActiveX as a set of technologies and services based on COM that are optimized for the Internet.

ActiveX Versus ActiveX Controls

Most people think that the terms *ActiveX* and *ActiveX controls* are synonymous. Actually, whereas ActiveX refers to several technologies, ActiveX controls represent a specific means of implementing ActiveX. Another way of putting it is that ActiveX controls are reusable software components written using these technologies.

Advantages of ActiveX Controls

Before deciding whether ActiveX is right for your Internet or intranet application, you need to know what the different advantages and disadvantages are. The lists of advantages regarding the use of ActiveX controls are

- Multiplatform support
- User-defined security
- Performance
- Intelligent download capability
- Availability

Multiplatform Support

Multiplatform support is something that could qualify as either an advantage or disadvantage depending on your specific needs. Microsoft will tell you that ActiveX is a multiplatform technology. In reality, although ActiveX is currently supported on all 32-bit Windows operating systems (Windows 95, Windows 98, and Windows NT) and the Macintosh, it has yet to be ported to platforms such as UNIX or Digital. Therefore, the Microsoft definition of multiplatform support might differ from your own.

User-Defined Security

Here again, security is a gray area regarding whether ActiveX provides an advantage over other component-based technologies. Because ActiveX controls have access to the client system's resources, some say that ActiveX controls present an obvious danger to the client's machine. However, Microsoft's take on this is that ActiveX controls give you the best compromise possible through the concept of a digital signature.

As opposed to simply not allowing any piece of code to interface directly with the client system, ActiveX controls are signed by their authors with a digital signature. This signature is certified by neutral third-party services that attach a digital certificate to the control. Although this process doesn't guarantee the control's quality, it does at least give you piece of mind in knowing that the control's developer can be tracked down in the event that the code does intentionally or unintentionally cause your system harm.

When you attempt to download a Web page that contains an ActiveX control, you might see a message similar to that shown in Figure 8.1. As you can see, this dialog not only enables you to decide for yourself whether you trust the company or individual that developed the ActiveX control in question, but it also enables you to specify that you trust all content from that particular company or individual. This way, security can be configured to meet your personal needs.

FIGURE 8.1

Example of the prompt that Internet Explorer displays before down-loading a signed ActiveX control.

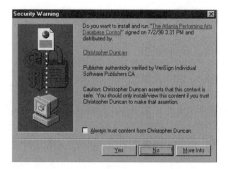

As an example of this, take a look at Figure 8.2, where I attempted to view a Web page that contains an unsigned, uncertified ActiveX control. In this situation, the browser (in this case, Internet Explorer) warns you that the control's author cannot be determined. It is usually prudent to heed the browser's warning and decline the page's offer to download the control.

FIGURE 8.2

An example of the warning that Internet Explorer displays when it encounters an unsigned ActiveX control.

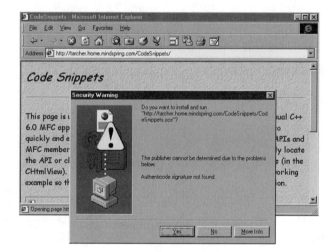

Intelligent Download Capability

Another big advantage that ActiveX controls have over other technologies such as Java applets is that they are more intelligent with regards to when they are downloaded. When a Web page is displayed that contains a Java applet, that applet is downloaded to the client each time the page is refreshed or visited. However, in the case of an ActiveX control, it is only downloaded the first time the Web page is viewed. From then on, the ActiveX control will only be downloaded again if it is removed from the client machine or if the control is out-of-date and the Web page contains a more recent version.

Performance

ActiveX controls are compiled into the native code of the target operating system and, as such, are optimized for the system on which they are running. Therefore, they enjoy a tremendous advantage over other technologies with regard to their performance.

Availability

Although it used to be true that ActiveX controls were difficult to find, the past couple of years have seen their numbers grow exponentially. It has gotten to the point now where you can find an ActiveX control for everything from fancy UI controls, to nonvisual business objects, to entire applications. With Microsoft fully backing ActiveX, there is no doubt that this technology is going to play an even more important role in Internet development.

Disadvantages of ActiveX Controls

As you've seen, there are many advantages to using ActiveX controls on your Web pages. However, in order to depict a realistic view of the Web world, it is necessary to mention the downside to ActiveX controls:

- Limited multiplatform support
- Security—Access to system resources
- Browser support

Limited Multiplatform Support

Although it is true that the different Microsoft Windows platforms comprise over 90 percent of the operating systems running on desktop computers, that might not be enough to sway everyone. After all, the intent of Web-based application development is that the resulting application(s) can be run on *any* platform; not just the ones from Redmond. Whether this is a disadvantage to you depends entirely on two things. Firstly, how important are the unsupported platforms (for example, UNIX, Digital, and so on) to your business? Secondly, if these platforms are important, can you trust Microsoft when they say that development is underway to have these platforms support ActiveX?

Security

As mentioned previously, your users have the right to configure their own browser security settings so that they can enable the downloading of ActiveX controls on a one-off basis or on a company-by-company basis. However, your users could just as easily disable the downloading of ActiveX controls altogether. In this case, any Web pages you've developed that make extensive use of ActiveX controls wouldn't function correctly. Therefore, before making a final decision on whether to use ActiveX controls on your Web pages, it is imperative that you know what stance you are going to take with your users.

Lack of Browser Support

The last issue with ActiveX controls that I'll cover is one of browser support. Currently, Microsoft Internet Explorer is the only browser to natively support ActiveX controls. Therefore, if your users are using Netscape Navigator, you need to realize that they will need to purchase a plug-in from NCompass called ScriptActive in order to properly run your Web pages.

Inserting an ActiveX Control on a Web Page

Now you can dive into seeing exactly what it takes to insert an ActiveX control into a Web page. Using Visual InterDev, there are two ways to define an ActiveX for a Web page. The first way is to manually insert the necessary HTML directly into the page's source code. The second way is to use the Design view of the Visual InterDev HTML editor and simply drag an ActiveX control onto the Web page.

Manually Inserting the HTML Code

Although the manual coding of the HTML needed to define an ActiveX control requires a bit more work on your part, the extra effort you put into understanding exactly what is happening "under the hood" will be well worth it.

ActiveX controls are defined on a Web page using the HTML <OBJECT> tag. An example of the HTML used to define a progress bar ActiveX control is shown in Listing 8.1.

LISTING 8.1   HTML Necessary to Define an ActiveX Control

```
 1: <OBJECT classid=clsid:0713E8D2-850A-101B-AFC0-4210102A8DA7
 2: id=ProgressBar1>
 3: <PARAM NAME="_ExtentX" VALUE="2646">
 4: <PARAM NAME="_ExtentY" VALUE="1323">
 5: <PARAM NAME="_Version" VALUE="327682">
 6: <PARAM NAME="BorderStyle" VALUE="0">
 7: <PARAM NAME="Appearance" VALUE="1">
 8: <PARAM NAME="MousePointer" VALUE="0">
 9: <PARAM NAME="Enabled" VALUE="1">
10: <PARAM NAME="OLEDropMode" VALUE="0">
11: <PARAM NAME="Min" VALUE="0">
12: <PARAM NAME="Max" VALUE="100">
13: </OBJECT>
```

The first attribute of note here is the CLASSID. As you can see in the previous example, the CLASSID for the progress bar is clsid:0713E8D2-850A-101B-AFC0-4210102A8DA7. This value is stored in the Windows Registry and is used to uniquely identify this control. The next attribute is the ID. As you've learned in the hours on writing JavaScript, the ID is used to identify a control within script so that its properties and methods can be used. The last attribute that you see in Listing 8.1 is PARAM and it is used to pass parameters to the ActiveX control at runtime. At this point, you will see just how easy it is to insert an ActiveX control onto a Web page, as shown in the following:

1. Create a new Visual InterDev project called ActiveXTest.

2. After the project has been created, add a new HTML page to it named Manual.htm. This is the page that will house your very first ActiveX control.

3. Open the Manual.htm file in Source view.

4. Insert the code you see listed in Listing 8.1 between the <BODY> tag and its terminating </BODY> tag.

When you're finished, click the QuickView tab on the HTML editor, and you will see the control. Obviously, you haven't set any of its properties or called any of its methods in order to make it actually perform any tasks as of yet, but you can now see how incredibly easy it is to insert an ActiveX control into any of your Web pages. However, as easy as that was, you haven't seen anything yet.

Using the Visual InterDev Toolbox

Visual InterDev wouldn't be very visually oriented if you had to always type in every line of HTML in order to do such a routine task as defining ActiveX controls. After all, one control isn't such a big deal, but think about developing several dozen Web pages with a couple of ActiveX controls on each one, and you'll definitely appreciate the Visual InterDev Toolbox.

At this point, open the Toolbox window by selecting the View, Toolbox menu option. Just as there is a tab for HTML controls, there is also one dedicated to ActiveX controls. At this point, click the ActiveX control to unveil the ActiveX controls that are automatically installed with Visual InterDev. Using these controls works just like using the HTML controls. You simply open a Web page in Design view, place the caret where you want the control to appear, and double-click the desired ActiveX control. The following example will illustrate how easy it is to drop one of the standard ActiveX controls on a Web page.

Using the Standard ActiveX Controls in the Toolbox

At this point, complete the following:

1. Create a new HTML page called Automatic.htm.

2. Open the Automatic.htm file in Design view.

3. Display the Toolbox window by selecting the View, Toolbox menu option.

4. When the Toolbox window is displayed, you will see several tabs that each contains a type of element that can be dragged and dropped onto a Web page. Click on the ActiveX Controls tab to display all the controls that Visual InterDev installs and provides for you automatically (see Figure 8.3).

FIGURE 8.3

Visual InterDev ships with several ActiveX controls to make creating attractive, functional Web pages a snap.

5. Double-click on the Progress Bar control just as you did with the HTML controls. A quick glance at the source code will reveal what you manually typed into Manual.htm (only with much less work!). Once again, your little ActiveX control isn't doing much because you haven't changed any of its properties or called any of its methods. That's going to change very shortly.

Adding ActiveX Controls to the Toolbox

Now that you've seen the standard ActiveX controls, you're probably wondering how you can add more to the Toolbox window. All you have to do is simply right-click on the Toolbox window and select the Customize Toolbox menu option. When the Customize Toolbox dialog is displayed (see Figure 8.4), click the ActiveX Controls tab to display a list of all the ActiveX controls that are currently registered on the system. Notice that the controls installed on the Toolbox have a check mark next to them. Therefore, in order to add an ActiveX control to the Toolbox that is already registered on your system, you need only click on that item's check box in the Customize Toolbox dialog.

However, what if you just downloaded this really great ActiveX control and you want to use it? You still open the Customize Toolbox dialog, but this time because the control is not yet registered, you would need to click the Browse button to tell Visual InterDev where your new ActiveX control is located. After you locate and select the desired control, Visual InterDev will update the Customize Toolbox with the new control and automatically check it so that it is included in the Toolbox.

Figure 8.4

The Customize Toolbox dialog displays all the registered ActiveX controls on the system.

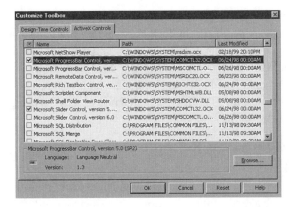

8

 When adding items to the Visual InterDev Toolbox, make sure to display the Customize Toolbox while on the tab where you want the new item to appear. Otherwise, you'll have to remove the item and add it back again to the correct tab.

Setting the Properties of an ActiveX Control

Every ActiveX control has a set of properties used to control such characteristics as the way the control looks and behaves. Some properties are obvious such as color, font, and size. You will generally see such properties implemented for almost all ActiveX controls. However, other properties will be unique to a specific control: Therefore, they can only be documented by that control. For example, a credit card validation ActiveX control might have properties for specifying the type of card and card number to be verified. Regardless of the property, there are two ways in which to set an ActiveX control's properties: at design time and at runtime.

Setting Properties at Design Time

Earlier you saw how to use HTML to specify the parameters (via the PARAM attribute) for an ActiveX control. These parameters are one way of setting the initial values for a control's properties. For example, in the example credit card validation ActiveX control, I said that it had a property for specifying the credit card type and the credit card number. Going with that example, the following HTML could be used to initialize those properties:

```
<PARAM NAME="CreditCardType" VALUE="AMEX">
<PARAM NAME="CreditCardNumber" VALUE="372123457632107"
```

Obviously, in the previous example, the property names were made up because they are named by the ActiveX control developer. So, how does Visual InterDev know how to display those properties in the Properties window so that you can set them like you do the HTML control properties? The answer is: It doesn't.

In order to allow the design-time setting of its properties, ActiveX controls support something called *property pages*. Right-click the Progress Bar control and then click the Properties menu option. This is an example of an OLE property page because it is not something that Visual InterDev is displaying. What has happened is that the control itself is displaying this dialog and allowing you to set its properties. When you've finished editing the properties, the HTML will be updated to reflect your changes just as if you had manually typed in the <PARAM> attributes yourself.

Setting Properties at Runtime

When you talk about setting an ActiveX control's properties at runtime, it is usually in response to a given event. The previous example isn't very realistic simply because you wouldn't initialize a credit card validation control's credit card type and number when you created the control. Those properties would be more dynamic and would be the types of properties that would be set as a result of some action taken by the user. For example, say that you had a page that did nothing but validate credit cards. You might have a drop-down control that contained a list of all credit cards that could be validated by your ActiveX control. Then you would also have an Edit control that would allow the user to type in a credit card number to be validated. Lastly, there would have to be some means of having the user initiate the validation routine. In this case, you would need a means other than property pages and <PARAM> attributes to specify the control's property values.

Luckily, setting an ActiveX control's properties in Visual InterDev is as easy as setting any component's properties. Here is the syntax to do just that:

```
ControlName.PropertyName = Value
```

As discussed earlier, the ControlName is the value assigned to the ID attribute in the <OBJECT> tag. In fact, to see something really nice about Visual InterDev, perform the following steps:

1. Open the Automatic.htm file and click the Design tab.

2. Add a HTML Button control to the page called btnDecrement. Set the button's Value property to Decrement.

3. Add another HTML Button control called btnIncrement. Set this button's Value property to Increment.

4. Open the Script Outline and add an onload handler for the Window object.

5. At this point, modify the window_onload function so that when finished, it appears as follows. This initializes the progress bar's minimum and maximum values and sets its current value. It also calls a function that enables or disables the Increment/Decrement buttons based on the progress bar's current value in relation to its Min and Max settings.

8

```
function window_onload() {
 ProgressBar1.Min = 0;
 ProgressBar1.Max = 100;
 ProgressBar1.Value = ProgressBar1.Min;
 setButtonState(ProgressBar1.Value);
}
```

6. Add a handler for the `btnDecrement` `onclick` event and modify it so that when finished, it looks like the following. As you can see, this function simply decrements the progress bar's value if it is greater than its defined `Min` value (set in `window_onload`).

```
function btnDecrement_onclick() {
 if (ProgressBar1.Value > ProgressBar1.Min)
 {
  ProgressBar1.Value -= 10;
 }
 setButtonState(ProgressBar1.Value);
}
```

7. Add a handler for the `btnIncrement` `onclick` event and modify it so that when finished, it looks like the following. As you can see, this function simply increments the progress bar's value if it is less than its defined `Max` value (set in `window_onload`).

```
function btnIncrement_onclick() {
 if (ProgressBar1.Value < ProgressBar1.Max)
 {
  ProgressBar1.Value += 10;
 }
 setButtonState(ProgressBar1.Value);
}
```

8. Now add the `setButtonState` function as follows:

```
function setButtonState(iValue)
{
 btnDecrement.disabled = (ProgressBar1.Min == iValue);
 btnIncrement.disabled = (ProgressBar1.Max == iValue);
}
```

9. Now that you've finished scripting the ActiveX control, click the QuickView tab and test your new Web page (see Figure 8.5).

FIGURE 8.5

Using ActiveX controls, you can plug literally any functionality into your Web page in minutes.

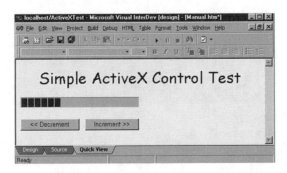

Calling the Methods of an ActiveX Control

ActiveX controls *expose* methods in order to allow you to direct how and when they need to
perform a given task on your behalf. For example, using the credit card validation ActiveX
control example, such a control would certainly need to expose a method called something
like Validate. This would use the values of the properties (credit card type and credit card
number) that you had already set in order to determine if the combination proved valid.

In order to invoke an ActiveX control method from JavaScript, you need to adhere to the
following syntax:

```
ControlName.MethodName(parameter1, parameter2, ...);
```

Once again, ControlName represents the name of the control as you defined it via the ID
attribute in the <OBJECT> tag. By now, you should be realizing why it so important to
give your controls meaningful names. It makes for much more maintainable code. After
all, the default names given by Visual InterDev such as Text1 and ProgressBar1 don't
really give you much to go on when looking at the code regarding logical context.

Using the Object Browser to Interrogate Controls

One of the most functional, yet least used, Visual Studio tools is the Object Browser. The
Object Browser is displayed by selecting the View, Other Windows, Object Browser
menu option (see Figure 8.6). This incredible tool not only allows you to view the methods and properties of any registered control on your system, but it also has quite a wealth
of filters and options to make finding what you need very easy.

FIGURE 8.6

*The Object Browser
offers a good deal of
flexibility in querying
your system's installed
controls for their prop-
erties and methods.*

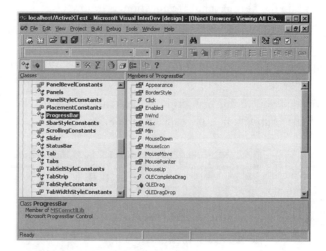

At this time, open the Object Browser and click the Select Current Packages/Libraries toolbar button. When the Select Packages/Libraries dialog appears, click the Add button. This action causes the Add New Packages/Libraries dialog to appear. At this time, you will see the entire list of COM objects that are registered in your system's registry. All you have to do is simply click on the objects for which you want more information. When you return to the Object Browser, you will see that its list has been updated with the newly selected controls. At this point, click on any control to view the full list of properties and methods that it exposes for your usage.

Developing an Image Processing Application with ActiveX

This example will use the ImageObject ActiveX control (provided courtesy of Infinite Vision Technologies) to illustrate how easily you can write a full-featured Web using the right tools.

The first thing you will need to do is to create the Web page and add the necessary controls by performing the following steps:

1. Add a new HTML page to your ActiveXTest project and call it ImageProcessing.htm.

2. Open the ImageProcessing.htm Web page in Design view.

3. Open the Toolbox window and click on the ActiveX Controls tab.

4. Right-click the Toolbox window and select the Customize Toolbox menu option.

5. When the Customize Toolbox dialog appears, click the ActiveX Controls tab.

6. Now, click the Browse button to locate the Image Class ActiveX control.

7. Click the Files Of Type drop-down control and select the All Files entry.

8. Browse to the ImageObject folder on the companion CD-ROM and select the ImageObjectControl.dll file.

9. When you return to the Customize Toolbox dialog, a new entry entitled Image Class will be listed and checked. Click the OK button to return to Visual InterDev. You should now be able to scroll through the list of ActiveX controls until you find the Image control (see Figure 8.7).

10. From the Design view, double-click the Image entry on the ActiveX tab of the Toolbox to insert it into the ImageProcessing Web page. Don't worry if you don't see anything at this point. You will shortly.

FIGURE 8.7

Adding ActiveX controls to the Visual InterDev is a simple point-and-click procedure.

11. Click on the HTML tab of the Toolbox and add a Button control to the bottom of the page. Name the Button control btnOpenImage and change its value property to read Open an Image.

12. Next, click the Source tab of the HTML editor.

13. Open the Script Outline window and add an event handler for the btnOpenImage Button control's onclick event.

14. In order to cause the Image control to allow you to browse for an image to open, simply call the Image control's Load method. When finished, your onclick method should look like the following:

```
function btnOpenImage_onclick() {
Image1.Load();
}
```

15. Now, return to the Design view and add a Button control called btnInvertImage with its value property set to Invert Image.

16. Add an onclick event handler for the btnInvertImage that calls the Image control's Invert method.

17. At this point, clicking on the QuickView tab and opening any image file will allow you to view and invert images like you see in Figure 8.8.

So as you can see from this little exercise, you were able to write a little image processing application by doing nothing more than dragging an ActiveX control onto a Web page and calling some of the control's methods at the appropriate times.

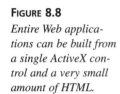

FIGURE 8.8

Entire Web applications can be built from a single ActiveX control and a very small amount of HTML.

8

ActiveX Resources on the Internet

As mentioned earlier, the ActiveX controls market is growing by leaps and bounds seemingly every day. As such, it is quite easy to get information on ActiveX programming and scripting as well as actual controls themselves (some are even free).

There are an incredible number of sites that have a wealth of useful information on programming ActiveX controls, including the following:

- http://www.microsoft.com/ActiveX—The obvious first place to look for information is at the Web site of the company that invented ActiveX. Here you will find everything from the actual COM and ActiveX specifications, to documentation on writing ActiveX controls and scripting them to full-blown sample code to help get you started.

- http://www.experts-exchange.com—For years, developers have turned first to CompuServe forums and then to Internet newsgroups when they've found themselves in need of help. However, this little-known Web site is the first place I look when I'm stuck. Without going into a lot of detail, the concept is simple. When you first log on and register, you get "points." You can then use these points when asking questions of the Web site's experts. Because you only award your points when the question has been answered to your satisfaction, trust me when I say that the competitiveness of getting your points definitely encourages far better help from this site than you'll ever get from a newsgroup.

- http://www.codeguru.com—Being the Web administrator and main section manager here, I might be a bit biased. However, if you're looking for great articles and sample code from real programmers doing real work with just about any technology you can name, this is the place to start.

Now that you've enjoyed playing around with the ActiveX controls that come with Visual InterDev, here's a list of places on the Internet where you can download many more controls:

- `http://www.developer.com/directories/pages/dir.activex.html`—This extremely popular developer Web site has literally hundreds of ActiveX controls that you can download.
- `http://www.zdnet.com/devhead/filters/activex/`—This site not only contains tons of ActiveX controls for download, but it also contains some very informative articles on the subject of ActiveX. Not being affiliated with Microsoft, it's a great resource for unbiased information regarding the past, present, and future of ActiveX and ActiveX controls.
- `http://browserwatch.internet.com/activex.html`—Sports a comprehensive list of ActiveX controls, all of which are neatly categorized by type.

Summary

In this hour, you learned about ActiveX controls, how to insert them into your Web pages, how to set their properties, and how to call their methods. You then fortified what you learned by working through several examples that showed you how ActiveX controls can make your life as a Web developer easier by providing a means of incorporating already developed and tested functionality into your Web page with just a few lines of code.

You have learned a tremendous amount about programming the client side of a Web application the past couple of hours. In the next hour, you will learn one more client-side programming skill that will help you develop a dynamic, intuitive type of Web site and will set your site apart from your competitors: Dynamic HTML.

Q&A

Q Can I write an ActiveX control with JavaScript?

A Unfortunately, no. Although JavaScript is great for scripting a Web page, in order to develop an ActiveX control, you will need something a little more heavy duty than a scripting language. Examples of this are Visual C++, Visual Basic, and Borland Delphi.

Q What reputable companies are responsible for certifying ActiveX controls, and where can I get more information?

A By far, VeriSign is the most widely accepted third-party certification company. VeriSign's Web site is `www.verisign.com`.

Workshop

The Workshop is designed to help you anticipate possible questions, review what you've learned, and begin thinking ahead to put your knowledge into practice. The answers to the quiz are in Appendix A, "Answers."

8

Quiz

1. What is the difference between ActiveX and ActiveX controls?
2. What are some of the advantages of using ActiveX controls?
3. What are some of the disadvantages of using ActiveX controls?
4. Why does Microsoft seem to disagree with some experts' opinions that ActiveX controls are unsafe?
5. When Internet Explorer prompts the user regarding the downloading of an ActiveX control, what are the user's options?
6. What HTML tag is used to define an ActiveX control?
7. In very general terms, what is the CLASSID attribute used for?
8. What does the PARAM attribute do, and how does it differ from setting an ActiveX control's properties at runtime when responding to an event?
9. How are new ActiveX controls added to Visual InterDev so that they can be dropped onto a Web page?
10. What is an OLE property page?

Exercise

Add some additional buttons and controls to the ImageProcessing demo to make it more of a full-fledged image-processing application.

Hour 9

Using Dynamic HTML

In Hour 7, "Document and Form Processing with Client Scripts," you learned a bit about the basics of the document object and how it can aid you in creating dynamic content with your Web pages. This hour you will take what you learned from that hour another step further (actually a very large leap forward) and discover what it is to write truly dynamic Web pages using Dynamic HTML (DHTML).

The highlights of this hour include

- Learning how to use Dynamic HTML to create professional Web pages
- Discovering Dynamic Styles to provide visual feedback to user interaction with your Web pages
- Learning how to dynamically change a Web page's text
- Discovering how to use the TextRange object
- Using JavaScript to find and replace text in a document
- Creating dynamic menus
- Creating Web pages with watermarks

Dynamic HTML Basics

Before jumping into Dynamic HTML, now would be a good time to delve into exactly what Dynamic HTML is and how it aids you in creating truly innovative, visually appealing Web pages.

Dynamic HTML is a browser feature that enables you to write truly dynamic Web pages. It is important to realize a distinction here between a couple of technologies that you've learned up to this point. Dynamic HTML is not any one specific technology such as JavaScript or ActiveX. Nor is it an HTML tag or a plug-in. Dynamic HTML uses a myriad of different technologies inherent to the browser to create HTML that can change even after a page has been loaded into a browser. The technologies that help make this all possible are JavaScript, the Document Object Model (DOM), layers, and Cascading Style Sheets (CSS).

Using Dynamic HTML, you can do some pretty incredible things with your Web site. For example, a paragraph could turn any color you want when the user moves the cursor over it. A header could slide across the screen in any direction and at any speed you desire. Want to place a menu on your Web page, but you can't find room for it? No problem. With Dynamic HTML, you can do things like making that menu appear when the user clicks on an image or when the cursor moves over a certain area of the page. With Dynamic HTML, you can create a page that scrolls automatically at predefined intervals and even create windows of scrolling text (such as news events and bulletins) that the user can pause and restart with a click of the mouse. Basically, what all this means is that anything that can be done in HTML can be redone after the page loads.

Browser Support for Dynamic HTML

Dynamic HTML is a browser feature that is natively supported by both Netscape Communicator and Microsoft Internet Explorer (IE) 4 (and above). However, three important topics should be taken into consideration when making the decisions of if and how to incorporate Dynamic HTML into your Web pages:

- Supporting previous browser versions
- Handling Netscape and Microsoft IE incompatibilities
- Selecting a scripting language

Supporting Previous Browser Versions

If there is the possibility that some of your users are going to view your work with an older version of Netscape Communicator or Microsoft IE, you want to at least make sure that your Web page degrades gracefully when viewed. The term *degrading gracefully* simply means that even though your Web pages might take advantage of the "bleeding edge" features of a browser, that same Web page will still function when viewed by a previous version of the same browser. As an example, say that you have defined a hierarchical, tree-like menu that automatically expands and contracts when the user moves the cursor over the different items in the menu. Say that you accomplished this using Dynamic HTML provided by Microsoft IE 4. In order for your Web page to still function correctly when viewed by previous versions of Microsoft IE, you could simply use the Navigator object that you learned about earlier in the book to determine the browser name and version the page it is currently being viewed with. Then, if the browser didn't support Dynamic HTML, you could simply display a menu that automatically has all its branches expanded. As you work your way through this hour, you will see how this is accomplished.

Handling Netscape and Microsoft IE Incompatibilities

The World Wide Web Consortium (www.w3.org) is a group that is responsible for endorsing the standards that govern the World Wide Web. Also referred to as W3C, this group has not endorsed Dynamic HTML as a standard as of the time of this writing. However, it has issued a standard for the Document Object Model. The relevance here is that the W3C Document Object Model Level 1 Specification (http://www.w3.org/TR/1998/REC-DOM-Level-1-19981001) does explicitly mention that Dynamic HTML was the ancestor of the Document Object Model.

The problem is that without a definitive standard for Dynamic HTML, Netscape Communicator and IE are currently at very different stages in terms of support for DHTML. An example of the different approaches they have taken can be seen in how elements are dynamically positioned. With Netscape, you use the <LAYER> and <ILAYER> tags for dynamic positioning, whereas with IE, you use CSS positioning. Additionally, IE grants the Web developer complete dynamic access to any HTML tag. In other words, it doesn't rely on any single HTML tag. Rather, all HTML elements in a document can be dynamically accessed and modified after the document has been loaded.

This glaring weakness in Netscape's support of Dynamic HTML means that Web developers have choices and compromises to make. If you are developing an intranet application in which you know that the client browser will always be Microsoft IE, this is not an issue. However, if there is a possibility that your site might be viewed from Netscape Communicator, you basically have two choices to ensure that your page can be viewed from either of these browsers. First, using the Navigator object, determine the current browser type. Then you can use script to conditionally display the page content that is compatible with the detected browser. This works great only if you have a relatively small amount of Dynamic HTML that is incompatible. Otherwise, you would end up with a page that is so full of conditional logic that it would make debugging and maintaining the source code very difficult. In the latter case, you would be better off redirecting the user to completely different Web pages, depending on the detected browser type.

Visual InterDev 6 is, for obvious reasons, biased towards the Microsoft IE flavor of Dynamic HTML. Therefore, because this book's focus is Microsoft Visual InterDev 6, the majority of the examples in this hour use techniques that are only available if the client browser is IE.

Selecting a Scripting Language

As mentioned in Hour 6, "Empowering Your Site with Client Scripting," Microsoft IE supports JavaScript, JScript, and VBScript. However, Netscape only supports JavaScript. Therefore, if cross-browser compliance is important to you, you will need to use JavaScript. In addition, the majority of Dynamic HTML scripts you will find on the Internet are written in JavaScript even when the author notes that the script will only work in Microsoft IE. For these reasons, I would strongly recommend using JavaScript. Therefore all the examples in this hour do, in fact, use JavaScript.

Using the Document Object Model

The W3C defines the Document Object Model as a hierarchy of objects within a Dynamic HTML document (see Figure 9.1). Each object within this lattice has its own methods, properties, collections, and associated events that it can fire. In order to access a given object within the hierarchy, you need to use the "dotted syntax."

For example, if you define a form for your Web page named MyForm and then define a text control within that form named txtMyField, the following could be used in order to display the value of txtMyField:

```
alert(document.MyForm.txtMyField.Value);
```

Now look at Figure 9.1 again and notice that many of the objects in the DOM have names that end in the letter s. These objects are actually collections of objects. For example, the Forms collection contains all the Form objects that are defined for the current Document object. In addition, each Form object has an embedded Elements collection that contains an Element object for every single HTML element defined for that form. Because an element in a collection can be referenced by its subscript, you can then use the following syntax to display the value of the third element on the second form for a particular document. Note that all collection subscripts are relative to zero. Therefore, the following would refer to the third element's value on the second form.

```
alert(window.document.forms[1].elements[2].value);
```

9

FIGURE 9.1

The Document Object Model gives you complete control over your Web page's appearance even after the page has been downloaded.

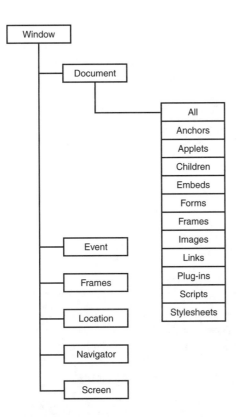

Collections come in very handy when you either don't know the specific ID of the element you are attempting to manipulate (something that is very common in dynamic situations), or you need to iterate through an entire collection. The following code iterates through all the HTML elements in the form named MyForm and displays the value of each found element:

```
len=document.MyForm.elements.length;
for (i = 0; i < len; i++)
{
 alert(document.MyForm.elements[i].value);
}
```

In the previous example, MyForm is the first form defined for the document. Therefore, the following code would accomplish the same thing:

```
len=document.MyForm.elements.length;
for (i = 0; i < len; i++)
{
 alert(document.forms[0].elements[i].value);
}
```

As you can see, fully qualifying each element name can get a bit tedious when you're talking about a Web page with several forms and controls. Luckily, a collection called All enables you to specify just the element name. The browser is then responsible for searching across the different forms to find your uniquely defined element.

Therefore, the following three lines of script all accomplish the same thing with the use of the All collection simply making for less typing:

```
alert(document.MyForm.txtMyField.value);
alert(window.document.MyForm. txtMyField.value);
alert(document.all.txtMyField.value);
```

Dynamic Styles

The first usage of Dynamic HTML that you'll learn is that of Dynamic Styles. As the term implies, *Dynamic Styles* simply refers to the ability to change the style of a Web page or one of its HTML elements after the page has been loaded on the client browser. This feature is often used to provide immediate feedback to the user because he is working his way through the page. An example of when to use Dynamic Styles is if you want to show the same content to all your users, but you also want to highlight certain sections of the page—based on some dynamic factor such as runtime options the user can make or the current date and time.

An Example of Dynamic Styling

Therefore, in this hour's first example, you will create a very simple cinema Web page that lists the movies to be shown for a given day. Each movie will be represented as a separate line of text. In addition to the list of movies, you will add a set of check boxes to the top of the page that allows the user to specify which kind of movie (action, drama, or comedy) that she is interested in seeing. You will then add JavaScript so that when the user clicks on one of these check boxes, the appropriate movie title will be shown in bold. This use of Dynamic Styling illustrates a perfect example of the benefits of Dynamic HTML because it allows the Web page to dynamically provide feedback to the user based on user input. It does all this on the client side without incurring the overhead of retrieving information from the server. To do this, perform the following steps:

1. At this point, create a new project named DynamicHTML using the Artsy theme.

2. Create a new HTML page called Cinema.htm.

3. Add a <FORM> element named MyForm to the Cinema.htm page.

4. After you have created the Web page, create the content for the page as shown in Figure 9.2.

FIGURE 9.2

*Dynamic styling enables
you to change the style
of an entire HTML page
or HTML element at
runtime in response to a
user's action.*

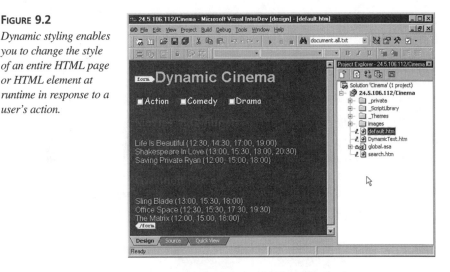

5. Set the ID of the Action, Comedy, and Drama controls to chkAction, chkComedy and chkDrama, respectively.

6. Although you haven't done it yet in this book, you can set the ID property of a text item so that you can reference the item in your HTML or script. Open the Source view and place each movie title in a <NOBR> element. Here's an example (notice that the name of this text is txtSaving):

```
<nobr id=txtSaving>Saving Private Ryan (12:00, 15:00, 18:00)</nobr>
```

In a real application, you would probably want to fully qualify each movie title with the name of the cinema in which it is playing. But then again, in a real application you would also be reading this information from a database. Therefore, please keep in mind that this example has been kept simple by design in order to concentrate on the DHTML.

7. Now you're ready to see how easy this stuff really is. Open the Script Outline window and add an onclick handler for the Drama check box. Remember that the Web page has to be in Source view in order for you to view its objects and scripts in the Script Outline window.

8. Now add the following code to the chkDrama_onclick handler. Notice that, if you're using controls that are on the same page as the handler, you can omit prepending the document.all qualifier.

```
if (true == MyForm.chkDrama.checked)
{
 txtLife.style.fontWeight = "bold";
 txtSaving.style.fontWeight = "bold";
 txtSling.style.fontWeight = "bold";
```

```
    }
    else
    {
     txtLife.style.fontWeight = "normal";
     txtSaving.style.fontWeight = "normal";
     txtSling.style.fontWeight = "normal";
    }
```

9. When you've finished coding the `chkDrama_onclick` event handler, do the same for the
   other two check boxes and test your new Web page. You will find that now when you
   click on a button, your users will see feedback similar to what you see in Figure 9.3.
   Obviously, this is an incredibly simple example (by design). However, now that you've
   seen how to dynamically set the styles of any item on a Web page, you can easily do
   the same for your pages regardless of the complexity of your actual application.

FIGURE 9.3

*Click on the check
boxes to see how the
styles of the different
text items are dynami-
cally modified.*

Dynamic Text

In the previous section, you saw how to change the style of an HTML element after the
page had been loaded. In fact, after a page has loaded, you can even change the textual
content! This is all done using the `innerText`, `outerText`, `innerHTML` and `outerHTML`
properties. Unfortunately, although being very useful, using these particular properties
can be extremely frustrating because of their ambiguous names. Therefore, take a look at
the `innerText` and `outerText` properties first.

Say that you have a piece of text defined within a pair of container elements. You might
have a heading to a Web page between `<H1>` and `</H1>` tags. In order to change just the text,
you would use the `innerText` property. Therefore, if the element is defined as the following:

```
<h1 id="myHeading">This is my Heading</h1>
```

The following use of the `innerText` property would change the `myHeading` text, but not its style:

```
myHeading.innerText = "This will change the text, but not the style"
```

Now look at another example where you can see the effect that the `outerText` property would have on your page's content. Assuming the following definition:

```
<H1 id="myHeading2">This is my second Heading</H1>
```

The following use of the `outerText` property would change the myHeading2 text *and* its style:

```
myHeading2.outerText = "This will change the text and the element's style"
```

Although the `innerText` and `outerText` properties provide you with the contents of the text target without the tags, the `innerHTML` and `outerHTML` include the tags. Actually, the way it works is that the `innerHTML` property will enable you to set or retrieve the text (including any HTML tags) between a set of tags that are defined for a given element. To clarify, say that you have the following text item defined:

```
<H1 id="myHeading3"> This is my <i>third</i> Heading</H1>
```

Now, set the `innerHTML` property of the `myHeading3` element as follows:

```
myHeading3.innerHTML = "This is my <U>third</U> Heading</H1>"
```

The result will be that the entire text will still be in Heading 1 style and the word `third` will be italicized.

Finally, that brings us to the `outerHTML` property. This property is used to set or retrieve the HTML content of an element. Therefore, assuming that once again you have the following element defined for your page:

```
<H1 id="myHeading4"> This is my <i>fourth</i> Heading</H1>
```

Now, set the `outerHTML` property of the `myHeading4` element as follows:

```
myHeading4.outerHTML = "This is my <u>fourth</u> Heading"
```

This time, you not only will replace the text, but you will have also effectively removed the outer tags from the text. Therefore, the user will see the entire text in the normal style with the word fourth italicized.

At this point, an example Web page might help to clarify things, so perform the following steps:

1. Add a Web page to the Dynamic HTML project called TextOperations.htm.
2. Open the TextOperations page in Design view and add the directions and horizontal bar you see in Figure 9.4.

FIGURE **9.4**

*Add this heading for
the text properties
example.*

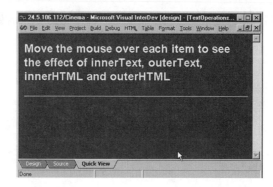

3. Sometimes it's easier to add named text items manually, so switch to the Source view
   and insert the following definitions after the `<HR>` tag and just before the `</BODY>` tag:

```
<H3 id="InnerText" onmouseover="innerTextOver();"
➥onmouseout="innerTextOut();">
innerText will change the text (but not the style) of an
➥element</H3>

<H3 id="OuterText" onmouseover="outerTextOver();">
outerText will change the text (and style) of an element</H3>

<H3 id="InnerHTML" onmouseover="innerHTMLOver();"
➥onmouseout="innerHTMLOut();">
innerHTML will change the text and style
➥(excluding the element's tags)</H3>

<H3 id="OuterHTML" onmouseover="outerHTMLOver();">
outerHTML will change the text and style
➥(including the element's tags)</H3>
```

4. Now, enter the following script to handle the different `onmouseover` and `onmouse-
   out` events. This code should be inserted just before the `</HEAD>` tag.

```
<SCRIPT ID=clientEventHandlersJS LANGUAGE=javascript>
<!--

// innerText methods
function innerTextOver() {
InnerText.innerText = "You just changed the text (but not style)
➥via the innerText property";
}
```

```
function innerTextOut() {
InnerText.innerText = "innerText will change the text
➥(but not its style) of an element";
}

// outerText methods
function outerTextOver() {
OuterText.outerText = "You just changed the (and style)
➥via outerText";
}

// innerHTML methods
function innerHTMLOver() {
InnerHTML.innerHTML = "Notice that this is <i>italicized</i>,
➥but still the style is still Heading 1";
}

function innerHTMLOut() {
InnerHTML.innerHTML = "innerHTML will change the text and style
➥(excluding the element's tags)";
}

// outerHTML methods
function outerHTMLOver() {
OuterHTML.outerHTML = "Notice that this is <i>italicized</i>,
➥and no longer a Heading 1";
}

//-->
</SCRIPT>
```

5. Now when you test your Web page, it will look like that shown in Figure 9.5.

FIGURE 9.5

Dynamic HTML allows you to easily modify any text on a page (including its HTML tags).

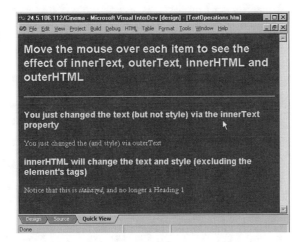

Using the `TextRange` Object

The `TextRange` object is used to work with all the text in a document or a specific range of text such as a paragraph. With this object, you can perform such tasks as completely replacing whole blocks of text, searching and replacing specific text, and highlighting key text.

The `TextRange` is a very robust and flexible class and could easily take up an entire hour by itself. Therefore, it should be noted that this section is not intended to cover every aspect of this object. Rather, the intention here is to at least cover the basics of this object and its functionality so that you can see what it can do for you and whether you feel as though it warrants further investigation.

Creating the `TextRange` Object

A `TextRange` object is initialized by calling the `createTextRange` method of a `BODY`, `BUTTON`, `TEXTAREA` element, or an `INPUT` element whose type has been defined as `TEXT`. For example, the following code would return a `TextRange` object that contains all the text within the `<BODY>` and `</BODY>` tags of a page:

```
myTextRange = document.body.createTextRange();
```

If you accidentally call the `createTextRange` method without including the parenthesis, you might find that something interesting happens. For example, say that you call the `createTextRange` like this:

```
alert(document.body.createTextRange);
```

In this case, through the omission of the parenthesis, you have instructed the browser to display the `createTextRange` method itself as opposed to calling it. Therefore, if after calling the `createTextRange` method, what appears to be a prototype is returned to you, it probably means that you simply need to verify that you are calling the method correctly.

Retrieving the Value of a `TextRange` Object

When you have obtained the `TextRange` object through the `createTextRange` method, its contents minus the HTML tags can be retrieved by referencing the `TextRange` object's Text property. Figure 9.6 shows you an example of a Web page that contains a letter.

The button at the bottom of the page simply made the following code in order to display the Web page's content:

```
textRange = document.body.createTextRange();
alert(textRange.text);
```

If you want the entire text (including the HTML tags), simply use the `TextRange` object's `htmlText` property.

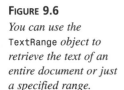

FIGURE 9.6

You can use the `TextRange` *object to retrieve the text of an entire document or just a specified range.*

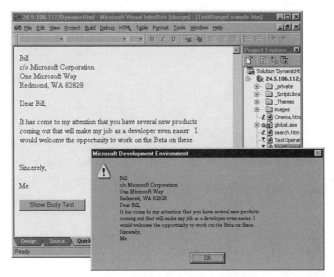

Searching for Text

The `TextRange` object defines a method called `findText` that allows for the searching of text throughout a document.

The following code shows the syntax for the `TextRange` object's `findText` method. Notice that the parameters match what you would expect on your typical Find dialog. The difference, of course, is that with the `TextRange` object, you can perform this same type of search from within your script.

```
findText (sText [,iSearchScope] [,iFlags])
```

In this syntax, *sText* is the text to be found, *iSearchScope* indicates the number of characters to search through (negative numbers represent a backward search), and *iFlags* is any combination of the following (2 = match whole words only, 4 = match case).

Listing 9.1 is a code snippet that illustrates how you might provide a user with the capability to find text on a given document. Notice that if the desired text is found, it will be highlighted via the `TextRange` object's Select method.

LISTING 9.1   Example Usage of `TextRange`

```
1: <SCRIPT ID=clientEventHandlersJS LANGUAGE=javascript>
2: <!--
3: function btnFindText_onclick()
4: {
5:   textRange = document.body.createTextRange();
```

continues

LISTING 9.1   continued

```
 6:  if (true == textRange.findText(txtFindText.value))
 7:  {
 8:   textRange.select();
 9:  }
10: }
11: //-->
12: </SCRIPT>
13:
14: <P>
15: <INPUT id=txtFindText name=text1>  <INPUT id=btnFindText
➥name=button2 type=button value="Find Text" LANGUAGE =javascript
➥onclick="return btnFindText_onclick()">
16: </P>
```

Replacing Found Text

Now that you've seen how easy it is to find text within a document using the TextRange object, its time to look into how you would replace found text.

Actually, there's no need to call another method. As you saw from Listing 9.1, when a search is performed via the TextRange object's findText method, its value is returned in the TextRange object itself. Therefore, you need only to set the TextRange object's text property. Listing 9.2 shows how you might provide the user with the capability to find a specific text string and replace it with another.

LISTING 9.2   Find-and-Replace Example

```
 1: <SCRIPT ID=clientEventHandlersJS LANGUAGE=javascript>
 2: <!--
 3: function btnFindText_onclick()
 4: {
 5:  textRange = document.body.createTextRange();
 6:  if (true == textRange.findText(txtFindText.value))
 7:  {
 8:   textRange.select();
 9:  }
10: }
11:
12: function btnReplaceWith_onclick()
13: {
14:  textRange = document.body.createTextRange();
15:  while (true == textRange.findText(txtFindText.value))
16:  {
17:   alert(textRange.text);
18:   textRange.text = txtReplaceWith.value;
19:  }
```

```
20: }
21:
22: //-->
23: </SCRIPT>
```

Creating Dynamic Menu Bars

Another very popular way to use Dynamic HTML is with menu bars. UI designers have always faced a difficult dilemma regarding elements like these simply because on the one hand a menu does provide quick navigation capability to the user. However, they also take up a lot of screen real estate. Therefore, in this section, you will see how to use Dynamic HTML to develop a cool menu bar. A cool menu bar that automatically slides open from the left edge of the screen as the surfer moves the cursor over it. Moving the cursor out will cause the bar to slide back in. Here's how to incorporate this cool feature into a Web page:

1. Create a new HTML page or open an existing one to which you want to add a menu of hyperlinks.

2. Insert the following code just before the `</HEAD>` tag. This code will define the styles that will be used for the presentation of the menu bar. It is the code that you will modify if you want to change the visual aspects of the menu bar itself (size, position, border color, and so on).

```
<style>
<!--

#slidemenubar, #slidemenubar2{
position:absolute;
left:-155px;
width:160px;
top:170px;
border:1.5px solid green;
background-color:lightyellow;
layer-background-color:lightyellow;
font:bold 12px Verdana;
line-height:20px;
}
-->
</style>
```

3. Now, insert the following code immediately after the `<BODY>` tag. You might recall from earlier that the document write method is used to set a document's content. Here the script is simply stipulating what methods are to be called when the mouse cursor is moved over the menu's edge (pull) and what method is called when the cursor is moved off of the menu (draw). Notice the DIV and Layer tags that you learned about earlier.

```
<script language="JavaScript1.2">

if (document.all)
document.write('<div id="slidemenubar2" style="left:-150"
➥onMouseover="pull()" onMouseout="draw()">')
</script>
<layer id="slidemenubar" onMouseover="pull()" onMouseout="draw()">
<script language="JavaScript1.2">
```

4. Now define the menu text and hyperlinks by declaring two arrays and filling them up with your values:

```
var sitems=new Array()
var sitemlinks=new Array()

//extend or shorten this list
sitems[0]="Tom Archer's MFC Web Page"
sitems[1]="CodeGuru"
sitems[2]="Dynamic Drive"
sitems[3]="Experts Exchange"
sitems[4]="Web Monkeys DHTML Guide"

//These are the links pertaining to the above text.
sitemlinks[0]="http://tarcher.home.mindspring.com"
sitemlinks[1]="http://www.codeguru.com"
sitemlinks[2]="http://www.dynamicdrive.com"
sitemlinks[3]="http://www.experts-exchange.com"
sitemlinks[4]="http://www.hotwired.com/webmonkey/dynamic_html/"
```

5. Now add the code to actually iterate through the menu item and hyperlink array and write them out to the menu document:

```
for (i=0;i<=sitems.length-1;i++)
document.write('<a href='+sitemlinks[i]+'>'+sitems[i]+'</a><br>')
</script>

</layer>
```

6. Finally, add the methods that are responsible for the actual drawing of the menu bar:

```
<script language="JavaScript1.2">
function regenerate(){
window.location.reload()
}
function regenerate2(){
if (document.layers)
setTimeout("window.onresize=regenerate",400)
}
```

```
window.onload=regenerate2
if (document.all){
document.write('</div>')
themenu=document.all.slidemenubar2.style
rightboundary=0
leftboundary=-150
}
else{
themenu=document.layers.slidemenubar
rightboundary=150
leftboundary=10
}
function pull(){
if (window.drawit)
clearInterval(drawit)
pullit=setInterval("pullengine()",50)
}
function draw(){
clearInterval(pullit)
drawit=setInterval("drawengine()",50)
}
function pullengine(){
if (document.all&&themenu.pixelLeft<rightboundary)
themenu.pixelLeft+=5
else if(document.layers&&themenu.left<rightboundary)
themenu.left+=5
else if (window.pullit)
clearInterval(pullit)
}
function drawengine(){
if (document.all&&themenu.pixelLeft>leftboundary)
themenu.pixelLeft-=5
else if(document.layers&&themenu.left>leftboundary)
themenu.left-=5
else if (window.drawit)
clearInterval(drawit)
}
</script>
```

7. Figure 9.7 shows you what you will see when you've finished inserting the cool
   menu bar code.

9

FIGURE 9.7

FIGURE 9.7

*Dynamic HTML allows
you to create cool
menu bars that auto-
matically show and
hide themselves when
the user moves the cur-
sor around the page.*

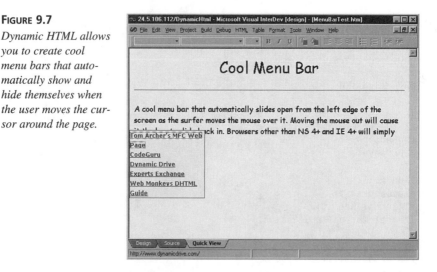

Creating Watermarks

Another cool effect that Dynamic HTML can help you add to your Web page is a watermark. If you've ever been to a Web page hosted by GeoCities, you've seen this neat little
feature. As opposed to a simple background that gets tiled or stretched in accordance with
the document's size, a watermark is an image that is defined to appear in a specific place on
the Web page. Then when the user scrolls the document's content, the watermark doesn't
move! Watermarks give you the ability to keep your company's logo in front of the user at
all times, but in a very low-key, subtle way.

To add a watermark to a Web page, simply do the following:

1. Create a new Web page or open an existing Web page on which you want to create
   your watermark.

2. Using what you learned in Hour 1, "Creating Your First Web Page with Visual
   InterDev," add an image to the project that will serve as the watermark.

3. Open the Web page in Design view and insert the following script after the <BODY>
   tag. Notice the override of the background color via the cssText (Cascading Stylesheet
   Text) property. Also notice the last three values (fixed, center, center). These values
   specify that the image is to be fixed (non-moving) and that it is to be centered both
   vertically and horizontally.

```
<script language="JavaScript1.2">
if (document.all)
 document.body.style.cssText="background:white url
 ➥(images/ov_main.gif) no-repeat fixed center center"
</script>
```

4. Figure 9.8 illustrates an example of how your page will look when you've finished adding this script.

FIGURE 9.8

Dynamic HTML allows you to add a water-mark image to your Web page with a couple of lines of script.

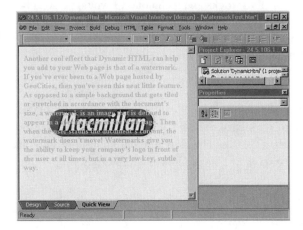

Summary

In the course of this hour, you have not only learned the basics of Dynamic HTML, but you also put them to use in several examples ranging from Dynamic Styling to Text Manipulation. You then learned several techniques regarding the TextRange object and finally, you wrote a cool menu bar and added a Web page watermark.

Although you have learned a tremendous amount in the last hour, you should be cognizant of the fact that Dynamic HTML is a very large and complex topic and obviously cannot be adequately covered in a single hour. Therefore, if you are serious about becoming even more fluent in this very exciting technology, I would recommend purchasing a book that is dedicated solely to the subject of Dynamic HTML.

Q&A

Q What are the chances that Netscape and Microsoft will ever make it easier to develop cross-browser Dynamic HTML?

A With the W3C's standardization of the Document Object Model, it appears very likely that at some point in the near future these competing browsers will finally have a standard from which they can both work.

Q Where can I learn more about Dynamic HTML on the Internet?

A There are quite a few very good Web sites that provide information on the latest Dynamic HTML tricks and techniques. I would personally recommend the Dynamic Drive site (`www.dynamicdrive.com`) because they contributed both the cool menu bar and watermark code to this effort as well as the Web Monkeys DHTML Guide (`www.hotwired.com/webmonkey/dynamic_html`).

Workshop

The Workshop is designed to help you anticipate possible questions, review what you've learned, and begin thinking ahead to put your knowledge into practice. The answers to the quiz and exercise are in Appendix A, "Answers."

Quiz

1. What is Dynamic HTML?
2. What is a technique for gracefully degrading to a browser that doesn't support Dynamic HTML?
3. What is the main difference between how Dynamic HTML is defined in Netscape and how it is defined with Microsoft IE?
4. What is the benefit of Dynamic styles?
5. What is the difference between the `innerText` and `innerHTML` properties?
6. What is the `TextRange` object used for?
7. How is a `TextRange` object created?
8. What is the difference between the `TextRange` properties, `text` and `htmlText`?
9. What `TextRange` method is used to search a document?
10. What Document Object Model property is used to create a watermark?

Exercise

Create a Web page that provides a template letter in which the user can enter the values (To Address, From Address, Subject, and so on) that will be used in the letter itself.

Hour 10

Writing Scriptlets

In the last hour, you learned about the exciting browser feature known as Dynamic HTML and how it can aid in developing truly dynamic Web pages whose content can change even after being downloaded to the client. With all the talk lately about object-oriented, or component-based programming, you might be wondering if there's any way to take these scripts you've been writing and turn them into encapsulated components that can be reused in other Web pages or even other Visual InterDev projects. Well, now you can, and it's done via an exciting technology called scriptlets.

In this hour, you will learn

- What scriptlets are
- How scriptlets enable componentized Web programming
- How scriptlets differ from similar technologies
- How to build a scriptlet
- How to use a scriptlet as you would any object
- How to create your own scriptlet properties
- How to raise standard HTML events from a scriptlet
- How to raise standard custom events from a scriptlet

Scriptlets Overview

In September 1997, Microsoft formally announced that they had created a new technology called scriptlets that use Dynamic HTML and scripts to create reusable objects for Web-based development. What is so exciting about this is that, with scriptlets, Web developers finally have all the benefits of object-oriented programming without the learning curve associated with Java or ActiveX controls. In fact, Microsoft is so supportive of this new innovation that in the same press release (`http://www.info-sec.com/internet/internet_091597c.html-ssi`), they announced that Java applets were being banned from their site in favor of this Dynamic HTML-based technology.

So what exactly are scriptlets? Scriptlets are fully contained objects written using a scripting language (usually JavaScript). Scriptlets allow Web developers to create commonly used elements—such as navigation bars, rotating ad banners, and even advanced UI elements like calculators—only once using a scripting language. These scriptlets can then be stored in the form of Web pages and reused on other Web pages or another Web so that all the benefits of code reuse can be realized.

Component-Based Programming

So far, you have used many component-based concepts to get to this point in the book. For example, you've set the properties of HTML controls, called the methods of ActiveX controls, and handled events raised by objects of the Document Object Model (DOM). However, because Visual InterDev hides a lot of the details from you with its visual interface to Web-based development, you've never really had to understand what is at the core of component-based programming. Therefore, before jumping into writing your own scriptlets (which are components), it would be a good idea to first take a look at some component-based programming concepts. Although this will take a few minutes, it will be time well spent because an understanding of the theories and concepts behind components and component-based programming is essential to developing self-contained, reusable scriptlets.

Understanding the Basics

The main buzzword in software development today is components. Components can be defined as units of software that are self-contained and provide some sort of black box functionality through exposed methods or properties. The term *black box* simply refers to the fact that the user of a component should not have to know anything about the inner workings of a component. For example, if one developer writes a component that allows for the verification of credit card numbers, the user of that component shouldn't have to understand how that component goes about doing its job. The internal workings of the component should be hidden, so the only thing the user of that component has to be concerned with is what properties can be set, what methods can be called, and what component-raised events can be handled.

In the beginning, most components were designed to present some visual appearance. Examples of these components are UI elements such as fancy buttons, toolbars, and grids. However, as the concept of component-based development began to take hold, developers began to realize that business logic could also be encapsulated. Therefore, now you will see many components that do everything from validating a vehicle identification number (VIN) to balancing a customer's order, which has no visual interface whatsoever.

Properties, Methods, and Events

Although the functionality that can be provided by components is literally endless, most component architectures rely heavily on three concepts: properties, methods, and events.

- Properties—Properties are used by components to allow a developer to set or retrieve certain design time or runtime attributes, or values. Although components usually incorporate numerous internal values that are not viewable outside the component, the term *properties* is used to refer to the values that can be set or retrieved from a user of the component. For example, a button component might have properties for setting and retrieving its size, position on the screen, background color, and text.

- Methods—Methods are the operations that can be executed by the user of a component. For example, an invoice component might have methods called `AddDetailLine`, `CalculateTotal`, and `Print`. A component's actions are generally manipulated through its methods.

- Events—Components are normally created within a container such as a Web page. Events are named runtime notifications to the component's container that something of interest to the container has occurred. For example, a button would send a notification to its container via an `onclick` event when the user has clicked the button. An example using a nonvisual component would be an invoice component sending notification via a `hasPrinted` event when an invoice has completed its printing.

Benefits of Components

Now that you know what a component is, you might be wondering, "What are the tangible benefits of components?" The two main advantages that writing components (such as scriptlets) affords you as a developer are encapsulation and code reuse.

Encapsulation refers to a component's ability to isolate its internal workings from the rest of the program. This goes back to the black box behavior mentioned earlier. The benefit to be gained from this is that errors elsewhere in an application (or in the case of scriptlets, a Web page) will not affect the working of a component and vice versa. Therefore, debugging errors in your code becomes much easier because you can exclude whole pieces of code when tracking down the cause of the error. For example, say that you have an intranet Web page that allows for the entering of customer orders through an order component. When

10

completed, an invoice component might be created that prints itself to a specific printer. If something were to go wrong with the printing of the invoice, it would be much easier to narrow down the possible culprit because only one section of code is responsible for the printing.

Code reuse refers to the ability to write a component one time and use it over and over again in similar programmatic situations. However, it can't be stressed enough that the promise of code reuse can't be realized unless a good amount of forethought and planning are put into the design of the component. For example, if your invoicing component is hard-coded to do things such as print to a specific printer and use a specific font, your component won't be nearly as reusable as an invoice component that allows for the settings of these variables through its exposed properties.

Comparing Scriptlets to Other Component-Based Technologies

So far the definition of a scriptlet might sound very much like that of a Java applet or an ActiveX control. After all, all three provide a means of writing an encapsulated, reusable component; exposing public methods and properties; and raising events to the component's container. However, depending on your needs, scriptlets just might be the best choice for developing components for your Web site.

Scriptlets Versus Java Applets

Java applets are based on a very robust, powerful language (Java). Therefore, Java applets will always be able to perform much more advanced functions than an object-oriented scripting technology such as scriptlets. However, scriptlets have the following three major advantages over Java applets:

- Security
- Download time
- Learning curve

Scriptlets Are Secure

Although most people (including me) believe that Java applets are completely safe to use, many corporate IS departments still refuse to allow the downloading of Java applets from the Internet for fear of some heretofore undiscovered security breach. Scriptlets don't cause this concern because they are built on Dynamic HTML and script, which is considered to be completely safe.

Scriptlets Don't Take Any Time to Download

The main factor that Microsoft pointed out regarding the removal of Java applets from their Web site in favor of scriptlets was the time it takes to download a Java applet to the client. Scriptlets, on the other hand, are usually very small code snippets with a very finite purpose. Therefore, downloading a page with scriptlets defined is no different in terms of speed than downloading any page with client-side script. In other words, the few lines of textual script code that define the scriptlet won't even be noticed with regard to its impact on downloading a Web page.

Writing Scriptlets Can Be Learned Quickly

To use today's vernacular, this one's pretty much a "no-brainer." Writing a Java applet takes a considerable investment of time and money in order to learn the Java language. In a perfect world, that isn't a problem. You simply tell your boss that you need a couple of weeks to get up to speed on Java, and you'll be cranking those Java applets right out. However, we as software developers don't live in this programming Utopia and therefore have to deal with real (or unreal) deadlines that usually prevent us from taking the time to learn an entire language in order to complete a particular project. This is where scriptlets offer their best advantage because they can be written by anyone who is already comfortable writing in a scripting language. This fact alone makes scriptlets a perfect tool for the Web developer.

Scriptlets Versus ActiveX Controls

ActiveX controls are a very exciting technology in many respects. Once again, you can't compare ActiveX controls to scriptlets based on their capabilities because ActiveX controls are built using full, robust languages such as C++, Visual Basic, and even Java. In fact, as you learned earlier, ActiveX controls provide even more functionality (at the expense of security) because they give the developer complete access to the system upon which the control is executing. However, that having been said, scriptlets have the following advantages over ActiveX controls:

- Security
- Download time
- Learning curve
- Truly multiplatform

Security

Despite Microsoft's best efforts, ActiveX controls have (up to this point) not become very popular outside of controlled environments (such as intranets). The problem is that because of the ActiveX control security model, ActiveX controls suffer from an even greater paranoia regarding the general consensus that they represent a real security threat. Therefore, once again, many corporate IS departments will not allow the downloading of ActiveX controls from the Internet. Once again scriptlets do not generate any concern regarding security because they are based only on Dynamic HTML and scripting code.

Download Time

Although ActiveX controls have the advantage over Java applets in that they are only downloaded when they don't exist on the client machine or they are out-of-date, they can still take a considerable amount of time to download that first time. Once again, scriptlets don't have this problem because they are simply scripting code embedded in the Web page itself.

Learning Curve

Although more and more development platforms are providing the capability to create ActiveX controls, nothing is as easy to learn as something already known. Therefore, for the Web developer already proficient at scripting, scriptlets will always have an advantage in this area.

Truly Multiplatform

In spite of Microsoft's statements for future extension to other platforms, ActiveX controls remain to this day a standard for Win32 platforms and the Macintosh only. Scriptlets, however, can be used on any platform that supports Microsoft Internet Explorer (IE) 4 and above.

Scriptlets Versus Includes

Actually the include statement provides nothing more than the ability to simply state that you want a particular piece of code inserted into a specific location in the Web page. Therefore, although the include does give you the ability to reuse your scripts in a very simple, rudimentary manner, it doesn't provide any of the benefits that you've learned can be gained by componentizing your scripting code.

Building Your First Scriptlet

Enough talk! Now get down to writing that first scriptlet. The first scriptlet you will build is very basic. However, most of what you learn here can be carried over and used in building scriptlets of any complexity.

Creating a scriptlet and using it can be accomplished by following these three easy steps:

1. Create the HTML page that will be the scriptlet.
2. Define the HTML page as a scriptlet to Visual InterDev.
3. Create a container to test the scriptlet.

Creating the Scriptlet

The first thing you need to do in order to write your scriptlet is create a Web page that will contain the scriptlet itself. Remember that a scriptlet is basically a Web page that is used like a component. To do this, perform the following steps:

1. Create a new Visual InterDev project called `MyFirstScriptlets`.

2. Now, add an HTML page to your new project and name it `DisplayMessage.htm`.

3. After switching to Source view, right-click on the background of the HTML editor after the `<HEAD>` tag and select the Script Block, Client menu option.

4. Now insert the following code between the `<SCRIPT>` and `</SCRIPT>` tags. By using the word public to prefix the method name, you are specifying that this method will be exposed to any users of this scriptlet. Therefore, the actual name of the method is not `public_whoami`. To any users of this component, the name of the exposed method is simply `whoami`. Notice also the use of something called level. Actually, it isn't defined at this point, but will be in the next step via the `DIV` tag.

```
function public_whoami(strLevel)
{
 level.innerText = strLevel;
}
```

5. After entering the `whoami` method, insert the following code after the `<BODY>` tag. Notice the `DIV` tag. This defines your variable named `level`. When you've finished, your DisplayMessage.htm file should resemble Listing 10.1.

```
<h3>I am a
<DIV ID="level"></DIV>
in writing Scriptlets.</h3>
```

LISTING 10.1   DisplayMessage.htm

```
 1: <HTML>
 2: <HEAD>
 3: <META NAME="GENERATOR" Content="Microsoft Visual Studio 6.0">
 4: <TITLE></TITLE>
 5: </HEAD>
 6:
 7: <SCRIPT LANGUAGE=javascript>
 8: <!--
 9: function public_whoami(strLevel)
10: {
11:  level.innerText = strLevel;
12: }
13: //-->
14: </SCRIPT>
```

continues

LISTING **10.1** continued

```
15:
16: <BODY>
17: <h3>I am a
18: <DIV ID="level"></DIV>
19: in writing Scriptlets.</h3>
20:
21: <P> </P>
22:
23: </BODY>
24: </HTML>
```

Defining an HTML Page as a Scriptlet to Visual InterDev

The last thing you need to do after you've created your scriptlet is to let Visual InterDev know about it, by implementing the following steps:

1. Open the Project Explorer window and locate your DisplayMessages.htm file.

2. After right-clicking on it, select the Mark as Scriptlet menu option. This will add an entry to the Scriptlets tab on the Toolbox window.

3. Open the Toolbox window and click on the Scriptlets tab. You should see your new DisplayMessage.htm scriptlet as shown in Figure 10.1.

FIGURE **10.1**

After you've created a scriptlet, Visual InterDev enables you to easily view and manage it via the Toolbox window.

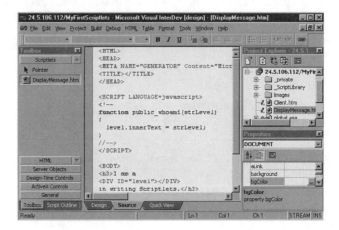

Creating a Test Container

After you've created the scriptlet and added it to the Toolbox, it's time to create the container to actually use your newly created component. To do so, follow these steps:

1. Using the same MyFirstScriptlets project, add an HTML page called Client.htm and open it up in Source view.

2. Open the Toolbox window and locate the DisplayMessage.htm scriptlet.

3. After placing the caret before the </BODY> tag, simply double-click your new scriptlet, and it will automatically be added to the page. At this time, you can size the scriptlet object just as you would any HTML or ActiveX control that you add to your Web page.

4. If the scriptlet is displayed in the page's source code as a rectangle as opposed to its HTML, simply right-click the HTML editor background and select the Always View as Text menu option.

5. At this point, you will see that in order to use a scriptlet, you simply need to create an OBJECT element in your HTML with the associated PARAM keyword values.

6. Notice that there are two ways to set these PARAM values. You can either manually key them into the OBJECT element or you can do so via the Properties window.

> It can be difficult to get all of a scriptlet object's properties to display in the Properties window when the Always View as Text option is turned on. Therefore, when attempting to set a scriptlet's properties via the Properties window, I would recommend unchecking the Always View as Text option and then clicking the component.

7. After you've included a scriptlet into your container, you can call any of its public methods. At this point, open the Script Outline window and add an event handler for the window object's onload event.

8. Insert the following script for the onload event handler (substituting the ID of your scriptlet object for the WebBridge1):

```
a = WebBridge1.whoami("BEGINNER")
```

9. When you're finished, click the QuickView tab to see your very first scriptlet (see Figure 10.2). Although this might have seemed like a lot of steps to go through, when you get the hang of it, you will realize how much easier (and more productive) creating scriptlets is than copying and pasting your scripts from page to page.

Figure 10.2

Scriptlets enable you to easily componentize HTML pages so that they can be easily reused in other Web pages. Hopefully by the end of this hour, you will be changing this text to read GURU.

Taking a Close Look at the OBJECT Element

As you saw previously, when you add a scriptlet to a container Web page from the Toolbox window, Visual InterDev automatically inserts the OBJECT element for you into that page's HTML. Here's the OBJECT element that was previously created:

```
<OBJECT height=187 id=WebBridge1
style="HEIGHT: 187px; LEFT: 0px; TOP: 0px; WIDTH: 283px"
➥type=text/x-scriptlet
width=283 VIEWASTEXT>
 <PARAM NAME="URL" VALUE="http://24.5.106.112/MyFirstScriptlets/
➥DisplayMessage.htm">
 <PARAM NAME="Scrollbar" VALUE="0">
</OBJECT>
```

Of special interest here is the type parameter. This parameter defines a new MIME type and is what allows a Web page to contain an embedded HTML page as a scriptlet.

Also note that the URL parameter is used to determine the exact address of the scriptlet page itself. Therefore, if you move a scriptlet, you will need to remember to update all other pages that reference it by its address.

Creating Scriptlet Properties

Properties are exposed from a scriptlet by creating a function that contains the word get (for retrieving) or put (for setting) prepended to the name of the property. Additionally, as you saw when you created your scriptlet's whoami method, you also need to prepend the word public so that users of your scriptlet will have access to it. Therefore, the syntax for exposing a property so that it can be set is as follows:

```
function public_put_property(input)
```

The syntax for setting this property would then be the following. Notice the omission of the public prefix and the put prefix.

```
scriptlet_id.property = input;
```

Because this can definitely be a bit confusing, here's an example. Take a scriptlet that only has two public properties (first name and last name) and a public method that will concatenate them and display them.

One unfortunate thing I have found with investigating scriptlets and how to use them is that most examples on the Web are so complex that it's impossible to just learn the fundamentals. Therefore, this is an intentionally simple example so that it is easier to concentrate on the task at hand, which is how to define and expose properties.

Exposing the Properties

To expose the properties of a scriptlet, follow these steps:

1. Create a new Web page called `DisplayName.htm` and open it in Source view.

2. Insert a Script Block into your code.

3. Define two variables to hold the first name and last name values as follows:
```
var m_firstName;
var m_lastName;
```

4. Immediately after the variable declarations, create two functions that will be used to set the two variables you just created. Take special note of the formatting of the function names.
```
function public_put_firstName(firstName)
{
 m_firstName = firstName;
}

function public_put_lastName(lastName)
{
 m_lastName = lastName;
}
```

5. Finally, add a method that will cause the first name and last name values to be concatenated and displayed. When you are finished, your code should look like that presented in Listing 10.2.
```
function public_displayName()
{
 alert("Hi " + m_firstName + " " + m_lastName);
}
```

10

LISTING 10.2   Example of Exposing Properties from a Scriptlet

```
 1: <script LANGUAGE="JavaScript">
 2:
 3: var m_firstName;
 4: var m_lastName;
 5:
 6: function public_put_firstName(firstName)
 7: {
 8:   m_firstName = firstName;
 9: }
10:
11: function public_put_lastName(lastName)
12: {
13:   m_lastName = lastName;
14: }
15:
16: function public_displayName()
17: {
18:   alert("Hi " + m_firstName + " " + m_lastName);
19: }
20: </script>
```

Accessing the Properties

Now that your component exposes the properties, it's time to look at how they are accessed, by performing the following steps:

1. Add a Web page called DisplayNameClient.htm and open it in Source view.

2. Add the following OBJECT element in the <BODY> segment of the HTML. You can also use the Toolbox technique you learned earlier, but I wanted to cover both techniques of defining a scriptlet. Which one you use will generally come down to a choice of whatever you're comfortable doing.

   ```
   <OBJECT ID="scriptlet"
   TYPE="text/x-scriptlet"
   DATA="DisplayName.htm"
   STYLE="width:100%; height:100;">
   </OBJECT>
   ```

3. Using the Script Outline window, add an event handler for the window object's onload event and modify it as follows. This will simply cause a method you're about to add to be called when the window is loaded.

   ```
   function window_onload() {
    useScriptlet();
   }
   ```

4. Finally, add the following function immediately after the window_onload function you just created. *Here's the important part:* Notice that even though the functions

in the scriptlet are called `public_put_firstName` and `public_put_lastName`, they are actually used as though they were functions (using the = operator) and sans the `public` and `put` prefixes.

```
function useScriptlet()
{
 scriptlet.firstName = "Tom";
 scriptlet.lastName = "Archer";
 scriptlet.displayName();
}
```

Firing Events from a Scriptlet

The last thing you will learn about scriptlets in this hour is how to raise events to the scriptlet's container. Scriptlets raise events when they want to notify the container that something happened in which the container might be interested.

Bubbling Standard HTML Events

Whenever a scriptlet receives a standard HTML event, it can choose to handle that event and "eat it" (not let the container see the event), or it can perform whatever processing is necessary and pass the event up to the container. The act of passing the event up to the container is sometimes referred to as *bubbling*.

Take an example in which the container wants to know whenever the user clicks the mouse on the scriptlet component (assuming that it's a visual component). The scriptlet component would simply handle the document object's `onclick` event and call the window object's `bubbleEvent` method:

```
function document_onclick() {
 window.external.bubbleEvent();
}
```

The container can then handle the event from the scriptlet. For example, if the scriptlet has an ID of myScriptlet, the following function could be inserted into the container to handle the bubbled up `onclick` event:

```
function myScriptlet_onclick() {
 alert("the scriptlet was clicked");
}
```

Defining Custom Events for a Scriptlet

Bubbling standard HTML events is easy enough if you want to define your own custom events. For example, say you have an invoice component that exposes a `balanceInvoice` method. In that situation, you would almost certainly need the capability to raise an `outOfBalance` event if the invoice didn't total correctly.

Luckily, Microsoft foresaw this obvious need and made it very easy to accomplish. In order to define a custom event for a scriptlet, you simply need to call the window object's `raiseEvent` method, passing to it the name of the event you want to raise.

Therefore, the syntax for raising a custom event to the container is the following:

```
window.external.raiseEvent(eventName, eventObject)
```

The container then catches the event by implementing a handler with the following syntax:

```
function scriptletId_OnScriptletEvent(eventName, eventObject)
```

Because all raised events will result in the same container event handler being executed, in cases where a scriptlet might raise more than one type of event, the container would need to look at the `eventName` parameter to decide what action to take.

```
function scriptletId_OnScriptletEvent(eventName, eventObject)
{
 if ("outOfBalance" == eventName)
 {
  // process out of balance event
 }
 else
 {
  // process other event types
 }
}
```

Summary

In the last hour, you've learned the basics of component-based programming as well as the benefits that can be derived from componentizing your script. You then learned how to define scriptlets, how to add them to the Visual InterDev Toolbox, and how to incorporate them into another Web page. You finished up this tutorial on scriptlets by discovering how to create your own scriptlet methods, properties, and custom events.

Q&A

Q Can a scriptlet have a context menu?

A Yes. Actually, this is quite easy. Simply use the `window.external.setContextMenu` method.

Q **Where can I find more information on scriptlets using the Internet?**

A There are several great examples of scriptlets to learn from on the Internet, including a calculator scriptlet (`http://home.earthlink.net/~itsinc/cal4.0.htm`), a navigation bar scriptlet (`www.datssoftware.com/top.html`), and a label scriptlet (`www.sis.pit.edu/~jcarlson/scriptlets/logo.html`).

Workshop

The Workshop is designed to help you anticipate possible questions, review what you've learned, and begin thinking ahead to put your knowledge into practice. The answers to the quiz and exercises are in Appendix A, "Answers."

Quiz

1. What are scriptlets?
2. How are scriptlets safer than Java applets and ActiveX controls?
3. What are the three basic concepts of almost any component architecture?
4. What is the difference between a scriptlet and an include?
5. Using JavaScript, what is the syntax for defining a `public` method in a scriptlet?
6. How do you define an HTML page as a scriptlet in Visual InterDev so that it appears in the Toolbox window?
7. What HTML element is used to access a scriptlet from another HTML page?
8. What is the syntax for defining a `public` property that can be set in a scriptlet in JavaScript?
9. How are standard HTML events bubbled up to the scriptlet's container?
10. How are custom events defined for a scriptlet?

Exercises

1. Create a scriptlet that represents a VIN verification component.
2. Create a scriptlet that represents a rotating ad banner component.

10

HOUR 11

Developing Active Server Pages

Over the past few hours, you've learned a great deal about developing scripts that run on the client side. In this hour, you will combine what you've learned about scripting and creating dynamic content to write scripts that will run on the server. As you will see, these scripts, called Active Server Scripts, will enable your Web applications to do things such as access server-side data and perform system level functions that cannot be done on the client.

The highlights of this hour include

- Learning why server-side processing is needed
- Learning about alternative means of providing server-side processing
- Discovering what an Active Server Page is
- Creating an Active Server Page in Visual InterDev
- Writing server script for an Active Server Page
- Using the Request object to retrieve form data
- Submitting a form to an Active Server Page
- Validating a form before submitting it to the server

An Overview of Active Server Pages

If you look up the term Active Server Page, you will find a definition similar to the following:

> An Active Server Page is script that executes on the server and dynamically generates HTML code to run on the client (the user's browser).

This definition is fine if you're answering a question on an exam. However, like most textbook-like definitions, it falls well short of explaining the true essence of what an Active Server Page is, what problems it helps to solve, and how it fits in with the other Web development technologies you've learned so far in this book. Therefore, a brief overview is in order to help clarify all of this.

The first thing you will see in this overview is a list of some of the technologies you've learned so far and how each piece fits together to enable the Web developer to write dynamic, interactive Web applications. Because the primary function of an Active Server Page is to provide for server-side processing, you'll then see what server-side processing is and how it can help to create a professional Web site. Then, you'll be introduced to a brief history of the attempts to allow Web pages to interact with server-side processes. After all, you can't decide for yourself whether Active Server Pages are for you if you don't know what the alternatives are. Finally, after you've seen what problem Active Server Pages are meant to solve and what alternatives exist, you'll learn how Active Server Pages solve the inadequacies of these other technologies to provide for a much better solution to the problem of server-side processing with a Web application.

Technologies Learned So Far

With the use of that *dynamic* word again, you might be wondering how Active Server Pages fit in with the technologies you've learned so far in this book. Therefore, take a quick look at what you've learned up to this point regarding which technology is for what purpose.

In the very beginning of this book, you saw that HTML is used to generate and publish a page of information. Included in HTML is the ability to set a style (font name, size, and so on) for a given area of text to be displayed. Cascading Style Sheets then provide the ability to define a set of styles at different levels of your Web site. HTML controls and script can be used to add programmatic functionality to the Web page and, therefore, create truly interactive Web applications. ActiveX controls enable you to add prepackaged functionality to a Web application. Dynamic HTML and the Document Object Model define a means of creating dynamic content on the client side of the Web application after the page has been loaded. And finally, Scriptlets are a means of componentizing Dynamic HTML pages so that they can be treated as objects in a single Web application or across multiple Web applications.

Therefore, a slightly more detailed description of an Active Server Page is that it enables the Web developer to accomplish server-side processing that simply isn't available with code (HTML, script, ActiveX, Dynamic HTML, Scriptlets, and so on) that runs only on the client. Now, take a look at what a server-side process is and how it provides a benefit to a Web application.

Server-Side Processing

As the name implies, a server-side process is code that runs on the server. Remember that browsers will not enable direct access to the system from a Web page (except with the use of ActiveX controls). However, even if system access were possible from the Web page, it wouldn't solve the problem of developing a real world Web application. As an example, say that you're writing a system that will allow users to peruse your company's inventory and purchase items online. In this situation, the database would exist on the server and each client would be used to display the inventory items and some sort of order form. However, how is the client going to be able to read the data from the server's database or create a new order on the server? This is accomplished by having the Web page make requests of a server process to do the actual database I/O. In a nutshell, this is what is known as client/server programming (see Figure 11.1).

11

FIGURE 11.1

A client/server applica-
tion allows you to move
processor intensive
tasks such as database
I/O to the server.

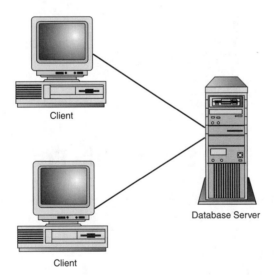

Client

Database Server

Client

Therefore, any time you have code that needs to execute on the server, you would write a server process. However, let me throw a few more terms at you. When speaking of client/server development, many times you will hear the terms 2-tier, 3-tier, and n-tier. Figure 11.1 depicts a very standard 2-tier client server scenario. It is called 2-tier because the client and server are the only two components. The term 3-tier simply means the addition of another tier, or component. Typically, this means that the system architects decided to move the business logic, or rules, into their own component, so you have a solution that looks similar to what you see in Figure 11.2. In this situation, both of the server components can be running on the same server or they can be running on completely different machines in order to balance the workload for more efficient processing. Taking that a step further, the term n-tier simply means the breaking out of the business rules and database I/O into multiple tiers. This is usually only done in very complex situations in which you need to have these different processes running on different machines because the workload is simply too great to get decent performance.

FIGURE 11.2

The n-tier client/server is used to define a client/server scenario in which the server components are broken in several pieces to improve performance.

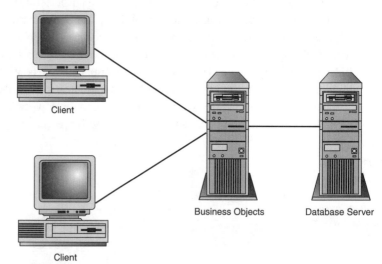

Client

Client

Business Objects

Database Server

The Evolution of Server-Side Processing

Now that you've seen what server-side processing is, take a look at a brief history of the attempts to allow Web pages to interact with server-side processes. You will start by looking at traditional HTML Web pages that are static in nature.

Static HTML Web Pages

In the early days of the World Wide Web, Web pages consisted of only static information. Take a look at how a browser processes a static Web page. As an example, say that you have a home page (www.yourisp.com/you.htm) that contains such things as pictures of your house and family, your resume, and other such personal goodies. You know that when a user types that URL into the browser's address field, the browser will display your Web page. However, what actually happens when a Web surfer types in the URL to your home page? Take a look at the following:

1. The browser (running on the user's machine) locates the Web server (in this case, www.yourisp.com).

2. The browser then requests that the www.yourisp.com Web server return a page named you.htm.

3. The www.yourisp.com Web server locates the page named you.htm and sends it back to the browser.

4. Upon receiving the you.htm Web page from the server, the browser then uses its built-in HTML engine to parse the file for valid HTML tags and display the results of the HTML.

This is all wonderful and presents an incredibly easy way to distribute static information to the masses. However, this type of communication is one way. In other words, the server sends information to the client and the browser displays that information. What is needed is a way of sending information back to the Web server for processing. To do this, next you will look at forms and the Common Gateway Interface (CGI).

Forms and CGI

In order to allow for the client to send data back to the server, a new HTML tag called a FORM tag was introduced. This tag enables Web developers to define a group of controls or fields whose data can be sent as a single, logical unit to the server. However, the problem was never really on the client side. A technology had to be invented to enable the server to do more than simply handle requests for Web pages and send out those Web pages. The server needed to be able to receive this new Form object and know how to process it. That's where CGI comes in.

CGI enables the Web server to communicate with another application that can handle the Form object's data when it's sent back. When the CGI application receives the Form object's data, it can then do whatever it wants with it. The data can be validated, saved in a database, or even sent to another server. The CGI programmer has complete control at that point. As great as this sounds, CGI has a couple of major disadvantages.

The first problem is an economic one. Although CGI applications can be written in myriad languages, most often they are developed using a language called Perl. The problem with this is that it involves learning yet another language (outside of the HTML and a scripting language that you already must know just to create your Web pages). As you know, learning any new language takes time. Unfortunately, that usually results in delayed deliverables, which directly affects how expensive the Web site or application is to build. As we've all seen too often, presenting management with an expensive solution typically means an otherwise good project idea never seeing the light of day.

11

The second problem is a technical one. A copy of the CGI application is created for every single form that is being submitted to the server. This means that if 100 people submit a form to the server, 100 different copies of the CGI application have to be running on the server to handle each of those requests. Needless to say, this isn't exactly the optimum choice for a Web site that expects moderate to heavy traffic. To correct this, server APIs are used.

Server APIs

Because of the problems outlined previously with using CGI to process form data, server APIs were introduced. The term API stands for *Application Programming Interface* and simply refers to a means of programmatically controlling or manipulating something. For example, in order to write a Windows application, you must use the Windows API, which has functions to do such things as create a window, display a menu, and respond to the keyboard and mouse events. Microsoft's server API is called Internet Server Application Programming Interface (ISAPI).

Like CGI, ISAPI enables the Web server to communicate with other applications running on the server machine. However, the advantage ISAPI has over CGI is that it doesn't launch a separate application each time a form is sent to the server. ISAPI applications also give the developer much more flexibility in how the server can respond to the browser.

Alas, ISAPI still doesn't solve one of the main problems with server-side processing because you must still learn a new programming language to write these ISAPI applications. Additionally, ISAPI is anything but easy to learn. A quick look at some of the resume services on the Internet will show you very few programmers with ISAPI experience and very few companies looking for it. The reason for this is simple. ISAPI applications are a pain to write and maintain. Because of these problems, very few companies have bought into the Microsoft server API because it represents too expensive a solution. Therefore, for several years, most companies simply accepted the fact that they could not have a truly interactive Web site with server-side processing. That was until the introduction of Active Server Pages.

Active Server Pages

Active Server Pages solves all the problems associated with CGI and server APIs. In addition to being just as efficient as ISAPI applications, Active Server Pages are much simpler to learn and much easier to use because they are written using the same scripting languages that are used on the client side. Like writing client script, with an Active Server Page, you simply insert your script directly into the HTML page itself. The HTML tags and the code are side by side.

Using an Active Server Page, the Web page can programmatically interact with code on the server in order to have tasks processed on its behalf (for example, reading data from a database, accessing OLE servers, and so on). In addition, when executed, the server-side code can dynamically generate HTML that is downloaded and processed on the client. The fact that an Active Server Page creates standard HTML to be executed on the client means that the client can be running any browser and doesn't even know that an Active Server Page is being used. Therefore, it is an optimum solution when you are attempting to write Web applications that are cross-browser compliant.

Installing Active Server Page Support

Active Server Page is not a product that you can buy by itself. Rather, it is a technology, or feature, that is built into the Web server. Therefore, in order to write an Active Server Page, you need either Microsoft Internet Information Server (IIS) version 3 or above or the Microsoft Personal Web Server.

Windows NT Server ships with its own copy of the IIS. IIS is a full-fledged, robust, powerful Web server that while being free, can handle Web sites of any size. If you have Windows NT Server installed, simply install the IIS from your Windows NT Server CDs or from the MSDN Windows NT Option Pack.

On the other hand, if you are using Windows 95, Windows 98, or Windows NT Workstation 4, you will need to install the Microsoft Personal Web Server. However, there are a couple of very important things to realize here regarding Personal Web Server. Firstly, it was never intended be a Web server for a large Web site. It simply lacks the capability to scale to a large number of users and still provide decent performance. Secondly, if you have Personal Web Server installed, you will need to also install the Microsoft FrontPage 98 extensions.

11

Writing Your First Active Server Page

Now that you've learned about the basics of developing Active Server Pages, it's time to write your first one! In this example, you will accomplish the following:

- Create an Active Server Page in Visual InterDev
- Write VBScript in an Active Server Page
- See how server script is sent to the client's browser as HTML to be displayed
- Learn the steps involved in processing an Active Server Page

Creating an Active Server Page with Visual InterDev

In this example, the Active Server Page will simply display the current time to the user and a message based on that time. Although simple, this Active Server Page allows you to see several basic things. First, you'll see how to create the Active Server Page. Second, you'll see how to write JavaScript that is executed on the server only. Finally, you will see how this JavaScript results in HTML that is sent back to the client's Web page for displaying. At this point, complete the following to make all this happen:

1. Open the Project Explorer and right-click the MyFirstServerScripts project.

2. From the context menu, select the Add, Active Server Page menu option to display the Add Item dialog (see Figure 11.3).

FIGURE 11.3

Creating an Active Server Page.

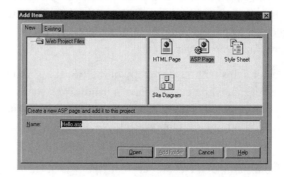

3. From the Add Item dialog, simply make sure that the ASP Page is selected and type the value DateTime.asp into the Name field. When finished, click the Open button to create your new Active Server Page.

4. At this point, the Active Server Page will be opened in Design view (see Figure 11.4). Notice that VBScript is the default scripting language. This is because Visual InterDev defaults the client scripting language to JavaScript and the server scripting language to VBScript. You'll see how to change this Active Server Page option and several others shortly.

Writing Server Script in VBScript

Because VBScript is the default scripting language (and you haven't seen it yet in this book), the first Active Server Page example will be written using it.

FIGURE 11.4

*A bare-bones Active
Server Page created by
Visual InterDev. Notice
that Visual InterDev
highlights any code to
be executed on the
server in yellow.*

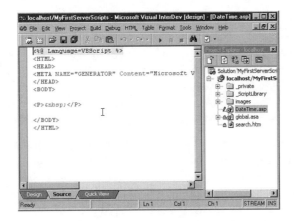

At this point, open the DateTime.asp file in Design view and insert the following script
after the <BODY> tag and before the </BODY> tag:

```
<H1 align=center>My First Active Server Page</H1>

<P><H2>The time is <%=Time%>.

<% If Time>- #12:00:00 AM# And Time < #12:00:00 PM# Then %>
Good Morning!!!

<% ElseIf Time>- #12:00:00 PM# And Time < #6:00:00 PM# Then %>
Good Afternoon !!!

<%Else%>
Good Evening !!!

<%End If %>

<br><br>Thanks for coming

</H2>
```

Most of this should look familiar because you learned about client scripting in Hour 6,
"Empowering Your Site with Client Scripting." For example, the page has a (centered)
title and uses a H1 tag to display the fact that this is your first Active Server Page. You
can also see some other familiar HTML tags and styles that you've used throughout this
book such as <H2>, <P>, and <BR>.

11

However, what are <% and %>? These are called delimiters. The script that is inside these delimiters is server-side script. Anything outside is either HTML or client-side script. Also notice that as you type this code in, every time you type <% or %>, those particular characters are displayed by Visual InterDev in yellow. This is a visual cue that the code being entered will only be executed on the server.

Examining the Entire Active Server Page Process

Now you are ready to execute your first Active Server Page. Normally at this point, you would click on the QuickView tab to see the results of your work. However, Visual InterDev does not support the processing of server-side script from within its environment. Therefore, you will need to either select the View, View in Browser menu option or manually view the DateTime.asp page from your particular browser. When you do, you will see results similar to those shown in Figure 11.5.

FIGURE 11.5

Active Server Pages enable you to write code that will execute only on the server.

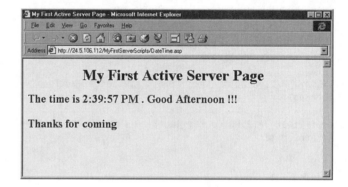

When you run the DateTime.asp file from your browser, select the Browsers View Source option. With Microsoft Internet Explorer, that option is under the View menu option. The code you will see is shown in Listing 11.1.

LISTING 11.1 Client-Side Results of DateTime.asp

```
 1: <HTML>
 2: <HEAD>
 3: <META NAME="GENERATOR" Content="Microsoft Visual Studio 6.0">
 4: <title>My First Active Server Page</title>
 5: </HEAD>
 6: <BODY>
 7:
 8: <H1 align=center>My First Active Server Page</H1>
 9:
10: <P><H2>The time is
11: 2:39:57 PM
12:  .
```

```
13:
14:  Good Afternoon !!!
15:
16: <br><br>Thanks for coming
17:
18: </H2>
19:
20: </BODY>
21: </HTML>
```

Notice that the only thing that can be viewed on the client side is the actual HTML generated as a result of the server-side script. In other words, none of the actual script itself (the conditional statement used to determine the time of day and use of the Time function) is seen. This is another advantage to writing server-side script as opposed to client-side script: the user can never see your proprietary code. She only sees the resulting HTML.

Now that you've written your first Active Server Page and seen it in action, take a look at the steps that the browser and Web server went through in order to process the request. This is what happens:

1. A user requests that an Active Server Page be loaded in his browser.

2. The browser attempts to locate the Web server.

3. When the Web server is located, the browser requests the appropriate Active Server Page.

4. You should recall from earlier in the hour that so far this is exactly how any static HTML page is processed. However, at this point, something different happens. As opposed to simply returning the requested page to the browser, the Web server executes the page. In other words, the Web server parses the Active Server Page for any server-side script (remember the <% and %> delimiters) and executes that code.

5. After the server-side script is executed, all the Active Server Code is stripped out of the page and only the remaining client-side script and HTML are returned. This is why your DateTime.asp file and the resulting HTML seen in the browser look so different.

6. The resulting HTML is then sent to the browser.

Advantages of Using Active Server Pages

After writing your first Active Server Page, you should now understand the following advantages that Active Server Pages provide:

- Active Server Pages are easy to write. They are written using a scripting language such as JavaScript, JScript, or VBScript.

- Active Server Pages are easy to maintain because the code is inserted into the Web page. Therefore, there is no need to keep up with a completely isolated set of source code that is stored separately from the Web page's HTML and client script.

- The code is executed on the server. Therefore, it is not limited by the browser's security policy such as not being allowed to have system level access to the file system or database.

- The server script is stripped out before it is sent to the browser as pure HTML. Therefore, your proprietary applications can't be easily stolen.

- Because only pure HTML is sent back, Active Server Pages will work regardless of the type of browser that the client computer is running.

Submitting Forms to an Active Server Page

In the DateTime Active Server Page, no information was sent from the client computer. However, most Active Server Pages are written to process information that is gathered from the client via the Web page. You might recall the form object from earlier in the hour. This is the object that is normally used to convey information from the client to the server. Therefore, at this time, look at a more realistic example. Say you own a company, and you want to provide a means by which your users can request additional information about your products. In this example, you will create this Web page and upon the user's clicking a Submit button, your Web page will send user entered information to an Active Server Page and have the Active Server Page confirm that the information was received.

Creating a Web Page that Is Submitted to the Server

Because you will need to create a Web page that will be ultimately submitted to the Active Server Page, follow these steps:

1. Create a new Web page for your MyFirstServerScripts project named `RequestForProductInfo.htm` and open it in Source view.

2. Insert the following FORM tag after the <BODY> tag. This is what will be eventually submitted to the Active Server Page.

   `<FORM NAME = MyForm>`

3. Insert the following before the </BODY> tag:

   `</FORM>`

4. Now, switch to Design view and, looking at Figure 11.6, drag from the Toolbox the necessary HTML controls to create your user interface for the Web page. Note that the two buttons are not regular buttons: They are the Submit and Reset buttons that can also be found on the Toolbox window.

5. Name the Textbox control, Select (combo box) control, and Text Area control `txtName`, `cboProducts`, and `txtRemarks`, respectively.

FIGURE 11.6

Viewing the
`RequestForProduct-`
`Info.htm` *Web page in*
Visual InterDev.

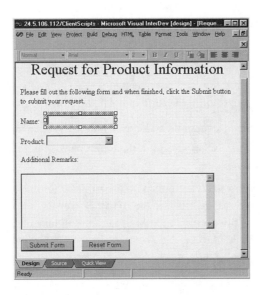

6. Right-click the Products Select control and then select the Properties menu option. This will cause the Select control's Properties dialog to be displayed (see Figure 11.7). This dialog enables you to graphically (as opposed to manually) code the properties for the control. You can even enter the data that will be seen by the user implementing this dialog. At this point, add the entries you see in Table 11.1 to the Select control.

11

FIGURE 11.7

The Select control's
Property Page allows
you to graphically
configure the Select
control (including
initializing its data).

TABLE 11.1 Values to Be Entered for the Product Select Control

Text	Value
Windows Widgets	Windows Widgets
ActiveX Add-Ons	ActiveX Add-Ons
Catalog	Catalog

Using the ACTION Attribute to Send a Form to the Server

Now that the Web page has been created, you need some way of telling the browser that
the entered information will be submitted to an Active Server Page when the user clicks the
Submit button. To do that, you will only need to make a small modification to the FORM tag
you created in the RequestForProductInfo.htm file, as shown in the following steps:

1. Make sure that the RequestForProductInfo.htm file is open and switch to Source view.

2. Open the Properties window and in the combo box at the top of the window, locate
   the <FORM> entry.

3. Locate and set the ACTION property to the value of RequestConfirmation.asp. This
   property specifies to the browser the Active Server Page that must be loaded in
   order to process this form. The Submit button will take care of making sure that
   the form is submitted to the file specified by the ACTION property.

4. Very Important: Make sure that you also set the form's method property to POST.

5. When finished, click the Source tab and locate the FORM tag. It should look like the
   following.

   ```
   <FORM Name=MyForm ACTION=RequestConfirmation.asp method=post>
   ```

Processing a Form on the Server

Now that you've seen how to submit a form to the server, it's time to take a look at how
the Active Server Page receives and processes it. This is illustrated in the following steps:

1. Add an Active Server Page to your project named RequestConfirmation.asp.

2. Open the newly created RequestConfirmation.asp file in Source view.

3. Insert the following server script between the <BODY> and </BODY> tags. As you can
   see, the Active Server Page can access the form's data via the Request object. This
   object contains another object (the Form object) that contains all the items on the form.

   ```
   <H1 align=center>Confirmation of Product Information Request
   ➡</H1>
   Thank you very much, <b><%=Request.Form.Item("txtName")%></b>.
   The information regarding our <b><%=Request.Form.Item
   ➡("cboProducts")%></b>
   will be sent to you within the next 2 business days.
   ```

> You will learn more about the Request object as well as the other Active
> Server objects in the next hour.

4. Displaying the page, entering the data, and clicking the Submit button will produce results similar to what you see in Figure 11.8.

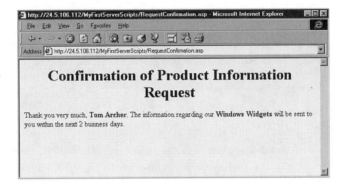

Confirmation of Product Information Request

Thank you very much, **Tom Archer**. The information regarding our **Windows Widgets** will be sent to you within the next 2 business days.

Validating the Form Before Submitting It

Besides the database I/O, the only thing left to add to this example in order to make it a practical application is the issue of validation. After all, if the RequestConfirmation.asp Active Server Page is going to use the values on the form, the Web page must validate that they have been entered.

In order to handle validation and then stop the ACTION attribute from loading the Active Server Page if there is an error, you will need to implement a handler for the form object's onsubmit event. To do so, complete the following steps:

1. Open the RequestForProductInfo.htm file and switch to Source view.

2. Open the Script Outline window.

3. Locate and expand the MyForm object.

4. Double-click the onclick event in order to add an event handler. If you look at the MyForm definition now, you will see code similar to the following. Notice that the onsubmit handler needs to return a value. This value is how you specify to the browser whether the file specified on the ACTION attribute should be loaded.

```
<FORM Name=MyForm ACTION=RequestConfirmation.asp method=post
LANGUAGE=javascript onsubmit="return MyForm_onsubmit()">
```

5. In the MyForm_onsubmit function, insert the following script to validate the form. (The code you need to add is in bold.) Notice that if the name has not been entered, focus is set to that field. Little things like this go a long way, so the user perceives your Web page as being professional.

11

```
function MyForm_onsubmit()
{
 bSuccess = true;

 if ("" == MyForm.txtName.value)
 {
  alert("Please enter your name in order to continue.");
  document.MyForm.txtName.focus();
  bSuccess = false;
 }

 return bSuccess;
}
```

6. Now if you display the Web page and click the Submit button without entering a name value, you will receive an error (see Figure 11.9), and the Active Server Page will not be loaded.

FIGURE 11.9

Form validation can be performed on the client when the user attempts to submit the form to the server.

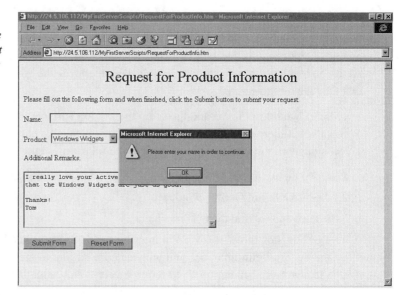

Summary

In this hour, you discovered what Active Server Pages are and how they can be used to provide for server-side processing. You then wrote two Active Server Pages that illustrated how server-side script is written and how to submit and process a form's data on the server. Congratulations! You've have learned one of the most vital parts of developing a Web site or Web application.

Q&A

Q Say that I have a Web page that accepts data from a user. This data is then passed to an Active Server Page. Obviously, in this case, I need the user to go through the Web page first. However, if the user does directly navigate to my Active Server Page (bypassing the Web page), is there a way to redirect the user back to my Web page so that everything is processed correctly?

A In this hour, you learned about the `Request` object. However, as mentioned, several other objects can be used by the Active Server Page to process an incoming form (you'll learn more about them in the next hour). One of those objects is the `Response` object. Among several useful methods is a method called `Redirect`. This is what you would use in order to direct the user to the Web page.

Workshop

The Workshop is designed to help you anticipate possible questions, review what you've learned, and begin thinking ahead to put your knowledge into practice. The answers to the quiz are in Appendix A, "Answers."

Quiz

1. What was the first technology introduced to process forms on the server?

2. What is Microsoft's server API that is used to write server-side applications?

3. If you are running Windows 95 or Windows 98, which Web server must you install in order to develop and deploy Active Server Pages?

4. If Visual InterDev can't process server-side script, how can you view the results of your work?

5. When writing server script, what do the `<%` and `%>` commands do?

6. In order to submit a form to the server, what form attribute must be set?

7. In order to submit a form to the server, what must the form's method property be set to?

8. What object does the Active Server Page use to get values from the form being passed?

9. What event do you need to handle to validate the form when the user is attempting to submit the form to the server?

10. What are some of the advantages of using Active Server Pages as opposed to using CGI or ISAPI?

11

Exercise

Write a simple logon Web page that requires that the user enter a password, which is then validated on the server.

Hour **12**

Using the Active Server Page Object Model

In the previous hour, you learned the basics of Active Server Pages and how they can be executed on the server to process the information entered on a Web page. You also learned about the Request object, which is used by the Active Server Page to retrieve the values of the submitted form. However, what you might not know is that this object is one of several objects defined by the Active Server Page Object Model. Therefore, in this hour, you will learn how this robust object model enables you to develop Active Server Pages much more efficiently by providing a very powerful, intuitive interface to ASP scripting.

The highlights of this hour include

- Configuring the Visual InterDev Active Server Page options
- Learning about the Active Server Object Model
- How to use the Request object to retrieve user information
- How to use the Response object to send information to the user

- How to use the `Session` object to store session-level information
- How to use the `Application` object to share common data across multiple users
- Using the GLOBAL.ASA file

Setting the Visual InterDev Active Server Page Options

Before you jump into working with Active Server Pages, it is important to verify that you have the proper settings for Visual InterDev. To do so, follow these steps:

1. Open any Visual InterDev project.

2. Open any Active Server Page file in the project. If you haven't yet created one for this project, you can simply open the global.asa file for purposes of this demonstration. This file contains the global routines for your Active Server Pages. You will see examples of how to use this file later on in the hour.

3. After you have opened an Active Server Page (or the global.asa file), select the View, Property Pages menu option to display the Properties dialog (see Figure 12.1).

FIGURE 12.1

Setting the Active Server Page options in Visual InterDev.

As you can see, the Properties dialog is where you set the Active Server Page options such as the default language to use, whether you want to use transactions, and if you want the Scripting Object Model enabled. More detail on these options can be found in the following sections.

Default Language

Just as you saw in Hour 6, "Empowering Your Site with Client Scripting," you can specify the default scripting language to use when writing server-side script. Visual

InterDev defaults this value to VBScript. If the default scripting language is set to VBScript, Visual InterDev will insert the following line of code into the top of any Active Server Page that you create:

```
<%@ language=VBScript %>
```

If the default language is set to JavaScript (ECMAScript), the following line of code will be inserted into each newly created Active Server Page:

```
<%@ language=JavaScript %>
```

Enable Transactions

Transactions, or commitment control (as it is known in some circles), give the developer the ability to logically group a set of operations into a single logical operation so that if any of the operations fails, the entire set of operations fails. As an example, say that you are writing a banking application. If a customer wants to transfer some amount of money from his checking account to his savings account, you will need to first debit his checking account for the specified amount and then credit his savings account. Now say that after you debit the checking account, for some reason the attempt to credit the savings account fails. What happens now? At this point, the money is not in checking *or* savings. Obviously, your client is going to have one very unhappy customer if you don't somehow restore the money to checking. This is where transactions come in. By grouping both the credit and debit operation in a transaction, you are specifying that either both operations must succeed or both must fail. In this example, the first operation would be rolled back when the second operation failed. Therefore, to the system, it would appear as though no transactions whatsoever had transpired.

This option specifies whether the Microsoft Transaction Server (MTS) should consider changes that occur in an Active Server Page as transactions, such as database manipulation (through ODBC or OLE DB) or MSMQ message transmission. Actually, MTS uses the Microsoft Distributed Transaction Coordinator (MS DTC) to accomplish this task. This is why, if you installed Microsoft Internet Information Server (IIS), you would have seen MTS and MS DTC installed automatically. Note that this capability is not applicable for Microsoft Personal Web Server (PWS). If you do select this option, the following code will be inserted into the top of the currently open Active Server Page:

```
<% @ Transaction=required%>
```

Because the topic of MTS and MSDTC is way beyond the scope of this book, let alone this hour, I would recommend reading the section "Creating Transactional Scripts" in the IIS documentation.

12

Sessionless ASP Pages

A *session* is defined as a user's visit to a Web site. As you will learn later in this hour, the `Session` object is used to store information about a user's session with your Web site. This option, therefore, is used to specify that the Web server will not allow `Session` object support for maintaining this information. The following tag is inserted into the top of the Active Server Page:

```
<%@ EnableSessionState=FALSE %>
```

Enable Scripting Object Model

As you can probably guess from the name, this option simply specifies that you do not wish to have support for the Scripting Object Model. This object model was introduced with Visual InterDev 6 and allows the Web developer to treat Web pages as objects. Therefore, you can reference any other page on your Web site as an object from within the Active Server Page script. In addition, the Scripting Object Model enables a concept known as remote scripting. The cool thing about remote scripting is that if you have created the Active Server Pages as page objects, you can call methods on those pages from the client page. In other words, you can execute a method on an Active Server Page while the client page is loaded without navigating away from the client page.

Programming with the Active Server Page Object Model

In the previous hour, the second example retrieved the values from a submitted form using the `Request` object. Little did you know at the time that this object is actually one of several in a lattice known as the Active Server Page Object Model (referred to simply as the ASP Object Model from this point on). Not only do these objects provide a very easy, intuitive way to write server code, but also Visual InterDev's IntelliSense awareness of them makes using them a breeze. The ASP Object Model defines the following objects. Each of these objects contains collections, properties, and methods that are used to create very powerful and robust Active Server Pages.

- The `Request` object
- The `Response` object
- The `Session` object
- The `Application` object
- The `Server` object
- The `ObjectContext` object

The Request Object

You will start out by learning about the Request object because it is probably the object you will use most when developing your Active Server Pages. This is because it contains information such as the form values, the user's browser information, and cookie information you might have stored on the user's machine.

The Request object contains five collections. A collection is simply a logical grouping of semantically related properties and methods. Table 12.1 lists the Request object's collections.

TABLE 12.1 Collections of the Request Object

Collection Name	Purpose
Form	Used to retrieve the values of a submitted form
Cookies	Used to retrieve the values stored in a client-side cookie file
ClientCertificate	Used to retrieve certification fields from the browser request
QueryString	Used to retrieve the values of variables passed in the HTTP string
ServerVariables	Used to retrieve the values of predetermined environment variables

Using the Form Collection

The Form collection contains the values of the form that was submitted to the Active Server Page. These values are extracted using the following syntax:

```
Request.Form(item [(index)¦.Count]
```

Because this syntax is as convoluted as most, here are three examples that might help to clarify things:

- Retrieving a single value—Say you have a form that contains two fields to retrieve the user's first and last name. If the field names were txtFirst and txtLast, respectively, the following code would be used to display a hello message to the user:

  ```
  Hello <%=Request.form.Item("txtFirst")%> <%=Request.form.Item
  ➡("txtLast")%>!
  ```

  Therefore, if the txtFirst field had a value of Bill and the txtLast field had a value of Gates, the result would be the following:

  ```
  Hello Bill Gates!
  ```

- Retrieving multiple values—Now say you have another form that can contain multiple values for a single field (for example, a multiselect Listbox control). If the field (named FavoriteHobbies) contains several values, the following code could be used to extract all the values. Notice the use of the Response object. This object will be covered later in the hour.

12

```
<%For Each item In Request.Form("FavoriteHobbies")
Response.Write item & "<BR>"
Next%>
```

Therefore, if the selected hobbies were Roller Blading and Golfing, those items would be displayed on the Web page.

In addition, the following code would accomplish exactly the same thing:

```
<%For i = 1 to Request.Form("FavoriteHobbies").Count
Response.Write Request.Form("FavoriteHobbies")(i) & "<BR>"
Next%>
```

The only difference in the two preceding code snippets is that in the first one, each item was extracted as an object whereas in the second snippet, each item's value was extracted.

- Retrieving the raw form information—When a form is submitted to an Active Server Page, all the information is passed as text in an HTTP request. If you combine the previous examples, you would have a form that is submitting a first name, a last name, and a list of hobbies. Therefore, the following code could be used to print out the entire list of form field and value pairings:

```
The unparsed data is as follows: <%=Request.form%>
```

The results would then be as follows:

```
The unparsed data is as follows: txtFirst=Bill&txtLast=
➥Gates&FavoriteHobbies
```

Using the Cookies Collection

Files, called cookies, are stored on the user's machine when the Web application needs to store information about the user. This information can then be recalled the next time the user visits the Web site. An example of when a cookie would be used is if your site allows the user to set certain preferences. These values would be saved on the user's machine so that they are "remembered" each time the she visits the site, so she doesn't have to keep configuring the preferences each time. This incredibly useful collection will be covered in much more detail in Hour 21, "Tracking and Maintaining User Information."

Using the ClientCertificate Collection

The ClientCertificate collection is used to retrieve the certification fields from a request issued by the browser. If the browser is using the Secure Sockets Layer (SSL) protocol (that is, it uses the https:// syntax as opposed to the http:// syntax) to connect to the server, the ClientCertificate will contain the values of the certificate such as the certificate serial number, certificate expiration date, and issuer. Because this collection is really only of interest if you are using SSL, it will be covered in the hour on security (Hour 22, "Security, Digital Certificates, and Authentication").

Using the QueryString Collection

The QueryString collection is very similar to the Form collection. The main difference is that when processing a `Request` object, you are retrieving the information returned by the client. The QueryString collection, however, is used to retrieve the data that is specified after the URL.

As an example, say that the following HTTP request is sent to the Web server:

```
http://YourWebSite.com/teams.asp?T=Rockets&T=Kings
```

The following use of the QueryString collection could then be used to iterate through this list and print out the specified values:

```
<%For Each item In Request.QueryString("T")
Response.Write item & "<BR>"
Next%>
```

Because these values can be added to the URL by script, the biggest advantage of the QueryString collection is that it makes passing data between pages very easy. All you have to do is simply append the question mark to the page's URL and then add the field and value pairs as you saw previously.

Using the ServerVariables Collection

The last `Request` object collection that you'll look at is the ServerVariables collection. The ServerVariables collection is used to retrieve the environment variables that pertain to the client request. The syntax of this collection is the following:

```
Request.ServerVariables(variable)
```

The following script shows you how to iterate through the entire list of server variables and insert them into a table. As a bonus, you also get to see the HTML involved in dynamically creating and filling a table:

```
<table border=1 cellspacing=2 cellpadding=2 align=center valign=top>
<% For Each Item In Request.ServerVariables %>
<tr><td><% = Item %></td>
<td><% = Request.ServerVariables(Item)%>
</td></tr>
<% Next %>
</table>
```

This script, when run, will produce something similar to what you see in Figure 12.2.

12

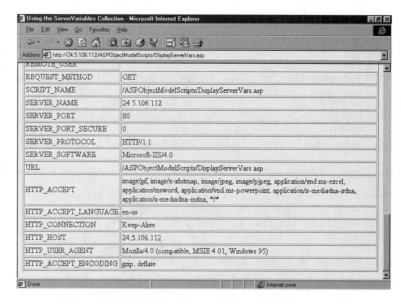

The Response Object

The Response object is used to send information back to the user. This very powerful object can be used to perform tasks such as redirecting a user to a Web page and sending cookie information back to the user's machine. In fact, the Cookies collection is the Response object's only collection. Once again, this collection won't be covered here because it is covered in great detail in Hour 21.

Although the Response object only contains a single collection, it does contain several properties and methods as shown in Tables 12.2 and 12.3, respectively.

TABLE 12.2   Properties of the Response Object

Property Name	Purpose
Buffer	This property (set to TRUE or FALSE) is used to specify whether to buffer page output. When this value is set to TRUE, the server does not send a response to the client until all the server scripts on the current page have been processed (or until the Flush or End method has been explicitly called).
CacheControl	This property is used to determine whether proxy servers are able to cache the output generated by ASP.
CharSet	Appends the name of the character set to the content-type header.
ContentType	Used to specify the HTTP content type. This is a string that represents the type of file being sent.

Property Name	Purpose
Expires	This is a really cool property that enables you to specify (in minutes) how long before a cached page expires. Therefore, if the user leaves your Web page and then returns and the amount of elapsed time exceeds this value, the page will be refreshed from the Web server.
ExpiresAbsolute	This property is similar to the Expires property except that it is used to specify an absolute date and time used to determine when a cached page expires.
IsClientConnected	Boolean flag that indicates if the user is currently connected to the server.
Status	This property specifies the value of the status line returned by the server. The different valid values for this property are defined in the HTTP specification.

TABLE 12.3   Methods of the Response Object

Method Name	Purpose
AddHeader	This is a very advanced method of the Response object and enables you to dynamically create an HTTP header.
AppendToLog	This method is used to write to the Web server log.
BinaryWrite	Writes the given information to the current HTTP output without any character-set conversion.
Clear	This method clears any buffered HTML output.
End	Use this method when you need to stop the processing of the .asp file and return the current result.
Flush	Sends buffered output immediately and empties the buffer.
Redirect	This is the method that you would use in order to redirect the user to a given page.
Write	This method is used to write directly to the page.

12

The Session Object

So far, all the Web application work you have done has dealt with information that has been handled at the page level. The Session object is used to store information needed for a particular user session. A *user* session is defined as a single visit to a Web site.

A practical example of when you would use the Session object is the shopping cart application. This application enables visitors to a Web site to purchase items as they browse through the different pages of the site. The pages are like aisles in a grocery store. As you move from aisle to aisle, you don't lose all your groceries nor are you forced to purchase the items at that time. You are free to roam around for as long as you want until you decide to leave the store (the Web site), at which time you must decide whether you want to purchase the items in your shopping cart or discard them. Just as in real life, values stored in the Session object are not discarded when the user navigates to other pages in the application (see Tables 12.4–12.6).

TABLE 12.4 Collections of the Session Object

Collection Name	Purpose
Contents	Used to store the items that you add via script commands.
StaticObjects	Used to store the objects that you create via the <OBJECT> tag at the session level.

TABLE 12.5 Properties of the Session Object

Property Name	Purpose
CodePage	Used to identify the codepage to be used for the session.
LCID	Used to identify the locale.
SessionID	This property is used to retrieve the unique Session identifier for a user session. The data type for this property is a LONG. A Session object is automatically created for each session with its own unique SessionID.
Timeout	Used to specify (in minutes) the amount of time a session can be idle before being automatically ended by the browser.

TABLE 12.6 Methods of the Session Object

Method Name	Purpose
Abandon	This method is used to explicitly drop, or end, a session.

Storing and Retrieving Values in a Session Object

As mentioned previously, a Session object is used to store information pertaining to a given user session. Any information you store within this object, therefore, is available throughout the session. The following code snippet illustrates how to store two session variables:

```
<%
Session("userID") = "tarcher"
Session("userNumber") = 1234567
%>
```

Storing and Retrieving Objects in a `Session` Object

The ability to easily store variables on one page and access them from any other page in a given session gives the Web developer a tremendous amount of flexibility. However, the `Session` object also enables you to store objects as well as simple values. If you are using VBScript as the server scripting language, you simply use the VBScript `Set` method and the `Server` object's `CreateObject` method (more on this object later) to create an instance of the desired object.

```
<% Set Session("myObjectBeingStored") =
➡Server.CreateObject("MyComponent.class1") %>
```

When the object is stored in the `Session` object, any page can reference that object's exposed methods or properties with the following syntax:

```
<% Session("myObjectBeingStored").MyMethod %>
```

or

```
<% Session("myObjectBeingStored").MyProperty %>
```

Alternately, you can also extract a local (page level) copy of the object using the following VBScript:

```
<%
Set myLocalCopy = Session("myObjectBeingStored")
myLocalCopy.MyMethod
myLocalCopy.MyProperty
%>
```

Using Arrays with a `Session` Object

If you store an array of values in the `Session` object, you cannot directly alter those values. You must first extract a local copy of the array, work with the local copy, and restore the array into the `Session` object. Listings 12.1 and 12.2 illustrate (in VBScript) how you would create an array of strings on one page and then retrieve and manipulate that array on another page.

LISTING 12.1 Page1.asp

```
1: <%
2: 'Create the array
3: Dim productsToBePurchased()
4: Redim productsToBePurchased (5)
5: productsToBePurchased (0) = "Delirium CD"
6: productsToBePurchased (1) = "Baz Luhrmann CD"
7:
8: 'Store the array in the current Session object
```

continues

12

LISTING 12.1 continued

```
 9: Session("productsToBePurchased") = productsToBePurchased
10:
11: 'Redirect the user to another page
12: Response.Redirect("Page2.asp")
13: %>
```

LISTING 12.2 Page2.asp

```
 1: <%
 2: 'Retrieve a local copy of the array from the Session object
 3: productsToBePurchased = Session("productsToBePurchased ")
 4:
 5: 'Replace the second item in the array (relative to zero)
 6: productsToBePurchased(1) = "Front Line Assembly CD"
 7:
 8: 'Restore the array in the Session object with its new values
 9: Session("productsToBePurchased") = productsToBePurchased
10: %>
```

The `Application` Object

The `Application` object is used to share data among users of your application. In this context, the term application refers to all the .asp files (Active Server Pages) in a virtual directory and its subdirectories (see Tables 12.7 and Table 12.8).

TABLE 12.7 Collections of the `Application` Object

Collection Name	Purpose
Contents	Used to store the items that you add via script commands.
StaticObjects	Used to store the objects that you create via the `<OBJECT>` tag at the session level.

TABLE 12.8 Methods of the `Application` Object

Method Name	Purpose
`Lock`	Because this object is used for all the users of a Web application, the Lock property allows synchronization of access to the `Application` object.
`Unlock`	Unlocks the `Application` object so that it can be accessed.

Using the `Application` Object

Values and objects are stored in the `Application` object in the same way they are stored in the `Session` object. The only difference is that with the `Session` object, its values are for a single user session, whereas the values associated with the `Application` object are global to all users and sessions. Examples might be the image that is used as the watermark for all Web pages or the URL that represents the Feedback and Registration Web pages.

> Although you can store objects in the `Application` object, you cannot store any predefined objects such as the `Request` or `Response` objects. Therefore, all the following attempts to store objects in the `Application` object are invalid:
>
> ```
> <%
> Set Application("request") = Request
> Set Application("response") = Response
> Set Application("session") = Session
> Set Application("application") = Application
> Set Application("server") = Server
> Set Application("objectContext") = ObjectContext
> %>
> ```

The `Server` Object

The `Server` object provides utility functions such as the ability to create an object from a scripting language and set the timeout value of any executing script (see Tables 12.9 and 12.10).

TABLE 12.9   Properties of the `Server` Object

Property Name	Purpose
ScriptTimeout	Specifies in seconds the maximum amount of time that a script can run before it is automatically aborted by the server.

TABLE 12.10   Methods of the `Server` Object

Method Name	Purpose
CreateObject	This method is used to create instances of a given object on the server.
HTMLEncode	Applies HTML encoding to a string.
MapPath	Used to map a virtual directory to its physical OS path on the server.
URLEncode	Applies URL encoding rules to a string.
URLPathEncode	Applies URL encoding rules to the specified string, up to the first question mark encountered.

12

Creating Objects with the Server Object

In order to create an instance of an object from an Active Server Page, you must use the Server object's CreateObject method. The syntax for this method is as follows:

```
Server.CreateObject(progID)
```

The format for progID is then broken down as follows:

```
[Vendor.]Component[.Version]
```

By default, objects created by the Server.CreateObject method have page-level scope. In other words, the object is automatically destroyed when the page in which it is created goes out of scope. In order to create an object with session-level or application-level scope, you must do one of the following:

- <OBJECT> tag and set the SCOPE attribute to SESSION or APPLICATION
- Store the object in a Session or Application object's variable

Here's an example of how to create an object that exists at the user session level. In this example, the object's lifetime will be controlled by the lifetime of the session. Therefore, it will not be destroyed until the session has ended.

```
<% Set Session("ra") = Server.CreateObject("Real Audio ActiveX
➥Control Library")%>
```

When you have set an object's value, you can always reset it to another value or destroy it by setting to a value of Nothing. This snippet effectively destroys the object by setting its value to Nothing:

```
<% Session("ra") = Nothing %>
```

When the object is created, you are then free to call any of its methods and properties as you would for any built-in script object.

Remember that Visual InterDev contains an Object Browser (accessed via the View, Other Windows, Object Browser menu option) that enables you to find ActiveX controls and COM objects on your system. Using this incredibly powerful tool, you'd be surprised at all the functionality that is already on your system. Therefore, before you nix that cool idea for a Web application because you can't or don't have the time to write the necessary controls, take a look at the Object Browser first. You might already have the control you need and don't even know it. Also, because Active Server Page script runs on your server, you no longer have the hassle of worrying about whether your users have turned off the browser's ability to download ActiveX controls.

The `ObjectContext` Object

It has been my experience that the `ObjectContext` object is not used much, but I wanted to mention it because it is part of the ASP framework. For additional information on this, check out Microsoft's Active Server Page site.

Using the Global.asa File

As you learned earlier in the book, the global.asa file is a file that is generated automatically for you when you create a new Visual InterDev project. This file is used to handle the global event and object information for the application. For example, using the global.asa file, you can define the method that will be called every time a new session starts. That way, you can easily do such things as track users and log sessions.

The global.asa file can contain only the following items:

- Application events
- Session events
- <OBJECT> declarations
- TypeLibrary declarations

There will probably be times when you want to control the user's navigation through your Web site. For example, if your site requires that each user log in to the system, you don't want the user to directly navigate to any Web page on your site without having first logged in.

With the global.asa file, it is very easy to handle this situation. Simply write a handler for the `Session_OnStart` event. This event is fired each time a new session is started. That way, you can verify if the user's first page is, in fact, the login page. If not, you can then redirect the user to the login page. This guarantees that each user on your system has correctly logged in with a valid userid and password.

Listing 12.3 is a sample code snippet of how all that would be done.

LISTING 12.3 Verifying That the User Logs In

```
1: <SCRIPT RUNAT=Server Language=VBScript>
2: Sub Session_OnStart
3:
4:    `Verify that the current page is the login page
5:    loginPage = "Login.asp"
6:
7:    `Get the current page
8:    currentPage = Request.ServerVariables("SCRIPT_NAME")
```

12

continues

LISTING 12.3 continued

```
 9:
10:  `If user tried to skirt the login, redirect them
11:  'to the login page
12:  if strcomp(currentPage, loginPage, 1) Then
13:    Response.Redirect(loginPage)
14:  End If
15: End Sub
16: </SCRIPT>
```

Creating Applicationwide Functions

Any functions that are defined in the global.asa file can only be called from one of the scripts associated with the Application_OnStart, Application_OnEnd, Session_OnStart, and Session_OnEnd events. In other words, these functions are not available to any other Active Server Page in the Web application.

In order to create a function that can be called from any Active Server Page across the Web application, simply do the following:

1. Create the page with the script.

2. Save the file with an .inc extension. This is not mandated by the specification, but is a filenaming convention for this type of file.

3. Use the Server-Side Include (SSI) statement to include the file in the Active Server Pages that needs to call the file's functions.

Summary

In this hour, you extended your knowledge of developing Active Server Pages by discovering the Active Server Page Object Model. You learned that this object model includes several objects that facilitate the creation and maintenance of named variables and objects, and the page, session, and application levels. You also learned how to create and reference COM objects and how to use the global.asa file to create global event handlers for such events as the application being started and a new user session being created.

Q&A

Q How can I check for the existence of an image before attempting to use it? I can't stand that stupid little box with an 'x' in it being displayed to my users!

A The following script shows how to use the FileSystemObject to access file system information on the server:

```
<%
On Error Resume Next
Set fileObject = CreateObject("Scripting.FileSystemObject")

' This uses the MapPath method to map the virtual
' path to the server's physical OS path. You would
' need to change this to point your actual images
' folder and image file. When finished FileString
' will contain the valid path to the file.
FileString = Server.MapPath("/")&"\images\yourImage.gif"

' open the file using the OpenTextFile method
' of the Scripting.FileSystemObject object
Set CheckFile = fileObject.OpenTextFile(FileString)

FileString = CheckFile.Read(5)

If (FileString <> "GIF89") Then
 ' the file DOES NOT EXIST
 ' report error or use another image
End If

%>
```

Q How can I log information to the Web server log from an Active Server Page?

A By using the `Response` object's `AppendToLog` method. Here's the syntax:

`Response.AppendToLog yourText`

Q Obviously Active Server Pages are too complex to completely cover in two hours. What are some good resources to continue my education?

A In my opinion, the best books on the subject of Active Server Page development are *Sams Teach Yourself Active Server Pages 2.0 in 21 days* (Sams Publishing) and *Professional Active Server Pages 2.0* (Wrox Press, Inc.). Regarding the Internet, the best Web sites that I know of are The ASP Toolbox (`www.tcp-ip.com`) and `www.ActiveServerPages.com`.

12

Workshop

The Workshop is designed to help you anticipate possible questions, review what you've learned, and begin thinking ahead to put your knowledge into practice. The answers to the quiz and exercise are in Appendix A, "Answers."

Quiz

1. What object and collection are used to retrieve the information from a submitted form?

2. What Request collection can be used to pass variables in the HTTP string?

3. What Request collection is used to determine things like the browser name and version?

4. What two Response properties enable you to specify the amount of time that a cached page can exist before it needs to be refreshed?

5. What unique identifier is created every time a new user session is created for a Web application?

6. How can the Web application explicitly terminate a user's session?

7. What are the special circumstances regarding the modification of an array's data after it has been added to a Session object?

8. What methods are used in order to synchronize access to the Application object?

9. How are COM objects created in script?

10. What sort of global events can be handled in the global.asa file?

Exercise

Write the script necessary to maintain the number of times that a Web page is visited.

HOUR 13

Debugging Your Scripts

So far, things have proceeded along nicely. You've learned how to build Web pages, you've added HTML and ActiveX controls to those pages, and you've written script on the client and the server to make it all work together. However, there's one important aspect of scripting that hasn't been covered yet: debugging. In this hour, you will not only learn the basics of debugging, but also how Visual InterDev 6 turns what was previously a pain-staking, laborious task into an intuitive, iterative process of locating and resolving bugs in your Web application.

The highlights of this hour include

- Discovering the typical bugs of a Web application
- Configuring Visual InterDev for client and server script debugging
- Attaching to and debugging running Web pages
- Performing just-in-time debugging
- Debugging server script locally and remotely

An Introduction to Debugging

 This section is intended for developers that are new to debugging. If you are already familiar with basic debugging concepts, you might want to jump ahead to the section "Configuring Debug Support in Visual InterDev."

Face facts. Bugs happen. No matter how good you are or how good you hope to be, bugs inevitably happen to the best of us. Unfortunately, these insidious creatures typically creep up on us at the worst of all possible times: like the day before the big demo or the week before the release of a new product. Therefore, just as bugs are a fact of (a programmer's) life, so is the need for a decent debugger within any professional development environment.

Types of Errors

Before jumping into how to debug using Visual InterDev 6, have a look at the types of errors you're most likely to be dealing with regarding Web applications:

- Syntax errors
- Typographical errors
- Errors of omission
- Logical errors
- Runtime errors

Syntax Errors

When applied to a programming language, syntax refers to the rules that govern the way in which a method, or function, is to be used. Included in those rules is the spelling and capitalization of a method or property name, the number of arguments a method has, the order of the arguments, and the types of those arguments. Therefore, a syntax error is the breaking of one or more of those rules.

As an example, say that the function foo has the following syntax:

```
foo(int iVar, char* lpszText);
```

As you can see, this function takes as its arguments an int and a char pointer. Therefore, calling this function with a pair of values of type int would result in a syntax error because the function is being called incorrectly, or not in accordance with its syntactical rules.

Typographical Errors

Typographical errors can sometimes be the most difficult types of errors to catch. In HTML, these types of mistakes are especially easy to commit because of the fact that many tags have very similar names. An example of a typographical error is typing in an HTML tag such as <SPIN> instead of <SPAN>. Because this is perfectly valid HTML, the browser will not report an error. However, you certainly won't get the desired results and will most assuredly be left wondering why.

Errors of Omission

Errors of omission occur when you forget to specify or include something in your code. An example of errors of omission is leaving off a closing tag. If you use heading style for a heading and then forget to close that style, it's going to be fairly obvious when you preview the page. However, if you use the <DIV> tag in order to name a region of a document and omit the closing </DIV> tag, you're likely to end up with very unpredictable results from the point of the omission to the end of the document.

Logical Errors

Logical errors are one type of error that most debuggers aren't going to be able to pinpoint for you. This is because there is nothing syntactically incorrect in these situations. Logical errors are situations in which the code is correct according to the definition of the language being used, but the developer simply made an incorrect decision or assumption. Examples of logical errors include calling an incorrect method or using an incorrect property.

Configuring Debug Support in Visual InterDev

This hour differs significantly from the other hours that you've read up to this point for two very important reasons. The act of debugging in Visual InterDev (setting breakpoints, watching variables, and so on) is not difficult. What is difficult is the incredible number of things you must do in order to configure your system, so you can get to the point in which you can debug a Web application. This—coupled with the fact that the number one complaint I constantly hear from my fellow software developers is that books never take the time to explain how to install and configure the software—is why the rest of this hour is dedicated to doing just that.

13

Debugging is much simpler when all the code for the application is running on the same machine because debugging tools have been designed to handle this scenario for years. However, in the case of a Web application, programming logic is typically split into several different layers, many of which are running on different machines. Although this multitiered approach to development is certainly not new, most development environments have been slow to incorporate robust debuggers in their products that handle this type of programming paradigm.

Another problem with debugging Web applications is the use of multiple programming languages. As an example, a typical Web application might have JavaScript embedded in a Dynamic HTML page on the client's browser that communicates with an Active Server Page on a server that was written in VBScript and communicates with an ActiveX component written in Visual C++.

Therefore, what was needed with Visual InterDev was a tool that not only allowed for the debugging of both client and server scripts, but could also handle the different languages being used today in order to create Web applications (for example, HTML, Dynamic HTML, JavaScript, VBScript, and so on). With Visual InterDev 6, Microsoft succeeded in both of these areas.

Debugging Client Script

The first thing you need to know about debugging client script is that you need to use Microsoft Internet Explorer (IE) 4 or higher. If you do, there are several options to debugging client script. These options include the following:

- Debugging a Visual InterDev project
- Debugging a Running Document
- Just-in-time (JIT) debugging

Debugging a Visual InterDev Project

Debugging client script from a Visual InterDev project can get tricky because you need to be able to debug straight client script (the kind you type into your .htm files) as well as the client script that is generated from an Active Server Page. We will look at debugging normal client script first because it is the simpler of the two.

If you are working in a Visual InterDev solution, you can debug a file by following these steps:

1. Open the Project Explorer and select the page you want to debug.
2. Right-click the page and select the Set As Start Page menu option.

Unfortunately, when you right-click a page and select the Set As Start Page menu option, Visual InterDev doesn't give you any kind of cue that this page is now the start page (such as placing a check mark next to the menu option). However, the start page for a project can be verified by right-clicking the project in the Project Explorer and clicking the Launch tab.

Another feature that aids greatly in debugging is that from the Launch tab, not only can you see the start page, but you can also specify any parameters that need to be passed to that page when it is loaded. That way, you can mimic the page being called and pass data from another page.

3. Set a breakpoint on the line of code in which you want to stop execution in order to verify variable values. You can set a breakpoint in Visual InterDev by simply positioning the caret on the line of code where you want execution to stop and pressing the F9 key. The F9 key is a toggle, so it will also turn off a breakpoint if one currently exists for that line of code.

4. After setting the desired breakpoints, press F5 or select the Debug, Start menu option in order to bring the page up in Internet Explorer.

5. When a line of code is hit that contains a breakpoint, the debugger will interrupt execution of the page, and you can then query the system about things such as current variable values.

As you can see, that was fairly easy. Now that you've seen how to debug a page from the Visual InterDev development environment, let's look at how you would attach to and debug a document that is already running.

Debugging a Running Document

Thanks to the interoperability of Visual InterDev and Microsoft Internet Explorer, you can debug a document that is already open in the browser. Actually, you have two options available to you in that you can attach to and debug the running document from Visual InterDev, or you can start a debug session from within Internet Explorer. In order to attach to a running document, you will need to enable that feature in Visual InterDev:

1. From Visual InterDev, select the Tools, Options menu option.

2. When the Options dialog box is displayed, you will see a list of categories in a tree view on the left side of the dialog. Select the Debugger item to show the debugging options that you can modify (see Figure 13.1).

13

FIGURE **13.1**

Enabling the ability to attach to a running document.

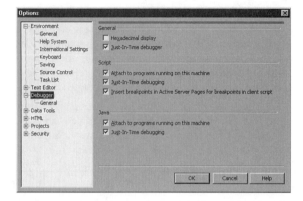

3. At this point, check the option that reads Attach to Programs Running on This Machine (within the Script section).

When you have enabled the ability to attach to open documents, the process by which you actually attach is as follows:

1. Now open the desired page in IE.

2. From Visual InterDev, select the Debug, Processes menu option (see Figure 13.2).

FIGURE **13.2**

Attaching to a running document from Visual InterDev.

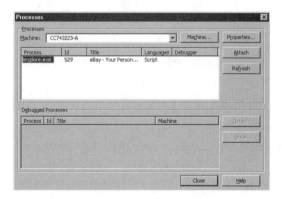

3. As you can see, Visual InterDev shows you all running instances of Internet Explorer and gives you the opportunity to attach to them. Simply select the desired instance and click the Attach key.

Make sure to turn off the Active Desktop feature if you want to be able to debug client scripts this way. For some reason this feature causes all kinds of unpredictable behavior when trying to debug scripts.

At this point, you're attached and can begin debugging. However, what if the code you want to debug has already run? Because you're attached, simply set the breakpoint where you want and press the F5 (Refresh) key. (If you don't know yet how to set breakpoints, see the next section.)

If you have already attached to a running document and simply want to interrupt its execution, you can do the following:

1. From Visual InterDev, select the Debug, Processes menu option (just as you did to attach to the process).

2. Now you will see the attached process listed in the Debugged Processes list view at the bottom of the Processes Dialog.

3. Simply click the Break button in order to interrupt execution of the running document.

In order to debug a running script from Internet Explorer, you will need to do the following:

1. From Internet Explorer, select the View, Script Debugger, Break At Next Statement.

2. At this point, do whatever you need to do in your Web page in order to cause the code you want to be debugged to execute. As soon as the first line is read by the browser, execution will be halted, and you can start debugging the page.

Another technique that does the same thing is the following:

1. From Internet Explorer, choose the View, Script Debugger, Open menu option.

2. This causes a new instance of Visual InterDev to be launched.

3. Now, simply open the file you want to debug and set any applicable breakpoints.

As you can see, Visual InterDev in cooperation with IE gives you several options for attaching to and debugging a page that is already running in the browser. In the next section, you'll see how to stop the execution of a page and invoke the debugger from code.

Just-in-Time Debugging

Another great advantage of developing with Visual InterDev and IE is just-in-time debugging. Simply stated, this feature gives you the ability to start a debug session in Visual InterDev when an error has occurred in your page.

For an example of this, create an HTML page, add any bogus line of script to the page, and then run the script from the browser. You will see a dialog similar to one shown in Figure 13.3. For this figure, I simply added a call to a nonexistent function called stop to my page. As you can see, the dialog tells me both the line where the error occurred and the nature of the error. (In this case, the function stop doesn't exist.)

13

FIGURE 13.3

When IE encounters an
error in your script, it
displays an error asking
if you want to debug the
offending page.

When you receive an error like this, you have the option of debugging the offending page using Visual InterDev. However, this option works only if you've turned on the option to use JIT.

> If you receive the dialog that asks you if you want to debug a page and you select No, this generally results in your having a very unstable instance of IE. For example, in some cases, I didn't have any history in the IE Address combo box, and my Favorites were missing completely! At that point, I didn't have a lot of confidence in IE; if you reach a similar point, I suggest shutting IE down and starting a new instance.

To turn on the option to use JIT, simply follow these steps:

1. From Visual InterDev, select the Tools, Options menu option.
2. Select the Debugger tree view entry to display the debugging options that can be modified.
3. When you've done that, simply check the Just-In-Time Debugging option, as shown in Figure 13.4.

FIGURE 13.4

Enabling just-in-time
debugging.

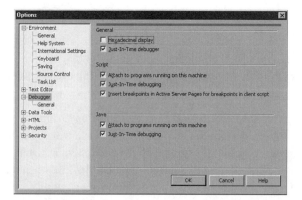

After you have JIT enabled, you will be able to debug your Web pages on-the-fly as errors occur. One thing to note is that, if you aren't running Visual InterDev at the time an error like this occurs (and you click the Yes button), IE will launch Visual InterDev automatically and you will be asked if you want to have Visual InterDev open the project for debugging. If you reply Yes to this dialog (see Figure 13.5), the project will be loaded, the page in error will be opened, and you will situated at the offending line of code. If you reply No to this dialog, the offending page will still be loaded (because you've already indicated that you wanted to debug the page), but the Visual InterDev project won't be.

FIGURE 13.5

When JIT is invoked, Visual InterDev will prompt you as to whether you want to open the associated Visual InterDev Web project.

If you already have an instance of Visual InterDev running, another instance will be loaded automatically. However, if the other instance of Visual InterDev already has the project open that contains the page in error, you will not be able to open the project. Instead, only the page will be opened.

Debugging Server Script

To debug server script, you must be using Microsoft Internet Information Server (IIS) 4 (or higher) as the Web server. If not, you can stop reading at this point. The fact that you've seen this limitation throughout this hour is why I always stress that the only time you should be using Microsoft Personal Web Server (PWS) is when you are testing a very simple Web page in an isolated situation. PWS simply has too many limitations (such as debugging) to be used in developing a serious Web site.

There are two ways to debug server script. The first way is to debug locally. This is the case when you are developing on the same machine that contains the Web server. The second way is remote debugging. However, whether you're debugging remotely or locally, the following steps need to be completed.

As you learned in the last hour, when an Active Server Page is processed, the results are sent to the client browser as pure HTML. The results, therefore, are always considerably different from what you see when you edit the Active Server Page source code in the editor. Sometimes a few lines of server script produce dozens or even hundreds of lines of HTML to be run on the client, and sometimes several lines of server script generate just

13

a couple of lines of HTML. The bottom line is that any breakpoint you set in the Active Server Page code won't match up correctly with regard to line numbers when the client page is generated.

As a solution to this, there is an option with which you can enable client-side debugging of Active Server Pages. When you select this option, it causes IIS to keep track of the location of client script breakpoints in the Active Server Page. IIS is then responsible for passing the correct location of your breakpoints to IE so that IE can stop at the specified lines of code.

To enable client script debugging of Active Server Pages, complete the following steps:

1. In the Project Explorer of Visual InterDev, right-click the project and choose the Properties menu option.

2. When the IDispWebProject Properties dialog appears, select the Launch tab (see Figure 13.6).

FIGURE 13.6

Enabling client script debugging of Active Server Pages.

3. At the bottom of the tab, you will see a group box labeled Server Script with a single check box called Automatically Enable ASP Server-Side Script Debugging on Launch. Check this option to enable it.

As mentioned earlier, there are two ways to debug server script: locally or remotely. The next two sections cover both of these options.

Debugging Server Script Locally

Debugging server script locally is identical to debugging client script because you are debugging code that is running on the local machine in both cases. Therefore, simply refer to the previous sections for help in that area.

However, if the Web server is on a different machine, the process is called *remote debugging*, which requires a bit more work, as you'll see in the next section.

Debugging Server Script Remotely

Without remote debugging, the only means of debugging Active Server Pages would be to install Visual InterDev on the Web server itself and then debug the code locally. Needless to say, this technique will not work for a lot of companies. Therefore, remote debugging was introduced.

> To debug script in an Active Server Page, you must be running Microsoft Internet Information Server 4 (or later). Unfortunately, at this time, Personal Web Server doesn't provide this functionality. In addition, you can perform remote debugging only from a computer running Windows NT.

In order to configure remote debugging, you must verify that the full-server version of Visual InterDev was installed on the Web server. This can be done through the following steps:

1. On the Web server, run the Visual Studio Enterprise setup application.

2. Under Add/Remove Options, choose Server Applications and Tools and click the Next button.

3. Then select the Launch BackOffice Installation Wizard and click the Install button. This causes that particular installation program to run.

4. When the BackOffice Business Solutions wizard is displayed, choose Custom option and click the Next button.

5. Proceed through the wizard until you see the page offering you a list of components to install. From here, you will want to uncheck all the components except the Remote Machine Debugging and Visual InterDev Server. They are the components that are needed for remote debugging to work.

6. When prompted for a username and password, you must provide the username and password of a user that has admin privileges for the server. Therefore, all users who will be doing remote debugging must be set up with admin rights.

In addition to installing the Visual InterDev server on the Web server, you must also ensure that DCOM is configured correctly by performing the following:

1. Run the dcomcnfg application from Windows Start or any command prompt.

If you are using PWS in conjunction with Windows 95 or Windows 98, you
will need to make sure that you have user-level security defined for the
server. This can be accomplished by running the Network applet from the
Control Panel. When the Network applet starts, click the Access Control tab
and select the User-Level Access Control option (see Figure 13.7).

FIGURE 13.7

You must have User-Level Access Control enabled if you want to perform remote debugging with a Web server running on Windows 95 or Windows 98.

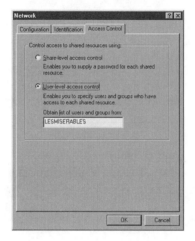

2. When the Distributed COM Configuration Properties dialog appears, select
   Machine Debug Manager, and then choose Properties to display the Machine
   Debug Manager Properties dialog.

3. From there, select the Security tab and then Use Custom Access Permissions.

4. Click the Edit button.

5. From the Registry Value Permissions dialog, verify that Allow Access is selected in
   the Type of Access list, and then click the Add button.

6. When the Add Users and Groups dialog is displayed, select the Web server's name
   from the List Names From list box.

7. Under Names, choose Administrators, choose Add, and then click OK.

8. When that is finished, return to the Security tab and choose the Use Custom
   Launch permissions and click the Edit button.

9. Verify that Allow Launch option is selected in the Type of Access list, choose Add
   option, and then add administrators.

The last thing that you'll need to do in order to configure remote debugging is to turn on
the option to enable debugging for Active Server Pages. To do so, implement the following:

1. From Visual InterDev, open the Project Explorer.

2. Display the Properties dialog for the project you want to enable remote debugging for.

3. When the Properties dialog is displayed, choose the Launch tab.

4. Under Server Script, make sure that the Automatically Enable ASP Server-Side Debugging on Launch option is checked. When you set this option, it can take a few moments to complete. Therefore, be patient and let it finish.

When you have done all this, you are finally able to start remotely debugging your server scripts. Thank goodness, the act of actually debugging a remote server (when you've survived the configuration) is exactly the same as debugging client script or debugging server script locally. Therefore, at this point, simply follow the instructions in the previous section depending on how you want to debug (that is, from Visual InterDev, by attaching to a running document, and so on).

A Sample Debugging Case Study

Now that you've seen what it takes to configure debugging, take a look at the simple stuff: the actual act of debugging! Instead of simply regurgitating the online help for each menu option and dialog that pertains to debugging, this section walks you through a sample debugging session in which you will see the menu options and dialogs that you will most often use as you build and debug your Web applications.

Building the Case Study Demo

Because I want to concentrate on the debugging options, I'll keep the demo simple. At this point, perform the following steps to create the new Web page that you will debug:

1. Create a new Visual InterDev project called Debugging.

2. After the project has been created, add a new HTML page and call it Calc.htm.

3. Add a form to the page called frmCalc.

4. Add the HTML controls as they are shown in Figure 13.8.

5. After you have added the controls, name them (from left to right on the Web page) txtValue1, txtValue2, btnMultiply, and txtAnswer.

6. When you are finished naming the controls, open the Project Explorer and after right-clicking the Calc.htm page, select the Set As Start Page menu option.

7. Now that this little example is done, look at the different types of errors situations that you can debug using Visual InterDev's debugging capabilities.

13

FIGURE 13.8
*A test page for debugging
purposes.*

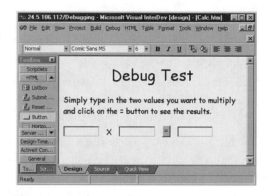

Handling Runtime Errors

Runtime errors occur when a line of script attempts to perform an invalid action. To see
an example of this, add an event handler for the `onclick` event of the `btnMultiply`
Button control and insert the following code:

```
frmCalc.txtAnswer = frmCalc.txtValue1 * frmCalc.txtValue2;
```

When you've finished, select the Debug, Run menu option. At this point, entering any
values into the two value fields and clicking the = button will result in the runtime error
you see in Figure 13.9. This is because the operation being attempted (the multiplication
of two text fields) is invalid.

FIGURE 13.9
*Runtime errors occur
when an invalid action
is attempted from
script.*

After you have clicked OK to the error message, you will be placed in the program at the
location in which the error occurred. (By default, the offending line will have a yellow
background.) No doubt as you've entered the examples while reading this book, you've
encountered the occasional runtime error because of a typo and had no choice but to keep
looking back and forth between the book and the screen until you finally located the typo.
Now you can locate the exact line where an error is occurring using the debugger.

Setting Breakpoints

Breakpoints enable you to define on which line of code the script should stop executing. As
an example, replace the body of the `btnMultiply` `onclick` handler with the following code:

```
var v1 = parseInt(frmCalc.txtValue1.value);
var v2 = parseInt(frmCalc.txtValue2.value);
var a = v1 * v1;
frmCalc.txtAnswer.value = stringToNum(a);
```

Now, run the code and type in the values 3 and 4 for the first and second text fields, respectively. You will see that the page incorrectly shows the result as being a value of 9. Although you can easily see the problem, I will walk through how you would debug this if the problem is not quite so obvious.

Breakpoints are created by positioning the caret on the desired source code line and pressing the F9 key (or selecting the Debug, Insert Breakpoint menu option).

This will create a breakpoint at the point of the caret. Notice that a small red dot is placed in the left margin on the same line as the breakpoint. This is just a visual reminder that you have a breakpoint set at that location.

Now, press the F5 key to run the page again. This time, immediately after you enter the two values and press the = button, the debugger will kick in and halt execution, whereupon you're caret will be placed on the first line of code in the `onclick` method where you had set the breakpoint.

At this point, you can do such things as inspect variables and step into called functions (both covered later) in order to further debug the problem.

In addition to F9 being used to set a breakpoint, it is also used to turn a breakpoint off when a breakpoint has already been set for the current line.

You can get a list of all the breakpoints that have been set throughout the Web application by selecting the Debug, Breakpoints menu option (or pressing Ctrl+B). The result is the dialog you see in Figure 13.10. As you can see, the Breakpoints dialog enables you to do everything from jumping to the code where the breakpoint is set to disabling and removing individual or all defined breakpoints.

FIGURE 13.10

The Breakpoints dialog makes it easier to keep track of the breakpoints that you have set across several scripts in your Web application.

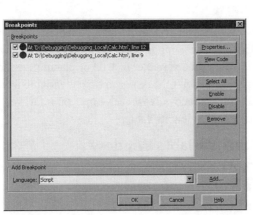

13

A very handy shortcut that I've always used with Microsoft development environments is the Shift+Ctrl+F9 combination. This removes all breakpoints from the current application, so you don't have to go through the extra steps of invoking the Breakpoints dialog, clicking the Select All button, and then clicking the Remove button.

Inspecting Variables

Breakpoints don't help much unless you can do something useful when you get there. Therefore, take a look at how to inspect variables and at the same time correct the bogus code so that it functions correctly.

At this point, make sure that the only breakpoint you have is on the last line of the `onclick` event handler and press the F5 key to run the application. When the browser reaches the line of code that contains the breakpoint, execution will be stopped and you will then have the ability to inspect your variables.

Viewing a Variable's Value

The quickest way to ascertain the value of a given variable is to simply place the cursor over that variable. When you do, the variable's value will display in a ToolTip below the mouse cursor.

Immediate Window

The Immediate Window can also be used to inspect variables on-the-fly. However, this window (displayed by selecting the View, Debug Windows, Immediate menu option) is generally used when you want to change a variable's value for testing purposes. Using this window, you can either type in hard-coded values or even mathematical formulas in order to interactively test your application without restarting it over and over again.

Watch Window

The Watch window enables you to define which variables you want to watch constantly. For example, say that you are going to set several breakpoints and that each time you are going to want to view the same variable. Instead of placing the mouse cursor over the variable in order to view it each time, you can drag a variable from the actual source code editor into the watch window. Now each time you hit a breakpoint and that variable is in scope, you can quickly view its value.

Locals and Autos Variable Window

Two last windows that you should pay attention to are the Auto and Local windows. Like the Immediate window, both of these windows can be displayed from the View, Debug Windows menu option.

These windows have a very similar function. The Locals window is used to view variables that are in the current scope (for example, the current method), whereas the Autos windows is used to view variables that are defined for all threads of the current process.

Summary

Although debugging can be a pain-staking, laborious task that is exacerbated with the element of server and remote debugging, Visual InterDev has come a long way in delivering a tool that can at least make this necessary process easier. In this hour, you have learned not only the principals of debugging, but also how to configure the debugging of client script, local server script, and remote server script. This knowledge, combined with what you've already learned about scripting, should enable you to confidently move forward in your script development endeavors.

Q&A

Q What is the difference between removing and disabling a breakpoint?

A When you disable a breakpoint, its definition remains. In other words, when you close the file and open it again, you can still see an icon that marks that line as having a disabled breakpoint. Therefore, disabling a breakpoint doesn't require opening the file back up, locating where you had the breakpoint and setting it again. Instead you can just open the Breakpoints dialog and re-enable it when you need to. This is especially useful if you know that you are going to have to set and unset a given breakpoint several times.

Q How can I set a breakpoint in order to debug methods in the global.asa file?

A Because the global.asa file can not be defined as the start page, you must request an Active Server Page. When that page is processed, the Web server will process the global.asa file.

Workshop

The Workshop is designed to help you anticipate possible questions, review what you've learned, and begin thinking ahead to put your knowledge into practice. The answers to the quiz are in Appendix A, "Answers."

Quiz

1. What are some types of errors that you can encounter in your applications?
2. What are some reasons that debugging a Web application is more difficult than debugging other types of applications?

13

3. What must you do to the page you want to debug from the Visual InterDev environment?

4. What is the feature that enables you to dynamically start a debug session when the browser encounters an error on a page?

5. What is the utility to help configure DCOM for remote server script debugging?

6. What is a quick way to remove all breakpoints from a Web application?

7. How do you set a breakpoint?

8. How can you change a variable at runtime?

9. What is the Watch window used for?

10. What is the difference between the Locals and Autos windows?

Exercise

Using what you've learned here, attempt to create your own case study for a remote debugging session.

Part III

Creating Database-Driven Web Sites

Hour

HOUR 14

An Introduction to Database Design

This is the first hour of the database section. In the next few hours, you will discover how the Database Designer enables you to create and modify your database structure and how the Query Designer enables you to build and execute almost any query against those databases. After you learn that, you will spend the remaining hours learning the more advanced tasks of writing stored procedures and triggers. However, all these hours assume at least an intermediate level of relational database knowledge. Therefore, instead of interrupting the flow of these hours to stop and explain the different parts of database design a little bit at a time, I've dedicated this hour to the task of teaching you the basics of relational database design.

Another thing to add is that database analysts (DBAs) enjoy talking about such things as relational algebra, tuples, normal form, and natural composition. If you're one of these people, this hour is definitely not for you. Rather, this hour focuses on the basics of relational databases for the rest of you who are accustomed to having those DBA types do the database work for you and now find yourselves with this great Visual InterDev tool that finally puts some of the database power in your hands. However, with power comes responsibility, hence, the purpose for this hour. In this hour, you will learn the core elements of relational database management systems (RDBMS) and how they work together to give you the whole picture of your data. Next, you will learn the language all RDBMS systems use—SQL. If you're not already familiar with SQL, you will want to read these sections because the following hours will assume a certain level of SQL knowledge.

The highlights of this hour include

- Learning the advantages and disadvantage of stored procedures and triggers
- Learning the steps required in designing a relational database
- Learning about artificial keys
- Discovering the rules of data normalization
- Learning about referential integrity

An Introduction to Relational Database Management Systems

The first thing to understand about relational databases is why they're called relational. In simple terms, a relational database is a set of related objects, such as tables, views, and indexes that constitute your data. In other words, unlike a flat file, which simply stores raw data, a relational database stores the data in tables and enables you to define how the data in each table is related.

Tables

As I already mentioned, tables store the data in a database. Actually, there are two facets to tables. The first is the schema, or physical definition of the table. Because tables are meant to store real-life data, think about the information you might want to store with a real-life entity: your customers.

Obviously, your application will have some specific things you want to store regarding your customers, but almost all customer tables have to store the basics, such as customer number, customer name, and customer address information. In relational database terminology, you will create each of these items as columns in the table. Therefore, in your Customer table, you might define a CustomerNumber column, a CustomerName column, and so on.

Each column is defined as being of a certain type. Because different databases support different types, I'm not going to attempt to list all possible types here. In general terms, types are usually things, such as text, number, memo (very long text), and image. More advanced database systems further break these types down to have many different categories. For example, SQL Server 7 defined about half a dozen different numeric types. However, when you design your tables, you must think about what data will be stored, such as what columns to add and the types of columns to add.

The actual data is the second aspect of tables. In relational databases, data is stored in rows. Therefore, if you have two customers stored in your Customer table, they will be represented by two data rows. Think of tables in terms of a grid, or spreadsheet of information, in which the columns are defined horizontally across the top of the grid and each row contains the data for the table.

Indexes

Indexes are a complex subject, especially when I start talking about things such as B+ trees, clustered indexes, and hashing algorithms. However, for purposes of this discussion, it's enough to understand that indexes are relational database objects used internally to make processing more efficient. But how do indexes speed up performance?

Suppose that you want to read only the rows from the Customer table where the customer resides in a particular state or group of states. Without an index, the database would have to read through every single row in the table to retrieve the desired results. This would be similar to reading through the entire phone book in order to find the phone book entries of all the people who live on Main St. This might not be a problem if you live in Mayberry, R.F.D. However, obviously, this approach does present a serious problem with any real amount of data.

Indexes are the answer to this. Obviously, databases can't guess how you are going to use your data; therefore, when you design your database, it's important to give some thought to how the data will be accessed. In the preceding example, you would have told the database you wanted an index created on the Customer table using the State column. In logical terms, the database will not only keep track of the customer data in the Customer table, but it will also maintain an ordered list of the states for which a customer row exists. Each entry in the index will point back to a real row in the table. Figure 14.1 illustrates this example. Note that the way in which indexes are actually stored is much more complex than this. This should convey the logical manner in which indexes are defined and maintained.

14

FIGURE **14.1**

FIGURE **14.1**

*A logical example of a
set of indexes being
used for a Customer
table.*

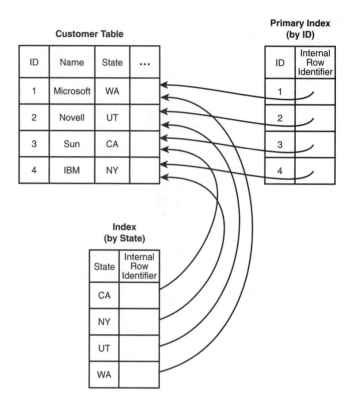

By defining a State column index, you make sure that each time a record is added or
removed from the Customer table, the database updates this index. In addition, each time
a Customer row is updated and the State column is modified, that index is also updated.
Therefore, you need to be careful in deciding what indexes to create and exactly which
columns to use in those indexes. Not having indexes built can result in poor performance;
however, having too many indexes can be even worse (due to all the indexes being
updated in the background of every applicable database operation).

Primary Indexes

Most relational database systems mandate the definition of a primary key, or index. A
primary key guarantees uniqueness in your table. For example, you might state that each
customer in your Customer table has a unique identifier stored in the CustomerNumber
column. In this case, you will define this column as the primary key for the table. The
important thing to realize is that the column(s) which are defined for the primary key
cannot be defined with the NOT NULL attribute. This means that those columns can never
have a NULL value. The primary key is so important because it is used to help enforce
referential integrity, which I'll discuss soon.

> If you are a C or C++ developer, you've certainly worked with NULLs before. However, it's important to realize that the NULL you've worked with in programming is different from the database definition of the same term. In programming, the term NULL almost always means a 0, or empty value. However, in database terms, a NULL value means having no value at all.

Views

Views are basically queries that reference one or more columns of one or more tables. Views are powerful objects because they are persistable. In other words, after you define a view, it is stored in the database for future use. You might use a view, if you find that you often need to read the same columns from a table that uses the same columns to search with. For example, suppose that you define a report that lists all the customers by state. Because this is something you would probably be using quite frequently, you would want to save the SQL needed to generate this report in the form of a view. Views are sometimes called logical files because they can be treated as tables. In this example, you would simply instruct the database that you want to read all the rows from the saved view.

Security is another benefit of views. Say that you store the customer's credit card in the Customer table. You might not want anyone in the company to be able to view that particular column of information. In this case, you could secure the Customer table so that it could not be used at all. You would then define a view for the Customer table that included only non-sensitive data. Because a view looks like a table (from a programmatic standpoint), it can be referenced just like the original table with the sensitive data being protected.

Stored Procedures

Stored procedures are precompiled statements stored in the database. The main benefit of stored procedures is that because they are precompiled, they perform much better than a query or dynamically prepared SQL statement. The following are some benefits of defining stored procedures:

- Stored procedures encapsulate business rules. The reason this is so important to many companies is two-fold. First, the business rules are stored apart from the application's source code. This is important because if a business rule changes, the client workstations don't have to be updated with a new version of code that will have to be updated if the business rules are defined within the application's source code. Note that this advantage assumes a two-tier client/server model. In distributed n-tier architecture, this isn't an advantage. I'll touch on that shortly. Second, if the business rules are stored in the database, multiple applications can make use of these rules, thereby, creating a consistent interaction between the applications and the company's data throughout the system.

14

- Stored procedures are easier to maintain than code because they are localized to a single place (the database). For example, suppose that every time inventory is changed, you want to create a row in a transaction (or log) table detailing the change to inventory because many things update inventory (order entry, picking ticket update, receiving, parts inquiry, and so on). With this in mind, you go about changing every single one of those applications to write out this new record. Now, what happens when the schema for that transaction table changes? You have to update every one of those source code modules. If, on the other hand, you create a stored procedure for creating this record, you will have to change the code in only one place (in the stored procedure).

- As mentioned previously, stored procedures provide significant performance benefits over alternative methods of database interaction. This is especially true if the database supports procedure caching. This means that after executing the stored procedure the first time, any subsequent attempts to execute the same stored procedure (in the same session) will result in the stored procedure being run from a cache. SQL Server 7 supports this type of caching.

- Similar to a view, stored procedures are named database objects that can be executed either interactively or programmatically. For example, you might have a stored procedure that calculates the balance owed on a set of loans. You might typically run this process in batch during end of day processing. Using a stored procedure, you can call the stored procedure using the syntax of the database you are using.

Stored procedures are one of those things that usually spark impassioned debates among DBAs because they have their disadvantages. Some of those disadvantages are as follows:

- The biggest drawback to stored procedures (and the argument that is becoming louder as more companies move towards distributed applications) is that they don't work with n-tier systems. In a standard 2-tier client/server system, a fat client resides on the client's workstation and accesses a database on the server. However, with today's move towards Microsoft DNA and its distributed application technologies, the business rules are moving away from the client (leaving a thin, UI-only client) and onto one or more servers. This accomplishes two things. First, deployment is greatly simplified because the client workstation contains only UI code. Second, the business logic and database are spread across multiple servers for load balancing and scalability. Obviously, defining stored procedures becomes much more difficult to spread the server-side processing to multiple servers.

- Another big disadvantage to using stored procedures is that they are extremely database dependent. Each database defines its own unique, proprietary version of SQL that is used to define such objects as stored procedures. For SQL Server, that language is called Transact-SQL (T-SQL). In Oracle, it's called PL/SQL. Therefore, if you decide to write a lot of stored procedures, be cognizant of the fact that if you want to move to another database at a later date, it might not be as easy as you think. On that account, if database independence is an important goal to your overall system design, you will be better off not using stored procedures.

Triggers

Triggers are similar to stored procedures; however, triggers are stored, precompiled codes that are executed as a result of a predefined action. These objects are incredibly useful items that help to enforce business logic within the database. For example, take the preceding situation in which you had to write a transaction record every time inventory was changed. Instead of having the programmer perform this task in the source code, you could create a trigger that would write this record every time the inventory table is updated. So, how is this different from having a stored procedure write the transaction record when it updates inventory? Each time the inventory table is updated, your trigger will fire and the transaction record will be written. This is guaranteed because it is enforced by the database. The stored procedure, although convenient, isn't quite as foolproof because there's no guarantee that everyone who updates inventory will do so by calling the appropriate stored procedure. For example, if someone opens the database and manually enters an item into the inventory table, the stored procedure technique will circumvent, yet the trigger will fire and the expected result realized.

Triggers enjoy most of the same advantages as stored procedures, with the added benefit that they are run automatically. However, before deciding whether you want to use them, keep in mind that they too have disadvantages, such as not being database independent and not being the best solution for n-tier applications.

Designing Relational Databases

Now that you've seen the different physical elements that make up a relational database, take a look at some issues regarding how to design your database. Follow these basic steps when designing your databases:

1. Analyze the application's needs. As you speak with the users of the system, start getting a feel for how you think the user wants the application to look and document the ways in which you see that the database should be designed.

2. Investigate the existence of similar systems from which you can glean ideas or pointers. The best way of avoiding pitfalls is to listen to people who have already made these mistakes. Rarely will you ever be asked to create a system unlike any created previously.

14

3. Decide on normalization rules (covered shortly in the section "Data Normalization"). It's important to decide this up front instead of continually redefining your tables and views every time you realize that you want to put an integrity check into the system.

4. Create the database objects. These include all tables, views, indexes, stored procedures, and triggers.

5. Extremely Important: Write SQL scripts to automate the creation of your database. You never know when you might have to duplicate the database or recreate it from scratch. Therefore, it's always a good idea to think about the steps that recreating your database would entail should you ever need to do so.

In addition to these high-level tasks, you should also consider the following topics, in case you are in charge of designing your database:

- Artificial keys
- Data normalization
- Referential integrity

Artificial Keys

One decision you'll have to make is whether you want to use artificial keys when defining your tables. An artificial key is a column the system creates to guarantee uniqueness in a table. Suppose you have a Customer table and you have to decide what the primary key will be. You might be thinking, "Why not use something like a CustomerName column?" Actually, doing so would present two problems. First, using text fields (especially large ones) as primary keys is inefficient and can negatively affect performance. Second, some developers (myself included) are opposed to defining primary keys that are modifiable by either the users of the system or the system itself. In the case of a CustomerName column, obviously, the company can change names, but every table that uses this key will have to be updated. By using an artificial key (almost always a numeric value), you guarantee a value that will never change for the life of the system.

The only drawback to using artificial keys is that you must maintain them. For example, in the Customer table example, you had to define a CustomerId column somewhere in your system and then keep track of incrementing it each time a new customer was added to the system. Most developers create a special table (sometimes called a system control table) to keep track of these special keys.

Data Normalization

Aside from the actual schema, normalization is one of the biggest decisions you'll make. In a sense, normalization is what relational databases are all about because by definition, normalization is the process of organizing data into related tables.

Three accepted rules of normalization exist for the purpose of aiding you in designing your database so that the data stored in it remains an accurate representation of your system throughout the life of your system. These rules are called forms and are explained in the following paragraphs. As you read through this form section, realize that when describing a table or set of tables, these rules define the degree to which your data is normalized.

First Normal Form

The first normal form (FNF) eliminates repeating groups. This means that you must make a separate table for each set of related attributes and give each table its own primary key (see Figure 14.2).

FIGURE 14.2

An example of FNF.

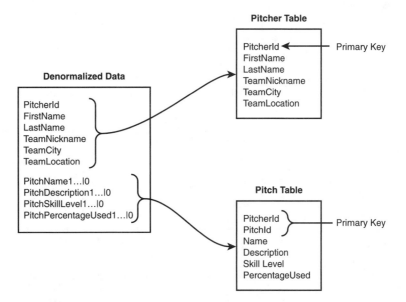

In the original list of data, each baseball pitcher's description and the team he plays on is followed by the pitches he has in his arsenal. Obviously, some pitchers have mastered some pitches, whereas others have not. To answer the question, "Can Tom Glavine throw a curveball?," find Tom Glavine's record and then scan every pitch column in the row. This is both awkward and extremely inefficient. Moving the pitches into a second table helps tremendously.

Using the Tom Glavine example, the first advantage is that now you simply need to join the Pitchers table and the Pitches table, where the pitcher id is that of Tom Glavine. Now, not only is the code for finding if a pitcher has mastered a particular pitch easier to write, but it also eliminates any concerns over how many pitch columns to create. For example,

14

if you define ten pitch columns, what will you do five years from now, when the baseball establishment recognizes another two or three pitches? By adhering to FNF, you'll never have to worry about that.

By the way, if you do not adhere to at least FNF, your data is said to be *denormalized*.

Second Normal Form

The second normal form (SNF) eliminates redundant data. This means that if an attribute relies on only part of a multivalued key, you must remove it to a separate table. Figure 14.3 illustrates this using the baseball pitcher example carried over from the description of FNF.

FIGURE 14.3

An example of SNF.

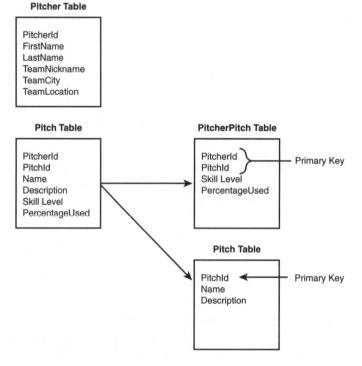

In the Pitches table, the primary key consists of the `PitcherId` and the `PitchId`. This makes sense for the PercentageUsed and SkillLevel columns because they can be different for every Pitcher and Pitch combination. The problem is that the PitchName and PitchDescription columns depend only on the `PitchId`.

So where's the problem? Suppose you want to assign a different description, the slider pitch. You must update every single Pitch record with the new description. If you miss one, you will have what is known in database parlance as an *update anomaly* because the update produces inconsistent data. In this case, the same pitch has different descriptions depending on which records you manage to update.

Now, I'm going to give you another textbook example of why not adhering to SNF is bad. What if the last pitcher who knows a particular pitch retires (assuming that you're dealing only with active pitchers)? In this case, the removal of his Pitcher table record and any of his Pitch table records will effectively remove that particular pitch from the system, as though it never existed! This is known as a *delete anomaly*.

To avoid update anomalies and delete anomalies, move the attributes that depend only on a part of a multivalued key to another table. Because the PercentageUsed and SkillLevel columns depend on both the PitcherId and the PitchId columns, they must stay in the Pitches table. However, because both the PitchName and the PitchDescription columns depend only on the PitchId column (and not the PitcherId column), they can be moved to another table.

Third Normal Form

The third normal form (TNF) eliminates columns not dependent on a the table's primary key. That rule translates to the fact that if an attribute doesn't contribute to the description of a key, it must be moved to another table. Figure 14.4 shows how applying third normal form would change the baseball database example.

FIGURE 14.4

An example of TNF.

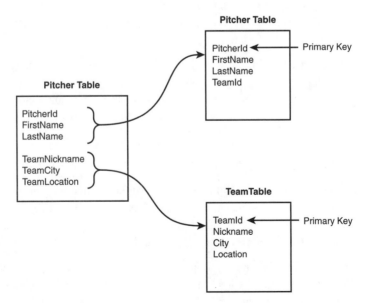

14

The Pitcher table looks great so far. It adheres to FNF because it contains no repeating groups. It also adheres to SNF because it doesn't contain any columns that are dependent on only a part of a multivalued key. However, the primary key to this table is `PitcherId`. Both FirstName and LastName depend on this key, but TeamNickname, TeamCity, and TeamLocation do not. The problem is that these columns describe a team and not a pitcher. Therefore, they must be moved to another table (Teams). To be consistent with the other tables, replace the Pitcher table's Team columns with a TeamId column. Move these displaced columns into a Team table for which a TeamId column represents the primary key. Doing this means that your Pitcher table now adheres to TNF.

However, it's important to realize that the goal here is to make your data consistent and avoid the certain database anomalies. Let's look at some possible scenarios with the Pitcher table not adhering to TNF. Suppose, for the sake of argument, that no Houston Astro pitcher currently exists in the database. There would be no record of the team. Although my favorite team's hitters usually disappear come playoff time, removing the last Astro pitcher would result in a delete anomaly because there would be no record of the team's existence.

Fourth and Fifth Normal Form

I won't go into a lot of detail on the fourth and fifth forms because they are so rarely implemented in today's database designs. However, for completeness, I will at least define them; that way, you can investigate them further if you find that they are of interest to you.

Fourth normal form eliminates multiple independent relationships. In plain English, this means that no table can have more than one many-to-one or many-to-many relationships that aren't directly related.

Fifth normal form means isolating logically related many-to-many relationships. This particular form can get quite complex, and because it's almost never used, I'm not going to go into any more detail here. For those of you who want a more detailed explanation of this particular form, I recommend the well-known book *An Introduction to Database Systems* by Chris Date.

Referential Integrity

Referential integrity is a relational database feature that prevents users from entering inconsistent data. Said another way, it helps to ensure data integrity within your database. Referential integrity works hand-in-hand with how you decide to normalize your data and is defined by the specification of how the database is to react to certain changes to data.

Using the preceding baseball pitcher example, pretend that you want to add a PitcherPitches record without having an existing Pitcher. The database would prevent this because part of the PitcherPitches table's primary key would include a valid `PitcherId` (from the Pitcher table) value. This would guarantee that you will never be in a situation where you have a record without a record on which it depends.

However, what happens if you delete a pitcher from the Pitcher table? Well, that depends on what you want to happen. Obviously, you don't want the pitcher's pitch records to remain, or else your database will be in an inconsistent state. Therefore, you must define to the database that those records have to be deleted. This is done by specifying to the database that these two tables are linked by the PitcherId column, and you want to enable something called *cascading deletes*. Cascading deletes means that if a row's dependent record is removed, the depending record will also be removed. This way, you are not left with an invalid data set.

Another similar example is a linked column changed in one table causes all records in a dependent table to also be updated to reflect the change. This is called *cascading updates*. This is not as big of an issue if you are using artificial keys, and they are the only columns being used to link the different tables.

Summary

In this hour, you discovered the core elements that constitute a relational database and how they work together to give you the whole picture of your data. Next, you learned that data normalization is more than just a buzzword and what it means to have a normalized database. Finally, you finished the hour by learning how decisions, such as which rules of referential integrity to apply, whether to use artificial keys, and what level of normalization to use, will affect how you design your database.

Q&A

Q What if I want to use SQL Server or Oracle? Can I define the relationships between my different tables using Visual InterDev, or do I have to learn yet another tool?

A So far, you've only worked with Web projects. However, Visual InterDev enables you to create Database projects. The combination of this and the Database Designer (which you'll learn about in the next hour) enables you to work with any OLE DB- or ODBC-compliant database in a uniform manner.

Q Are there other normal forms?

A Yes. Originally, only three normal forms were defined for relational databases, but an additional two (forth normal form and fifth normal form) were added later. However, these forms can result in the exponential growth of the number of tables and views in your system and are therefore considered to be difficult to implement because of performance concerns.

14

Q **Now that Visual InterDev finally gives application programmers a decent tool with which to design and maintain a database, where should I look to learn more about database design?**

A Unfortunately, there aren't too many places on the Web for this. Your RDBMS vendor would be one place to start. For example, Oracle has an excellent line of technical books to help the beginner-level DBA. If you're not really interested in becoming a DBA but just want to improve your database knowledge, that might be one avenue to consider. Another would be any classic texts by either E.F. Codd or C.J. Date. I personally recommend a book entitled *An Introduction to Database Systems* (ISBN: 020154329X). I will warn you, however, that this book is very difficult to follow. But, if you want the definitive text on relational database theory, this book is it.

Workshop

The Workshop is designed to help you anticipate possible questions, review what you've learned, and begin thinking ahead to put your knowledge into practice. The answers to the quiz and exercise are in Appendix A, "Answers."

Quiz

1. What disadvantages do stored procedures and triggers have regarding n-tier applications?
2. What is an artificial key?
3. Why is normalization so important?
4. What is it called if a table is not normalized?
5. What is first normal form?
6. What is second normal form?
7. What is third normal form?
8. Under what conditions is it considered to be okay if a table is denormalized?
9. What is a delete anomaly and an update anomaly?
10. What is a cascading delete and a cascading update?

Exercise

Using what you've learned in this hour, create a contact information database that adheres to third normal form. Some ideas for the data that you need to store are artist, album, and tour information.

HOUR **15**

Using the Database Designer

Now that you have discovered the basics of relational database theory and learned quite a bit about the SQL language, this hour concentrates on the next logical step: adding database support to your application.

All database examples in this book are based on the SQL Server 7 sample databases, Pubs and Northwind. Therefore, although the lessons being taught are generic in nature and will work across all OLE DB– or ODBC-compliant databases, you will need to be using SQL Server 7 in order to work through the examples. For instructions on how to install and configure SQL Server 7, see Appendix B, "Installing and Configuring SQL Server."

The first part of the hour has you concentrating on what it takes to define and connect to a database via OLE DB. After that, you will learn how the Database Designer enables you to manipulate the physical schema of a database. You will do this by taking a hands-on approach and making several changes to the Northwind sample database.

The highlights of this hour include

- Creating a Visual InterDev database project
- Configuring an OLE DB data connection
- Creating database diagrams
- Creating tables
- Modifying columns
- Defining table and column constraints
- Defining indexes
- Specifying table relationships
- Generating SQL change scripts

Creating a Database Project

So far in this book, you've created numerous Visual InterDev projects. However, all these projects have been Web projects that did not contain any type of database support. In this section, you will learn how to create a new type of project called a Visual InterDev database project.

To create a new database project, select the File, New option from the main menu. You will see the familiar New Project dialog (see Figure 15.1). However, at this point, double-click on the Visual Studio entry in the tree view on the left side of the dialog. This expands that branch to reveal three new project types: Database Projects, Distribution Units, and Utility Projects. After clicking on the Database Project item, simply type in the name of the project to be created and click the Open button as you would with any type of Visual InterDev project that you are creating.

FIGURE 15.1

Visual InterDev gives you the ability to create several other types of projects besides Web projects.

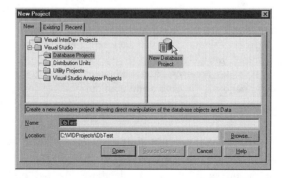

Configuring the Data Connection

After the database project has been created, the Data Link Properties dialog is displayed (see Figure 15.2). This dialog contains four separate tabs with which you can define everything from the OLE DB provider to connection attributes such as timeout values and username and password information.

FIGURE 15.2

The Data Link Properties dialog enables you to select an OLE DB provider.

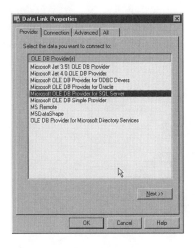

For this hour, I assume that you're using Visual Studio Service Pack 3. If you aren't, the dialogs shown here will be substantially different. If you are using an earlier version of Visual Studio, refer to the online documentation or MSDN in order to create an ODBC-based data connection.

If you are using a true relational database management system (RDBMS) such as SQL Server or Oracle, make sure that the database is running before you attempt to connect to it. With SQL Server, this can be accomplished by executing the SQL Server Service Manager, selecting the MS SQL Server Service and clicking the Start button.

Selecting an OLE DB Provider

As you can see, the first tab (Provider) of the Data Link Properties dialog enables you to select which OLE DB provider will be used to connect to your data source. Notice the inclusion of Microsoft OLE DB Provider for ODBC Drivers. This is great for databases that have an ODBC driver, but not an OLE DB provider. For the purposes of the examples in this book, you will be using the Microsoft OLE DB Provider for SQL Server. After you have selected the provider, select the Connection tab.

Defining the OLE DB Connection

The Connection tab enables you to define database-specific connection attributes (see Figure 15.3). For example, if you are using SQL Server, you must specify which server you are using and what database you want to connect this connection to. The different items that you need to specify on this tab are broken into three sections and numbered on the tab itself.

FIGURE 15.3

You can define and test an OLE DB connection using the Connection tab.

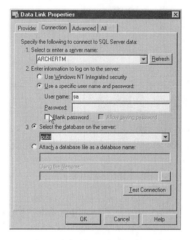

The first step involves the specification of the database server name. If you drop down the list box portion of the server name combo box, you will see several choices. In Figure 15.3, you see the entry ARCHERTM because I installed my copy of SQL Server 7 on a machine with the name ARCHERTM. Therefore, this is a valid server name for me to use when specifying where my target database is located. At this point, select the server name where your database is located.

The next step on this tab is to define how you will log on to the database server. There are two options here. The first is to use Windows NT integrated security; this means that the user ID and password for your current session will be used to log on to the database server. Alternatively, you can enter a specific username and password. I used the username sa for this example because I know that the SQL Server ships with this username with no password. Obviously, in a real-world environment, you are going to want to either specify a username with a password or change the sa user's password for a more secure environment.

The last step on this tab is to define which database you want to use. As mentioned earlier, the databases that have been used throughout this book's data examples are the Northwind and Pubs databases. If you have specified a valid database server name and a valid username/password, when you drop down the database combo box, you will see these two databases (along with a few others).

When you have finished filling out the Connection tab, you can test the connection by clicking the Test Connection button. A successfully completed test will result in the message box shown in Figure 15.4.

FIGURE 15.4

A successful test of your defined OLE DB connection will be indicated by this message box.

Defining Advanced OLE DB Properties

The Advanced tab displays properties such as the Connect Timeout value and Access Permissions (see Figure 15.5). The Connect Timeout value (specified in seconds) enables you to specify how long OLE DB should take in attempting to connect to the data store before giving up. The Access Permissions options enable you to specify exactly what the connecting application will be able to do when connected to the data store.

FIGURE 15.5

The Advanced tab of the Data Link Properties dialog.

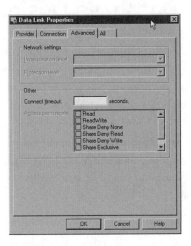

Specifying Data Store–Specific Properties

The All tab enables you to define numerous data store–specific properties for the new data connection. As you can see in Figure 15.6, most of these properties are either properties that you have already set on previous tabs or properties that you would generally never have to change (for example, Locale Identifier, Packet Size). However, if you do need to change any of these, you can do so by selecting the desired property and clicking the Edit Value button. This results in a small dialog box that allows you to type in a new value.

FIGURE 15.6

The All tab of the Data Link Properties dialog.

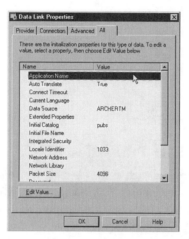

Working with the Database Designer

After you have created a connection to a database, you will see that Visual InterDev is now displaying a new window. The Data View window is only available to you when you've connected to a database (see Figure 15.7). This window not only provides a graphical means of managing and working with the connection to the database but also allows you to modify the database's physical schema and its data, as you will soon see.

Using Database Diagrams

The first element that is listed under the database name in the Data View is Database Diagrams. Database diagrams are used to help you graphically create and modify database elements such as tables, columns, relationships, indexes, and constraints.

Creating a Database Diagram

Because the best way to learn something is by doing, this section walks you through creating a new database diagram. Simply follow these steps to create a database diagram:

FIGURE 15.7

The Data View window enables you to create, view, and edit database elements graphically.

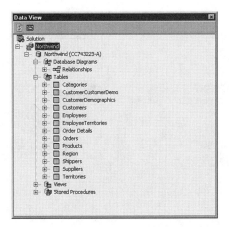

1. Locate the Data View window. If the Data View window is not open, it can be displayed by selecting the View, Other Windows, Data View menu option.

2. Right-click on Database Diagrams and then select the New Diagram menu option from the ensuing context menu. This can also be achieved by selecting the Project, Add Database Item, Diagram menu option.

3. At this point, you will see that a blank window has appeared in Visual InterDev. Think of this window as a playing field for graphically editing a database's schema.

4. You should also notice that Visual InterDev has automatically given the new diagram a default name of DatabaseDiagram*n* (where n = a sequential number in order to guarantee uniqueness). This name can be overridden when you save the diagram. Go ahead and do so at this point and name the diagram Orders.

When you attempt to save your work, you will see that no object is added to the Data View. Also if you were to exit Visual InterDev and reopen it, you would see that the Data View would not contain your newly created database diagram. This is because despite you're having elected to save the diagram, Visual InterDev will not save an empty diagram.

Adding Tables to a Database Diagram

Adding tables to a diagram couldn't be easier. Simply drag the desired tables from the Data View onto the diagram. Visual InterDev will automatically display any relationships between that table and any other related tables already present in the diagram. For example, if you

drag the Orders table and the Order Details table over to the diagram, you will see a line
connecting them (see Figure 15.8) that shows how these tables are related (in this case as
one-to-many).

FIGURE 15.8

*The database diagram
allows you to view
table relationships.*

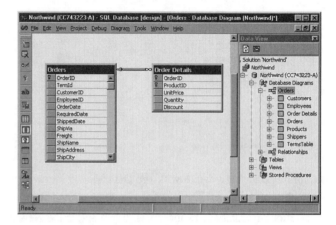

Customizing the Database Diagram

At this point, it's easy to see that after adding a few tables to the diagram, it could
become very difficult to visually navigate. Therefore, Visual InterDev includes a
Database Diagram toolbar that can be used to filter which elements are displayed in a
diagram and how they are displayed (see Figure 15.9). This toolbar can be displayed by
right-clicking on the main menu bar and selecting the Database Diagram menu option.

FIGURE 15.9

*The Database
Diagram toolbar
enables you to more
easily manage the
visual layout of your
database elements and
their relationships.*

To illustrate this, open the Database Diagram toolbar. Now, alternately click on the two
objects (Orders and Order Details) in the diagram. You will see that the toolbar is sensitive to which object is currently selected. Also notice that you can select any object(s) in
the diagram by "rubber banding" them or by clicking Ctrl+A to select them all.

In order to view the different things you can do with the toolbar, simply move the mouse
cursor over each toolbar icon in order to view a ToolTip describing what each button does.

Because there are an infinite number of viewing and filtering combinations, look at the following example to give you an idea of what you can do with the Database Diagram toolbar:

1. Select both the Orders and Order Details objects.

2. From the Database Diagram toolbar, click the Add Related Tables button. This causes all related tables to automatically be added to the diagram. However, there are a couple of problems with regards to being able to view everything.

3. The first problem is that the newly added tables overlap one another. Therefore, click the Arrange Tables button. This causes all the tables in the diagram to be displayed in a manner that is much easier to view.

4. The second problem is that now you have to scroll down to view all the tables. To remedy this, simply click Ctrl+A and then click the Show Table Names button. This causes only the name of the table to be viewed (hiding the column names and properties). Now click the Arrange Tables button to achieve the same results as shown in Figure 15.10.

FIGURE 15.10

Using some of the Database Diagram toolbar's options, you can more efficiently use the screen in order to view more of what is important to you.

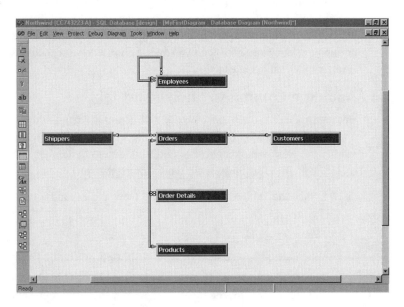

Adding Text to a Diagram

Because database diagrams also serve as a great documentation tool, you can even add text to a diagram for such things as specifying a title or date. To do that simply right-click on the background of the database diagram and select the Diagram, New Text Annotation menu option.

This creates a large text field on the diagram where you can type any text that you desire. When finished, simply click somewhere outside of the text field because pressing the Enter key only causes newline characters to be entered into the text field.

Also, you will find that deleting one of these text annotations is not as easy as you would think. If you simply select the text field and click the Delete key, the only thing that will happen is that each character to the right of the caret will be removed with each pressing of the Delete key. In order to delete the actual text annotation itself, you must select it in such a way that Visual InterDev does not position the text caret inside the text field (for example, by rubber banding a corner of the field). After you've done that, select the Edit, Delete menu option.

Altering the Database Schema

So far you've seen that Visual InterDev allows you to connect to a database and even view the layout and relationships between the different database elements. This is where most development environments leave off. After all, to most people, database administrative tasks are performed using a tool provided by the DBMS vendor. Luckily for us, the developers of Visual InterDev didn't feel this way. As you are about to see, if you need to perform such database admin chores as changing an existing table's definition, creating a new table, or creating a relationship between two tables, you can do so without ever having to leave the comfort of Visual InterDev.

Adding a Column to an Existing Table

Because none of us are perfect, there will be times when—after creating and populating a table—you will want to modify that table's definition. As an example, you will now modify the Northwind database to add a column to Orders table that will track the terms of an order. To do so, implement the following:

1. Locate the Tables entry in the Data View and expand it to display a list of the existing tables.

2. Now, right-click the Orders table.

3. When the table's context menu is displayed, select the Design menu option.

4. This results in the grid you see in Figure 15.11. This grid displays the columns and their properties for the table. In this grid, each row represents a single column or field in the table, and each column represents an attribute of that column (for example, datatype, length, and precision).

FIGURE 15.11

The Database Designer provides a very easy, intuitive means of adding and modifying a table's columns.

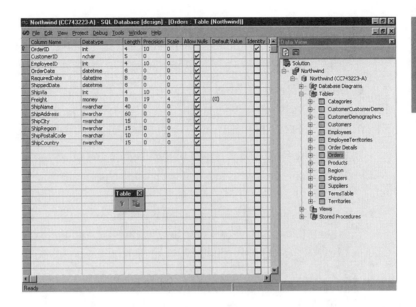

5. Now, click in the first grid column (the one that does not have a heading) of the second row. This is how you select the column of a table. As visual feedback, Visual InterDev will highlight the row to show that it is currently selected.

6. Right-click to display the context menu for this column and after the menu has been displayed, select the Insert Column menu option.

7. Now you can type in the properties that you want to give your new column. In this case specify a Column Name of TermId and a Datatype of int.

8. When you have finished, save your work. You have just added a new column to the Orders table of the Northwind sample database.

Removing a Column from an Existing Table

Removing a column from a table is even easier than adding a new column. To do so, follow these steps:

1. Locate the desired table in the Data View and right-click on it.

2. Select the Design menu option.

3. Select the desired column and after right-clicking on it, select the Delete Column menu option.

Modifying the Properties of a Column in an Existing Table

To modify the properties of a column, do the following:

1. Locate the desired table in the Data View and right-click on it.

2. Select the Design menu option.

3. Each row in the grid represents a column in the table. Therefore, locate the desired column and make the necessary changes to the desired properties.

Creating New Tables

To continue the example of adding terms to the Northwind database, you will now create the Terms table to illustrate how to add new tables to a database, using the following steps:

1. Right-click the background of the diagram and select the New Table menu option.

2. When the Choose Name dialog appears, type in the value of Terms and click the OK button.

3. Just as you saw when you added a column to the Orders table, a grid will be displayed that enables you to create and modify columns to the table. At this point, add the columns found in Table 15.1.

TABLE 15.1   Columns for the Terms Table

Column Name	Datatype
TermId	int
TermDesc	char(50)
DueInDays	int
DiscDays	int
DiscPctg	real

4. When finished, save your work to complete the addition of this new table to the database.

 When you attempt to save the work you've done in the Database Designer, you will see a dialog that asks you to confirm that you want those changes made to the physical database. This area of Visual InterDev will be covered shortly. For now, whenever you get this dialog while saving your work, simply click the Yes button.

Specifying the Primary Key for a Table

To uniquely identify each record in a table, a primary key must be defined. To do this, follow these steps:

15

1. Select the desired table column(s) that will constitute a unique row of data in the table. In this case, that would be the TermId column you just created. Keep in mind here that a primary key cannot consist of any columns where a Null value is valid.

2. Now, select that column and click the Set Primary Key menu option. This causes a small key icon to be displayed to the left of the column name(s), indicating that this/these column(s) is/are the primary key(s) for the table.

Creating a Relationship

A relationship defines how the records in one table relate to records in another table. To create a relationship, follow these steps:

1. Open the Orders database diagram.

2. Open the Data View window and drag the Terms table to the diagram.

3. Position the Orders table and the Terms table next to one another.

4. Click on the Orders table title bar with the right mouse button and select the Column Names menu option so that its columns are also displayed in the diagram.

5. Select the Terms table's primary key (TermId).

6. Now, drag that row and drop it on the Orders table's TermId column.

7. The ensuing dialog allows you to specify a meaningful name for the relationship and other properties that will govern how SQL Server manages the two tables with respect to one another. Figure 15.12 shows your newly created relationship.

FIGURE 15.12

Relationships between tables can be created with a couple mouse clicks.

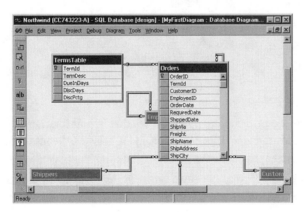

Creating an Index

Technically speaking, when you created the Terms table's primary key, you created an index. However, in the name of performance, you will certainly need to create other indexes in the future. As an example, say that at some point, you want to run reports on which terms are being used the most on your orders. In order to make that query run more efficiently, you might want to add an index to the Orders table for the TermId column. Do that now by implementing the following steps:

1. From the Orders database diagram, right-click the title bar of the Orders table.

2. When the context menu is displayed, select the Property Pages menu option.

3. When the Property Pages dialog is displayed, select the Indexes/Keys tab (see Figure 15.13).

FIGURE 15.13

Named indexes can be created using one or multiple columns of a table in order to achieve more efficient data access.

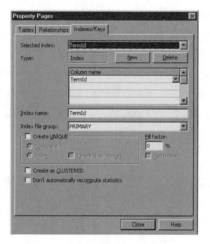

4. Click the New button to create a new index.

5. At the top of the dialog, you can see that Visual InterDev has automatically named the index for you. This can be changed. However, you must define the index first by selecting the columns that constitute it.

6. At this point, using the down arrow in the first row of the columns list box, select the TermId column.

7. Now, change Index Name to something more meaningful such as TermId. Notice that the Selected Index combo box automatically reflects your change.

8. The Create UNIQUE check box allows you to specify that the index will be a unique one. Obviously, because the same term code can be used on multiple

15

orders, you wouldn't want that here, but it is an option that will certainly come in handy in situations in which you want the database to help guarantee uniqueness of a given column.

9. Click the Close button and then save your work.

Defining Constraints

Constraints allow you to specify that the database needs to do certain validation before allowing data to be added or modified. For example, you might set a constraint on a numeric column that stipulates that a value of no greater than 100 can be saved.

To define a constraint, follow these steps:

1. Select the desired table in a database diagram.

2. Right-click on the table's title bar.

3. From the context menu, select the Property Pages menu options.

4. After the Property Pages dialog has been displayed, select the Tables tab.

5. Notice that all the fields in the Check Constraints For Tables And Columns group box might be disabled if no constraints have been created.

6. To create a new constraint, click the New button.

7. Now, using SQL, simply type in the constraint. For example if you want to ensure that a column named Quantity could not be less than 1 and not be greater than 1000, you would enter the following SQL:

```
Quantity > 0 AND Quantity <= 1000
```

8. As with an index, you can give a meaningful name to a constraint.

Saving Changes to a Database Schema

One very handy feature of the Database Designer is that it allows you to test making changes to a database diagram without actually making those changes to the physical database itself. In other words, all the things you do regarding new tables, columns, indexes, and so on aren't actually done to the real database until you explicitly specify that you want them to be. In fact, even when you choose to save your changes, Visual InterDev displays a message box detailing all the database elements that will be affected. Because an inadvertent change could result in lost data or break existing code that is built around the database schema, this dialog gives you one last opportunity to make absolutely certain that you do want to represent these changes in the database.

Generating SQL Scripts

Remember that although you are editing the database using the Database Designer, these changes won't be realized until you save your changes to the physical database. Visual InterDev also gives you the ability to save the SQL required to make those changes in addition to making those changes permanent. This can be done by selecting the File, Save Change Script menu option.

Say that you want to document the exact steps you used to create a database. This would definitely come in handy when you need to create a duplicate of the database. Another great advantage would be with version control. As you learned in Hour 5, "Protecting Your Investment with Version Control," you can set labels on releases of code that enable you to easily revert back to previous releases of your code base. However, what do you do about the database? After all, it does you no good to rollback your software to last month's version if that code base won't work with today's database definition. Therefore, the ability to save your scripts could come in very handy here.

As you make changes to your database definition, you could simply save the scripts to a text file and check those into version control as well. Now if you ever have to roll back your system, you simply create a blank database and run all the scripts that have been accumulated up to that point to produce a database that is 100 percent compatible with the rolled back code base.

Take a look at the process of generating an SQL script. As an example, say that the only change you made was to add a constraint for the Terms table that stipulated that the DueInDays column must have a value between 1 and 90. If you were to choose the File, Save Change Script menu option, Visual InterDev would display the dialog you see in Figure 15.14. This confirmation dialog simply gives you the opportunity to back out of saving the script. It also allows you to specify that you want to always generate a save script when a database change has occurred in the Database Designer. If you click the Yes button to have the script saved, Visual InterDev then displays a dialog that advises you of the filename and location where the script was saved.

FIGURE 15.14

Any database changes made in the Database Designer can be saved to a text file in the form of SQL commands.

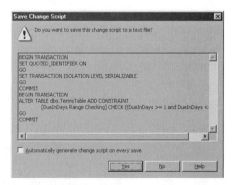

15

Summary

In this hour, you learned what it takes to define and connect to a database via ODBC. After that, you learned how the Database Designer enables you to manipulate the physical schema of a database by making several modifications to the Northwind sample database. Finally, you learned about saving these changes as scripts that can be run against the database at a later time.

Q&A

Q What are some other types of constraints that can be created in the Database Designer and what are they for?

A A check constraint is used when you want the system to verify that the new values meet certain criteria. You saw this type of constraint earlier when you created a constraint for the TermId column of the Terms table. The default constraint is used if you want the system to automatically provide a default when the user or application does not. A foreign key constraint allows you to specify that if the value in a foreign key column does not exist in the foreign table, you do not want to add or update the record. A primary key constraint ensures that a column is unique and does not have a value of NULL. A unique constraint is the same as the primary key constraint with the exception that the column can have a NULL value.

Workshop

The Workshop is designed to help you anticipate possible questions, review what you've learned, and begin thinking ahead to put your knowledge into practice. The answers to the quiz are in Appendix A, "Answers."

Quiz

1. Aside from a Web project, what other kinds of projects can be created with Visual InterDev?
2. How can you use OLE DB if there isn't an OLE DB provider for your database?
3. When defining a data connection, what are the two ways you can log on to the database server?
4. What window is used (among other things) to display relationships between tables?
5. How do you add a caption to a database diagram?
6. What is a primary key?

7. What is a relationship?

8. How do you define an index (other than the primary key)?

9. What is a constraint?

10. How can you generate the SQL script that represents changes made in the Database Designer?

Exercise

Create an ODBC data source for the Pubs database and using what you've learned in this hour, make some of the same changes to that database. See if you can figure out where it would make sense to add more columns and then relate them to another table as you did in this hour with the Terms table.

Hour **16**

Using the Query Designer

Last hour, you learned how to create and manipulate the elements that make up a database using the Database Designer. As you will learn in this hour, the Database Designer is just one of the Microsoft Visual Database Tools that makes working with databases a much easier task. Now that you know how to define the schema for a database using the Database Designer, this hour focuses on retrieving data from a database using a tool called the Query Designer.

The Query Designer is another one of the Visual Database Tools, and it allows you to create SQL commands using an intuitive graphical interface. Using this powerful tool, you can create SQL queries that range from simple SELECT statements to complex, multitable queries via simple drag-and-drop operations with the mouse.

The highlights of this hour include

- Graphically designing queries
- Creating queries directly with SQL
- Creating queries from multitable joins

- Setting the search criteria for your queries
- Ordering the results of your queries
- Editing the results of your queries
- Creating queries that modify data

Query Designer Layout

The Query Designer consists of four panes (see Figure 16.1) to aid you in graphically creating, executing, and viewing the results of your database queries:

- The Diagram pane
- The Grid pane
- The SQL pane
- The Results pane

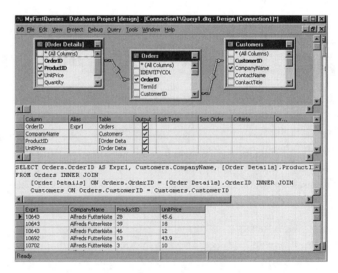

The Diagram Pane

The main pane that is used with the Query Designer is the Diagram pane. This pane contains the different input sources (tables and views) that are being used in the query. Each window in the diagram pane represents a single input source and lists the available data columns as well as icons that indicate how each column is being used in the query.

When two or more input sources are being joined, lines are displayed connecting the participating tables or views. You will see how this is done later in the hour.

The Grid Pane

The Grid pane is used to define the different query options such as the sort order, how to group rows, and the search criteria to use in selecting rows.

The SQL Pane

The SQL pane displays the SQL code for the current query. This is a real treat for those of us who sometimes find it easier to type in the actual SQL rather than click around in a graphical interface. In addition, some queries simply cannot be created graphically and must be defined using the SQL pane. An example of this is a Union query.

The Results Pane

The Results pane uses a grid in order to display the results of an executed query. However, not only can you simply view the results, but you can also edit the actual data within the grid cells as well as add and remove rows. These changes are then realized in the query's underlying database.

Creating Queries

The process of creating a query can be as simple as the following steps:

1. Create the query.
2. Specify the input sources.
3. Specify the columns.
4. Execute the query.
5. Analyze the results.

Creating the Query

The Query Designer makes creating queries a snap in Visual InterDev. To illustrate how this is done, simply following these steps:

1. Open the Project Explorer of a project that contains a database connection. If necessary, you might want to create a database project and use one of the sample databases that is supplied with your DBMS.

2. Right-click the database connection icon and select the Add Query menu option to display the Add Item dialog (see Figure 16.2).

FIGURE 16.2

The Add Item dialog allows you to quickly create new queries.

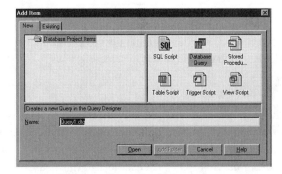

3. At this point, type the name of the query and click the Open button to create the query.
4. After the query has been created, the four Query Designer panes will be displayed (see Figure 16.3), and you can now select the query's input sources. Notice (in the SQL pane) that the query defaults to a SELECT FROM query.

FIGURE 16.3

The default query type is a SELECT FROM query that can be seen in the SQL pane of the Query Designer.

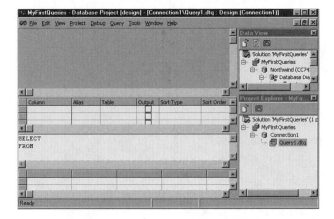

Specifying the Input Sources

A query is built on items called input sources, which can be tables or views. This section will illustrate how to add and remove input sources from a query.

Adding Input Sources

In order to add an input source to a query, you need only to add it to the Diagram pane by implementing the following steps:

1. Open the Data View window.
2. Expand the desired database connection.

3. Select the tables and views that you want to include in the query, and then drag them onto the Diagram pane. Notice that if a relationship exists between two or more input sources, a line connecting the applicable input sources is displayed with icons representing cardinality.

> Query Designer synchronizes the different panes as you update the query regardless of which pane you are using. As an example of this, if you manually type SQL into the SQL pane that references a table or a view that is not currently present in the Diagram pane, Query Designer will automatically add that input source to the Diagram pane.

16

In addition to adding each input source one at a time, you can also add whole predefined groups of input sources. In the last hour, you learned how to create a database diagram that defines a logically related grouping of tables. In order to use one of these groups with a query, just follow these steps:

1. Locate the desired database connection within the Data View and expand it to display the Database Diagrams folder.
2. Expand the Database Diagrams folder to list all the available diagrams.
3. Simply drag the desired diagram folder from the Data View and drop it on the Diagram pane. Each table that had been defined within the diagram will automatically be displayed.

> The Query Designer will not display data columns for an input source if you do not have sufficient access rights to the input source or if the ODBC driver cannot return information about an input source you are using (for example, if no such table currently exists). In such cases, only a title bar is displayed for the input source window and the * (All Columns) check box.

Removing Input Sources

An input source can be removed from a query by doing the following:

1. Right-click the title bar of the desired input source in the Diagram pane.
2. From the context menu, select the Remove menu option.

The act of removing an input source simply removes it from the current query. The underlying database schema is not affect by this. In other words, this action does not delete the table or view from the actual database.

If you have joined multiple tables, the removal of one of the tables in that join will automatically result in the join being removed as well.

Specifying the Columns

So far, you know how to create a query and add input sources to it. Now you will see how to specify which columns you want added to the query's resultset.

Several options for adding columns to a query are as follows:

- Adding individual columns
- Adding all columns of an input source
- Adding all columns of all input sources

Adding Individual Columns

When input sources are added to the Diagram pane, a list of their column names is also displayed. To the left of these column names is a check box that is used to specify whether that column should be included in the query. Therefore, in order to add a column from an input source that already exists on the Diagram pane, simply locate the column name within that input source and click the check box to the left of it. Notice that as you check column names, they are added to the Grid pane automatically.

 So far you've learned that you can drag an input source from the Data View to the Diagram pane and then check the desired column names that you want included in the query. Instead of going through that two-step process, you can also expand an input source in the Data View and directly drag only the desired columns (instead of the input source) to the Diagram pane. Query Designer will automatically add the input source to the Diagram pane and place a check next to the columns that you had dragged over.

Adding All Columns of an Input Source

The very first entry in any input source that is added to the Diagram pane is the * (All Columns) entry. This gives you a very easy and fast way to specify that you want all of an input source's columns used in the current query.

One important thing to know here, however, is that although individually checked items are added to the Grid pane automatically, columns that are added via the * (All Columns) check box are not. Therefore, instead of seeing a row added to the grid for each column of an input source, you will see a single row in which the Table name equals the input source name and the Column name equals a value of *.

Adding All Columns of All Input Sources

To select all the columns of all the input sources, simply do the following:

1. Click the background of the Diagram pane (to deselect any selected items).
2. Right-click the background in order to display the Diagram pane's context menu.
3. Select the Property Pages menu option.
4. From the Property Pages dialog, click the Output All Columns check box (see Figure 16.4).

FIGURE 16.4

Using the Diagram pane's Property Pages dialog, you can specify that you want the entire pane's input source's columns to be included in the current query.

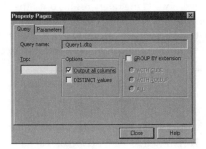

5. Click the Close button to apply this change to the current query.

Doing this will have the same effect on the Grid pane as if you had manually selected each input source and clicked its * (All Columns) entry.

Executing the Query

After you have specified the input source and desired columns, you can execute the query by either selecting the Query, Run menu option from the main menu or by right-clicking the Diagram pane and selecting the Run menu option. Doing this results in the query being run against the database and the results being displayed in the Results pane.

Analyzing the Results

When you've executed a query, the results will be displayed in a grid in the Results pane. At this point, there are a number of things you can do with these results, as follows:

- Print the results
- Modify the data

- Jump to a specific row
- Clear the results

Printing the Results

In order to print the results of a query, you need to do the following:

1. Select the desired rows in the Grid pane. You can select all the grid's rows by making sure that the Grid pane has focus and pressing Ctrl+A.
2. Select the Edit, Copy menu option to copy the data to the Windows Clipboard.
3. Switch to another Windows application such as Microsoft Word for Windows and paste the data.
4. Using the other Windows application, format the data to your liking and then print it.

> The Query Designer inserts the query results onto the Clipboard using tabs as delimiters between columns and carriage return and linefeed characters as delimiters between rows. Therefore, I have found that when printing query results, a spreadsheet program like Microsoft Excel works best.

Modifying the Data

The Query Designer not only allows you to query existing data, but actually gives you the ability to modify the data that is returned as well. The data is changed by simply modifying the values in the different cells of the Results pane's grid. However, whether the database allows you to save your modifications to the data depends on the type of query you have defined and on any constraints, triggers, and permissions that have been defined for the database. For a list of the rules that govern when the results of a query can be updated, refer to the Visual InterDev documentation in Books Online or the MSDN Library Edition.

In order to modify data in a resultset, do the following:

1. Locate the row and cell that you want to modify.
2. Type in the new data value for the cell. Obviously, any properties of the column (for example, datatype, maximum length, and so on) are going to be enforced.
3. Move to another row in the grid in order to attempt to save the changes you've made. The changes will not be saved if you simply set focus to another Query Designer pane. If you want to cancel the change, simply press the Esc key.

In order to enter the database value of NULL, press Ctrl+0.

You can edit a column defined as having a datatype of memo if the column does not display <Long Text>. The Results pane's grid will not allow you to type in more than 900 characters of text in a memo column.

Columns defined as a datatype of BLOB cannot be edited.

16

Jumping to a Specific Row

When the Query Designer executes a query, it caches the results. In other words, it doesn't attempt to write all the rows into the grid because you might never even attempt to view all the rows. Therefore, it writes a few rows to the Results pane's grid and won't write the others until you scroll down to them. This is obviously very good for performance and normally works great. However, it creates a noticeable lag if you are attempting to scroll down through hundreds or even thousands of records. Therefore, an option exists that allows you to jump to a specified row by its row number. To implement this option, follow these steps:

1. Right-click the background of the Results pane.

2. Select the Row menu option.

3. When the Go To Row dialog appears, type in the number of the row that you want to become the current row in the Results pane grid and click the OK button.

Notice that when the Go To Row dialog is displayed, Query Designer has no idea what the last row is. That's because Query Designer itself hasn't read all the rows from the ODBC or OLEDB resultset.

Also, the Query Designer will allow you to type in any value greater than zero. If the value you enter is greater than the total number of returned rows from the query, Query Designer simply places the cursor on the last row in the grid. Now if you were to display the Go To Row dialog, you would see that Query Designer knows how many rows were returned. This is because it had to sequentially read every single row until it got to the one you requested. Therefore, be careful what you ask for! Especially with very large resultsets.

Clearing the Results

If you modify the current query, the Query Designer dims the Results pane to indicate that the contents of the pane are out of synch with the current query definition. What's really interesting here is that it is intelligent. If you make a change (for example, add another column), the Results pane dims. However, if you remove that very same column, the Query Designer is smart enough to realize that you reset the query to its original state and, therefore, the font color of the text in the Results pane returns to normal.

In order to clear the contents of the Results pane, you need to perform the following steps:

1. Right-click the background of the Results pane.
2. Select the Clear Results menu option.

Sorting the Data

After you have added the columns to a query, the Query Designer allows you to order the results of that query in two ways: by the values of a column (or group of columns) or by an expression. The order is controlled by the Sort Order and Sort By columns of the Grid pane. Setting either of these values will be reflected in the ORDER BY clause in the SQL pane.

1. In the Grid pane, locate the row containing the first data column or expression by which you want to sort.
2. Click in the Sort Type column of that row.
3. You will see a small arrow appear in the right corner that allows you to specify whether the sort is ascending or descending. Do this for each column and expression that will act as a sorting agent for the query.
4. Notice that as you do this, the Sort Order field is being updated with a number that is increasing with each column or expression you select. This column allows you to easily change the order of your sort criteria. As an example, say that you wanted to sort the invoices by customer ID and then date. If you inadvertently selected the date column as your first sort column and then the customer ID column, your query will not produce the desired results. However, instead of having to redo your work in this case, all you have to do is reset the Sort Order number to accurately reflect how you want the query to be sorted.

Setting Search Criteria

Search criteria refers to the SQL WHERE clause and can be used to restrict the rows that are returned by a SELECT statement or to restrict the rows affected by any SQL statement that modifies data (such as an UPDATE or DELETE statement).

In order to specify search criteria, simply perform the following steps after you've added the desired input sources to the Diagram pane and selected the desired columns to be used in the query:

1. Using the Grid pane, locate the first row that will be used in the search criteria.

2. Now, locate the Criteria column of the Grid pane. This column is used to specify the search condition of the query. In this column, you can either type in the full expression to use as the search criteria, or you can simply type in a value. If you do not specify an operator, Query Designer automatically inserts the default operator of =.

Figure 16.5 shows an example of a join between the Orders table and Order Details table. The only columns that have been selected for this query are Order ID, Product ID, Unit Price, and Quantity. If you look carefully at the Grid pane, you will see that a search criteria has been defined for the Quantity column where the only records that will be returned are detail records in which the Quantity value is greater than 10. Also notice the SQL WHERE clause in the SQL pane.

FIGURE 16.5

Search criteria can be easily defined using the Grid pane.

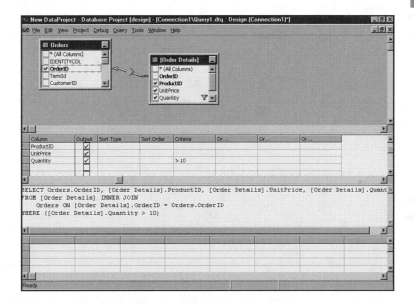

Writing Queries That Modify Data

You learned earlier how to manually modify a given data row in the Results pane after running a query. This works fine if you are going to be modifying a relatively small amount of data. However, if you need to modify many rows, it is much more efficient to simply write a query that can do the necessary modification for you.

Types of Queries That Modify Data

Query Designer allows you to create the following query types that can either modify a database's schema or data:

- Insert query
- Insert Values query
- Update query
- Delete query
- Make Table query

Creating Insert Queries

An Insert query is used to copy data from one table to another or to copy data from one row to another within the same table. Here is how you would create an Insert query:

1. Add the table you want to update to the Diagram pane.
2. Select the Query, Change Type, Insert menu option from the main menu. If you have more than one table in the Diagram pane, Query Designer displays a dialog (see Figure 16.6) whereupon you must select which table is being updated.

FIGURE 16.6

Select the target table of the INSERT INTO...SELECT *statement.*

3. Select the table from the Append To combo box that will receive the new data and click the OK button.
4. After you click OK, the caret will be positioned in the SQL pane with the SQL that has been created by default for an INSERT INTO...SELECT statement.
5. From the input source in the Diagram pane, choose the columns that you want to select.
6. At this point, you've specified the source and target tables as well as the source column(s). Now its time to specify the target column(s). This is done by specifying a column name (of the target table) in the Append column of the Grid pane.
7. Set the necessary search criteria. If no search criteria is specified, all the data will be copied from the source table to the target table.
8. Execute the query by selecting the Query, Run menu option to copy the data.

Insert Values Query

The Insert Values query is used to insert a new row into a table and can be create visually by doing the following:

1. Select the Query, Change Type, Insert Values menu option from the main menu.

2. If you had only one table already in the Diagram pane, the SQL will automatically be set to refer to that table as the target of the data to be inserted.

If you have more than one table already in the Diagram pane, you will see the Insert Values dialog shown in Figure 16.7. Simply select the desired input source and click the OK button.

FIGURE 16.7

The Insert Values dialog allows you to specify which table you want to use as the target table for the new data.

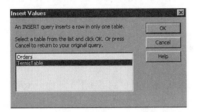

If you did not have a table already in the Diagram pane, select one now. When you do, Query Designer will update the SQL to point to that table as the recipient of the data to be inserted.

3. Click the desired columns in the Grid pane and as you click each column, enter the column's data in the New Value column of the grid.

Update Query

An Update query is used to update the rows that correspond to a particular query. For example, if you receive a shipment of inventory, you would have to update each item received as to the new quantity now available for sale. To create this type of query, follow these steps:

1. Add the table you want to update to the Diagram pane.

2. Select the Query, Change Type, Update menu option from the main menu. If you have more than one table in the Diagram pane, Query Designer displays a dialog whereupon you must select which table is being updated.

3. Select the columns that will be updated.

4. In the New Value column of the Grid pane, specify the value to which the column must be set. This can be a literal, another column name, or an expression.

5. Define which rows are to be updated by specifying the search criteria.

6. Execute the query.

Delete Query

The Delete query allows you to delete rows as a result of a query or expression. To create this type of query, simply follow these steps:

1. Add the desired table to the Diagram pane.

2. Select the Query, Change Type, Delete menu option from the main menu. The Delete query is another type of query that can only be run against a single input source at a time. Therefore, if you have more than one input source on the Diagram pane, Query Designer prompts you to select which input source to use.

3. At this point, running your query will delete all the records from the specified input source. If needed, specify the desired search criteria at this point to limit which rows are deleted.

4. Execute the query to delete the desired rows.

Make Table Query

The last query type that you'll look at is the Make Table query. This type of query allows you to copy rows into a new table. An example of using this would be when you want to create a subset of data work by copying some of the columns of one table into another (new) table. To do so, follow these steps:

1. Add the desired source table to the Diagram pane.

2. Select the Query, Change Type, Make Table menu option from the main menu.

3. At this point, the Make Table dialog will be displayed (see Figure 16.8). This is the target table of the query. Simply name the new table and click the OK button.

FIGURE 16.8

You can create a table and copy data from another table in one step using a Make Table query.

4. Select the desired columns from the source table to be copied into the target table.

5. Execute the query in order to create the new table.

If you have the Data View open when you execute a Make Table query, the database connection's table list will not be updated to include the new table automatically. In order to view the new table in the Data View, you must right-click the database connection icon and select the Refresh menu option from the context menu.

Verifying Your Query's Syntax

The last thing you'll look at in this hour is the ability to verify a query's syntax. This is especially useful when you don't want to actually run the query at this time, but do want to make sure that the SQL is understood by the data source.

In order to verify the syntax of a query, simply open the Query toolbar and click the Verify SQL Syntax button. Query Designer will display a dialog box indicating whether the data source returned an error for the current query's SQL. It's also important to realize that the only thing being verified here is the SQL syntax. In other words, whether the query will violate any defined constraints is not checked.

16

Summary

In this hour, you learned how to use the Query Designer to graphically create single table queries as well as multitable queries. In addition, you used the Grid pane to define the search criteria and ordering of the results for your queries. Finally, you discovered how to modify the returned data and save your queries as script for later use.

Q&A

Q Are there any SQL Server- or Oracle-specific issues I need to know about when using the Query Designer?

A Absolutely. These issues are covered in your Visual InterDev documentation and cover such topics as using synonyms, identifying database objects, and creating outer joins.

Q Can I use the Query Designer with any database?

A You can use any of the Visual InterDev Visual Database Tools against any database, as long as you have either an ODBC driver or an OLE DB provider for that database.

Workshop

The Workshop is designed to help you anticipate possible questions, review what you've learned, and begin thinking ahead to put your knowledge into practice. The answers to the quiz and exercise are in Appendix A, "Answers."

Quiz

1. What are the four panes of the Query Designer?

2. Which pane shows the relationships between two or more tables?

3. How is a new query created for a data connection?

4. How are input sources added to a query?

5. How are single columns added to a query?

6. How can you add all the columns for all the input sources in the Diagram pane to a query?

7. What are the two ways in which you sort the data returned by a query?

8. What are the two ways in which you specify the search criteria for a query?

9. What are the different types of queries that modify data?

10. How can you test a query to make sure that its syntax is correct?

Exercise

Practice what you've learned in this hour by creating different queries that will execute against either the Northwind or the Pubs sample databases.

HOUR 17

Using SQL Scripts, Views, Stored Procedures, and Triggers

In the past couple of hours, you learned about managing tables and queries using the Database Designer and Query Designer, respectively. In this hour, you will focus on several key elements necessary to implementing database connectivity with your Web application. First you will learn how to create SQL scripts so that you can easily automate tedious and time-consuming tasks. After that, you will learn about creating and saving views. Finally, you will discover the wonderful world of stored procedures and triggers and how they make database programming much easier than it would be without them.

The highlights of this hour include

- Working with SQL scripts
- Creating views with the View Designer

- Creating stored procedures
- Debugging stored procedures
- Creating triggers

Working with SQL Scripts

An SQL script is simply an external text file that contains SQL statements. Aside from being external to the database, SQL scripts differ from views and stored procedures in that scripts typically contain the SQL necessary to create your database objects. These statements are then saved so that you can re-create or duplicate your database simply by running the script.

Another advantage of SQL scripts is that they can be used to execute SQL against a database in order to perform tasks that aren't supported by the Visual InterDev user interface. An example of this is granting access rights to users for a given database object.

There are two ways to create SQL scripts in Visual InterDev. One way is to create a blank SQL script file and manually type the needed SQL. The second way is to create the SQL script file from a Visual InterDev SQL script template.

Creating an SQL Script from Scratch

To create an SQL script from scratch, follow these steps:

1. Open a project that contains a data connection.
2. Right-click the data connection from the Project Explorer and select the Add SQL Script menu option.
3. At this point, you will see the Add Item dialog, which enables you to select the type of item you want to create (see Figure 17.1). Because you selected the Add SQL Script menu option, the SQL Script object is highlighted by default. Type in a meaningful name and click the Open button to create the new script.

FIGURE 17.1

The Add Item dialog is used to create a new SQL script.

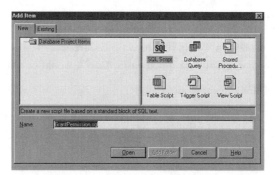

4. Visual InterDev will now display a blank dialog into which you can enter your SQL. If this looks a bit intimidating to you, don't worry. In the next section, you'll see how Visual InterDev enables you to create a new SQL script from a template script. However, because there can't be a template for every possible SQL script, this option at least enables you to manually compose the needed SQL.

In the SQL Editor window, enter the SQL statements that define the database objects you want to add or manipulate.

5. Execute the SQL script via the Tools, Execute menu option or simply save it to be run at a later time.

Creating an SQL Script from a Template

In addition to giving you the ability to create SQL scripts from scratch, Visual InterDev provides several template scripts for you to use. You can use these templates when you want SQL script to create such standard database objects as tables, views, stored procedures, or triggers. To use an SQL script template, follow these steps:

1. Open a project that contains a data connection.

2. Right-click the data connection from the Project Explorer and select the Add SQL Script menu option.

3. The same Add Item dialog shown in Figure 17.1 appears; you can see that Visual InterDev provides several templates from which to pick. At this point, pick the appropriate template for the SQL that you want to create.

4. Listing 17.1 shows the SQL that is generated from the Table Script object. As you can see, the SQL script templates provide a huge benefit over manually typing in the SQL. In this case, the Table Script template checks to see if the table already exists, deletes (drops) the table if it does exist, creates the new table, and provides a block of code in which you would grant rights to the newly created table. The code even includes a comment block so that you can enter a description as to the purpose of the script.

LISTING 17.1   SQL Table Script

```
IF EXISTS (SELECT * FROM sysobjects WHERE type = 'U' AND name = 'Table_Name')
 BEGIN
  PRINT 'Dropping Table Table_Name'
  DROP  Table Table_Name
 END
GO

/***************************************************************************
```

continues

LISTING 17.1 continued

```
**        File:
**        Name: Table_Name
**        Desc:
**
**        This template can be customized:
**
**
**        Auth:
**        Date:
****************************************************************************
**        Change History
****************************************************************************
**        Date:          Author:                    Description:
**        --------       --------                    -----------------------------
**
****************************************************************************/

PRINT 'Creating Table Table_Name'
GO
CREATE TABLE Table_Name
(

)
GO

GRANT SELECT ON Table_Name TO PUBLIC

GO
```

5. Next, modify the code the template provided. Using the Table Script template as an example, at a minimum, you will need to specify the new table name (replacing all occurrences of the placeholder Table_Name).

6. Execute the SQL script using the Tools, Execute menu option or simply save it to be run at a later time.

Managing Views

In the previous hour, you learned that a query is an SQL statement. A view is a virtual table whose data contents are based on the results of a predefined query. A view resembles a table in that it contains a set of named columns and rows of data. However, a view does not exist as a stored set of data values in a database. Instead, a view is a query resultset that is maintained on the server and is updated each time it is opened.

Although the data that a view presents is not technically stored in the view object itself, it is modifiable. When the data that a view displays is modified, the data in the underlying database tables is what is actually being changed. Therefore, changes to data in those underlying tables are automatically reflected in any other views that are based in part or whole on those same tables.

Advantages of Views

Now that you know what a view is and the difference between a view and a query, take a look at some advantages of using views:

- Can limit access to table columns
- Eliminates redundant SQL
- Faster development
- Performance

Can Limit Access to Table Columns

Using a view, you can limit the columns of a table or tables that are accessible by other developers or users. For example, say that you have a database that contains a table called Employees that includes as one of its columns the pay rate of each employee. Because you wouldn't want just anyone to be able to view this column of data, you could define a view that would not contain this column.

Eliminates Redundant SQL

Views enable you to centralize commonly used query results. As an example, say that you have a book publishing database that includes three tables: Titles, Authors, and AuthorTitles. In all likelihood, these tables are going to be joined many times for a variety of reasons. Instead of having each developer write her own query in order to access this data, you could define a view one time and have each developer reference the view as part of her query.

Faster Development

Views enable faster development because other developers can use resultsets that have already been defined. Therefore, if you find that similar queries are being created, you can create a view instead and have the developers reference them. This means less work and fewer bugs because they are using something that has already been tested and used in other situations.

Performance

Say that you have a set of tables that are indexed on certain columns. If other developers don't understand exactly how to express their SQL statements to take advantage of how these indexes have been created, this could result in poor performance. However, if you

17

create a view that takes into account exactly how the SQL statement needs to be formed in order to take advantage of the existing indexes, the other developers can use that view to ensure optimal performance.

Creating a View with the View Designer

Creating a view is done via the View Designer, which works almost identical to the Query Designer except that it creates views instead of queries. To create a view, perform these steps:

1. Open the Data View.

2. Expand the desired database connection and locate the Views folder.

3. Right-click on the Views folder and select the New View menu option.

4. From this point, you will see that the View Designer has the exact same interface as the Query Designer (see Figure 17.2). Simply create your view using the same techniques you learned in the previous hour. In the query shown in Figure 17.2, a view was created that joined the titles, authors, and titleauthor tables of the SQL Server Pubs sample database.

FIGURE 17.2

Creating a view is very similar to creating a query.

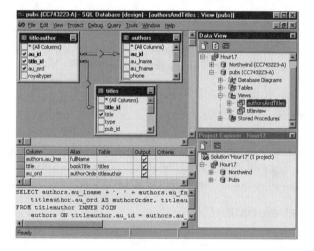

5. When you have finished constructing the view, select the View, Open menu option from the main menu. The results of the view will then be displayed in the Results pane of the View Designer. You can then iteratively test and tweak the view until it yields the desired results.

6. When you are content with the view, you can save it by selecting the File, Save <view name> menu option and entering a name for the view when prompted. As opposed to a query that is saved in an external file associated with the Visual InterDev project, a view is stored in the actual database itself.

7. When you have entered the view name and clicked the OK button, the view will appear under the Views folder in the Data View window.

8. Select the Query, Run menu option in order to view the results of executing the view's SQL.

Encrypting a View

In another example of how Visual InterDev integrates very well with Microsoft SQL Server, the View Designer gives you the ability to encrypt SQL Server views. When you encrypt a view, other users cannot edit it nor can its definition be viewed. Therefore, this is a very powerful feature that enables you to protect the definition of sensitive views.

> After you have encrypted a view and closed it, you will not be able to open that view again in design mode. Therefore, be extremely careful in deciding whether to encrypt a view. Also, because you can specify the encryption option only when the view is open in design mode, you will not be able to reverse this action.

17

To encrypt a view, follow these steps:

1. Open the Data View window.

2. Locate the desired database connection and then expand its Views folder.

3. Right-click the view that you want to encrypt and select the Design menu option.

4. When the view is open in the View Designer, select the View, Property Pages menu option from the main menu.

5. When the Property Pages dialog is displayed, click the Encrypt View check box and the Close button (see Figure 17.3).

FIGURE 17.3

Encrypting a view is a means of ensuring that a view's definition cannot be displayed or modified.

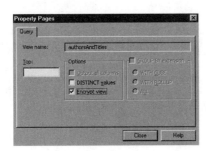

6. Save the view.

Working with Stored Procedures

Stored procedures are precompiled SQL statements that are stored in the database. Because stored procedures are named database objects, they can be referenced from an external application just like a table or a view.

The main difference between a stored procedure and a query is that a stored procedure is written in a database specific language that allows user-declared variables, conditional statements, the use of other database objects (such as queries and views), and many other powerful features supported by the language.

Stored procedures provide the following advantages:

- Any number of SQL statements can be stored and executed from a single stored procedure.
- Other stored procedures can be referenced from within a stored procedure. The advantage here is that a very complex set of database interactions can be broken into a series of simpler stored procedures.
- With the capability for one stored procedure to use another stored procedure, you can reuse common SQL code.
- Because the stored procedures exists and is executed on the server, network traffic is kept to a minimum.
- The performance of stored procedures is much faster than that of queries because stored procedures are precompiled on the database, thereby being optimized by the time they are run.

Creating a Stored Procedure

As with the other database objects that you've seen presented throughout this book, Visual InterDev provides a very simple, intuitive way of creating stored procedures.

1. Open the Data View.
2. Expand the desired database connection and locate the Stored Procedures folder.
3. Right-click on the Stored Procedures folder and select the New Stored Procedure menu option.
4. At this point, Visual InterDev will create a template stored procedure from which to work (see Figure 17.4).

FIGURE 17.4

Stored procedures are written in a superset of the SQL language that allows for parameters, variables, and condition logic.

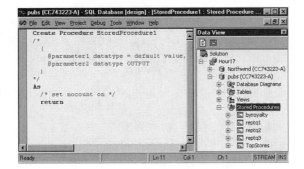

5. Notice that the first line contains the name of the stored procedure in the format of StoredProcedure*n*, where *n* is used to make the name unique. If you want, you can change this name at any time.

   Write the SQL as needed to perform the necessary work.

> Microsoft SQL Server defines a language called Transact-SQL (TSQL) that is used to write stored procedures. This language is an enhanced version of SQL and would take several hours to cover adequately. Therefore, if you want to learn more about TSQL than you can figure out by simply playing with the sample databases that are installed with SQL Server, I would recommend referencing the Microsoft SQL Server Programmer's Toolkit.

6. When finished, the stored procedure can be saved by selecting the File, Save <stored procedure name> menu option from the main menu and entering a unique name for the stored procedure when prompted.

7. After you have entered the name of the stored procedure and clicked the OK button, it will appear under the Stored Procedures folder in the Data View window.

8. In order to execute the stored procedure, select the Tools, Execute menu option.

Permissions and Stored Procedures

In some cases, other users will not be able to use the stored procedure until you have set the execute permission for the stored procedure. This can be done at a user level and a group level using the SQL GRANT EXECUTE command.

> When a stored procedure is created in an Oracle database, execute permission must be explicitly granted. Therefore, if a user who needs to execute a stored procedure hasn't been given explicit permission to do so, that user must have the EXECUTE ANY PROCEDURE system privilege.

To grant permission to a user or a group of users, you first create a new SQL script as you learned earlier in the hour. Next, enter the following SQL in the script file:

```
GRANT EXECUTE ON <stored procedure name> TO PUBLIC
```

Then save and execute the SQL script file.

To grant permission to all users, you first create a new SQL script and then enter the following SQL in the script file:

```
GRANT EXECUTE ON <stored procedure name> TO <userid or group name>
```

Save and execute the SQL script, and you are finished.

Working with Triggers

Say that you have a distribution system in which you want a transaction record created every time inventory is changed. Because many applications affect inventory (for example, order entry, picking ticket update, receiving, backorders, and so on), it would mean that every one of those programs would have to write a transaction record when they've finished doing their work. This design has several flaws:

- Every programmer who writes code that updates inventory has to remember to add the logic to also write the transaction record or call a function that will.
- If the way the record is written changes, all these disparate applications and functions must be updated.
- What do you do if the system on which your distribution application is running allows interactive SQL to be executed against the database?

As you can see, what is needed in cases like this is a way for the database to execute the necessary code when a user-defined event happens (such as a certain table being modified). This is what triggers were invented for.

A *trigger* is a type of stored procedure that executes (fires) when data in a specified table is modified. As with any stored procedure, triggers can query other tables and can include complex SQL statements and condition logic. Triggers are generally used to enforce complex business rules or requirements.

Creating a Trigger

To create a trigger, first open the Data View window. For the desired database connection, expand the Tables folder. Right-click on the table that you want to be monitored for any modification. When the context menu appears, select the New Trigger menu option.

At this point, Visual InterDev will open the SQL editor and create the skeleton trigger code that you see in Figure 17.5.

FIGURE 17.5

Visual InterDev allows for the easy incorporation of triggers into your database development.

As you can see, Visual InterDev automatically names the trigger for you in the format of *tableName*_Trigger*n*, where *tableName* is the name of the table that will be monitored for modification by the database and *n* is used to create a unique trigger name.

The syntax is very easy to follow on a trigger. The For clause simply allows you to specify what type of modification you want to monitor for (that is, Insert, Update, or Delete). The As clause allows you to specify the transactions that will take place when any of those modifications occur to the specified table.

Select the File, Save <trigger name> menu option from the main menu. Notice that when you save the trigger, it appears in the Data view under the table being monitored. Now you need to test the trigger.

All you have to do in order to test a trigger is simply simulate the actual event that is being monitored. For example, if you have written a trigger that will write a record into a summary table every time an item record is updated, simply create a dummy item record and modify it. This should cause the trigger to fire and the summary table record to be written.

Summary

Over the past hour, you learned several key elements necessary to incorporate database connectivity into your Web application. First you learned how to create SQL scripts to automate routine tasks. After that, you learned about creating and saving views. Finally, you discovered the stored procedures and triggers and how they make the task of database development much easier.

Q&A

Q Can I create an SQL script that calls a stored procedure, and if so, how?

A You can create an SQL script that runs any of your stored procedures or even the built-in stored procedures of your database. For example, if you are using SQL Server, you can run stored procedures such as sp_help or sp_who. To call a stored procedure from an SQL script, simply use the exec function, like this:

```
exec sp_who
```

```
exec_help
```

Q My company uses both SQL Server 6.5 and 7. How can I determine at run-time the version of SQL Server to which I am connected?

A You can use @@Version. Here's how you would print the version number to the Output window of Visual InterDev:

```
select @@version
```

Workshop

The Workshop is designed to help you anticipate possible questions, review what you've learned, and begin thinking ahead to put your knowledge into practice. The answers to the quiz and exercise are in Appendix A, "Answers."

Quiz

1. What is an SQL script?
2. What is a view?
3. What is the difference between a view and a table?
4. Can the data that a view displays be modified, and if so, what are the consequences regarding other views?
5. What are some advantages of views?
6. What is the purpose of encrypting a view, and how is it done?

7. What are stored procedures?

8. What is the difference between a stored procedure and a query?

9. How is permission given to other users so that they can run your stored procedures?

10. What is a trigger?

Exercise

Using the Pubs sample database, create a new summary table for sales. Then create a trigger that will automatically create a new summary record each time a sale is made.

17

HOUR **18**

Accessing Data with ADO

With the introduction of Visual InterDev 6, there are now several ways to interact with a database. These methods include manually writing script that implements the ActiveX Data Objects (ADO), using the new Visual InterDev Data Environment's (DE) database connections and database commands, and using the Design Time Controls (DTCs). Because at some level all these methods use ADO, this hour you will learn the basics of writing Active Server Pages and ADO.

The highlights of this hour include

- An introduction to ADO
- Using ADO from an ASP
- Writing server-side script to access data
- Inserting data into a database
- Writing an application to create new records

An Introduction to ADO

ADO is Microsoft's newest programmatic interface for data objects. ADO is a COM-based technology that has been designed to replace the older Data Access Objects (DAO) and Remote Data Objects (RDO). Unlike DAO and RDO, which are designed only for accessing relational databases, ADO is more general and can be used to access all sorts of different types of data, including ISAM database, spreadsheets, and any other types of documents. Because ADO was designed to allow access to any kind of data (not just databases), you will often hear the very generic term *data store* used in conjunction with ADO.

The ADO Object Model

As you can see in Figure 18.1, ADO is a simple object model consisting of only six objects and two collections. In this hour, however, I concentrate on the three objects that you will use most often in your ADO development (`Connection`, `Recordset`, and `Command`).

FIGURE 18.1
The ADO object model.

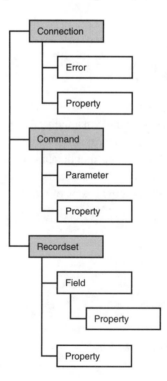

The `Connection` Object

The ADO `Connection` object creates a connection to a data provider (the equivalent of an Open Database Connectivity (ODBC) driver). Notice that this object is at the top of the ADO food chain, so you must create an ADO `Connection` object before you can do anything else with ADO.

The `Recordset` Object

The ADO `Recordset` object creates a set of records from a query. For example, if you want to retrieve all the invoices for a particular customer, you would run the appropriate query against the necessary tables in order to return the data in a recordset. If you're more familiar with ODBC and SQL, you might be accustomed to hearing the term *cursor* or *result set*. An ADO `Recordset` object provides this same functionality. After an ADO `Recordset` object has been returned from the database, the application can move (scroll) through it forward and backward.

The `Command` Object

The `Command` object is another object you will use quite often if you manually code script to access the ADO object model. This object is used to specify an SQL command, a stored procedure, or a query to execute on the database server.

The Errors Collection

The ADO Errors collection contains the errors that have occurred from the most recent failed database interaction. ADO defines a collection for containing the errors because a single SQL statement can result in multiple errors.

ADO Code Snippets

At this point, take a look at how the different tasks of connecting to a data provider, retrieving data, and writing data are achieved using ADO.

> All the code snippets and examples in this hour are written using VBScript. In addition, the SQL Server Pubs sample database is used as the data store for the examples.

18

Connecting to a Data Provider Using ADO

As mentioned previously, connecting to a data provider is done via the ADO Connection object. Listing 18.1 illustrates how to create, open, and close a connection using VBScript.

LISTING 18.1   Using ADO to Connect to a Data Provider

```
 1: 'declare a variable to hold the ADO Connection object
 2: dim DatabaseConnection
 3:
 4: 'use the Server object to create an instance of an ADO Connection
    ➥object
 5: Set DatabaseConnection = Server.CreateObject("ADODB.Connection")
 6:
 7: 'open the connection, specifying the user id and password
 8: DatabaseConnection.Open "DSN=Pubs", "sa", ""
 9:
10: 'Use database connection
11:
12: 'close the connection when finished
13: DatabaseConnection.Close
```

Using a Recordset to Retrieve Data

As mentioned previously, the ADO Recordset object can be used to execute a command against the data store that will return a group of records. This recordset can be iterated in order to obtain the returned data. Listing 18.2 shows how easy it is to write the VBScript and ADO that will read all the authors from the Authors table of the Pub database. Notice the mixing of HTML and script that you learned about earlier in the book. Figure 18.2 shows the results of running this code.

LISTING 18.2   Displaying All the Authors in the Authors Table

```
 1: <%
 2:  dim conn
 3:  Set conn = Server.CreateObject("ADODB.Connection")
 4:  conn.Open "DSN=Pubs", "sa", ""
 5:
 6:  dim rs 'recordset
 7:  dim sql 'sql statement
 8:
 9:  set rs=Server.CreateObject("ADODB.Recordset")
10:  sql = "select * from authors"
11:  rs.Open sql, conn
12: %>
13: <H1>Listing of all Authors</H1>
14: <%
```

```
15:  do while not rs.EOF
16:    Response.Write(rs("au_fname") & " " & rs("au_lname") & "<BR>")
17:    rs.MoveNext
18:  loop
19:
20:  rs.Close
21:  conn.Close
22: %>
```

FIGURE 18.2

The ADO Recordset
object in action.

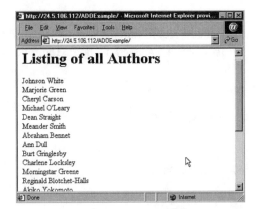

Listing of all Authors

Johnson White
Marjorie Green
Cheryl Carson
Michael O'Leary
Dean Straight
Meander Smith
Abraham Bennet
Ann Dull
Burt Gringlesby
Charlene Locksley
Morningstar Greene
Reginald Blotchet-Halls
Akiko Yokomoto

18

Updating Data Using the ADO Recordset Object

If the application had originally requested the data as part of a recordset, the data values of
the recordset can be changed and the Recordset.Update method called. In the following
simple example, the code opens a recordset based on the Authors table (notice the parameters passed to the Recordset Open method) and updates the first record. Obviously, this
isn't a very realistic example. However, the intention here is to show how the Update
method works, regardless of where in your code you actually use it.

```
dim conn
Set conn = Server.CreateObject("ADODB.Connection")
conn.Open "DSN=Pubs", "sa", ""

dim rs 'recordset
dim sql 'sql statement

set rs=Server.CreateObject("ADODB.Recordset")
sql = "select * from authors ore"

rs.Open sql, conn, 1, 2

rs.MoveFirst
%>

BEFORE=<%=rs("au_lname")%><p>
```

```
<%rs("au_lname") = CStr("Test Value")%>

AFTER=<%=rs("au_lname")%><p>

<%
rs.Update

rs.Close
conn.Close
```

If the application is saving a new record into the recordset, an additional step is required (the calling of the `Recordset` object's `AddNew` method). The following is an example of how to use the `AddNew` method:

```
<%
dim conn
Set conn = Server.CreateObject("ADODB.Connection")
conn.Open "DSN=Pubs", "sa", ""

dim rs 'recordset
set rs=Server.CreateObject("ADODB.Recordset")

rs.Open "authors", conn, 1, 2

rs.AddNew
rs("au_id") = CStr("123-45-6789")
rs("au_fname") = CStr("Tom")
rs("au_lname") = CStr("Archer")
rs("phone") = CStr("911")
rs("address") = CStr("www.SourceDNA.com")
rs("city") = CStr("Atlanta")
rs("state") = CStr("GA")
rs("zip") = CStr("30338")
rs("contract") = CInt(1)
rs.Update

rs.Close
conn.Close
%>
```

Notice how the `Recordset` is not being passed the `select *...` SQL string, but instead is simply being passed the name of the table to be opened. This has nothing to do with the `AddNew` method. I'm simply illustrating another way to open a recordset. This particular method is typically used when you are opening a recordset that returns all the records from a table or view.

Using the Command Object to Execute SQL Statements

Now, suppose that you want to execute an SQL statement against the database. For example, you might want to use the SQL INSERT statement instead of opening a record-set. This can be done using the ADO Command object by following these steps:

1. Create a Connection object in order to connect to the data provider.

2. Create a Command object.

3. Set the Command object's ActiveConnection property.

4. Format the SQL statement.

5. Set the Command object's CommandText property to the value of the SQL statement.

6. Call the Command object's Execute method to run the SQL.

7. Call the Connection object's Close method.

Listing 18.3 shows a partial example of inserting a record into the Title table of the Pubs database.

LISTING 18.3   Inserting a Record Using the Command Object

```
 1: Set DatabaseConnection = Server.CreateObject("ADODB.Connection")
 2: DatabaseConnection.Open "DSN=Pubs", "sa", ""
 3:
 4: set commandObject=Server.CreateObject("ADODB.Command")
 5: set commandObject.ActiveConnection=DatabaseConnection
 6:
 7: strInsertSql = "insert into Titles"
 8: strInsertSql = strInsertSql + " values("
 9:
10: strInsertSql = strInsertSql + "'" + Request.Form.Item("txtTitleID")
    ➥ + "',"
11: ' format sql string with remaining columns
12:
13: strInsertSql = strInsertSql + ")"
14:
15: commandObject.CommandText = strInsertSql
16: commandObject.Execute
17:
18: DatabaseConnection.Close
```

18

Example Maintenance Application

So far, I've talked a lot about ADO and how easy it is to use. However, the best way to learn something is by doing it. So, roll up your sleeves and prepare to create your first database-driven Web application!

Much as the "Hello, World" application is generally used to write your first application in a given language, a simple, straightforward maintenance application is typically used when interacting with a database for the first time from a new development environment. The reasoning is that a maintenance application is not going to be burdened with a lot of complex business rules that will make concentrating on the database I/O difficult. Therefore, your first Web database application will be used to maintain the Titles table of the Pubs sample database that ships with the SQL Server.

At this point, create a new Web project (in a new solution) called `TitleMaintenance`. This solution will house not only the Web project, but also the database connection to the Pubs database.

Creating the Menu Page

The menu page serves as this Web application's home page. In addition to the menu entries (hyperlinks to other pages), it can also serve as an introduction to the system. To add a menu page, follow these steps:

1. Add a new HTML page to your project called `default.htm`. As you learned earlier, anytime you have a Web application with a Web page named default.htm, the page is automatically loaded when the user surfs to the correct URL.

2. Add a title and several menu links to the menu page so that it appears the same as Figure 18.3 when finished.

FIGURE **18.3**

If your Web application is going to consist of several pages, it's a good idea to include a Web page with menu options.

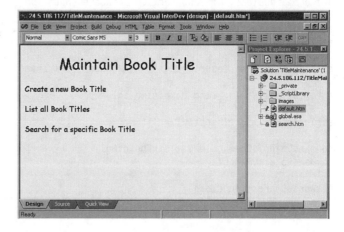

3. After you've created the menu page, you'll need to connect the menu entries to the appropriate pages. For now, you'll just do the first menu entry. Select the text Create a New Book Title and select the HTML, Link Menu Option from the main menu.

4. When the Hyperlink dialog appears, type in `CreateNewBookTitle.asp` as the name of the page that will be loaded when the user clicks on this menu option (see Figure 18.4).

FIGURE 18.4

The Hyperlink dialog enables you to easily create a link to an HTML page or an Active Server Page.

5. At this point, you would normally (especially for an Internet application) fix up the page by adding such things as banners, cool menus, and scrolling text. The techniques for doing these sorts of things is covered in the hours on scripting and DHTML. However, for the purposes of this demo, I've kept the UI as simple as possible in order to concentrate on the database interaction.

Creating the Data Entry Page

Now that you've created the main menu page and the database connection, it's time to create the page that will enable the user to enter the data which will be saved to the database. To do so, follow these steps:

1. Add an Active Server Page called CreateNewBookTitle.asp to the TitleMaintenance project.

2. Open the page in source view and add the following <FORM> tag after the <BODY> tag:

   ```
   <FORM name=frmCreateNewBookTitle>
   ```

3. Add a </FORM> tag immediately before the closing </BODY> tag.

4. Add a title as you did on the default.htm page with the text Create New Book Title.

5. One trick to creating a data entry form so that the controls are laid out in a visually appealing way is to use a table. Select the Table, Insert Table menu option to display the Insert Table dialog.

6. From the Insert Table dialog, set the number of rows to 10 (the number of fields in the Titles table) and the number of columns to 2 (to accommodate the prompt and the control). Click the OK button when finished.

7. In the first row and first column, type the text `Title ID:`. This is the prompt text for the Title ID Textbox control.

8. Open the Toolbox window. Position the caret in the first row and second column. Now, double-click the Textbox control. This is the control for the Title ID.

18

9. Display the properties for the Textbox control and change its ID and Name to `txtTitleID`.

10. At this point, using Table 18.1, create the prompts and controls it contains. Note that all controls should be Textbox controls except for the Notes control, which should be created as a TextArea control.

TABLE 18.1   Prompts and Controls to Be Added to the CreateNewBookTitle.asp Active Server Page

Prompt	Control Name and ID
Title:	`txtTitle`
Type:	`txtType`
Publisher ID:	`txtPubID`
Price:	`txtPrice`
Advance:	`txtAdvance`
Royalty:	`txtRoyalty`
YTD Sales:	`txtYTDSales`
Publication Date:	`txtPubDate`
Notes:	`txtNotes`

11. After the prompts and controls have been added to the page, select the Source view tab and locate the `<TABLE>` tag and change its border attribute to `0`. The table definition should look similar to Listing 18.4.

LISTING 18.4   Table Definition for Prompts and Controls

```
 1: <P align=left><FONT face="Comic Sans MS" size=6>
 2: <TABLE border=0 cellPadding=1 cellSpacing=1 height=386
 3: style="HEIGHT: 386px; WIDTH: 533px" width=88.54%>
 4:
 5:    <TR>
 6:        <TD>Title ID:</TD>
 7:        <TD>
 8:            <INPUT id=txtTitleID name=txtTitleID></TD></TR>
 9:    <TR>
10:        <TD>Title:</TD>
11:        <TD>
12:            <INPUT id=txtTitle name=txtTitle></TD></TR>
13:    <TR>
14:        <TD>Type:</TD>
15:        <TD>
16:            <INPUT id=txtType name=txtType></TD></TR>
```

```
17:     <TR>
18:         <TD>Publisher ID:</TD>
19:         <TD>
20:             <INPUT id=txtPubID name=txtPubID></TD></TR>
21:     <TR>
22:         <TD>Price:</TD>
23:         <TD>
24:             <INPUT id=txtPrice name=txtPrice></TD></TR>
25:     <TR>
26:         <TD>Advance:</TD>
27:         <TD>
28:             <INPUT id=txtAdvance name=txtAdvance></TD></TR>
29:     <TR>
30:         <TD>Royalty:</TD>
31:         <TD>
32:             <INPUT id=txtRoyalty name=txtRoyalty></TD></TR>
33:     <TR>
34:         <TD>YTD Sales:</TD>
35:         <TD>
36:             <INPUT id=txtYTDSales name=txtYTDSales></TD></TR>
37:     <TR>
38:         <TD>Publication Date:</TD>
39:         <TD>
40:             <INPUT id=txtPubDate name=txtPubDate></TD></TR>
41:     <TR>
42:         <TD>Notes:</TD>
43:         <TD><TEXTAREA id=txtNotes name=txtNotes style="HEIGHT:
    ➥ 38px; WIDTH: 349px">                         </TEXTAREA>
    ➥</TD></TR>
44:     </TABLE></FONT></P>
```

Notice that you can easily align controls on a page by placing them in a table and setting the table's border to 0 so that the table itself doesn't show up to the user.

12. Finally, add a Submit button (captioned Save Title) and a Reset button (captioned Clear Form) to the bottom of the page.

13. When you're finished, your page should look like Figure 18.5.

Submitting the Form for Processing

The last thing you need to do to the form is modify the <FORM> tag so that when you click the Submit button, the data is sent to another Active Server Page that will insert the data into the database. To modify it, follow these steps:

1. Open the CreateNewBookTitle.asp file in Source view

2. Locate the <FORM> tag and modify it so that when finished, it appears as follows:

```
<FORM name=frmCreateNewBookTitle method=POST action=
➥InsertBookTitle.asp>
```

18

FIGURE 18.5

A data entry form for the `TitleMaintenance` *application.*

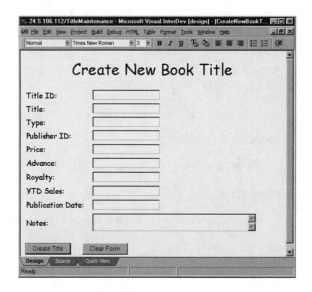

Inserting Data into a Database Using ADO

You can choose from several different methods in order to interact with a database from an Active Server Page. I've chosen ADO for this example, simply because it is the most widely used. First, create a new Active Server Page called InsertbookTitle.asp and open it in Source view. Insert the code shown in Listing 18.5 immediately after the <BODY> tag. If it looks like a lot of work, don't worry. As shown in the explanation that follows the code, all this code is simple, and most of it is nothing more than formatting the SQL string to be passed to the database in order to insert the record.

When typing in the code shown in Listing 18.5, do not forget the <% and %> tags that are on lines 1 and 51, respectively. As you learned in Hour 11, "Developing Active Server Pages," these are needed to tell the browser the code is script that must be executed on the server.

LISTING 18.5   Inserting a Record into the Titles Table Using ADO

```
1   <%
2   sub DisplayConfirmation
3     dim str
4     str = "Book title '" + Request.Form.Item("txtTitle") + "' has been
      ➥successfully written to the database. "
5     Response.Write(str)
```

```
6    Response.Write("Press your browser's Back button to return to add
     ➥more Book Titles")
7  end sub

8  sub WriteRecord
9   dim strInsertSql
10  dim commandObject
11
12  Set DatabaseConnection = Server.CreateObject("ADODB.Connection")
13  DatabaseConnection.Open "DSN=Pubs", "sa", ""
14
15  set commandObject=Server.CreateObject("ADODB.Command")
16  set commandObject.ActiveConnection=DatabaseConnection
17
18  strInsertSql = "insert into Titles"
19  strInsertSql = strInsertSql + " values("
20
21  strInsertSql = strInsertSql + "'" + Request.Form.Item("txtTitleID")
     ➥ + "',"
22  strInsertSql = strInsertSql + "'" + Request.Form.Item("txtTitle")
     ➥ + "',"
23  strInsertSql = strInsertSql + "'" + Request.Form.Item("txtType")
     ➥ + "',"
24  strInsertSql = strInsertSql + "'" + Request.Form.Item("txtPubID")
     ➥ + "',"
25  strInsertSql = strInsertSql + Request.Form.Item("txtPrice") + ","
26  strInsertSql = strInsertSql + Request.Form.Item("txtAdvance") + ","
27  strInsertSql = strInsertSql + Request.Form.Item("txtRoyalty") + ","
28  strInsertSql = strInsertSql + Request.Form.Item("txtYTDSales") + ","
29  strInsertSql = strInsertSql + "'" + Request.Form.Item("txtNotes")
     ➥ + "',"
30  strInsertSql = strInsertSql + "'" + Request.Form.Item("txtPubDate")
     ➥ + "'"
31
32  strInsertSql = strInsertSql + ")"
33
34  'Response.Write(strInsertSql)
35
36  commandObject.CommandText = strInsertSql
37  commandObject.Execute
38
39  DatabaseConnection.Close
40 end sub
41
42 '*******************************************
43 'Mainline of application
44 '*******************************************
45 if Request.Form.Count <= 0 then
```

18

continues

Listing **18.5** continued

```
46 Response.Write("You have entered this form incorrectly. "
    "This page is only accessible from the CreateNewBookTitle.asp page.")
47 else
48  Call WriteRecord
49  Call DisplayConfirmation
50 end if
51 %>
```

The first thing to note is where the page will begin processing (lines 45–50). As you can see, the page first checks to make sure that the only way this page was called was from another form. In other words, because this page relies on information being passed to it via the Request object, you cannot allow a user to simply navigate to it by supplying the URL on the browser address bar. Therefore, the Request object's form count is verified to be greater than zero. If it is, the WriteRecord subroutine is called (line 48), followed by the confirmation to the user that the write was successful (line 49).

The next thing to look at is the WriteRecord subroutine. In line 12, the Active Server Page's Server object creates an ADO Connection object. The ADO Connection object is used to open a specific data source (Pubs) on line 13.

After the page has connected to the database, it has to create a Command object with which it can execute an SQL command against the database. Therefore, a Command object is created (line 15) and its ActiveConnection property is set to the Connection object.

Lines 18 through 32 simply format the SQL string that will be used to insert the new record into the database. Notice that the formatting is single quotes used around the text fields. If this were a real application, you would need to verify that the user entered single quotes within the fields. Line 36 sets the Command object's CommandText property equal to the SQL string that has been formatted. At this point, the only thing left to do is tell the Command object to execute the command, which is exactly what line 37 does. After the command has been executed, line 39 closes the database connection and the WriteRecord subroutine ends.

Testing the Example Application

At this point, you should be able to run your application. As shown in Figures 18.6 and 18.7, I've entered some test data in the data entry form and saved a record. Upon successfully saving the data, you will receive confirmation that the record was written to the database.

FIGURE 18.6

The Create New Book Title Web page.

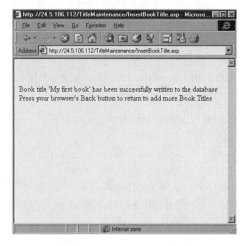

FIGURE 18.7

Confirmation of a successful write to the database.

As you learned in Hour 15, "Using the Database Designer," you can create tables with constraints that disallow a modification to an existing record or the addition of a new record if the data is not considered to be valid (per the constraint). The Titles table of the Pubs database is an example of this. For this reason, you might encounter errors when entering data into this application if you do not abide by these constraints. The values used in Figure 18.6, however, will work with these table constraints.

Summary

In this hour, you learned how to access data from an Active Server Page using ADO. You also learned about the ADO object model and the different ADO objects and collections that are used to connect to, read data from, insert data into, and disconnect from a database. You finished up the hour by writing a simple maintenance application that uses ADO to create new records in the Titles table of the Pubs database.

Q&A

Q **If I'm using VBScript, which is a subset of Visual Basic, can I use DAO to access data from my Active Server Pages?**

A Yes, you can. However, I would recommend using ADO for a couple of reasons. First, ADO performs much better than DAO. Second, ADO (and the underlying OLEDB) is definitely the future of programmatic data access.

Q **Why is it that, when I open a recordset and attempt to update a record or add a new one, I receive the error `The operation requested by the application is not supported by the provider`?**

A This is because you didn't open the recordset in a mode that allows updates. Try this instead. Notice the last two parameters:

```
<yourRecordset>.Open sqlStmt, connection, 1, 2
```

Workshop

The Workshop is designed to help you anticipate possible questions, review what you've learned, and begin thinking ahead to put your knowledge into practice. The answers to the quiz and exercise are in Appendix A, "Answers."

Quiz

1. What are the three ways in which to access data from an Active Server Page using Visual InterDev?
2. What are the three main objects in the ADO object model?
3. Why does ADO define an Errors collection instead of an `Errors` object?
4. What is a `Recordset` object used for?
5. How is a connection to a data provider created?
6. How are fields within a recordset specified?
7. How is a record added to a database using the `Recordset` object?

8. What is the Command object used for?

9. What Connection object method is used to run the SQL against the database?

10. What VBScript can be used to iterate through a recordset?

Exercise

Add to the TitleMaintenance Web application to enable the user to search for a specific title.

18

Hour 19

Using the Data Environment

Through ADO and ASP scripting, a Web application can connect to a data store to execute SQL statements, retrieve and update data, and (depending on the data store) use data objects such as stored procedures and queries. However, the main drawback against writing a script that directly accesses the ADO object model is that there's no inherent means of reusing the database code. For example, if you write the ADO necessary to read all the authors from the Authors table and then need to access that same list of data on another page, you basically have to copy the original code and paste it into the new page.

To help solve this problem, Microsoft introduced a technology called the *Data Environment* with Visual InterDev 6. The Data Environment not only makes it much simpler to access data from a server page, but it does so in such a way that the database code can be reused throughout the Web application. The Data Environment is actually composed of two parts. The first part is the object model, which you'll learn about in this hour, and the second is the data-bound controls, which you'll discover in the next hour.

The highlights of this hour include the following:

- Discovering the Data Environment
- Learning how to create data commands
- Writing script to execute data commands
- Writing script to retrieve data

Data Environment Overview

The Data Environment is a wrapper for ADO that allows for the definition and management of reusable data objects within a Web application. With the Data Environment, you can define one or more data connections, with each data connection referencing one or more data commands. Each of these data commands then represents a method for querying or modifying the database. When the Data Environment has been defined for a Web application, the information is stored in the global.asa file so that any defined data connections and commands can be shared by multiple Web pages in the application.

> The Data Environment is only available on the server. Therefore, if you're developing a Web application that uses client script in order to access data (not a recommended task), the Data Environment can't be used when the Web pages are viewed from the client.

The Data Environment introduces the following elements to aid in Web application database programming:

- Data connections
- Data commands
- The Data Environment object model
- Design-time controls (DTCs)

Data Connections

As you learned when you created a Visual InterDev database project in Hour 15, "Using the Database Designer," a *data connection* is a collection of information that's required to connect to a specific database. This information includes the data source name, user ID, and password. If the Web application needs access to multiple databases or multiple connections to a single database, this can be accommodated by creating multiple data connections.

Data Commands

Data commands are named objects that contain information used to access particular database objects. For example, one data command object might point to a table, whereas another data command might point to a stored procedure. Once defined, both of these commands would then be accessible from any page in the Web application.

Command objects can be seen as containing hierarchical information in that each command object contains metadata describing its structure. For example, if a command object is created that references a table, that command object will also contain a list of all the columns in the command's underlying database table.

Data Environment Object Model

The Data Environment defines its own object model, which can be used from script to manage the data for a Web application. The Data Environment object model is based on the ActiveX Data Objects (ADO) object model, but it's simpler to use.

ADO is made up of six objects and two collections. The three main objects primarily used in ADO programming are the `Connection`, `Command`, and `Recordset` objects. In addition, each of these objects defines its own set of properties and methods.

Listing 19.1 uses ADO to read and display all the records from the Authors table.

LISTING 19.1   An Example of Using ADO from Script (Without the Data Environment)

```
 1: <BODY>
 2: <%
 3: dim cn
 4: set cn=Server.CreateObject("ADODB.Connection")
 5: cn.Open "pubs", "sa", ""
 6:
 7: dim rs
 8: dim sql
 9:
10: set rs=Server.CreateObject("ADODB.Recordset")
11: sql = "select au_fname, au_lname from authors order by au_lname"
12: rs.Open sql, cn
13: %>
14:
15: <H1>Author List by Last Name</H1>
16:
17: <%
18: dim strName
19: Do While NOT rs.EOF
20:   strName = rs("au_lname") + ", " + rs("au_fname")
21:   Response.Write(strName)
```

19

continues

LISTING **19.1**   continued

```
22:   Response.Write("<br>")
23:   rs.MoveNext
24: Loop
25:
26: rs.Close
27: cn.Close
28: %>
29: </BODY>
```

Although there's certainly nothing overly complex about this code, several problems immediately jump out at you. First, look at all the hard-coding concerning the table name, user
ID, password, and so on. Second, this code can't be used on any other page than the one
it's written for. Before this hour is over, you'll see how the Data Environment improves
over the model.

The Data Environment object model isn't an object model in the typical sense, where you see
a hierarchy of objects and collections that each include their own methods and properties.
Actually, in this case, the Data Environment object model is even simpler to use and understand because the Data Environment itself is an object that can be used in script. Through the
Data Environment object, data command objects are exposed as methods. These data commands can then be called in order to execute the underlying data object, return the recordset
referenced by the command, or execute an SQL command or stored procedure.

If this sounds a bit confusing, don't worry. It will be cleared up when we get to the first
example on how to execute data commands using the Data Environment.

Creating Data Connections

In Hour 15, you saw how to create data connections as part of a database project. In this
section, you'll see how to add connections to a Web project (and the global.asa file). To
do so, simply follow these steps:

1. Create a new Visual InterDev Web project called DataEnv.

2. Open the Project Explorer. After locating the global.asa file, click it with the right
   mouse button to display its context menu.

3. Figure 19.1 shows the global.asa file context menu. As you can see, this menu can
   be used in order to create data connections as well as data commands for a Web
   application.

FIGURE 19.1

*Data connection
information is stored
in the global.asa file.*

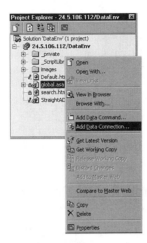

4. Select the Add Data Connection menu option. At this point, defining the data connection is done just as you did in Hour 15. Therefore, if you have any questions or need to brush up on how to do this, refer back to that hour. For the purposes of this example, create a data connection named g_dconnPubs and base it on the SQL Server database Pubs.

Surveying the Aftermath of Creating a Data Connection

Once you've created a data connection, you'll see that Visual InterDev has made numerous changes to the project. Not only have several folders and files been inserted into the project, but the global.asa file has been changed significantly as well.

Data Environment Folders and Files

Figure 19.2 shows the new folders and files that were created as a result of adding a data connection to the project.

FIGURE 19.2

*The Project Explorer
after the first data
connection has been
defined.*

19

The DataEnvironment folder located under the _private folder contains a single file (DataEnvironment.asa) that's used to hold the connection information for each defined data connection. You'll notice when you right-click this file that Visual InterDev has disabled the Open menu option. If you open this file with a hex editor, you can easily see the connection information, such as the database and user ID.

Now look at the DataEnvironment folder located under the global.asa file. This folder contains each defined data connection. The data connection's Properties dialog box, which you saw earlier when you created the data connection, can be displayed by right-clicking the desired data connection and selecting the Properties menu option.

Definitions of Data Environment and Data Connections in global.asa

Now, open the global.asa file by double-clicking it from the Project Explorer. Earlier in the book, you learned that this file is used to contain global variables and event handlers for a Web application. Listing 19.2 shows the modifications made to the global.asa file when a data command is added to a project.

LISTING 19.2   The global.asa File Modified with a Data Command

```
1.    <SCRIPT LANGUAGE=VBScript RUNAT=Server>
2.    Sub Application_OnStart
3.     '==Visual InterDev Generated - startspan==
4.     '—Project Data Connection
5.     Application("g_dconnPubs_ConnectionString")
       ➥= "Provider=SQLOLEDB.1;Persist Security Info=False;User
       ➥ID=sa;Initial Catalog=pubs;Data Source=CC743223-A;
       ➥Locale Identifier=1033;Connect Timeout=15;Use Procedure
       ➥for Prepare=1;Auto Translate=True;Packet Size=4096;
       ➥Workstation ID=CC743223-A;User Id=sa;"
6.     Application("g_dconnPubs_ConnectionTimeout") = 15
7.     Application("g_dconnPubs_CommandTimeout") = 30
8.     Application("g_dconnPubs_CursorLocation") = 3
9.     Application("g_dconnPubs_RuntimeUserName") = "sa"
10.    Application("g_dconnPubs_RuntimePassword") = ""
11.    '-- Project Data Environment
12.     'Set DE = Server.CreateObject("DERuntime.DERuntime")
13.     'Application("DE") = DE.Load(Server.MapPath("Global.ASA"),
       ➥"_private/DataEnvironment/DataEnvironment.asa")
14.    '==Visual InterDev Generated - endspan==
15.    End Sub
16.    </SCRIPT>
```

In lines 5 through 10, different application variables are set that directly reference the different data connection settings. Notice that each variable is prepended with the name of the connection. This is how each data connection property is resolved to. In other words, to access the runtime user ID for a particular data connection, you simply use the following syntax.

```
Application.Value("connectionNname_connectionPropertyName")
```

Also notice that the lines that define the Data Environment object (lines 12 and 13) are commented out by default. As you'll see in the next section, these lines are uncommented once you add a data command to the data connection.

Creating Data Commands

As mentioned earlier, *data commands* are simply objects that refer to database objects such as tables, queries, and SQL commands. Visual InterDev offers two different methods for defining data commands for a data connection:

- Drag and drop
- The Add Data Command menu option

Creating Data Commands via Drag and Drop

Drag and drop is the easiest method for creating a data command, but it's only applicable if the underlying database object already exists in the database. Follow these steps to create a data command for use in a Web application:

1. Open the Project Explorer and Data View windows. Position them side by side so you can see the elements of both windows.

2. From the Data View window, expand the Pubs data connection.

3. Once you've done that, expand the Views entry in order to display all views for this database.

4. Now, drag the titleview view in the Data View window and drop it either on the DataEnvironment folder located under the global.asa file or directly on the g_dconnPubs data connection.

5. When you've done that, the data command will be added to the Project Explorer and the global.asa file will updated so that you can now use that command in your Web application.

19

Creating Data Commands via the Add Data Command Menu Option

Another way of defining a data command is via the Add Data Command menu option. This is the method you'll use when you need the more advanced capabilities, such as using a database's catalog objects, specifying parameters for a stored procedure, or defining the different cursor properties at the data command level (as opposed to the data connection level). Follow these steps:

1. Right-click the g_dconnPubs data connection entry under the global.asa file.

2. When the data connection's context menu is displayed, select the Add Data Command menu option. This will display the command's Properties dialog box, as shown in Figure 19.3.

FIGURE 19.3

Creating a data command via the Add Data Command menu option allows for the setting of advanced options such as parameters and cursor settings.

3. Change the command name to cmdTitlesByAuthor. Notice that you can switch data connections at this point if you accidentally chose the wrong connection for which this data command is being created.

4. Click the SQL Statement radio button and type in the following SQL:

   SELECT * FROM titleview ORDER BY au_lname

   Notice that you can also create the SQL statement via the SQL Builder. Clicking this button will invoke the same interface used with the Database Designer and the Query Designer. This is a great tool to have when you're not 100 percent sure of the database objects that you need to use and want to view different ways of writing the SQL before creating the data command.

5. Click the OK button to indicate to Visual InterDev that you're finished defining the data command. When you do this, the data command will be inserted into the Project Explorer under its data connection.

6. As you can see in Figure 19.4, this project has two different data connections defined (g_dconnPubs and g_dconnNorthwind), and each data connection has its own data commands defined. Also notice the different icons that represent the different types of data commands created.

FIGURE 19.4

Multiple data connections and data commands can easily be added to a Web application.

Using the Data Environment from Script

Now that you've seen how to create a data connection and data commands, it's time to see just how easy it is use these data commands in your script. This process typically involves the following tasks:

- Initializing the Data Environment
- Executing the data command
- Retrieving the results

Initializing the Data Environment

In order to initialize the Data Environment, simply insert the following script into any Active Server Page:

```
<%
Set de = Server.CreateObject("DERuntime.DERuntime")
de.Init(Application("DE"))
%>
```

This will create an object named DE that can be used to access the different Data Environment methods and collections.

Executing a Data Command

Once you've initialized the Data Environment, all you have to do in order to execute a data command is reference it from the Data Environment object you've instantiated. Here's the syntax:

19

```
<Data Environment object>.<command object name>
```

Using the `cmdTitlesByAuthor` command object you created earlier, the data command can be executed with the following script:

```
<%
de.cmdTitlesByAuthor
%>
```

That's it! If the command object requires parameters, simply use this calling syntax:

```
<%
<Data Environment object>.<command object name> param1, param2, ...
%>
```

As an example of passing parameters to a data command, let's say you've created a command for retrieving the sales figures for a month that's to be determined at runtime. If the data command required a fiscal year and a fiscal period, the script to call it might look like this:

```
<%
de.cmdSalesFigures 99, 6
%>
```

If the data command being called returns a value, simply use this syntax:

```
<%
iReturnValue = <Data Environment object>.<command object name>
➥[param1], [paramn]
%>
```

Retrieving the Results of an Executed Data Command

The results of an executed data command are returned in a result set. All executed data commands return result sets. Even data commands such as updates and deletes that don't return actual data still return empty result sets. When a data command is executed, the Data Environment object automatically creates the result set object on your behalf. It's accessed using this syntax:

```
<Data Environment object>.rs<command object name>.<column name>
```

Notice that all you have to do is prepend the name of the data command name with the letters `rs` (for *result set*)!

In order to navigate through the result set, simply call the result set object's `MoveFirst`, `MoveLast`, `MovePrevious`, and `MoveNext` methods.

An Example of Using a Data Command

Using the `cmdTitlesByAuthor` data command you created earlier in the hour, Listing 19.3 shows a code snippet that can be plugged into an Active Server Page in order to display all the authors and titles in a table.

LISTING 19.3 Displaying Authors and Titles by Using `cmdTitlesByAuthor` Data Command

```
1.  <DIV align=center>
2.  <%
3.  Set de = Server.CreateObject("DERuntime.DERuntime")
4.  de.Init(Application("DE"))
5.  %>
6.
7.  <%
8.  de.cmdTitlesByAuthor
9.  set rs = de.rscmdTitlesByAuthor
10. %>
11. </DIV>
12.
13. <H1 align=center>Titles by author</H1>
14.
15. <TABLE border=1 cellPadding=1 cellSpacing=1 width=75%>
16.
17. <TR>
18.  <TD>
19.   <h2>Author</h2>
20.  </TD>
21.  <TD>
22.   <h2>Title</h2>
23.  </TD>
24. </TR>
25.
26. <%do while not rs.EOF%>
27.  <TR>
28.   <TD>
29.    <%Response.Write rs("au_lname")%>
30.   </TD>
31.
32.   <TD>
33.    <%Response.Write rs("title")%>
34.   </TD>
35.  </TR>
36.
37.  <%
38.   rs.MoveNext
39. loop
40. %>
41.
42. </TABLE>
```

Take away the fancy formatting with the styles and the table definition and you'll see that only seven lines of database code were needed to initialize the Data Environment, execute the data command, and navigate through the result set. Figure 19.5 shows what the application looks like when it's run.

FIGURE 19.5

Using the Data Environment, accessing and retrieving data can be accomplished in fewer steps and results in code that's reusable by other pages in the application.

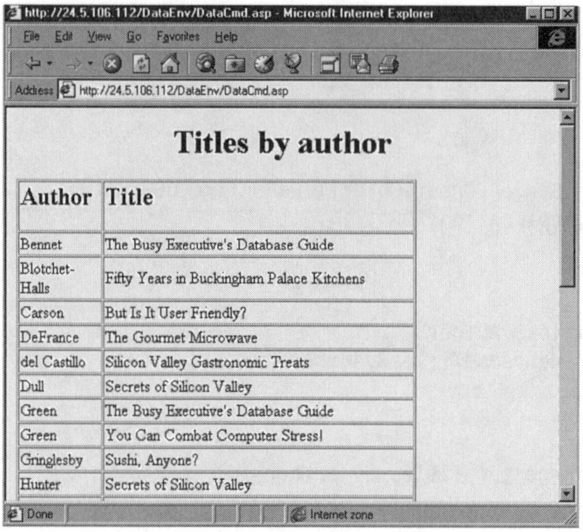

Summary

In this hour, you learned how much easier the Data Environment is to use than ADO in terms of accessing and retrieving data from a database. In learning about the Data Environment, you discovered how to create data connections and data commands. In the next hour, you'll learn an even more powerful means of implementing database access in your Web applications when you discover data-bound controls and design-time controls.

Q&A

Q How can I create a data command that is based on my database's system objects? In other words, I want to write an application that will display the SQL Server system tables like sysobjects and sysfiles.

A Select the Tools, Options menu option. On the left side of the Options dialog, select the Data Tools, Data Environment entry. This will result in the Data Environment options being displayed on the right side of the Options dialog. You should now see the Show System Objects check box. Check this and click the OK button. At this point, you've turned on the option to view system objects when creating or modifying data commands.

Now either create a new data command or right-click an existing data command and select the Properties menu option. From the General tab, you will see that the Database Object combo box now displays all the system objects of your database as well as the user database objects.

Workshop

The Workshop is designed to help you anticipate possible questions, review what you've learned, and begin thinking ahead to put your knowledge into practice. The answers to the quiz and exercise are in Appendix A, "Answers."

Quiz

1. What is the primary benefit programming with the Data Environment has over straight ADO scripting?
2. What are the two ways to use the Data Environment?
3. What is necessary in order to script the Data Environment object model on the client workstation?
4. How many Data Environments can a single application have defined?
5. What are data connections?
6. What are data commands?
7. How are the ADO objects represented from the Data Environment?
8. When you create a data connection, what file is updated with the new data connection's information, and what changes are made?
9. When creating a data command, what types of authentication settings can be specified?
10. How do you initialize the Data Environment in script?

19

Exercise

Create an application using the Data Environment that allows for the addition of records to a table.

HOUR **20**

Programming with Design-Time Controls

Over the course of this book, you've learned about several types of controls (such as HTML controls and ActiveX controls) that have aided you in creating the user interface for your Web applications. In this hour, you will learn

- How design-time controls differ from competing technologies and what benefits they provide you
- What steps are needed to incorporate these controls into your Web applications
- What data-bound controls are and the benefits they provide
- How to use the Recordset design-time control to quickly create database applications
- How to use the RecordsetNavBar to enable your users to scroll through data

A Design-Time Control Overview

Design-time controls (DTCs) are ActiveX controls that enable you to change their properties and behavioral characteristics from within the Visual InterDev environment at design time. These controls are manipulated at runtime via VBScript or JavaScript.

Although design-time controls existed in the first version of Visual InterDev, they did not have nearly the same level of maturity and robustness that they now enjoy in Visual InterDev 6. Specifically, they are now tightly integrated with the Scripting Object Model and the Data Environment (for the data-bound controls). For this reason, the majority of the design-time controls are used in conjunction with data access. Figure 20.1 shows the list of design-time controls (in the Toolbox window) that come stock with Visual InterDev. Notice that data-bound controls have icons that include the standard database symbol to differentiate them from non–data-bound controls.

FIGURE 20.1

Visual InterDev provides over a dozen design-time controls that aid in creating the user interface for your Web application.

Server-Side Design-Time Controls Versus ActiveX Controls

The main difference between ActiveX controls and server-side design-time controls is that ActiveX controls require a binary runtime component on the client workstation, whereas design-time controls do not.

To illustrate this point, let's say that you download an ActiveX control that allows for the validation of credit card numbers. In Visual InterDev, you would drag that ActiveX control onto a Web page and write the script to manipulate the control's properties and call its methods. In order for the page to work properly on the client workstation, the ActiveX control would have to be properly downloaded to the client workstation and registered. The downloading and registration happens automatically (as far as the Web application developer is concerned), but only if the browser supports ActiveX controls (only IE at this point) and if the user has not turned off ActiveX control support from within its browser.

With server-side design-time controls, the script runs only on the server and produces an HTML that is sent to the client's browser. For this reason, there is no binary runtime component on the user's machine to worry about, and no registration or concerns about whether the user's browser supports the component.

Developing Web Applications with Design-Time Controls

The key to design-time controls is understanding that when you drag a design-time control onto a page, the code that constitutes it writes script into that page. That script is responsible for creating a script object (using the Scripting Object Model) at runtime. (This is why no runtime binary component is needed on the client workstation.) You can then add your own scripting code to manipulate the control in terms of its properties and methods.

Because design-time controls are based on and tightly integrated with the Scripting Object Model, it is important that you realize what the Scripting Object Model is and why it is needed.

The Scripting Object Model

The Scripting Object Model was specifically designed to make Web application development a much easier process than it is using current technologies. This is accomplished by applying an object-oriented programming model to a standard HTML and script programming. The Scripting Object Model defines a set of objects with properties, methods, and events that can be manipulated to develop a Web application.

To illustrate the derived benefits of using an object-oriented approach to Web application development, let's take a look at how you would use the older, more traditional approach of creating a page using HTML and Active Server Pages. Then I will compare that with how you would accomplish the same thing using the Scripting Object Model.

As you've seen in many examples throughout this book, you can create a form by simply dragging the desired HTML controls (such as Textbox controls and Button controls) from the Toolbox window onto a page and writing script to manipulate them. One of these HTML controls is the Submit button control. When the user clicks this button, the

20

form's data is automatically submitted to a specified (in the <FORM> tag) Active Server Page. However, the Active Server Page has no intrinsic knowledge of what was done on the form or any state information regarding the form. In other words, the only thing the Active Server Page can do is manually examine the data that was passed, in hopes of determining the actions that it needs to take on behalf of the form.

In contrast, the Scripting Object Model enables you to place a button on the page and write a handler for its onclick method that processes the form. Because the Scripting Object Model abstracts events such as onclick, you can write handlers for these events in either client script or server script without the cumbersome, convoluted mechanism of submitting the form to another page.

Creating Forms with Design-Time Controls

The target platform is the first thing you must decide when using design-time controls. This dictates where the control will be instantiated and where the events will occur (that is, on the client or on the server).

Server-Side Controls

If you want to use server-side design-time controls, the controls must reside on an Active Server Page (not a regular HTML page). Using this technique, the script objects are created with server script, and any events, methods, or properties are available only from server script. It's also important to realize that any data binding occurs on the server.

Therefore, the biggest advantage to using server-side controls is that they enable the application to be cross-browser compliant.

Client-Side Controls

If you want to use client-side design-time controls, place the controls on either a regular HTML page or an Active Server Page. Using client-side controls, the properties, methods, and events are available only in client script. However, the data binding occurs on either the client or the server.

However, it is important to realize that this option requires that the Web application be used with a browser that supports Dynamic HTML (DHTML). Although this means that the application can take advantage of the Dynamic HTML object model, it isn't the best decision if the application must deploy on any browser. Because of this restriction, the examples in this hour will focus on server-side design-time controls.

Because script code is automatically inserted into a page when a design-time control is dragged on the page, you might be wondering where the script comes from. Actually, the template files used to generate the script that is later inserted into the pages is created automatically for you when you create the Visual InterDev project. These files are located in the _ScriptLibrary folder of the project on the Web server. For example, if you use Microsoft Internet Information Server (IIS), define the root for that server as wwwroot (the default), and then create a project called DTCExamples. These files will be located in `InetPub\wwwroot\DTCExamples\_ScriptLibrary`.

Specifying the Target Platform

After you have made the decision about the target platform, you must define that decision to Visual InterDev. To do this, simply follow these steps for a page that contains a design-time control:

1. Switch the page to Source view.

2. Right-click the <HTML> tag and select the Properties menu option.

3. In the Properties page, select the General tab (see Figure 20.2).

FIGURE 20.2

One of the first decisions you'll make regarding the use of design-time controls is which target scripting platform is right for your application.

4. In the group box entitled DTC Scripting Platform, click either the Server (ASP) radio button or the Client (IE 4.0 DHTML) radio button.

Adding Design-Time Controls to a Web Page

In order to insert a design-time control into a page, simply follow these steps:

1. Select the View, View Controls Graphically menu option from the main menu.

2. Create or open the page that will contain the design-time control. Remember that if your target platform is the server, you must add the control to an Active Server Page.

3. Open the Toolbox windows and click the Design-Time Controls tab.

4. Drag the desired control and drop it on the page. If you have not already enabled the Scripting Object Model, Visual InterDev will prompt you to do so. You cannot use design-time controls without applying this step.

Data-Bound Design-Time Controls

Data-bound controls are a special kind of design-time control. Data-bound controls enable you to write script to interface to your Web application's data more quickly and easily. Although a couple of design-time controls do not interface to a database, the majority of them do. Therefore, this hour concentrates on these controls (referred to as data-bound controls). With data-bound controls, specific columns in a recordset returned from a query against the database are bound, or associated with a specific control.

For example, say that you have a master table which contains a list of all the authors for a book publisher. Two of these columns might be first and last name. If you drop two design-time controls on a page that are bound to those two columns and issue a data command that returns a resultset of all authors, each time you navigate to a record in that resultset, the controls on the page will automatically be updated with the first and last name of that record without you having to do anything programmatically to make it happen!

Of all the data-bound design-time controls, you will use the Recordset control the most. Therefore, in this section, you will use it and a couple of other controls to write an example application illustrating both how to use design-time controls and why you would want to do so.

The other data-bound controls in the Visual InterDev arsenal include the Label, Checkbox, Textbox, OptionGroup, Listbox, RecordsetNavBar, Grid, and Form Manager. However, to use any of these controls, you must first place a Recordset control on the page. Next, add one of the data-bound controls and set its Recordset property equal to the name of the Recordset control.

The scripting target platform you chose determines where the script for the Recordset control executes. As you learned earlier, you can set this property at the project level or page level. However, you can also define this value at the Recordset control level. To do this, add the Recordset control to a page, right-click the control, and select the Properties menu option. From the Implementation tab, set the desired target platform.

Now, it's finally time to see how easily you can incorporate a design-time control into a Web application.

Adding a Recordset Control to a Page

The first thing you'll do to incorporate a design-time control to your Web application is add a Recordset control to a page and modify its properties. To do this, follow these steps:

1. Create a new Visual InterDev project called DTCExamples.

2. Because this control will be defined for the server target platform, create an Active Server Page and call it ViewAuthors.asp.

3. From the Project Explorer, right-click the project and select the Add Data Command menu option.

4. From the Data Link Properties dialog (see Figure 20.3), select Microsoft OLE DB Provider for SQL Server and click the Next button.

FIGURE 20.3

The Data Link Properties dialog enables you to specify which OLE DB provider you want to use.

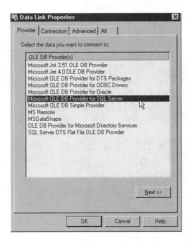

5. From the Connection tab of the Data Link Properties dialog (see Figure 20.4), specify the database server where your database is located, the username, and the password.

6. Although not strictly necessary, its always a good idea to click the Test button before continuing, just to make sure that the connection information you specified is correct and the database is responding correctly. If everything goes well, you will receive the confirmation message shown in Figure 20.5.

20

FIGURE 20.4

Specify the OLE DB connection and user authentication information via the Connection tab.

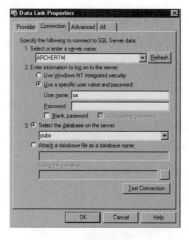

FIGURE 20.5

The Data Link Properties dialog enables you to test the connection to the specified database server.

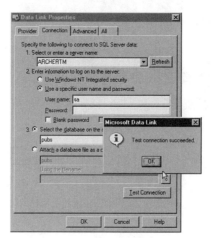

7. After you've received the confirmation of a good test, click the OK button to dismiss that message box, and then click the OK button to dismiss the Data Link Properties dialog.

8. Because you can't have a data command without a data connection, the Connection Properties dialog is the next dialog you will see (see Figure 20.6). Name the connection connPubs and click the OK button.

9. After the data connection has been created, the Command Properties dialog will be displayed. On this dialog, name the data command cmdAuthors. The connection should default to the newly created connPubs. If not, drop the Connection combo box down and select it. From the Database Object combo box, select the Table entry and select the dbo.Authors object from the Object Name combo box. When you're finished, the settings should look like those shown in Figure 20.7. Click the OK button to finish the data command creation process.

FIGURE 20.6

Name the connection using the Connection Properties dialog.

FIGURE 20.7

You can specify the different data command properties via the Command Properties dialog.

10. At this point, you might see a login dialog for SQL Server. Simply type in the username and password for your database and click the OK button.

11. As mentioned earlier, you will use the Recordset the most because it represents the actual data command and the data that is returned from the database. A Recordset DTC can be added to a page in two ways. However, doing this means that you'll also have to manually define the properties for the control. An easier way is to drag a data command from the Project Explorer and drop it on the page. This way, the majority of the Recordset DTC properties are set for you automatically from the data command's properties.

12. At this point, drag the cmdAuthors command and drop it onto the ViewAuthors.asp page. A Recordset DTC is created automatically when you do this. In addition, because the Scripting Object Model needs to be enabled before you can use DTCs, you will be prompted to enable the Scripting Object Model (see Figure 20.8). Simply click the Yes button to proceed.

20

FIGURE 20.8

*You must enable the
Scripting Object Model
to use DTCs on a Web
page.*

Although you can see the Recordset DTC control at the top of the page in design-time, the control won't be visible at runtime.

Adding Data-Bound Controls to a Recordset

Now that you've added the Recordset control to the page, it's time to see what it takes to add some controls that will reflect the data of the current record after executing the Recordset's associated data command.

As with the adding of the Recordset DTC, data-bound controls can be added via drag and drop with the Toolbox window or via the Project Explorer. In this section, you'll see how to do both.

Adding DTCs from the Toolbox

One way to add a data-bound DTC to a page is to drag the control from the Design-Time Controls tab of the Toolbox window and manually set its properties. Do so by implementing the following steps:

1. At this point, type in a heading of View Authors and press the Enter key to move to the next line. Remember to not worry about the appearance of the Recordset DTC when entering the title because it won't be visible at runtime.

2. Open the Design-Time Controls tab of the Toolbox window, drag a Label DTC, and drop it on the page.

3. Right-click the control and select the Properties menu option to display the Properties dialog (see Figure 20.9) specific to the type of DTC (in this case, a Label DTC) you are defining. Although each DTC has its own Properties dialog, the DTCs differ only slightly. Therefore, I'll use the Label DTC as an example.

4. The first tab of the Label Properties dialog enables you to specify the control's name. Unless you have to explicitly refer to the control in script, you can leave this name as it is, the Scripting Platform combo box. There are three options here. The first option is to select that you want this particular control to inherit its scripting platform option from that of the page. The other two options enable you to override

the page's definition and select either the Client or Server platform. You will almost always want to let this default to the Inherit From Page value. Finally, the last two fields enable you to specify with which Recordset DTC and field you want this field associated. For purposes of this example, select the Recordset1 Recordset and the au_fname field.

FIGURE 20.9

The Label Properties dialog.

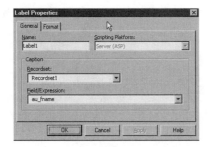

5. The second tab of the Label Properties dialog enables you to specify the different formatting options for the data when it's displayed on the page (see Figure 20.10).

FIGURE 20.10

Use the Format tab of the Label Properties dialog to set things, such as font, size, and color of the data value returned from the database.

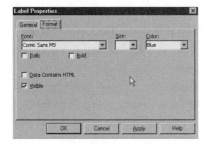

Adding DTCs from the Project Explorer

Now that you've learned how to create data-bound DTCs the manual way by using the Toolbox, take a look at the following steps to learn how to create them using the Project Explorer and the data command:

1. Open the Project Explorer and expand the global.asa file

2. From there, keep expanding the different levels of the tree from the DataEnvironment, to the connPubs data connection, to the cmdAuthors data command, to finally reveal the different columns that will return as a result of executing the cmdAuthors data command

3. Now, drag and drop any desired column onto the ViewAuthors.asp page.

20

4. Not only will Visual InterDev automatically create the appropriate DTC type (see Figure 20.11), but it will also create a prompt for that field. Unfortunately, because the actual database name for the column is used as the prompt, this might or might not be helpful. At least the DTC control is created and automatically connected to the correct Recordset DTC and the correct column.

FIGURE 20.11

Dragging a data command's field to a page automatically results in a data-bound DTC being created on your behalf.

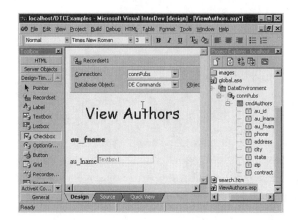

Using a Table to Properly Align Your Controls

Although the fact that you can drag and drop the fields from a data command is nice, the main problem I have with it is that the prompts and fields do not align properly. Therefore, I recommend creating a table for the page, setting its border to 0 (so that the border doesn't appear at runtime) and dragging and dropping the controls from the Toolbox into the appropriate table cells. This way, everything aligns nicely when finished.

At this point, add the remaining controls for this example so that when finished, your page looks like Figure 20.12. Notice that the last field is a Checkbox DTC because the contract column of the Authors table is defined as a Boolean type. Also, notice that this control's Caption property has been set to blank.

Adding a RecordsetNavBar

The RecordsetNavBar is a special DTC that contains the VCR-like buttons which enable the end user to scroll forward and backwards through the recordset. To incorporate this DTC into the ViewAuthors example, simply do the following:

1. Move to the end of the ViewAuthors.asp page.

2. Drag and drop a RecordsetNavBar DTC from the Toolbox window onto the page.

FIGURE 20.12

A table can be used to properly align the controls of a Web page.

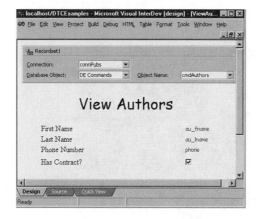

3. Right-click the control to display its properties (see Figure 20.13). Like the properties dialogs of the other DTCs, the RecordsetNavBar Properties dialog has two tabs (General and Format). At this point, the only change you need to make on the General tab is to select the Recordset1 entry in the Recordset combo box. Make the change at this time and then click the Format tab.

FIGURE 20.13

The RecordsetNavBar General properties dialog.

4. The Format tab of the RecordsetNavBar DTC is useful in that it enables you to specify which of the First, Previous, Next, and Last buttons you want on the control and what labels should be used. However, as you can see in Figure 20.14, you can also specify an image to display instead of text. Finally, you can define whether to display the control horizontally or vertically.

20

FIGURE 20.14
With the RecordsetNavBar DTC, you can select what text should be used on each button or even specify an image to be used on the different buttons instead.

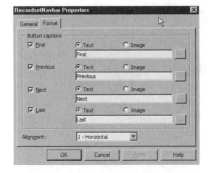

Making the Recordset Updatable

The last thing you'll do before testing this application is to allow the user to update the records. To do this, perform the following steps:

1. Open the ViewAuthors.asp page in Source view.

2. Right-click the RecordsetNavBar and select the Properties menu option (see Figure 20.15).

FIGURE 20.15
The RecordsetNavBar control can be configured to automatically updates its underlying recordset.

3. Now, check the Update on Move check box and click the OK button. Doing so causes the RecordsetNavBar control's script to automatically update the recordset each time the user moves from one record to another (if the current record has changed).

4. Right-click the Recordset control and select its Properties menu option.

5. Verify that the Recordset control's Lock Type is anything but Read-Only. Figure 20.16 shows the options I've selected for this particular sample application.

FIGURE 20.16

In order to have an updatable recordset, you must also specify the Recordset control's Lock Type as something other than Read-Only.

Now that you've created the application, let's see about giving it a test run.

Testing the Sample Page

At this point, save your work and select the View, View In Browser menu option. When the page is first displayed, the data command will be executed, and the first record's data will be displayed.

As you click on the RecordsetNavBar's buttons, notice how the application automatically iterates through the Pubs data command's resultset (of Authors records) and refreshes the different controls on the page with the appropriate values (see Figure 20.17). In addition, you can test the updatability of your application by changing some of the values, moving to another record, and returning to the changed record. As you will see, the database was updated automatically by the RecordsetNavBar control! Writing a simple maintenance application couldn't be easier.

FIGURE 20.17

Design-time controls aid in quickly and easily creating database applications.

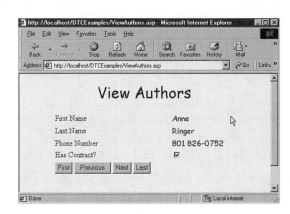

20

Summary

In this hour, you discovered the exciting new world of design-time controls. You began by discovering what these controls are and how they differ from competing technologies. You then learned how to incorporate these controls into your Web applications and reinforced that knowledge with a simple example in which data-bound design-time controls were used to view all the authors in the Pubs database.

Q&A

Q What is the difference between a design-time control and a FrontPage WebBot?

A Design-time controls were designed to work with any HMTL editor, whereas FrontPage WebBot controls were specifically created to work with FrontPage. In addition to requiring the use of the FrontPage editor, WebBot controls also require the installation of the FrontPage server extensions on the Web server.

Q Can I create my own design-time controls?

A Yes. Microsoft has released a design-time control SDK for doing just that. You can find information on it as well as a tutorial and samples at `http://msdn.microsoft.com/vinterdev/downloads/download.asp?ID=016`.

Workshop

The Workshop is designed to help you anticipate possible questions, review what you've learned, and begin thinking ahead to put your knowledge into practice. The answers to the quiz and exercise are in Appendix A, "Answers."

Quiz

1. What is a design-time control?
2. What support must first be enabled to use design-time controls?
3. How do design-time controls differ from ActiveX controls?
4. What are some advantages and disadvantages of specifying the server as the target scripting platform for a design-time control?
5. What are some advantages and disadvantages of specifying the client as the target?
6. Why don't you have to provide a runtime binary component for each design-time control used in your Web application if the design-time control is actually an ActiveX control itself?

7. What advantage does using the Scripting Object Model give you over using HTML and Active Server Pages?

8. What object is associated with a Recordset design-time control?

9. In order to use data-bound controls (such as a Textbox or Checkbox), which control must you also use on the same page?

10. Which design-time control enables the user to navigate through a resultset more easily?

Exercise

To solidify what you've learned in this hour, create an application that allows for the scrolling and modification of another table such as Employees.

20

PART IV

Deploying and Maintaining Your Web Site

Hour

Hour 21

Maintaining User Information

One common thread among professionally developed Web sites is the ability to maintain (or *persist*) user information so that each time you enter a Web site, your preferences are remembered. The Microsoft Web site is a good example of this. When you enter the Microsoft site, one of the options you're presented with is the ability to personalize the site based on your interests (for example, software development or sales). This information is then stored on your workstation so that each time you reenter the site, the type of information that interests you most is displayed.

Another example of maintaining user information is a Web site that requires you to log in. Although your user ID and password are typically stored in a database on the server, most of these sites allow you to save this information on your workstation so that you don't have to key it in each time you visit a site.

In both of these examples, cookies and session variables are being used to persist your user information on your workstation, retrieve it when you reenter a site, and share that information across the different pages of the application. This hour is dedicated to the subjects of writing and reading cookies and setting and retrieving session-level variables.

The highlights of this hour include

- Storing information in cookies
- Retrieving information from cookies
- Using the `Cookies` collection
- Setting and retrieving cookie attributes
- Writing a login example that uses cookies
- Using session-level variables

Working with Cookies

Even if you haven't worked with cookies programmatically yet, you've probably heard of this slightly controversial mechanism for maintaining, or *persisting*, state information. A *cookie* is a small file that's saved on the client's workstation in order to store information concerning the user's session with a given Web site.

If you're familiar with Windows development at all, you can think of a cookie as you would the Registry. In other words, the same sort of user- and application-level information that can be saved in the Registry for a Windows application can be saved to a cookie.

Syntax for Using Cookies

You may recall from Hour 12, "Using the Active Server Page Object Model," that cookies are implemented as collections of both the `Response` and the `Request` objects.

The `Response` object is the object that's used to send information to the user. Therefore, the `Response` object's `Cookies` collection is used to set the values of a cookie. Using the `Response` object, the syntax for setting a cookie's value is as follows:

```
Response.Cookies(cookie)[(key)¦.attribute] = value
```

The `Request` object, on the other hand, is the object that allows your script to obtain user and browser information. Therefore, its `Cookies` collection is used to retrieve information from a cookie. Using the `Request` object, the syntax for retrieving the value of a cookie is as follows:

```
value = Request.Cookies(cookie)[(key)¦.attribute]
```

Using this syntax, the `cookie` parameter represents the name of the cookie to be stored in the `Response` object or retrieved from the `Request` object. If any of this sounds a bit confusing, don't worry. You'll soon see some examples that will help you make sense of it all.

The `key` parameter is optional; it allows you to create multiple levels of keys within your cookies.

Finally, the `attribute` parameter is used in order to store or retrieve information about the cookie itself.

Programming Cookies with Server Script

Let's look at some very simple examples of how to use cookies. These examples should help illuminate how to use this very powerful feature. Note that all the examples in this hour are created using VBScript within Active Server Pages.

We'll start by looking at how information is stored in a cookie—after all, you can't retrieve information until you've saved it.

Let's suppose you want to store a single value containing the user's name. The following script accomplishes just that:

```
<%
Response.Cookies("userName") = "Tom Archer"
%>
```

In this example, the cookie's name is `userName` and its value is `Tom Archer`. In this case, no key is defined.

This example works in most cases; however, what if you want to save information at multiple levels? In other words, what if you want to store the user ID and password within one key and the user's preferences within another key?

This is accomplished by using the `Cookies` collection object's `key` parameter mentioned earlier. The `key` parameter enables you to store data as name/value pairs. Here's an example of storing several pieces of data in a cookie using keys:

```
<%
' get userid and password information
Response.Cookies("Authentication")("userID") = "Tom"
Response.Cookies("Authentication")("password") = "Archer"

' get user preferences
Response.Cookies("Preferences")("displayFrames") = "True"
Response.Cookies("Preferences")("displayTextOnly") = "False"
Response.Cookies("Preferences")("lastWebPage") = "OrderEntry"
%>
```

21

When you store information in a cookie, the script used to perform the action must be the only code in the Active Server Page or it must exist before any HTML. For this reason, one common technique used when creating Active Server Pages that read or write cookies is to have the Active Server Page do only the work of managing the cookie and then call the `Response.Redirect` method to display another page that's responsible for displaying any information to the user.

Retrieving cookie values is just as easy as storing them. Here are two sample scripts that retrieve the `userName` (assuming that the preceding script was used to store it) and write it out to a Web page.

The first example retrieves the cookie value into a variable and then uses the `Request Write` method to display it on the page (remember to place this code above the <HTML> tag):

```
<%
userName = Request.Cookies("userName")
Response.Write "User = " & userName
%>
```

The second example directly accesses the `Cookies` collection from script that has been embedded in a line of HTML:

```
User = <%=Request.Cookies("userName")
```

The following example retrieves the cookie values and then displays them on the page:

```
<%' get userid and password information%>
userID = <%=Request.Cookies("Authentication")("userID")%><BR>
pwd  = <%=Request.Cookies("Authentication")("password")%><BR>

<%' get user preferences%>
displayFrames = <%=Request.Cookies("Preferences")("displayFrames")%><BR>
displayTextOnly = <%=Request.Cookies("Preferences")("displayTextOnly")%><BR>
lastWebPage = <%=Request.Cookies("Preferences")("lastWebPage")%><BR>
```

Remember that if you need to use these values beyond the <HTML> tag, you need to first retrieve them into variables and then use the <%=varName%> syntax, as shown with the first example that retrieved the `userName` cookie into a variable also named `userName`. Here's an example of this:

```
<%@ Language=VBScript %>
<%
' get userid and password information
userID = Request.Cookies("Authentication")("userID")
pwd  = Request.Cookies("Authentication")("password")
%>
<HTML>
```

```
<HEAD>
<META NAME="GENERATOR" Content="Microsoft Visual Studio 6.0">
</HEAD>
<BODY>
userID = <%=userID%><BR>
password = <%=pwd%>
</BODY>
</HTML>
```

In order to allow your cookies to persist longer than the current user session, the Cookies collection provides a method for defining an expiration date. An example of when you would want to use this feature is if you provide a free service to people in return for their patronage and user information. For example, I frequently visit the Web site of my hometown's newspaper (Houston, Texas). This site writes a cookie to my workstation that's set to expire 30 days after my visit. This way, every 30 days, I'm forced to update my personal information with the site so that it always has my latest contact information.

For example, in order to set the expiration date for a cookie named MyCookie to December 31, 1999, you could simply use the following script:

```
Response.Cookies(MyCookie).Expires = 'December 31, 1999'
```

One thing that is extremely important to realize here is that the expiration date is set for all the keys of a cookie. Therefore, the following code would result in an error:

```
<%
' get userid and password information
Response.Cookies("Authentication")("userID") = "Tom"
Response.Cookies("Authentication")("userID").Expires = "December 31, 1999"
Response.Cookies("Authentication")("password") = "Archer"
Response.Cookies("Authentication")("password").Expires = "December 31, 1999"
%>
```

The following is the correct way to code this so that both keys belonging to the Authentication cookie will expire on December 31, 1999:

```
Response.Cookies("Authentication")("userID") = "Tom"
Response.Cookies("Authentication")("password") = "Archer"
Response.Cookies("Authentication").Expires = "December 31, 1999"
```

From time to time (especially when debugging your applications), you might find it necessary to remove or delete one of your cookies from a user's workstation. You'll probably be surprised to find out that no method exists to do this in a straightforward manner. Therefore, you'll have to use a bit of a trick to do it.

In order to delete a cookie, simply set the expiration date of the cookie (via its Expires attribute) to a date preceding the current date. A common technique for deleting a cookie is to simply set the cookie's expiration date to January 1, 1980. That way, no matter what the user's workstation time is set to, the cookie will expire immediately.

21

Displaying all the values of a cookie is a bit tricky because the Cookies collection doesn't work like most other collections. For example, the following attempt to iterate the Cookies collection won't work and will, in fact, result in a runtime error because the Contents property is not supported:

```
<%

'Declare a counter variable
Dim Item

'For each item in the collection, display its value.
For Each Item in Request.Cookies.Contents
 Response.Write Request.Cookies.Contents(Item)
Next
%>
```

In order to iterate through all the cookies in the collection, you can use this:

```
<%
'Declare a counter variable
Dim Item
'For each item in the collection, display its value.
For Each Item in Request.Cookies
 Response.Write Request.Cookies(Item)
%>
<BR>
<%Next%>
```

Here's something else that might throw you off at first: Each key is an item. In other words, suppose you've executed the following code:

```
<%
Response.Cookies("AddressInformation")("City")="Atlanta"
Response.Cookies("AddressInformation")("State")="GA"
Response.Cookies("AddressInformation")("ZipCode")="30338"
%>
```

If you then execute this code again to iterate through the collection and print out the results, you won't see three lines of values displayed. Instead, you'll see the following:

```
CITY=Atlanta&STATE=GA&ZIPCODE=30338
```

Note that all the values of the same key are considered to be one item in the collection. Now, suppose you execute the following code:

```
Response.Cookies("AddressInformation")("City")="Atlanta"
Response.Cookies("AddressInformation")("State")="GA"
Response.Cookies("AddressInformation")("ZipCode")="30338"
Response.Cookies("Name")("First")="Tom"
Response.Cookies("Name")("Last")="Archer"
```

The output from iterating through the Cookies collection would now be as follows:

```
CITY=Atlanta&STATE=GA&ZIPCODE=30338
FIRST=Tom&LAST=Archer
```

The last thing to notice about these code snippets is that the keys are stored in uppercase letters and, as such, are not case sensitive.

User Login Cookie Example

To illustrate how to store and retrieve cookie values, let's work through a simple login example. This example will have four pages.

Because this application contains several pages and a lot of redirection, let's walk through how the code will function before writing the script.

The first page is the default.asp page that the user will normally attempt to navigate to. At the top of this page, your script will attempt to verify whether the user's workstation contains a cookie from your site. If the cookie exists, the user will be redirected to the main menu page (MainMenu.asp), where the user will see a personalized greeting.

If, however, the cookie does not exist on the user's workstation, the user will be redirected from default.asp to the login page (Login.asp), where he will be able to specify a user ID and password. Additionally, this page contains a check box control so that the user can decide for himself if he wants his user ID and password saved to a cookie so that he doesn't have to reenter this information each time he visits your site.

Once the information is entered, the VerifyLogin.asp page is called and the information is verified. If the user ID is equal to Tom and the password is equal to Archer, the user will be redirected to the main menu page. Obviously, in a real-world application, the user ID and password would be compared against values stored in a database. Figure 21.1 shows the flowchart for this example.

Creating the Default Page

Let's get started by creating the project and default page. Here are the tasks you need to perform:

1. Create a new Visual InterDev Web project named CookieExample.

2. Add an Active Server Page to the project named default.asp.

3. Because the default page needs to verify whether the user has already logged into the site before and, if so, whether a cookie was saved, you need to insert the following script immediately after the first line of script that identifies the scripting language being used. Note that this example, like all server-scripting examples in this book, is created in VBScript. Notice how the user is redirected based on

21

whether a user ID is found. Obviously, in a real-world application, you would want to verify the user ID and password just in case. However, for this example, you're going to assume (for the sake of simplicity and because the database hours already cover accessing data from a Web page) that if a cookie is found that contains a user ID, the user ID and password are valid.

```
<%

'Retrieve the userid from the cookie
userID=Request.Cookies("Authentication")("userID")

if userID= "" then
' no cookie or blank userid
 Response.Redirect "Login.asp"
else
' cookie exists with userid
' for purposes of this demo, we assume
' the userid is value
 Session("currentlyLoggedInUser") = userID
 Response.Redirect "MainMenu.asp"
end if
%>
```

FIGURE 21.1

A flowchart of a simple login example that uses a cookie to store and retrieve user ID and password information.

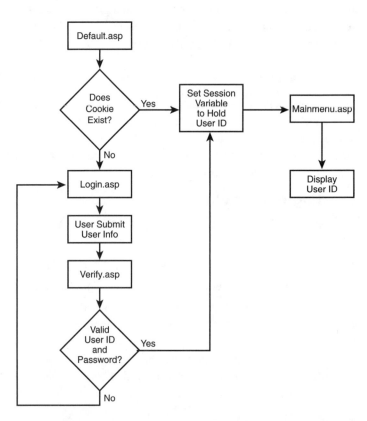

Creating the Login Page

Next, you'll add the login page to accept the user ID and password from the user. This page will contain a check box control that allows the user to control whether a cookie is to be created on his workstation. Here are the tasks you need to perform:

1. Add an Active Server Page named Login.asp to the project.

2. Add the HTML controls that will constitute the page's user interface (see Figure 21.2).

FIGURE 21.2

A login page that allows a user to specify whether he wants the application to save a cookie on his behalf.

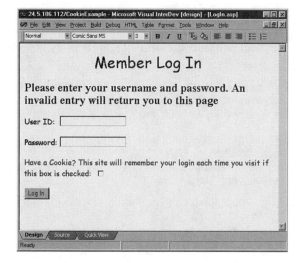

3. Name the User ID, Password, and check box controls `txtUserID`, `txtPassword`, and `chkSaveCookie`, respectively.

4. Switch to Source view and insert the following `<FORM>` tag immediately after the `<BODY>` tag:

```
<FORM action="VerifyLogin.asp" id=FORM1 method=get name=FORM1>
```

Verifying the Login

The verification page is invoked only from the Login.asp page and has the single responsibility of verifying the login information. Here are the tasks you need to perform:

1. Add an Active Server Page named VerifyLogin.asp to the project.

2. Immediately after the first line of script in the file, insert the following script. As you can see, this script simply retrieves the information from the submitting form (Login.asp), verifies the information, and saves the user ID and password to a cookie file (that is, if the user has indicated that the information can be saved).

21

```
<%
userID = CStr(Request("txtUserId"))
password = CStr(Request("txtPassword"))
saveCookie = CStr(Request("chkSaveCookie"))

' this would normally check the userid
' and password against a database
if userID = "Tom" and password = "Archer" then

 'only save the cookie if the user agreed to it
 if (saveCookie = "on") then
  Response.Cookies("Authentication")("userId")=userID
  Response.Cookies("Authentication")("password")=password
  Response.Cookies("Authentication").Expires = "December 31, 1999"
 end if

 'the user has been logged in, so direct them to the main menu
 Session("currentlyLoggedInUser") = userID
 Response.Redirect "MainMenu.asp"

else

 'make the user reenter the login information because it was invalid
 Response.Redirect "Login.asp"

end if
%>
```

Creating the Main Menu Page

Finally, you need to create the main menu page. This page simply displays a personalized greeting to the user using the user ID retrieved from the cookie. Here are the tasks you need to perform:

1. Add one last Active Server Page, named MainMenu.asp, to the project.

2. Insert the following script after the <BODY> tag:

```
<%Response.Write "Welcome back, " & Session
➥("currentlyLoggedInUser")%>
<A HREF="DeleteUserID.asp">Delete User</A>
```

Testing the Cookie Application Example

That's it! Now all you have to do is run the application. The first time through the application, you'll be redirected from the default.asp page to the Login.asp page. If you type in the correct values, you'll see a page similar to the one shown in Figure 21.3.

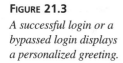

FIGURE 21.3

A successful login or a bypassed login displays a personalized greeting.

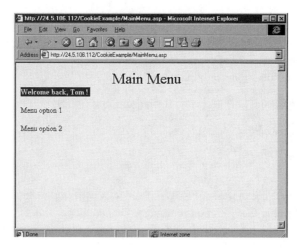

If you choose to have the cookie saved, you'll never see the login page again because it will be automatically bypassed for your workstation.

Using Session-Level Variables

Now that you've seen how easy it is to program cookies, you can see why they're so widely used. The simple fact is that with what you've learned so far in this hour, you can now save any type of data on a user's workstation regarding his visits to your site. For example, in addition to saving login information, you might also want to keep track of the last time the user visited your site or even keep a history log of which pages he visited. You can even get really fancy and write an application that looks at this log and attempts to determine whether the user is having trouble navigating your site. The possibilities are truly endless.

However, if you look closely at the login demo, you'll see that the user ID is stored in a Session variable called userID. This is done for the following simple reason: The user has the choice of whether to save the cookie. Therefore, after the user's ID is validated, that ID is stored in a Session variable for later display on the main menu. This way, even if the user doesn't want to save the cookie, the application can keep track of who the user is.

Making Sure That User Options Are Initialized

One major problem the CookieExample application suffers from is that assumption that each user will navigate directly to the home page of the application. Obviously, nothing guarantees that this will always be the case. Therefore, one way to handle this is to implement the Session_OnStart handler in the global.asa file. Remember that this method is called when a user first enters your Web site.

21

Here's an example of how you could force the user to go through the default.asp page to make sure that he has either logged on before (and the information was saved in a cookie) or logs on now:

```
<SCRIPT LANGUAGE=VBScript RUNAT=Server>
Sub Session_OnStart
 Session("startUrl") = Request.ServerVariables("SCRIPT_NAME")
 if Session("startUrl") <> "Default.asp" then
  Response.Redirect "Default.asp"
 end if
end sub
</SCRIPT>
```

Notice that in this example the `Request` object's `ServerVariables` collection is being used to determine the user's current page. This collection can be used with the following syntax:

```
Request.ServerVariables(server variable name)
```

As you can see in this example, session-level variables are stored and retrieved using the `Session` object. To store values in this object, simply use the following syntax:

```
Session("variable name")=value
```

In this example, the current URL is stored in a session variable named `startUrl`. This value can then be retrieved using the following call:

```
value = Session("startUrl")
```

By using `Session` variables, you remove the need to constantly reread the same values over and over again from the cookie(s). Also, by using the `Session_OnStart` method, you have control over exactly how a user enters your Web site.

One thing you'll need to keep in mind regarding storing values in the `Session` object is that if you're using VBScript and you're attempting to store an object in a `Session` object, you must use the `Set` command, like this:

```
<%
Set Session("myObject") = Server.CreateObject("myComponent.myClass")
%>
```

This object could then be retrieved with the following script:

```
<%
Set myObject = Session("myObject")
myObject.myMethod
%>
```

But what happens if the user tries to manually jump to the Main Menu page from the Login page? Simply add the following code to the top of the MainMenu.asp file:

```
<%
userID = Session("userID")
if userID = "" then
    Response.Redirect("default.asp")
end if
%>
```

You probably don't want to have to type that code into the top of every single page on your site. Therefore, a better way is to save this code snippet into a file called something like Check.inc and add the following `include` directive to the top of every file instead:

```
<!-- #include file="check.inc" -->
```

Congratulations! Now you have the ability to not only have your users log in to your application, but also to verify that they can't circumvent your security by typing in whatever URL they want.

Deleting the Cookie

As you test this application, you might want to be able to delete the cookie. To do so, follow these steps:

1. Open the MainMenu.asp file and add the following line before the `</BODY>` closing tag. This link will enable the user to delete the cookie from the main menu.

   ```
   <A HREF="DeleteUserID.asp">Delete User</A>
   ```

2. Add a new Active Server Page to the project called DeleteUserID.asp.

3. Insert the following lines of code just after the first line in the DeleteUserID.asp file. As you learned earlier in the hour, this code will set the expiration date so that the cookie will automatically be deleted by the browser.

   ```
   <%
   Response.Cookies("Authentication")("userId")=""
   Response.Cookies("Authentication").Expires = "January 1, 1980"
   %>
   <P>Deleted!
   ```

Summary

In this hour, you learned the importance of tracking user-level state information with cookies and session-level variables. After learning the basics of how to program cookies, you saw firsthand just how easy they are to incorporate into an application by writing a login sample application. After that, you learned how to remedy one of the sample application's shortcomings with the use of session-level variables.

21

Q&A

Q Can I program a cookie with client script?

A Technically, you can. However, as you've seen throughout this book, many complications and difficulties are associated with client scripting. As an example of one limitation, don't forget that the user can easily view any client script. Therefore, any user can view exactly what information is being stored and in what format. Depending on the information being stored, this could cause serious problems for an application that must rely completely on the integrity of that information. For this reason and many others, it's recommended that you use Active Server Page scripting in order to store and retrieve cookie values from the client workstation.

Workshop

The Workshop is designed to help you anticipate possible questions, review what you've learned, and begin thinking ahead to put your knowledge into practice. The answers to the quiz are in Appendix A, "Answers."

Quiz

1. What two Active Server Page Object Model objects contain cookie collections?
2. Show the two ways to store a cookie value from script?
3. Where must the script exist within an Active Server Page that stores or retrieves values from a cookie?
4. Are keys that are stored in a cookie case sensitive?
5. How is a cookie's expiration date set?
6. How is a cookie programmatically deleted?
7. What method is used to ensure session initialization?
8. What Scripting Object Model collection is used to store environment variables?
9. How are values set in the Session object?
10. How are objects stored and retrieved from a Session object when the scripting language being used is VBScript?

Exercise

Create a main menu that points to several pages. Write the necessary code to redirect users to the main menu regardless of which page they surf to.

HOUR **22**

Web Site and Web Application Security

Without a doubt, security, for many reasons, is the toughest of all the tasks you will have to deal with regarding your Web application. The first reason is the sheer number of places along a Web application's code path where you can choose to implement security. For example, if you are developing an intranet application, you might be concerned only with design-time as opposed to runtime issues. This can be handled using Visual InterDev security settings. If your application is an Internet application, do you want to secure your entire operating system against hackers or are you satisfied with the security your Web server provides? This might involve Windows NT security features, Microsoft Internet Information Server (IIS) security, and even file-level security (such as NTFS versus FAT). Are you concerned with hackers intercepting sensitive data as it is being routed to and from your client's workstations? This might entail some sort of encryption technique such as Secured Sockets Layer (SSL).

The second reason is the knowledge that if you don't institute security correctly, you are leaving yourself open to a limitless amount of danger. In other words, say that you create an Active Server Page and make a mistake in the HTML so that the fields don't show up on the form just right. No problem. If you don't catch it in quality assurance (QA), you'll find out about it the first time someone tries to use the page in production and will be able to correct it without much of a problem. However, if you make a mistake in protecting the integrity of your data or your Web site, you might walk into work one Monday morning and find that not only has someone broken into your server and trashed that weekend's orders, but you've also been locked out of your own server. Needless to say, security is an issue to which you need to pay special attention.

Having said all that, Web site security is an issue that can easily fill several books. Such a topic certainly can't be fully covered in a lesson designed to last a single hour. However, I will investigate the main security issues of a Web site and introduce some key concepts that illustrate at least how to begin securing your site. Finally, at the end of the hour, you'll see several good sources of information you can use to extend your knowledge so that when you go home on Friday, you'll know that you still have a server (and a job) when you arrive on Monday morning.

The highlights of this hour include

- Learning the importance of Web security
- Discovering how to secure your Windows NT Server
- Learning the security features of IIS
- Learning how to secure your Web applications
- Discovering how SSL enables you to securely transmit data

Security Overview

At its simplest, securing a Web site and its Web applications entails controlling who can use your application and what specific rights they have. In addition, Web security generally involves both the protection of the Web site's resources, as well as any sensitive data transferred between the Web server and any client workstations. To that end, the diagram in Figure 22.1 illustrates the points in the Web server where security can be implemented.

- Web server operating system (1)—Because this book focuses on Visual InterDev, this section assumes a server operating system of Microsoft Windows NT. This section covers the basics of the Windows NT security model.
- Web application (2)—When I speak of securing a Web application, I'm referring to the implementation of a user authentication page, as well as logging activities, such as an inordinate number of invalid logon attempts.

- Web server (3)—Obviously, the Web server is one of the first places you think about securing. In this hour, I'll assume a Web server of Microsoft Internet Information Server.

- Data transmission (4)—It's one thing to make sure that your site is secured; however, you're not going to keep many customers happy unless you can illustrate that their data is not only safe when it's on your server, but also when it's in transit to your server.

FIGURE 22.1

Security can be implemented at many different points on a Web server.

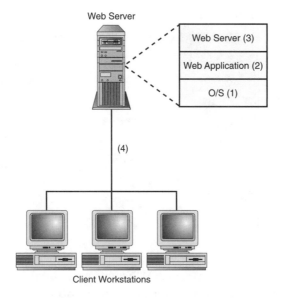

Windows NT Security Basics

You might be thinking, "Why do I have to worry about Windows NT security if my users will be going through my Web application?" Yes, application-level security is important (and will be covered shortly). However, when you host a Web server on your Windows NT box, you have to keep in mind that your box is on a huge TCP/IP network, and it is out there for anyone to hack into. Therefore, it is a huge (and possibly costly) mistake to assume that everyone who wants to attach to your server will do so via the applications that you write. As a result, it is vital to have at least a cursory understanding of the security model employed by your Web server's operating system.

Windows NT security is based on the concept of users and groups to which that user belongs. The different objects within the system (for example, files, registry keys, processes, threads, and so on) are available to a user only if that user has the appropriate rights, or privileges. To that end, user accounts, user groups, account policies, and user rights are the four keys to defining security in Windows NT.

User Accounts

You obviously know about user accounts because you have to supply a username and
password each time you log into your Windows NT system. Therefore, the first logical
thing to think about regarding safeguarding your system is the maintenance of these
accounts. Every user who has access to a Windows NT system has a user account
defined for that system consisting of a username, password, and other authentication-
level properties. These accounts are managed via the Windows NT User Manager
application (see Figure 22.2).

FIGURE 22.2

*The Windows NT User
Manager.*

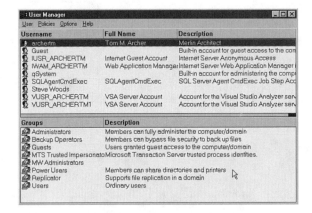

Notice that in addition to the user accounts you might have created, certain applications
such as Microsoft Transaction Server (MTS), Internet Information Server, and Visual
Studio Analyzer create accounts as well. It is extremely important to carefully read the
accompanying security documentation when you install software like this because sometimes applications such as these create user accounts you might not be aware of, which
can be used by other people to gain access to your system. More than a few systems have
fallen prey to hackers who knew of these loopholes. Just make sure that you know what
each and every user account on your system is capable of and only the absolute minimum number of people have access to its password.

Figure 22.3 shows the User Properties dialog used to define a user account. Notice the
different password properties you can set.

If you click the Dialin button to display the Dialin Information dialog (see Figure 22.4),
you will see that Windows NT enables you to specify whether a user can dial into this system from a remote location, and, if so, what restrictions are to be placed on this scenario.

FIGURE 22.3

The User Properties dialog.

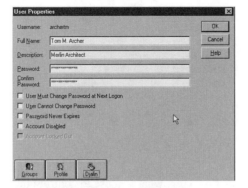

22

FIGURE 22.4

You can set whether a user can dial in via the Dialin Information dialog.

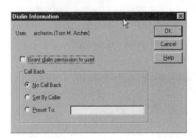

User Groups

Obviously, with a production Windows NT server that will be used by many users, you don't want to be forced to define the complete array of rights each user will have because that would be inefficient and take quite a bit of time. User groups enable you to define the rights and abilities of anyone who belongs to that group. That way, when you create a user, you can assign him to the particular groups that have the permissions he needs. Another advantage of user groups is that, when you modify the rights of a group, each participating member is automatically affected. Thus, you are saved the time that would be necessary to manually update each user if user groups didn't exist.

Examples of groups include the standard Administrators, Users, and Backup Operators groups. In addition, you might want to create your own groups, such as a group called Developers, whose members have access to only certain parts of the system.

One thing to keep in mind is that users and groups have a many-to-many relationship because any given user can belong to any number of groups. An example of this is the IWAM_COMPUTERNAME account that is created by IIS. However, MTS updates this account to include it in the MTS Trusted Impersonators group.

Figure 22.5 shows the Logical Group Properties dialog that is used to define a group. Notice that you can add users to the group via the Add button on this dialog or via the Groups button on the User Properties dialog shown earlier.

FIGURE 22.5

The Logical Group Properties dialog.

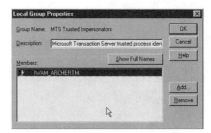

Account Policy

The Windows NT account policy is what you use to control how passwords must be used by all user accounts, and whether user accounts are automatically locked out after a specified number of incorrect logon attempts. Also displayed via the User Manager application is the Account Policy dialog, shown in Figure 22.6.

FIGURE 22.6

Using the Account Policy dialog, you can define how passwords and logons to the system should be managed.

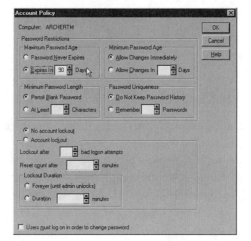

User Rights

User rights is the last thing I'll discuss in this brief introduction to Windows NT security. The User Rights Policy dialog enables you to specify high-level tasks to which a user or group has access (see Figure 22.7). For example, you can use this dialog to specify whether a particular user or group has the ability to log on locally and whether the group can access the system from another system on the network.

FIGURE 22.7
The User Rights Policy dialog.

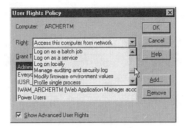

Securing Your Web Application

The easiest and most straightforward way to secure your Web application is to force users to go through a logon page where their usernames and passwords are verified and the functions of the system for which they have rights are resolved. Because of the need for security, almost all business Web sites have some sort of user logon process by which users are authenticated before they can interact with the application. This logon page acts as a gatekeeper to the rest of the application, such that if the user's logon information cannot be verified, the user is not granted access to any other part of the application.

The following steps show what you need to do in order to implement application-level security:

1. Add an HTML or Active Server Page to your application that is used to gather the logon information (typically just a username and password).

2. Upon the user submitting the form, send the form to an Active Server Page for validation.

3. In the validation Active Server Page, verify the passed logon information. This step generally involves reading a database and searching for an entered username and password.

4. If the user validation fails, report the error to the user and do not let him proceed to other parts of the application. If the user validation succeeds, display the next page per your application's needs (for example, a main menu or page).

5. After you have tested that the logon page is working, you will need to add script to your application to ensure that the user doesn't leap-frog your logon page by manually entering the URL of another page of your Web application in the address bar of the browser.

Although the preceding steps serve as an overview to securing a Web application, you will see firsthand at the end of this hour how this is done with an example application.

Defining Security for IIS

It's important to realize that IIS is neither an operating system nor an application with magic capabilities to ensure the safety of your system. IIS is just another application running on your Windows NT system that provides files for browsers that request them. Obviously, that's a bit of an exaggeration; however, in terms of security, that definition is valid for this discussion.

IIS works closely with Windows NT (which is why it runs only on Windows NT), in order to authenticate user information via the following methods:

- Anonymous Authentication
- Basic Authentication
- Windows NT Challenge/Response Authentication

Using IIS, you can select one or more of these authentication methods, but if you select a combination of the three, you must make sure that you understand the order in which they will be used. For example, IIS always tries the anonymous method first (if enabled). If that method fails or it is not enabled, IIS attempts to use the basic method if it is enabled. Finally, the last ditch resort is to use the Windows NT Challenge/Response method if enabled.

Anonymous access is generally used for Web applications that are being used on the Internet because in those situations you don't know who the user is. The Basic Authentication and Windows NT Challenge/Response Authentication methods are generally used only in conjunction with an intranet application in which you know the full list of users who can use the system.

Because defining IIS security properly is important to protecting your Web server, here's a breakdown of how each method works.

Anonymous Authentication

You can't create a user account on your Windows NT system for every user who might one day use your Internet-based Web application. For this reason, IIS defines what is called an anonymous user account. The account that is created for this purpose is called IUSR_*COMPUTERNAME*, and the only group to which it belongs (by default) is the Windows NT-supplied Guests group.

Whenever a user surfs to a site hosted by IIS and her browser requests a page, IIS first attempts to load that page using the anonymous account. If the items referenced by the page can be accessed by the anonymous account, the page is returned to the client's browser. This type of security is specified by enabling the Allow Anonymous option of IIS, and it is perfect for Web-based applications.

Basic Authentication

Basic Authentication is the technique of using clear text to transmit user security information to and from the client workstation.

Basic Authentication is enabled by checking the Enable Access Control check box on the Permissions tab of the Web Proxy service properties dialog. When enabled, this method of authentication is used only in the following situations:

- Either the anonymous user authentication is not enabled or could not be used.
- The Windows NT Challenge/Response method (described next) is not enabled.

When using Basic Authentication, the client is responsible for gathering the logon information and transmitting it to IIS. This information is typically encoded (not encrypted) before being sent. When received on the server system, the information is decoded and verified against the user accounts as defined within Windows NT.

Needless to say, Basic Authentication offers minimal protection for securing your application's data because the user's logon information is being sent in clear text. For this reason, you'll normally see this authentication method only with intranet applications.

Windows NT Challenge/Response Authentication

The Windows NT Challenge/Response method is a more advanced version of the Basic Authentication method. This method is used when the server and the client are located in either the same or trusted domains.

With the Windows NT Challenge/Response method, the client's Web browser attempts to use the Windows NT credentials that were used to log on to the client computer. If those credentials cannot be validated, the Windows NT Challenge/Response method prompts the user for a valid username and password. The username and password are then encrypted in a multiple transaction interaction between the server and the client. This is a drastic improvement over the Basic Authentication method because it protects against hackers attempting to monitor the data traffic between the server and the client.

However, as good as this sounds, the Windows NT Challenge/Response Authentication method has a couple of severe limitations to keep in mind:

- It cannot be used through a firewall via a proxy. If this is your situation, you need to use Basic Authentication.
- Unlike the Anonymous Authentication method in which all authentication occurs on the server, the Challenge/Response method involves the client. Therefore, you have to take into consideration that not all browsers support this authentication method.

- The Windows NT Challenge/Response method does not support delegation to third-party servers.

Because of these limitations, the Windows NT Challenge/Response Authentication method is typically used only with an intranet in which all communication occurs inside an organization's firewall.

Securing Data Transmissions

My father used to say that locking the doors and windows of a house serves to keep out the "honest" people. For anyone else who's really interested in getting in and taking what isn't his, you're going to have to get a little more creative. Unfortunately, that adage can be extended to Web applications. So far, you've seen enough information to help you in keeping the honest Web surfers from infiltrating your server. In other words, the ones who go about clicking a link here or typing a URL there just to see how lax the Web administrator was in doing his job. However, that doesn't work against the serious hacker. I'm talking about the types who stay up all night pouring over reports of every little security breach that can be exploited or writing applications to read the contents of (or sniff) network packets for sensitive information, such as passwords, credit card numbers, and personal identification numbers (pins). If you want to thwart these types, you have to learn about securing data transmissions.

> Let me just state once again that this hour is being used to introduce you to some concepts involving security. Therefore, don't think that by reading the next few sections that you will be prepared to fully protect yourself from every conceivable type of threat to your Web server's well-being. You should use this hour to familiarize yourself with the concepts and techniques used to provide a secure environment for your applications and their data. At the end of this hour, some additional resources will be referenced for those of you who want to pursue a more rigorous approach to securing your systems.

There are many different techniques to secure data transactions. Secured Sockets Layer (SSL) is the one covered here because it has been around the longest and is the most entrenched technology for securely transmitting data.

Secured Sockets Layer

So many books give only a superficial understanding of SSL, and the other books that give a decent explanation of this technology fail to explain how to use it from your Web applications. Therefore, the first thing I'll discuss is the technical side of how SSL works on both the server and the client side. After that, you'll learn what you need to do in order to implement SSL on your Web site.

How SSL Works

SSL is a protocol developed by Netscape for securing data transmissions across the Internet. SSL is application independent, and as such is used with other protocols, such as FTP, HTTP, and Telnet layered on top of it.

You can usually tell whether you are on a secured site when the URL begins with https (instead of just http). An example of such a URL is the Microsoft MSDN Web page (`https://msdn.one.microsoft.com/subscriber`), which enables you to log on to the secured area of the MSDN download site.

SSL uses public-key cryptography (PKC) to negotiate encryption keys and authenticate the server before any data is exchanged by the higher-level application. The SSL protocol uses encryption, authentication, and message authentication codes to secure the data being transmitted.

SSL includes something called the SSL Handshake Protocol, which consists of two phases: server authentication and (optionally) client authentication. In the server authentication phase, the server, in response to a client's request, sends its digital certificate and cipher preferences. Upon receipt, the client generates something called a master key, which the client encrypts with the server's public key. The client then transmits the encrypted master key back to the server. When the server receives and deciphers the master key, it authenticates itself to the client by a returned message authenticating the master key. Any subsequent data that is transmitted is encrypted and authenticated using keys derived from the original master key. Sometimes, the optional second phase is used where the server challenges the client to authenticate itself. In this situation, the client must return its digital signature as well as a public-key certificate for the server to authenticate.

If you are looking into processing credit card transactions over the Internet, realize that SSL doesn't do this for you. SSL simply secures the data transmitted between a client and a server. Therefore, although SSL will enable you to receive the customer's credit card information in a secure fashion, you will need to acquire a Merchant account from an accredited financial institution to process the transaction.

How to Implement SSL

The first thing you'll need to do to participate in an SSL connection is to obtain a digital certificate from one of the following Web sites:

- www.thawte.com
- www.verisign.com

After you have obtained the digital certificate to use with your site, you need to name the links to the secured URLs on your site with the https prefix. For example, if you have an order form HTML page on a domain called www.YourDomain.com that you want to link to from another page, the full URL would be https://www.YourDomain.com/OrderForm.html.

The next step is to write the script to save the transmitted data to a text file. After you've done that, you can access the data via a secure URL. As an example, say that you have every order to a uniquely named text file of the format OrderDataNNN.txt. After the order's data (including credit card information) is saved to the text file, you can reference the file with something like https://YourDomain/OrderData001.txt.

Summary

In this hour, you were introduced to the issues of Web site and Web application security. You also learned many key elements regarding the security of your server and the data it is responsible for transmitting to and from its client workstations.

Hopefully, after this hour, you have a new-found appreciation for the work that lies ahead of you in securing your site and the user's data. Although securing a site might not be the easiest or most fun part of developing a Web application, it just might be the most important.

Q&A

Q What are some additional resources for learning about security?

A Besides searching the Web for articles, I recommend the www.thawte.com and www.verisign.com Web sites because both of these companies make their money protecting sites. They also do a good job of teaching you why you need the protection in the first place. In addition, VeriSign also teaches seminars and does consulting on securing your Web site. Aside from that, another avenue is books specifically geared towards the topic of Web security. Richard Harrison's *ASP/MTS/ADSI Web Security* (ISBN: 0130844659) is, by far, the best book that I've read dealing with the newer technologies, such as Windows 2000 Active Directory Services Interface (ADSI).

Q **What if I want to sell products and services in a secure manner over the Internet without dealing with all the hassle of learning about security?**

A Luckily, companies will handle the security aspect of your transactions for a fee. That way, you are free to concentrate on the remainder of the application and can leave the security to a company that specializes in that area. An example of such a company can be found at `http://www.sslservices.com`.

Q **Where can I read more about the technical aspects of how SSL works?**

A One really good site for learning about some of the intricacies involving SSL is `http://www.rsa.com/standards/protocols`.

Workshop

The Workshop is designed to help you anticipate possible questions, review what you've learned, and begin thinking ahead to put your knowledge into practice. The answers to the quiz are in Appendix A, "Answers."

Quiz

1. What application is used to define users and groups in Windows NT?

2. What part of Windows NT security is used to define how passwords are used by all user accounts?

3. What are the three IIS authentication methods?

4. What is the IIS anonymous user account?

5. What must you do to enable Anonymous Authentication?

6. Why is the Basic Authentication method not considered to be a prudent security measure for a Web application?

7. What is the main difference between how data is transmitted using the Basic Authentication method and using the Windows NT Challenge/Response Authentication method?

8. What are the limitations of the Windows NT Challenge/Response Authentication method?

9. What technology does SSL use to encrypt information and authenticate other machines?

10. Where can a digital certificate be obtained to participate in an SSL connection?

Hour 23

Testing and Deploying Your Web Site

Up to this point, you've learned a great deal about the techniques and technologies involved in developing professional Web sites. However, one item I've only briefly alluded to is the all-important issue of testing your Web site (especially when multiple programmers are involved) and deploying the finished product to a production Web server. Therefore, in this hour, you'll learn about the Visual InterDev working modes, which enable you to isolate the work of individual team members until their work has been tested. After that, you'll then learn how to use the Copy Web Site functionality and the Deployment Explorer to quickly and easily copy or migrate one Web site from one Web server to another.

The highlights of this hour include the following:

- Discovering the project architecture and how it affects testing and deployment
- Learning about the different working modes
- Learning how the local working mode enables unit testing of the project

- Copying Web sites from one Web server to another
- Using the Deployment Explorer

Project Architecture

Before jumping into working modes and the Deployment Explorer, let's take a step back and look at the bigger picture of *project architecture*. You'll do this for a simple reason: The choices you make regarding working modes and deployment should come about as a direct result of your understanding of the overall architecture of your Web application.

Master and Local Application Files

A Web application or Web solution contains all the files that constitute that application's content and functionality. For example, a particular Web application may include files that contain HTML (.htm files), server script (.asp files), and image files. As you've created project after project in this book, you've certainly done your share of pointing Visual InterDev to the files that make up your Web applications. However, it's important to realize that when you create a Web project, the project file itself is not a part of the Web application. Instead, this file is a Visual InterDev–specific file that's used to define the files that make up your Web application as well as certain Visual InterDev–specific properties and settings.

Let's say that you have a team of developers who are all working on a Web-based distribution system. In this situation, it's important to realize that each developer creates a local Web project that will later be incorporated into the whole application. The Web project file remains on the developer's local computer and is not part of the Web application. In other words, when you deploy a Web application, the project file does not get copied with it, only the files containing your Web content and functionality.

When each of the developers in this example creates a Web project, he or she is actually working with two separate Web applications. One application is the *master* set of files on the production (or *master*) Web server. The second set of files is the local (to each developer) version of those files. Therefore, when a particular developer makes modifications to any of the Web application's files, those changes are made directly to the local files. This is why you'll sometimes hear people refer to a Visual InterDev project being a part of two separate Web applications (one master and one local for each developer). Figure 23.1 illustrates this architecture graphically.

Using this architecture, Visual InterDev affords the Web developer several advantages over working with other Web development tools that only allow working directly with the master set of files:

- Visual InterDev Project Explorer
- Team-based development
- Isolated development

FIGURE 23.1

The Visual InterDev project architectures is made up of a master set of files and a local set of files on each developer's workstation.

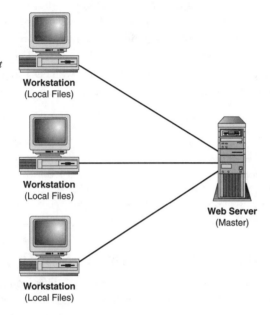

Workstation
(Local Files)

Workstation
(Local Files)

Workstation
(Local Files)

Web Server
(Master)

23

Visual InterDev Project Explorer

As you've experienced throughout your learning process with Visual InterDev, the Project Explorer gives you a tremendously flexible and robust means of graphically managing the files that constitute your Web application.

The Visual InterDev Project Explorer includes property windows and context-sensitive menus for each file type; powerful drag-and-drop interaction with the other Visual InterDev tools, such as Database Designer, Query Designer, and Site Designer; and the ability to define multiple Web and database projects within a single Web application.

Team-Based Development

By utilizing the local file set versus the master file set approach to Web development, Visual InterDev allows multiple developers to work on any given Web application concurrently. This is because each developer creates his or her localized version of the project that points to the master application on the production Web server. This way, developers can work independently on their local machines without fear of interfering with the work of the other developers on the team.

Isolated Development

That last point segues perfectly into the biggest advantage of the Visual InterDev project architecture: isolated development of individual developers.

Because each developer has his or her own local set of files, any modification made to a local file set is not replicated on the server until either the work is finished per the developer or the work has been certified to be functioning correctly using whatever metrics employed by the organization. This means that each developer has the freedom to develop, test, and debug without worrying about affecting others. Anyone who has had the nightmarish experience of having to directly modify code that's in production can certainly appreciate this functionality.

> Because of the isolated architecture of Visual InterDev Web applications, a developer can delete a project on his or her local workstation without impacting the master Web application files. Alternately, if desired, both the local and master versions of the application can be simultaneously deleted.

Multiple Projects Within a Single Solution

As you saw in Hour 15, "Using the Database Designer," when you learned about database projects, not only can a single Visual InterDev solution contain multiple projects, but each of these projects can be different types. This is because Visual InterDev supports Web projects and other Visual Studio–wide project types such as database projects and utility projects. The important point to realize here is that the Visual InterDev solution file (.sln) that points to its projects is also not considered to be a part of the Web application and therefore doesn't exist as a part of the master Web application file set.

Visual InterDev Project Architecture and Working Modes

Because you now know that a Web application consists of a master file set and a local file set, the question becomes, How do you tell Visual InterDev that you want to work with either or both of these file sets simultaneously? The answer is *working modes*. The project's working mode determines when changes made to the local files are sent to the master Web application.

Developers work on projects in one of two modes: local or master. Normally, the working mode for a project is defined when the project is created. However, Visual InterDev does allow you to change the working mode after you begin working on a project. You'll see how to do that shortly. Actually, in addition to the two main working modes, Visual InterDev supports a third working mode that works in conjunction with the other two. This mode is called the *offline mode*. The following sections outline the capabilities of each mode in more detail.

Local Mode

This is typically the mode you'll define for your projects when you want to develop in a local, isolated environment, such as when you're one member of a team of developers. Using the local working mode, any modifications you make and save only affect the local set of files on your workstation. In order to update the master Web application, you must explicitly specify that you're ready to do so. By working in this mode, you allow your developers the opportunity to completely test their work before attempting to merge it with production code on the production Web server.

Master Mode

The master working mode is the default working mode when a Visual InterDev project is created. This mode defines that when modifications are made to a project, these changes will automatically be replicated on the master Web application. In other words, Visual InterDev is responsible for making sure both sets of files remain in synchronization. Typically, you'll only want to use this working mode if you're developing in a standalone environment where you don't have to worry about merging your changes to the code base with other developers.

Offline Mode

The last working mode that I'll cover before looking at exactly how to set and change the working mode of a project is the offline mode. Although this mode isn't used by a large percentage of developers on a regular basis, it sure does come in handy when you need it.

Let's say your supervisor comes to you one afternoon and informs you that she's going out of town next week to demo your new system, which is all the talk around the office. You say no problem because, after all, it's a Web application. It can be run from any browser. However, then she drops the bomb: She wants you there because she wants to be able to incorporate, on the spot, any changes the customer can think of. Well, right off the bat, you would normally begin thinking of ways in which you can connect your laptop to the Web server from the customer site. However, what if you have problems connecting or the connection is slow? You're presenting the future of the company here. Luckily, for this reason and many more, Visual InterDev supports the ability to work offline, completely disconnected from the master Web server. With your project being in offline working mode, you can open a project, edit local copies of files, and run the application without a connection to the Web server. When you get back to the office, you can then decide which, if any, changes you want to upload to the master Web server.

Setting a Project's Working Mode

A project's working mode can be set in one of two ways. First, you can set the working mode when you create the project. The very first step of the Web Project Wizard allows for this selection (see Figure 23.2).

You can also change the working mode of a project during the life of that project. This is done by opening the Project Explorer and right-clicking the desired project. When the project's context menu appears, simply select the Working Mode menu option to display and select from the available working modes (see Figure 23.3).

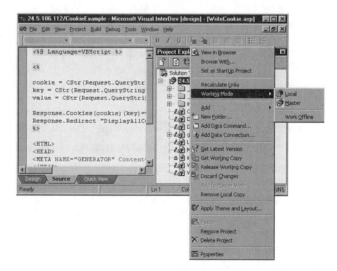

Deploying a Web Application

Now that you've seen how the local working mode enables the developing and testing of code in an isolated environment, let's take a look at how to deploy the Web application. *Web application deployment* means getting your application to the platforms on which it needs to run.

There are basically two distinctly different ways to go about deploying a Web application, depending on your needs as well as the complexity of the application and how it will be deployed. The first method involves simply copying the Web application from one Web server to another. This is sometimes referred to as *Web application duplication*. The second technique involves the Deployment Explorer. It provides much more control of which components of the Web application are copied and how.

23

Copying a Web Application

Visual InterDev's Copy Web Application feature enables you to duplicate an entire Web application between Web servers using either the master Web server or a local project as the source. Although this feature only enables you to copy to one Web server at a time, you can duplicate the following steps for as many Web servers as necessary:

1. Open the Web application that you want to duplicate.
2. From the Visual InterDev main menu, select the Project, Web Project, Copy Web Application menu item to display the Copy Project dialog box, shown in Figure 23.4.

FIGURE 23.4

Visual InterDev allows you to easily duplicate a Web project from one Web server to another using the Copy Web Application feature.

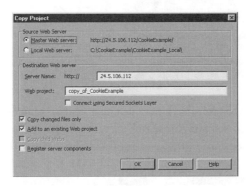

Notice that the first option on the dialog box is a set of radio buttons that allows you to specify which project (master or local) is the source of the duplication. As a convenience, the dialog box also shows the physical directory path of both projects.

3. After deciding which project will be the source, you need to specify the address of the Web server. As you can see in the example, this can be done via a URL in the typical format of www.myNewSite.com or via the Web server's IP address.

4. Once you've defined the target Web server, you can give the project the name that will identify it on the target machine.

5. Regarding security, you can specify whether you want to connect to the target machine using SSL (Secured Sockets Layer). In case you're interested, this protocol as well as other security issues are covered in Hour 22, "Web Site and Web Application Security."

6. The first check box at the bottom left of the Copy Project dialog box allows you to specify whether you only want to copy the files that have changed since the last time you copied the project. If you want to copy the entire project regardless, simply uncheck this option.

7. The next option enables you to specify whether the source project is being copied as a subfolder of an existing project on the target machine.

8. The Copy Child Webs check box is used if the source project is a root project and contains child projects. This option, therefore, enables you to copy all those projects at once.

9. The last option is used to specify whether you want Visual InterDev to automatically register any components such as ActiveX controls on the target machine once they're copied. At this point, you can click the OK button in order to start the copy. Notice that the dialog box doesn't give any real progress information (see Figure 23.5). However, if you look at the Visual InterDev status bar, you can track the copy's progress.

FIGURE 23.5

Visual InterDev Copy Web Application progress dialog.

10. When the copy has finished (and it can take several minutes, depending on the speed of your connection to the Web server), you'll see a message box that indicates whether the copy was successful (see Figure 23.6).

FIGURE 23.6

Visual InterDev confirms whether the copy was successful via a message box.

Using the Deployment Explorer

The last thing you'll look at in this hour is how to deploy a Web application to another Web server. In Visual InterDev, this feature is implemented via a tool called the *Deployment Explorer*. The main difference between the Copy Web Application feature and the Deployment Explorer is that the former is generally used to simply make a copy of a Web site, whereas the latter is typically used in order to deploy parts of a Web application that run on multiple Web servers.

In this section, you'll look at the following topics:

- Configuring a Web server as a deployment target
- Configuring the deployment target
- Specifying deployment outputs
- Deploying to the target

Configuring a Web Server as a Deployment Target

The first thing you need to do to deploy a Web application is make sure the target Web server is properly configured to be a deployment target. For starters, if the target Web server is running Microsoft Internet Information Server (IIS) or Personal Web Server (PWS), you do not have to install anything else *if* you're only deploying a Web application consisting of HTML code, HTML controls, and applets. However, if you're running either of these two Web servers and your Web application includes server-side components, you'll need to install the Microsoft Posting Acceptor (2 or later) on the Web server. The Microsoft Posting Acceptor product ships with both Visual Studio 6 and Visual J++ 6.

In addition to making sure that the prerequisite software is installed and configured on the server machine, you must also verify that you have read/write access to the Web server itself. It's always a good idea to get any user ID and password information *before* you begin the deployment because you won't be able to save a half-completed deployment attempt. In other words, once you begin the deployment, you'll need to either complete it or abort.

Configuring the Deployment Target

Once you've verified that the Web server is capable of being a deployment target, you need to configure it as a deployment target from within Visual InterDev. It's important to realize that the deployment target is not just a synonym for the target Web server. Rather, the deployment target itself contains several bits of information used to deploy an application, and one piece of that information is the target Web server HTTP address. The deployment target also defines the deployment services available on the specified Web server. As of version 6 of Visual InterDev, the following deployment services were defined:

23

- Client-side content—Defined as Web content, controls, and applets. These elements are referred to as client-side content because no additional support is needed on the Web server to make them operate correctly on the client workstation. This is why you don't have to have the Microsoft Posting Acceptor running if your application consists of only this type of content.

- Server-side content—Defined as any and all content executed on the Web server. The best example of server-side content is Active Server Pages.

Here's a step-by-step breakdown of how to define a deployment target:

1. Open the Visual InterDev project you're going to deploy.

2. Select the View, Other Windows, Deployment Explorer menu option from the main menu.

3. Notice that it's normal when you first display this window that the only entry it contains is the Deploy To My Computer option.

4. At the top of the Deployment Explorer, you'll see three icons. The first of these icons is used to create a new deployment target. Click this button to display the New Deployment Target dialog box (see Figure 23.7). Notice that the only target defined is the current Web master server.

FIGURE 23.7

The New Deployment Target dialog enables you to create deployment targets simply by specifying their HTTP address.

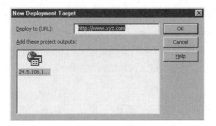

One important thing to note about the New Deployment Target dialog is that you need to provide the fully qualified address of the deployment target (including the virtual folder name), unless you want to copy the source application into the target's root folder.

5. At this point, type the HTTP address in the Deploy to (URL) field and click the OK button.

6. Once you've done that, Visual InterDev will query the target Web server about its capabilities and create a deployment target on your behalf. This deployment target is then added to the Deployment Explorer alongside the local computer entry.

7. Figure 23.8 shows an example of my Deployment Explorer after adding a deployment target. Notice that the available deployment services you learned about earlier are listed below each deployment target. In this case, you can see that although the specified server is running IIS 4, it does not have the Microsoft Posting Acceptor installed. Therefore, the only available deployment service is client-side content.

FIGURE 23.8

Visual InterDev automatically queries newly created deployment targets about their capabilities so that the Deployment Explorer accurately depicts the available deployment services for these targets.

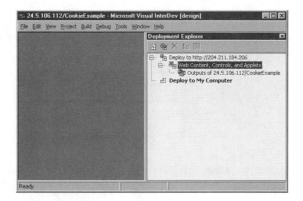

Specifying Deployment Outputs

In addition to the target Web server's HTTP address and that server's supported deployment services, the deployment target also contains a list of files to be deployed. To specify a project to deploy, follow these steps:

1. Open the project you want to deploy.

2. Open the Deployment Explorer window.

3. If you're including a full project to be deployed, right-click the desired deployment target's appropriate deployment service and select the Add Project Outputs menu option. This opens the Add Project Outputs dialog box. From there, simply select the desired projects and click the OK button.

4. Aside from including projects as part of a deployment, Visual InterDev also allows you to specify files that are not part of the project. To do this, right-click the desired deployment target's appropriate deployment service and select the Add File menu option. From there, simply browse to the desired files and select them.

Deploying to the Target

Once you've defined the deployment target and the files/projects you want to deploy, it's time run the deployment process. This is done with the following steps:

1. Open the Deployment Explorer.

2. Click the desired deployment target.

3. From the toolbar that runs along the top of the Deployment Explorer, click the Deploy button.

4. The Visual InterDev status bar will continually be updated as to the deployment's progress. When the deployment ends or is cancelled, Visual InterDev displays a list of any errors that occurred using the Task List window (see Figure 23.9).

FIGURE 23.9

The Task List window is used to display any errors that were encountered during the deployment.

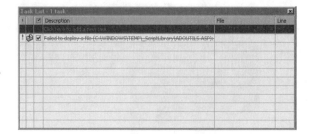

5. You can then walk through the list of errors and find out exactly what went awry with your deployment attempt. Notice that you can also mark the errors as handled by clicking the check box to the left of the error. Visual InterDev then grays out the error text and draws a line through it.

Summary

In this hour, you learned about the Visual InterDev project architecture and working modes and how they can be used in order to better test and deploy your Web application in a team environment. You then learned how to copy entire Web applications to remote Web servers using the Visual InterDev Copy Web Application feature. Finally, you finished up the hour by learning how to use Visual InterDev's deployment features to deploy your projects to Web servers for testing and production.

Q&A

Q Deployment sounds great for HTML and script, but what about my HTML references to Java applets? Won't they break if the directory hierarchy is different on the target machine?

A Actually, Visual InterDev automatically updates any HTML references to deployed Java classes so that changing the location of the file, through deployment, will not break the HTML link. Another point to note is that only the deployed HTML is updated on the Web server, not the HTML code in the source project.

Workshop

The Workshop is designed to help you anticipate possible questions, review what you've learned, and begin thinking ahead to put your knowledge into practice. The answers to the quiz and exercise are in Appendix A, "Answers."

Quiz

1. What two main Visual InterDev files that you work with all the time are not a part of the master Web application?

2. What is the difference between the master working mode and the local working mode?

3. What is the biggest advantage of the local working mode as it pertains to testing?

4. When would you use the offline working mode?

5. What information constitutes a deployment target?

6. When would you use the Deployment Explorer as opposed to simply duplicating the application via the Copy Web Application feature?

7. What are deployment outputs?

8. What are the supported deployment services?

9. What is needed on the target Web server to support the server-side content deployment service?

10. How does Visual InterDev communicate any deployment errors back to you?

Exercise

Now that you know about the Deployment Explorer, lay out the deployment strategy with regards to your own Web site.

23

HOUR **24**

Maintaining Your Web Site

In this, the last hour of your journey to discovering how Visual InterDev can be used to aid you in developing professional-quality Web sites, you will learn how to maintain your Web applications using the Link View tool. The Link View is an indispensable part of your toolbox because it enables you to graphically view your entire site in several ways by virtue of filters. In addition, this powerful tool is used to display and repair the nemesis of any Web site—broken links.

The highlights of this hour include

- Discovering the Link View tool
- Viewing link diagrams for a project
- Viewing link diagrams for any site on the Web
- Applying filters with the Link View
- Displaying and repairing broken links
- Using Link Repair to prevent broken links

Using Link View

The link diagram is the main element of the Link View tool. The link diagram enables you to graphically view the different elements, or items of your Web application, as icons. These link items, as they are called, are any files defined for the application, such as HTML files, Active Server Pages, or image files. In addition, a link item can also be Visual InterDev–specific elements, such as data commands and data connections.

A Web application's items are displayed on a link diagram with a line drawn between them and any other items to which they are programmatically linked. The Link View tool not only enables you to create link diagrams on your own Visual InterDev projects, but it also enables you to create link diagrams on any existing Web site for which you have a valid URL.

Creating a Link Diagram for a Visual InterDev Project

First, you will learn how to create a link diagram for a Visual InterDev project by following these steps:

1. Create a new project named LinkViewExamples.

2. After the project has been created, add an HTML file named default.htm.

3. Create an HTML file and an ASP file named about.htm and feedback.asp, respectively. Adding content to these files is unimportant for this exercise, so you can leave these pages blank.

4. Now, open the default.htm page in Design view and drag your newly created about.htm and feedback.asp files onto the default.htm page. Notice how Visual InterDev automatically creates the links for you.

5. When you are finished creating these files, open the Project Explorer and right-click the default.htm file.

6. When the default.htm file's context menu appears, select the View Links option. This causes Visual InterDev to open the default.htm file and parse it, looking for any links to Web items. When it has finished, these links will be displayed in a link diagram, like the one shown in Figure 24.1.

24

FIGURE 24.1

Link diagrams show the links between the different items in your Web application.

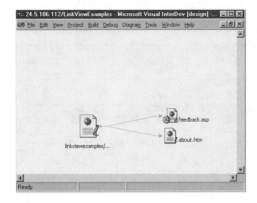

As you can see, the link diagram displays all three items that exist in your sample Web application and correctly diagrams the links between them. I'm going to add a bit of a twist here and show you how to add another link, using the following steps:

1. Open the Project Explorer.

2. Open the about.htm file in Design view.

3. Create a file named about-2.htm file. Again, you don't need any content on the page itself because the only thing you're concerned with here is showing how the different items link to one another, regardless of each item's content.

4. Drag the about-2.htm file from the Project Explorer onto the about.htm file in order to have Visual InterDev create the hyperlink between the two files.

5. Now, switch back to the link diagram if you have not closed it and select the View, Refresh menu item. If you have closed the link diagram, simply use the preceding technique and open a new link diagram based on the default.htm file. Figure 24.2 shows what your link diagram will now look like.

FIGURE 24.2

A multilevel Web application with the child items not expanded.

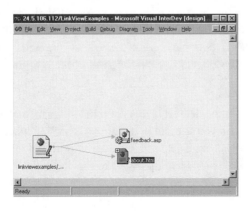

Notice the + sign next to the highlighted about.htm item. This means that the item has children items that are not being shown. Click the + sign in order to expand the child item so that you can see its links (see Figure 24.3).

FIGURE 24.3

A multilevel Web application with the child items expanded.

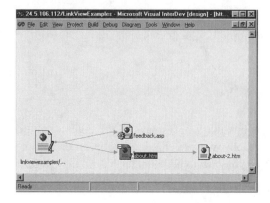

Creating a Link Diagram for Another Web Site

Follow these steps in order to create a link diagram for another Web site using that Web site's URL:

1. Select the Tools, View Links on WWW menu option.

2. When the View Links on WWW dialog appears, simply type in the URL of the desired site and click OK. If you chose a relatively large site, don't worry. In the next couple of sections, you'll see how to view large sites with a link diagram more easily.

Link Diagram Layouts

As you've seen, the link diagram provides an easy method of viewing which items in your Web application are linked. I will cover the different link diagram layouts next. Currently, link view supports two such layouts: the horizontal layout and the radial layout. You can toggle between these two layouts by selecting the Diagram, Change Diagram Layout menu option.

Horizontal Layout

The horizontal layout is the default layout for a link diagram and is used to display both *in links* and *out links*. As you learned in the previous section when you created your first link diagrams, this layout has each successive layer, or tier of your Web application being displayed along the x-axis (from left to right) of the diagram. Figure 24.4 shows a link diagram with a few more items added.

FIGURE 24.4

A link diagram in the horizontal layout.

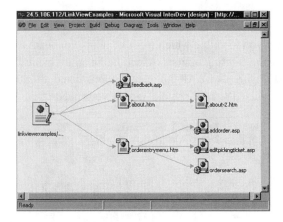

Radial Layout

A radial layout also shows both in links and out links for a Web application. However, both types cannot be viewed at the same time. The radial view shows the elements of the Web application arranged in a radial fashion around the central item of the diagram. Figure 24.5 shows an example of a link diagram with the radial layout. Notice that you can expand the child items in order to see their items as well.

FIGURE 24.5

A link diagram in the radial layout.

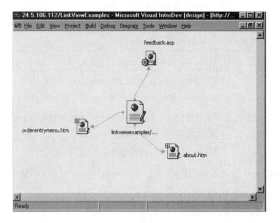

Managing the Viewable Content of a Large Link Diagram

As you might have guessed, link diagrams are easy to use for small Web applications. However, what if the Web application includes hundreds or even thousands of items? To help deal with this scenario, Link View provides two different means to enable you to manage the viewable content of a large link diagram. One way is to use filtering and the other is to use the zoom feature.

24

Filtering Link Diagrams

Filtering enables you to define which types of items you want to view in a link diagram. In order to view the filtering options, select the Diagram menu from the Visual InterDev main menu (see Figure 24.6). All the menu options listed after the Change Diagram Layout option are used to filter the diagram to your needs.

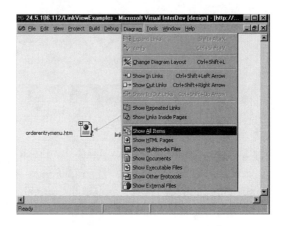

FIGURE 24.6

Visual InterDev provides several filtering options in order to deal with large link diagrams.

Table 24.1 provides a rundown of these options.

TABLE 24.1 Link Diagram Filtering Options

Filtering Option	Description
Show In Links	Enables you to specify that you want to view only the links that are coming into the main item of the link diagram
Show Out Links	Enables you to specify that you want to view only the items to which the main item is linked
Show In and Out Links	Displays both in links and out links
Show Repeated Links	Used in situations in which you have an item that is linked to by multiple items
Show Links Inside Pages	Displays the links inside the pages in the diagram
Show All Items	Displays all items
Show HTML Pages	Displays HTML pages
Show Multimedia Files	Displays multimedia files, such as images, sound files, and so on

Filtering Option	Description
Show Documents	Displays Office documents
Show Executable Files	Displays files that represent executable code (for example, DLLs, applications, batch files, and so on)
Show Other Protocols	Displays links that use protocols other than HTTP (for example, Mail, Telnet, and so on)
Show External Files	Displays all types of files that aren't defined as existing in the Web project

By default, all items are displayed on a link diagram. Selecting the desired menu option then toggles whether a given filter is in place when viewing the diagram. Note that some of these options can be combined in order to give you the precise view of the application that you need.

Using the Zoom Feature

The zoom feature is another way to manage how a large link diagram is viewed. This feature enables you to change the magnification of a link diagram. When you zoom in, items will appear larger and the labels can be read more easily. When you zoom out, you can view more content without having to scroll the diagram as much.

The zoom feature is controlled in two ways. The first way is via the link diagram's context menu, using the following steps:

1. Click the background of a link diagram with the right mouse button.
2. Select the Zoom menu option.
3. Select the exact zoom percentage that you want. Notice that the Zoom, Fit option causes the Link View to automatically set the magnification so that all items can be viewed within the viewable portion of the link diagram.

The second way is via the Site Diagram toolbar, using the following steps:

1. Display the Site Diagram toolbar by right-clicking the Visual InterDev main menu and selecting the Site Diagram menu option.
2. When the Site Diagram toolbar is displayed, you will see a combo box on the far right side (see Figure 24.7).
3. At this point, you can either select one of the predefined values included in this combo box or you can manually enter any percentage you want.

24

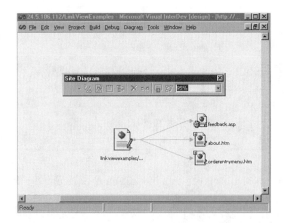

FIGURE 24.7

The Site Diagram tool-bar enables you to specify any magnification percentage for the zoom feature.

Displaying Broken Links

Obviously, broken links pertaining to the maintenance of a Web application are one of the biggest concerns of any Web administrator. To this end, Visual InterDev provides two different methods of displaying the broken links of an application: using the Broken Links Report or viewing them via a link diagram.

Using the Broken Links Report

The Broken Links Report is the first method I will discuss. To show how this works, perform the following steps:

1. Delete the about.htm and the feedback.asp files from the example project you created earlier in the hour.

2. After saving your work, select the View, Broken Links Report from the main menu.

3. When you run this report, you see output similar to that shown in Figure 24.8. Notice that not only are the broken links to the about.htm and feedback.asp shown, but this report also indicates the files that are present in the project but not referenced anywhere.

FIGURE 24.8

An example of the Broken Links Report.

```
Output                                                              ×
Broken Links Report                                                 ▼
Unused files in project:
   search.htm
   default.htm

Broken links in project:
   feedback.asp: broken link from default.htm
   about.htm: broken link from default.htm

Broken external links:

Broken links report complete. All items have been added to the ta
```

Viewing Broken Links with a Link Diagram

The link diagram is another way to display broken links. Using the preceding example, follow these steps to see how this works:

1. Open the Project Explorer.
2. Right-click the default.htm file and select the View Links menu option.

   Figure 24.9 illustrates how the link diagram displays broken links. Notice that the icons are red, the lines are red, and the icons representing the pages are broken. This might be a bit of an overkill, but it gets the point across.

FIGURE 24.9

The link diagram displays any broken links it finds with a special icon.

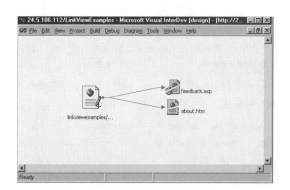

24

Using Link Repair and Preventing Broken Links

So far in this hour, you've learned how to use the Link View and link diagrams to view the current state of a Web application (including broken links). However, one thing that you haven't learned is how to prevent broken links *before* they occur. In Visual InterDev, this is done via the Link Repair feature.

Continually reorganizing a Web application by deleting and moving files and folders is a big problem because it inevitably leads to broken links. Luckily, Visual InterDev provides a way to automatically repair these links before they become the source of ugly emails from customers complaining that your site isn't working correctly.

Using Link Repair, all *relative links* in target files are automatically repaired when the target files are renamed, moved, or deleted. It's important to understand the distinction between explicit links and relative links. Explicit links specify the complete URL to the target file. In a relative link, however, the URL is relative to the current file.

To turn this feature on, follow these steps:

1. Select the Tools, Options menu option in order to display the Options dialog (see Figure 24.10).

FIGURE **24.10**

*Link Repair settings
are defined via the
Tools, Options menu
option.*

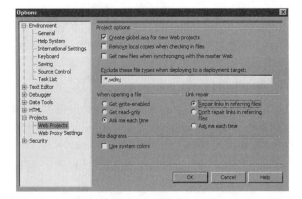

2. In the tree view on the left side of the dialog, expand the Projects entry and select the Web Projects entry.

3. On the right side of the dialog, you will see the different settings for the Link Repair feature.

4. As you can see, the default is for Visual InterDev to ask you each time a link might be broken as a result of deleting, renaming, or moving the target file of a link. Changing this option to Repair Links in Referring Files causes Visual InterDev to automatically repair all broken links without asking.

If you are using version control and you are going to delete, rename, or move a file that is the target of a link, you should also check out all files from version control that will be affected by the Link Repair.

Summary

In this hour, you learned about the Link View tool and how it enables you to graphically view the different element of your Web application. In addition to creating a link diagram of your project, you also discovered how to use the zoom feature and filters to manage large link diagrams. Finally, you learned how to find broken links using both the link diagram and the Broken Links Report and how to automatically prevent them using the Link Repair feature.

Q&A

Q If I can use the Broken Link Report to obtain a report of all broken links within a Web application, does the Link View really do that much for me?

A That depends on how you maintain and view your Web application. The main purpose of the Link View is to not only allow you to view broken links, but to also give you a tool that enables you to view all the items and see how they link to one another.

Workshop

The Workshop is designed to help you anticipate possible questions, review what you've learned, and begin thinking ahead to put your knowledge into practice. The answers to the quiz and exercises are in Appendix A, "Answers."

24

Quiz

1. What is a link diagram?
2. What are the different link diagram layouts?
3. What are the two methods of visually managing the content of a large link diagram?
4. What are in links?
5. What are out links?
6. What are the two ways to zoom a link diagram?
7. What are the two ways of displaying broken links?
8. What feature does Visual InterDev supply to help prevent broken links?
9. What are the three options for Link Repair?
10. What is the difference between an explicit link and a relative link?

Exercises

1. Open a complex Web site on the Internet (such as `www.microsoft.com` or `www.SourceDNA.com`) as a link diagram and see if you can spot any broken links.
2. See if you can view all the links from the home page of the popular Visual C++/MFC development site, `www.CodeGuru.com`.

PART V
Appendixes

APPENDIX A

Answers

This appendix provides the answers to the quiz and exercises at the end of each hour.

Hour 1

Quiz

1. What is the difference between a Visual InterDev solution and a Visual InterDev project?

   A Visual InterDev solution is a logical grouping of Visual InterDev projects. A Visual InterDev project is a grouping of files that make up a Web application.

2. Why are two sets of files created when you create a Visual InterDev project?

   One set of files resides on the Web server and can be thought of as "production files" in that they are implemented when a user browses to your Web site. The other set of files exists on the client (or local) machine. This enables you to work offline until you've tested your Web application so that you can debug any problems before affecting the production files.

3. Where do the files for a Visual InterDev project get created on the server?

   The files that get created on the Web server for a Visual InterDev project are created in a directory with the same name as the project. This directory can be found on the Web server in the directory that is designated as your Web server root directory. For example, because my Web server directory is defined as d:\Inetpub\Wwwroot, the files for the AddrBook project are located in d:\Inetpub\Wwwroot\AddrBook.

4. What is the Project Explorer used for?

   The Project Explorer is used to manage the files associated with a given Visual InterDev solution and its projects.

5. What is the difference between a pencil icon and a lock icon when shown next to an element in the Project Explorer?

   The pencil icon represents a read/write copy of the file that exists locally. The lock icon means that the local copy of the file is read-only.

6. What is a virtual root directory and what is it used for?

   The virtual root directory is the directory on the Web server that contains all the files for a Visual InterDev project.

7. What is the filename of the Web page that you must create in order to allow a user to browse to a project by specifying just `http://Web server/project name`?

   Both Microsoft Internet Information Server and Microsoft Personal Web Server define the default document for a Web application as either default.htm or default.asp. Therefore, either answer would be correct. However, if your Web application has both files, IIS will use default.asp, and PWS will use default.htm.

8. How do you create a hyperlink on a Web page in Visual InterDev?

   Open the Web page that you want to contain the hyperlink, type in the desired text using the WYSIWYG editor, select that text, click the Link toolbar button, and specify the desired URL.

9. What is an Active Server Page?

   An Active Server Page is a mixture of HTML and server-side scripting code that enables you to have active, or dynamic content in your Web site.

10. When viewing an Active Server Page in Quick View, why will Visual InterDev not run any of its embedded server-side scripts?

    Because by definition, server-side scripts and controls are designed to run on the server and not on the local machine.

Exercises

1. Try adding a new link to the default.htm file to point to an existing Web page such as http://www.microsoft.com.

   Open the default.htm file in the editor and type in the desired text. Then after selecting the text, click the Link toolbar button and specify http://www.microsoft.com.

2. Try adding more rows and columns to the table in the AddrBook.asp Active Server Page.

   Open the AddrBook.asp file in the editor. In order to insert new rows, place the cursor *after* the row where you want to insert the new row and select Table, Insert Row. In order to insert a column in an existing table, simply position the cursor in the column that is to the right of where you want the column to be located and select Table, Insert Column.

Hour 2

Quiz

1. Why is the use of styles so important in presenting a professional Web site?

   Defining different styles for different areas of the document (for example, headers, captions, footers, content, and so on), helps the user to more easily read through the document. Additionally, consistently using the same styles helps to produce a professional look and feel to the Web site.

2. When creating a hyperlink, how do you specify that the page being linked to should be opened in its own instance of the browser?

   By setting the TARGET keyword.

3. What is the difference between a hyperlink and bookmark?

   A hyperlink is used to jump to another Web page. A bookmark is used to navigate within to other sections of the current page.

4. How are dividers added to a Web page?

   By selecting the HTML, Div menu option.

5. What must you do before you can insert an image onto a Web page using Visual InterDev?

   The image must first be defined for the project before it can be used on any of the project's Web pages.

A

6. Which HTML tag is needed to define a background image for a Web page?

    The <BODY> tag is used to specify the image background for a Web page. Here's an example of how to do this:

    ```
    <body background=images/vintdev.JPG>
    ```

7. What benefits are derived from using the include directive?

    The main benefit is that it allows you to define HTML that will be used in multiple Web pages in one file. This makes maintenance of the Web site much easier and cuts down on errors.

8. What is the difference between the virtual and file keywords on the include directive?

    The virtual keyword is used to specify a filename that is relative to a virtual directory.

    The file keyword is used to specify a filename that is relative to the directory of the current Web page.

9. What are the keywords used to control when a video clip plays and how many times it plays?

    The START keyword is used to define when a video should start playing. For example, START=MouseOver indicates that the video should start playing only when the user moves the mouse over the image that represents the video.

    The LOOP keyword controls how many times the video will play. For example, specifying LOOP=Infinite will result in a continuous playing video.

10. When manually typing HTML tags into a Web page's Source view, how does Visual InterDev make remembering the different keywords unnecessary?

    When typing HTML code directly into a Web page's Source view, the Properties window will dynamically show the properties for the current tag or item being modified.

Exercises

1. Take a look at one of the articles on www.codeguru.com and see how closely you can make one of your Web pages match it.

    If you get stuck on this, one helpful trick is to view the source of one of the pages and compare it to what you have.

2. Now that you've seen most of the basic elements to a Web page, start thinking about how you want to lay out your Web site.

    Make sure to think about how the user will navigate from page to page, whether you'll want a search engine, and in what styles you'll want to present each page's content.

Hour 3

Quiz

1. How are layouts and navigation bars related?

   Layouts are used to define where the navigation bars will be positioned on a Web page.

2. How do you create a new template file?

   Simply by creating the desired file (HTML, ASP, or CSS) and copying it into the Visual InterDev template directory.

3. How can you create a file from a template?

   After you've created the desired file from which other files will be created, copy that file into the appropriate Visual InterDev template folder. Now, when you select the Add, Add Item menu option from the project's context menu, the newly created template will appear alongside the standard Visual InterDev templates such as HTML Page and ASP Page.

4. What are Cascading Style Sheets?

   Cascading Style Sheets enable you to define styles at different levels of your application so that you don't have to define each style every place it is going to be used.

5. Why are they called *cascading*?

   Because they can be overridden at different levels and therefore, cascaded with regards to order of precedence.

6. How do you link a Web page to an external Cascading Style Sheet file?

   Open the Web page in Source view and drag the desired Cascading Style Sheet between the <HEAD> and </HEAD> HTML tags.

7. How do you define document-level styles?

   There are two ways. The first way is to open a Web page in Source view and manually type in the <STYLE> tags between the <HEAD> and </HEAD> tags. An easier way is to create the styles using the Cascading Style Sheet editor and copy and paste the resulting source code into the Source view of a Web page.

8. How do you apply styles to an element of a Web page such as a division or span?

   Open the Web page in Design view; select the element, <DIV>, or <SPAN> that you want to style; display the Properties window; and specify that style's Class property.

A

9. What is the order of precedence regarding Cascading Style Sheets?

Styles applied to elements, divisions, and spans take precedence over document-level styles. Document-level styles take precedence over linked external Cascading Style Sheet files.

10. What are style classes and how are they defined?

Classes are used to implement a given style in more than one manner. For example, if you want to use the CODE style for both Visual Basic and Visual C++, you could define a CODE.VB and CODE.VC class. Classes are created in the Cascading Style Sheet editor.

Exercises

1. Create a template for a very simple bug-tracking Web site in which each bug is listed on one page that contains a link to another page detailing the nature of the bug. Remember to allow for input of information from the user as he creates his pages.

First, create a table of contents page that will contain the hyperlinks to the bug pages. Then create a template using the <%# and #%> tags to accept user input for things such as type of bug, priority, module, date, and so on. These values will be used to create the actual bug page. Because we haven't gotten into scripting yet, everything else such as the creation of the hyperlink from the bug list to a specific bug page would have to manually be done.

2. Give the users the ability to create either a Visual Basic page or a Visual C++ page in which the CODE styles of each page are completely different.

First, create two template HTML pages: one called something like vb_templ.htm and one called vc_templ.htm. Then create two Cascading Style Sheet files: one called vb.css and one called vc.css in which the CODE style on each is vastly different (at least enough to test with). Open the vb_templ.htm file in Source view and drag the vb.css file between the <HEAD> and </HEAD> tags. Do the same thing for the vc_templ.htm and vc.css files. Now when a user creates a new HTML page implementing the vb_templ.htm file, any text formatted with the CODE style will use the definition as per the vb.css file. Additionally, when a user creates a new HTML page implementing the vc_templ.htm file, any text formatted with the CODE style will use the definition as per the vc.css file.

Hour 4

Quiz

1. What is a site diagram used for?

Prototyping and designing the navigation of a Web site.

2. What are the different options for adding pages to a site diagram?

   Adding new pages, adding existing pages from the project, and adding links from other applications.

3. How do you add a link from another application to the site diagram?

   Open the other application, select the hyperlink, and drag it to the site diagram.

4. Can a project have multiple site diagrams?

   Yes.

5. How is the site diagram stored?

   The site diagram information is stored in a site structure file.

6. Can a project have multiple site structure files?

   No. Although a project might have multiple site diagrams, it can have only one site structure file.

7. What are the options when you attempt to remove a page from a site diagram?

   When attempting to remove a page from a site diagram, Visual InterDev displays a dialog that asks if you want to just remove the page from the diagram or if you also want to remove it completely from the current project.

8. How do you attach and detach a page that already exists on a site diagram to another page?

   Pages can be attached and detached to other pages via drag and drop from within the site diagram.

9. What DTC is used to create a navigation bar?

   The PageNavBar DTC.

10. What is the limitation Visual InterDev imposes when stipulating that a page is to be added to the global navigation bar?

    A page whose link exists on a global navigation bar cannot have a parent page. If it does when you attempt to add it to the global navigation bar, Visual InterDev displays a dialog that allows you to confirm that it's okay that the page be detached from its current page.

Exercise

Design a Web site that has several layers of Web pages to it and play around with the different layouts and PageNavBar properties. After you learn how to integrate these tools into your design of a Web site, you'll find that they are indispensable tools for getting a prototype of a Web site up quickly.

You're on your own for this one.

Hour 5

Quiz

1. Name some of the advantages of version control.

   Development team coordination, versioning, and the ability to share reusable components across software projects.

2. What is the biggest advantage of using Visual SourceSafe with your Visual InterDev applications?

   The Visual InterDev development environment is tightly integrated with Visual SourceSafe so that almost anything you need to do in the way of version control can be done without leaving Visual InterDev.

3. What must you do first before you can define project-level rights for each user?

   Run the SourceSafe Admin application. Select the Tools, Options menu option. When the Options dialog is displayed, select the Security tab and check the project-level security check box.

4. How do you specify that a given Visual InterDev project is to be added to version control?

   Display the Visual InterDev Project Explorer. Select the desired project. Then, select the Project, Source Control, Add To Source Control menu option and follow the prompts.

5. How do you remove a Visual InterDev project from version control?

   Display the Visual InterDev Project Explorer. Then, select the Project, Source Control, Remove [solution name] from Source Control menu option and click the OK button on the confirmation dialog.

6. How do you enable/disable version control for a Visual InterDev solution?

   Select the desired solution in the Project Explorer. Then, select the Project, Source Control, Change Connection menu option and fill out the ensuing dialog.

7. How do you add files to version control if they've been added to a Visual InterDev project while the project was disconnected from version control?

   Right-click on the file(s) in the Project Explorer. From the display context menu, select the Add To Source Control menu option. When the Add to Source Control dialog is displayed, specify the target Visual SourceSafe folder and click OK.

8. How do you enable the multiple-file checkout feature of Visual SourceSafe?

   Run the Visual SourceSafe Admin application. Select the Tools, Options menu option. Check the Allow Multiple Checkout check box and click OK to save your changes.

9. How do you create a label in Visual SourceSafe?

Open the Visual SourceSafe application. Right-click the desired folder. From the displayed context menu, select the Label menu option and then give the label a name as well as a descriptive comment.

10. How do you download from Visual SourceSafe the files that are specific to a given label?

Open the Visual SourceSafe application. Right-click on the desired project and select the Show History menu option. When the Project History Options dialog is displayed, check the Labels Only check box and click OK. When the History dialog is displayed, select the appropriate label and click the Get button to retrieve the files for that label.

Exercises

1. Test the automatic and manual merge capabilities of Visual SourceSafe.

This can easily be done by creating two Visual SourceSafe users and then having each user check out the same file. Have the first user change and check in the file. Then have the second user change the same file (not the same lines of code) and have that user check in the code. Visual SourceSafe should automatically accomplish this merge because there is no conflict.

Now, repeat the previous steps, but this time, have the second user change the same lines of code that the first user changed. Now, when you attempt to check in the second user's code, Visual SourceSafe should alert you that a conflict has occurred and prompt you to merge the files. At this point, you will be able to practice using the Visual SourceSafe visual merge editor.

2. Test the ability to label multiple versions of a project in Visual Source and retrieve only the desired versions.

Create a Visual InterDev project and using what you've learned in this hour, add the project to Visual SourceSafe. Now make some changes to a file such as search.htm and check in the changes. After you've done that, create a label called Version 1. When you've created the first label, check the file out again and make some more changes. Then, check the file back into version control and set a second label called Version 2. Now using what you've learned about retrieving specific labels, download the files for the Version 1 label. You will see that the changes you made in Version 2 are no longer present because you have retrieved a previous version of the file from version control.

A

Hour 6

Quiz

1. Why is scripting needed when you have HTML?

   HTML was originally designed to simply display static data. Scripting affords the Web developer the ability to write interactive Web applications so that information can be retrieve from the user and dynamically configured information can be displayed back to the user.

2. Why is script written as though it were a comment or series of comments?

   The reason script is written into HTML as an HTML comment is for backward compatibility with older browsers that were developed before the advent of scripting. That way, these browsers will simply see the script as a comment and not attempt to do anything with it. Newer, script-aware browsers, however, know that the "comments" between the <SCRIPT> and </SCRIPT> tags are to be interpreted as script code using the browsers' built-in scripting engines.

3. How do you add a JavaScript event handler for an HTML control?

   After dragging the desired control onto the Web page, you click the Source tab of the HTML editor. Then, after the Script Outline window is displayed, you locate the control and double-click the event you want to handle. Visual InterDev will automatically create the function for you and place the caret at the beginning of the function.

4. How can you change the default behavior of a TextBox or TextArea control to automatically select its contents upon receiving focus?

   By handling the object's onclick event and calling its select function.

5. How do you add items to a Select object using JavaScript?

   Items are added to a Select object by using the <OPTION> tag. Here's an example of how to add two items to a Select object named lbxCountries:

   ```
   <SELECT id=lbxCountries name=lbxCountries size=2 style=
   ➥"HEIGHT: 38px; WIDTH: 144px">
   <option value="United States">United States
   <option value="1">Germany
   </SELECT>
   ```

6. How do you make one of the entries in a Select object the default entry?

   Using the example in question 5, simply define one of the OPTION elements with the SELECTED keyword:

   ```
   <option selected value="United States">United States
   ```

7. How do you retrieve the value of the currently selected Radio Button control?

   By iterating through all the Radio Button controls having the same name in the group and querying each control for its `Checked` property. When you've located the one Radio Button control that has its `Checked` property turned on, you then query that object for its `Value` property. Alternatively, you can insert and use the `getRadioValue` function used in the Feedback example.

8. How is a CheckBox control's state retrieved?

   You can check the state of a CheckBox control by examining its `Checked` property. A string value of `false` is returned if the CheckBox is unchecked, and a value of `true` is returned if it is checked.

9. How do you insert a new JavaScript function into the source code of a Web page?

   Start by opening the Web page in Source view. Then right-click the background of the HTML editor and select the Script Block, Client menu option. This will insert the new block into the source code, whereupon you can start coding your new function.

10. What JavaScript function is used to display information to the user?

    To display simple messages to the user, use the `alert` function.

Exercise

Create a new Web page that has multiple groups of mutually exclusive Radio Button controls and figure out how to have them work correctly.

Remember that the trick here is that each group of Radio Button controls is made up of the controls that have the same `Name` value.

Hour 7

Quiz

1. What is the top-level object in the JavaScript object hierarchy?

   The `Window` object.

2. What two `Window` object events are typically the only ones you would use from JavaScript?

   The two most commonly used `Window` object events are `onload` and `onunload`. These two events allow you to perform initialization and deinitialization tasks for the window.

3. What `Document` object methods are used to write HTML to a Web page?

   The `Document` object's `write` and `writeln` methods are used to dynamically write HTML to a document.

4. How can you determine the current browser being used to view your Web page?

By using the following line of code:

```
var browser=navigator.appName;
```

5. How do you specify RGB values when setting any of the Document object's color properties?

By all three values (red, green, and blue) in hexadecimal (rrggbb).

6. What is the difference between the aLink and vlinkColor properties of the Document object?

The aLink property defines the color that will be used when the link is activated by the user clicking it (but not releasing the button). The vlinkColor property defines the color of a link that has been visited.

7. What is the ENCTYPE property used for in the <FORM> tag?

The ENCTYPE property defines the format of the data that will be sent.

8. How do you submit a form from a Web page?

By defining a Form object and specifying an action. Here's an example in which an email will be sent when the form's Submit function is called:

```
<FORM NAME="MyForm" ACTION="mailto:tarcher@codeguru.com" method=Get>
```

Once you have an action specified for the form, add a Submit button from the Toolbox. When the user clicks this button (whose Type property is set to Submit), the defined action for the form will be executed.

9. How do you send email using JavaScript?

The easiest way is to set an action for the form and then to either call the Form.Submit method explicitly or add a Submit button to the page.

10. How do you add the capability for the user to reinitialize a Web page?

By adding a Reset button to the page. This button automatically has its Type property set to Reset, which means that if you don't override its onclick event, the form's Reset code will run. This, in turn, will cause the form to initialize all its known child controls.

Exercise

Open the ClientScripts project you created in the last hour and modify the Feedback page so that it emails you the information from the form when the user clicks the Send Feedback button.

Use the technique you learned in this hour while developing the Registration page. Don't forget to specify ENCTYPE="text/plain" in the <FORM> tag.

Hour 8

Quiz

1. What is the difference between ActiveX and ActiveX controls?

   ActiveX refers to several COM-based technologies, whereas ActiveX controls represent a specific means of implementing ActiveX.

2. What are some of the advantages of using ActiveX controls?

   Multiplatform support, user-defined security, intelligent download capability, and availability.

3. What are some of the disadvantages of using ActiveX controls?

   Lack of multiplatform support, security, and lack of browser support.

4. Why does Microsoft seem to disagree with some experts' opinions that ActiveX controls are unsafe?

   Microsoft's view is that ActiveX controls give the users the best of both worlds. They can reject controls from unknown or distrusted sources while at the same time being able to use controls from sources that they do trust.

5. When Internet Explorer prompts the user regarding the downloading of an ActiveX control, what are the user's options?

   The user can reject the control, accept the control, or agree to accept all controls from the certified company or individual who wrote this control.

6. What HTML tag is used to define an ActiveX control?

   `<OBJECT>`

7. In very general terms, what is the CLASSID attribute used for?

   It uniquely identifies the control in the Windows Registry.

8. What does the PARAM attribute do, and how does it differ from setting an ActiveX control's properties at runtime when responding to an event?

   The PARAM attribute is used to set a control's properties in an HTML `<OBJECT>` tag. The difference is that the PARAM attribute is used when the control is being initialized and therefore, this attribute would not be used when setting a control's properties in response to a given event.

9. How are new ActiveX controls added to Visual InterDev so that they can be dropped onto a Web page?

   They are added via the Customize Toolbox dialog that is displayed via the Toolbox window's context menu.

A

10. What is an OLE property page?

An OLE property page allows the user of the control to set certain design-time properties.

Exercise

Add some additional buttons and controls to the ImageProcessing demo to make it more of a full-fledged image-processing application.

Take what you've learned and simply add more buttons and controls as you see fit. Use the Object Browser to see what methods and properties the Image class exposes.

Hour 9

Quiz

1. What is Dynamic HTML?

A feature of a browser that enables dynamic content to be displayed to the user even after the page has been downloaded.

2. What is a technique for gracefully degrading to a browser that doesn't support Dynamic HTML?

Use the Document Object Model's navigator (or clientInformation) object to determine the browser. If the browser is not capable of handling Dynamic HTML, display another version of the page that will work with the detected browser.

3. What is the main difference between how Dynamic HTML is defined in Netscape and how it is defined with Microsoft IE?

Netscape only allows the definition of Dynamic HTML through the HTML LAYER tag, whereas Microsoft enables any HTML element to be used in a dynamic fashion.

4. What is the benefit of Dynamic styles?

Dynamic styles enable the Web page to change the appearance of the textual content in response to runtime variables such as date and time or user input.

5. What is the difference between the innerText and innerHTML properties?

The innerText property is used to retrieve or set the text of an element (excluding HTML tags), whereas the innerHTML includes the HTML tags.

6. What is the TextRange object used for?

The TextRange object is used to manipulate the entire document of text or any specified range of text as an object.

7. How is a `TextRange` object created?

   A `TextRange` object is created by calling the `createTextRange` method of a `BODY`, `BUTTON`, `TEXTAREA` element, or an `INPUT` element whose type has been defined as `TEXT`.

8. What is the difference between the `TextRange` properties, `text` and `htmlText`?

   The `TextRange` object's `text` property is used to retrieve or set the text (excluding HTML tags). The `htmlText`, on the other hand, includes the HTML tags.

9. What `TextRange` method is used to search a document?

   The `TextRange` object's `findText` is used in order to search for text.

10. What Document Object Model property is used in order to create a watermark?

    The `document.body.style.cssText` property can be used to specify a document's watermark image.

Exercise

Create a Web page that provides a template letter in which the user can enter the values (To Address, From Address, Subject, and so on) that will be used in the letter itself.

Using what you've learned about the `TextRange` object, this should be relatively easy. Simply create the base content for the page. However, in the place of the values that the user will supply, enter a placeholder. For example, instead of typing in a To Address, you could enter something like *$$$ToAddress$$$*. Continuing in that vein, the placeholder for the subject might be *$$$Subject$$$*. When you've finished with the base page, add a Textbox control and a Button to the bottom of the page.

When the user first enters the page, the button might say something like Set To Address and when clicked on, the `onclick` method would search for occurrences of *$$$ToAddress$$$* and replace them with the text entered into the Textbox control. The script would then change the Button control's value to the next value to be set (for example, From Address).

Even with what you've learned from this hour, this exercise might be a bit difficult. However, it's definitely a good learning tool. Therefore, if you find yourself getting stuck, search the companion CD-ROM for the AddressTemplate Visual InterDev project to see one way that this can be implemented.

Hour 10

Quiz

1. What are scriptlets?

   Scriptlets are Dynamic HTML pages that are treated as components.

A

2. How are scriptlets safer than Java applets and ActiveX controls?

   Scriptlets are safer because they rely solely on the W3C standardized Document Object Model and scripting code.

3. What are the three basic concepts of almost any component architecture?

   Methods, properties, and events.

4. What is the difference between a scriptlet and an include?

   An include simply inserts the contents of the specified file into the specified location of the Web page, whereas a scriptlet is a true component in that it provides encapsulation, public and private method, and property definition and event raising capabilities.

5. Using JavaScript, what is the syntax for defining a `public` method in a scriptlet?

   `function public_YourMethodNameHere(vars)`

6. How do you define an HTML page as a scriptlet in Visual InterDev so that it appears in the Toolbox window?

   By right-clicking on it in the Project Explorer and selecting the Mark as Scriptlet menu option.

7. What HTML element is used to access a scriptlet from another HTML page?

   The `OBJECT` element.

8. What is the syntax for defining a `public` property that can be set in a scriptlet in JavaScript?

   `function public_put_yourPropertyName`

9. How are standard HTML events bubbled up to the scriptlet's container?

   Events are bubbled up to the scriptlet's container by calling the `window.external.bubbleEvent` method.

10. How are custom events defined for a scriptlet?

    Custom events can be raised from a scriptlet to its container by calling the `window.external.raiseEvent` method.

Exercises

1. Create a scriptlet that represents a VIN verification component.

   Use what you learned in writing your first scriptlet, along with what you learned about custom events to return error information when a VIN is invalid.

2. Create a scriptlet that represents a rotating ad banner component.

   The trick here is that you will want to use an <IMG> tag in the scriptlet and the window.setTimeout method in order to create a timer so that you can rotate the banners at regular intervals. Also, don't forget to expose some properties so that the container can configure things such as the images to be used and rotation interval.

Hour 11

Quiz

1. What was the first technology introduced to process forms on the server?

   Common Gateway Interface.

2. What is Microsoft's server API that is used to write server-side applications?

   Internet Server Application Programming Interface (ISAPI).

3. If you are running Windows 95 or Windows 98, which Web server must you install in order to develop and deploy Active Server Pages?

   Microsoft Personal Web Server.

4. If Visual InterDev can't process server-side script, how can you view the results of your work?

   Select the View, View in Browser menu option.

5. When writing server script, what do the <% and %> commands do?

   They are delimiters. All code with them is to be run on the server only. Any code outside of these delimiters is either HTML or client script.

6. In order to submit a form to the server, what form attribute must be set?

   The ACTION attribute is used to specify the server file that will process the form.

7. In order to submit a form to the server, what must the form's method property be set to?

   You must remember to set this value to POST in order to submit a form to the server for processing.

8. What object does the Active Server Page use to get values from the form being passed?

   The Request object is used by the Active Server Page to access form values passed from the Web page.

9. What event do you need to handle to validate the form when the user is attempting to submit the form to the server?

   The form object's onsubmit event is usually handled to do validation. Returning a value of false from this function will stop the form from being submitted to the server.

A

10. What are some of the advantages of using Active Server Pages as opposed to using CGI or ISAPI?

- Active Server Pages are easy to write. They are written using a scripting language, such as JavaScript, JScript, or VBScript.

- Active Server Pages are easy to maintain because the code is inserted into the Web page. Therefore, there is no need to keep up with a completely isolated set of source code that is stored separately from the Web page's HTML and client script.

- The code is executed on the server. Therefore, it is not limited by the browser's security policy, such as not being allowed to have system level access to the file system or database.

- The server script is stripped out before it is sent to the browser as pure HTML. Therefore, your proprietary applications can't be easily stolen.

- Because only pure HTML is sent back, Active Server Pages will work regardless of the type of browser that the client computer is running.

Exercise

Write a simple logon Web page that requires that the user enter a password, which is then validated on the server.

You're on your own for this one.

Hour 12

Quiz

1. What object and collection are used to retrieve the information from a submitted form?

   The Request object's Form collection is used to retrieve the information from a submitted form.

2. What Request collection can be used to pass variables in the HTTP string?

   The QueryString collection is used to retrieve the parameters that are passed in the HTTP string. For example, in the following URL identifier, the two variables (name and age) are being passed that are both accessible via the QueryString collection:

   ```
   http://teams.asp?name=Tom&age=34
   ```

   These values would then retrieve as follows:

   ```
   Request.QueryString("name")
   Request.QueryString("age")
   ```

3. What Request collection is used to determine things like the browser name and version?

The ServerVariables collection.

4. What two `Response` properties enable you to specify the amount of time that a cached page can exist before it needs to be refreshed?

`Expires` and `ExpiresAbsolute`.

5. What unique identifier is created every time a new user session is created for a Web application?

The `SessionID`, which is a property of the `Session` object.

6. How can the Web application explicitly terminate a user's session?

By calling the `Abandon` method.

7. What are the special circumstances regarding the modification of an array's data after it has been added to a `Session` object?

After you've inserted an array into the `Session` object, the only way to modify that array's data is to extract the array into a local variable, modify its contents, and then restore the array into the `Session` object.

8. What methods are used in order to synchronize access to the `Application` object?

The `Lock` and `Unlock` methods.

9. How are COM objects created in script?

Via the `Server` object's `CreateObject` method.

10. What sort of global events can be handled in the global.asa file?

- `Session_OnStart`
- `Session_OnEnd`
- `Application_OnStart`
- `Application_OnEnd`

Exercise

Write the script necessary to maintain the number of times that a Web page is visited.

The following example uses an application-level variable called nVisits to store the number of times that a particular page (or group of pages) has been visited. Note that the `Application.Lock` method is called to ensure that only the current client can modify the nVisits variable. When finished, the `Application.Unlock` method is called so that this other code can then access the `Application` object. Remember that the `Lock` and `Unlock` methods are object wide. In other words, you cannot lock access to a single variable. You must lock the entire `Application` object. Therefore, in a Web site with a lot of traffic, you shouldn't keep this object locked for very long.

```
<%
Application.Lock
Application("nVisits") = Application("nVisits") + 1
Application.Unlock
%>
```

Hour 13

Quiz

1. What are some types of errors that you can encounter in your applications?

   Logical, typographical, runtime, and syntactical.

2. What are some reasons that debugging a Web application is more difficult than debugging other types of applications?

   Web applications generally consist of multiple layers of code written in different languages and running on disparate machines. This makes debugging much more difficult than the traditional monolithic application that was written in one language and completely resided on a single machine.

3. What must you do to the page you want to debug from the Visual InterDev environment?

   You must define the page as the start page by right-clicking it in the Project Explorer and selecting the Set As Start Page menu option. After that, you can run the page by setting any applicable breakpoints and pressing the F5 key.

4. What is the feature that enables you to dynamically start a debug session when the browser encounters an error on a page?

   Just-in-time debugging.

5. What is the utility to help configure DCOM for remote server script debugging?

   dcomcnfg.exe.

6. What is a quick way to remove all breakpoints from a Web application?

   Shift+Ctrl+F9.

7. How do you set a breakpoint?

   By pressing the F9 key or selecting the Debug, Insert Breakpoint menu option.

8. How can you change a variable at runtime?

   By using the Immediate window.

9. What is the Watch window used for?

   The Watch window enables you to keep track of variables whose value you want to know through several breakpoints.

10. What is the difference between the Locals and Autos windows?

The Locals window is used to view variables of current scope, whereas the Autos window is used to view all variables that are defined for all threads of the current process.

Exercise

Using what you've learned here, attempt to create your own case study for a remote debugging session.

You're on your own for this one.

Hour 14

Quiz

1. What disadvantages do stored procedures and triggers have regarding n-tier applications?

Stored procedure and triggers that contain business logic make it difficult to separate all the business logic from the database server onto other servers.

2. What is an artificial key?

One that has no meaning to the business or organization and is created as a convenience to remedy situations where any other key would be large or complex. Artificial keys also guarantee a primary key that won't be modified by the user or application.

3. Why is normalization so important?

Data normalization ensures the integrity of the data so that updates or deletes to the system do not produce undesired results, such as delete anomalies and update anomalies.

4. What is it called if a table is not normalized?

Tables that do not even adhere to the first normal form are considered to be *denormalized*.

5. What is first normal form?

The first normal form dictates that all repeating groups of attributes or columns must be removed.

6. What is second normal form?

The second normal form dictates that all redundant data be removed from the system.

7. What is third normal form?

The third normal form dictates that columns, which are not dependent on the table's key, be moved to another table.

A

8. Under what conditions is it considered to be okay if a table is denormalized?

In the case of summary tables, a table can be denormalized.

9. What is a delete anomaly and an update anomaly?

A delete anomaly occurs when the deletion of a record results in the loss of history of a given business entity. An update anomaly occurs when an update to a table results in inconsistent data across the rows of a given table.

10. What is a cascading delete and a cascading update?

Cascading deletes and updates are both part of referential integrity. Say that you have two tables (TableA and TableB) and they are linked such that one too many rows in TableB are dependent on the existence of a row in TableA. By using cascading deletes, if a row is deleted from TableA, any dependent rows in TableB will be deleted automatically; thereby preserving the integrity of the data. Cascading updates work the same way. If the value of the column being used to link TableA and TableB is changed in TableA, all the dependent rows in TableB will be changed automatically.

Exercise

Using what you've learned in this hour, create a contact information database that adheres to third normal form. Some ideas for the data that you need to store are artist, album, and tour information.

The first thing you need to do is define what information you want to store about the different artists (such as name, band name, band origination date, and so on). Then you need to decide what you want to store concerning albums, such as release date, songs, and so on. The next task is to tie a particular artist to his albums. Because storing the different albums in an array within an artist table is a violation of first normal form, you need to move the album information into its own table and add the artist key to the album table. If you need help there, refer back to the part of the baseball database example in which the pitches that a pitcher knows were moved from the Pitchers table and into a Pitch table.

The third table you might want to create is the Tours table. Once again, an artist can have multiple tours, so you should handle this in exactly the same way as the Album table. That is, create a Tours table to contain all the information about a tour (date, location, and so on) and then add a column to it for the Artist key.

Hour 15

Quiz

1. Aside from a Web project, what other kinds of projects can be created with Visual InterDev?

   Database Projects, Distribution Units, and Utility Projects.

2. How can you use OLE DB if there isn't an OLE DB provider for your database?

   Microsoft realized that although it wants everyone to move to OLE DB, not every database is going to have an OLE DB provider immediately. Therefore, because all major databases do have an ODBC driver, Microsoft developed an OLE DB provider that interfaces to any ODBC driver. That way, you can use OLE DB to access any database for which there is an ODBC driver.

3. When defining a data connection, what are the two ways you can log on to the database server?

   One way is to use the Windows NT Integrated Security option on the Connection tab of the Data Link Properties dialog. This means that the user ID and password for your current session will be used to log on to the database server. Alternatively, you can enter a specific username and password that you know to be valid.

4. What window is used (among other things) to display relationships between tables?

   The Database Diagram window.

5. How do you add a caption to a database diagram?

   Text annotation can be added to a diagram by selecting the Diagram, New Text Annotation menu option from the diagram's context menu.

6. What is a primary key?

   A primary key enforces uniqueness for values entered into specific columns that do not allow NULLs.

7. What is a relationship?

   In an RDBMS, relationships are used to define how the records in one table relate to the records in another table in order to prevent things such as redundant or invalid data.

8. How do you define an index (other than the primary key)?

   Indexes for a table can be defined via a database diagram. Simply right-click the title bar of the desired table and select the Property Pages menu option. From there select the Indexes/Keys tab and define and name the index.

A

9. What is a constraint?

   Constraints are logic that the DBMS enforces. They limit the possible values that can be entered into specified columns.

10. How can you generate the SQL script that represents changes made in the Database Designer?

    When you've graphically made changes to a database via the Database Designer and you want to save the SQL needed to realize those changes, simply select the File, Save Change Script menu option.

Exercise

Create an ODBC data source for the Pubs database and using what you've learned in this hour, make some of the same changes to that database. See if you can figure out where it would make sense to add more columns and then relate them to another table as you did in this hour with the Terms table.

You're on your own for this one.

Hour 16

Quiz

1. What are the four panes of the Query Designer?

   Diagram pane, Grid pane, SQL pane, and Results pane.

2. Which pane shows the relationships between two or more tables?

   Diagram pane.

3. How is a new query created for a data connection?

   By right-clicking a data connection in the Project Explorer and selecting the Add Query menu option.

4. How are input sources added to a query?

   By dragging tables or views from the Data View onto the Diagram pane.

5. How are single columns added to a query?

   By clicking the check box to the left of the desired column in the Diagram pane or by dragging the columns from the Data View onto the Diagram pane.

6. How can you add all the columns for all the input sources in the Diagram pane to a query?

   By right-clicking the Diagram pane, selecting the Property Pages menu option, checking the Output All Columns check box, and clicking the OK button.

7. What are the two ways in which you sort the data returned by a query?

   By setting the Sort Type and Sort Order columns of the Grid pane or by manually coding the SQL ORDER BY clause.

8. What are the two ways in which you specify the search criteria for a query?

   By setting the Criteria columns in the Grid pane or by manually coding the SQL WHERE clause.

9. What are the different types of queries that modify data?

   Insert, Insert Values, Update, Delete, and Make Table.

10. How can you test a query to make sure that its syntax is correct?

    By clicking the Verify SQL Syntax button on the Query toolbar.

Exercise

Practice what you've learned in this hour by creating different queries that will execute against either the Northwind or the Pubs sample databases.

You're on your own for this one.

Hour 17

Quiz

1. What is an SQL script?

   An SQL script is simply an external text file that contains SQL statements.

2. What is a view?

   A view is a virtual table whose data contents are based on the results of a predefined query.

3. What is the difference between a view and a table?

   A view resembles a table in that it contains a set of named columns and rows of data. However, a view does not exist as a stored set of data values in a database. Instead, a view is a query resultset that is maintained on the server and is updated each time it is opened.

4. Can the data that a view displays be modified, and if so, what are the consequences regarding other views?

   Yes, the data being displayed by a view can be modified, and the data that is modified is the data that is stored in the view's underlying tables. Therefore, any other views that are also based on those tables will be affected as well.

A

5. What are some advantages of views?

- Views give you the ability to limit access to sensitive data.
- Views help to eliminate redundant SQL.
- Views provide for faster development regarding the SQL.
- Performance is sometimes better when using views.

6. What is the purpose of encrypting a view, and how is it done?

Views can be encrypted to prevent the viewing or modification of its definition by other users. A view is encrypted by setting the Encrypt View option on the view's Property Page dialog.

7. What are stored procedures?

Stored procedures are precompiled SQL statements that are executed on the server.

8. What is the difference between a stored procedure and a query?

A query can contain only SQL commands, whereas a stored procedure involves a superset of the SQL language so that sophisticated logic can be used in conjunction with the database I/O.

9. How is permission given to other users so that they can run your stored procedures?

You might need to run the SQL GRANT EXECUTE command in order to grant privileges.

10. What is a trigger?

A trigger is a type of stored procedure that executes in response to a specified table being modified in a predetermined manner.

Exercise

Using the Pubs sample database, create a new summary table for sales. Then create a trigger that will automatically create a new summary record each time a sale is made.

The answer to this exercise can be found on the book's accompanying CD-ROM.

Hour 18

Quiz

1. What are the three ways in which to access data from an Active Server Page using Visual InterDev?

Using script and the ADO object model, the Visual InterDev Data Environment, and the Visual InterDev design-time controls.

2. What are the three main objects in the ADO object model?

   `Connection`, `Command`, and `Recordset`.

3. Why does ADO define an Errors collection instead of an `Errors` object?

   Because a single data-access statement can return more than one error.

4. What is a `Recordset` object used for?

   To create a set of records from a query.

5. How is a connection to a data provider created?

   By calling the Server object's `CreateObject` method to instantiate an ADO `Connection` object.

6. How are fields within a recordset specified?

   With the following syntax:

   `<recordset>("column_name")`

7. How is a record added to a database using the `Recordset` object?

   By calling the `Recordset` object's `AddNew` method, setting the values of the columns, and then calling the `Recordset` object's `Update` method.

8. What is the `Command` object used for?

   To specify an SQL command, stored procedure, or query to execute on the database server.

9. What `Connection` object method is used to run the SQL against the database?

   The `Execute` method.

10. What VBScript can be used to iterate through a recordset?

    ```
    do while not <recordset>.EOF
    ' your code here
    loop
    ```

Exercise

Add to the TitleMaintenance Web application to enable the user to search for a specific title.

This basically uses a combination of what you learned in the hour's final example and what you learned about `Recordset` objects. Simply create a new Active Server Page that has the fields on which you want the user to search. When the user submits the form, call another Active Server Page that will perform the actual search. From this second page, use the `Record` object and the data the user entered to filter the Titles table to only the appropriate records. Finally, display the found records on the page.

Hour 19

Quiz

1. What is the primary benefit programming with the Data Environment has over straight ADO scripting?

   Reusability.

2. What are the two ways to use the Data Environment?

   Data Environment object model scripting and data-bound controls.

3. What is necessary in order to script the Data Environment object model on the client workstation?

   The Data Environment is available only on the server.

4. How many Data Environments can a single application have defined?

   Only one.

5. What are data connections?

   Data connections are collections of information used in order to connect to specific databases.

6. What are data commands?

   Data commands are named objects that contain information used to access particular database objects.

7. How are the ADO objects represented from the Data Environment?

   The Data Environment is a wrapper for the ADO object model, where each ADO object is exposed as a method of the Data Environment object.

8. When you create a data connection, what file is updated with the new data connection's information, and what changes are made?

   When a data connection is defined for a database, Visual InterDev modifies the global.asa file by inserting the necessary code to set application-level variables based on the data connection's settings.

9. When creating a data command, what types of authentication settings can be specified?

   When a data command is defined, the authentication properties that can be set are the user ID, the password, and the rules for deciding whether a prompt is displayed for these values. These settings can be adjusted for both the runtime and design-time environments.

10. How do you initialize the Data Environment in script?

    ```
    Set de = Server.CreateObject("DERuntime.DERuntime")
    de.Init("Application("DE"))
    ```

Exercise

Create an application using the Data Environment that allows for the addition of records to a table.

Remember the fact that, even though it's created automatically for you, the Data Environment recordset works just like the recordset you learned how to add records with in Hour 18, "Accessing Data with ADO." If you get stuck, check out the Data Environment example on this book's accompanying CD-ROM.

Hour 20

Quiz

1. What is a design-time control?

   Controls that enable you to view and change their properties from the Visual InterDev development environment at design-time.

2. What support must first be enabled in order to use design-time controls?

   The Scripting Object Model.

3. How do design-time controls differ from ActiveX controls?

   The biggest difference between a design-time control and an ActiveX control is that design-time controls require a binary runtime component to be downloaded to the client workstation, whereas ActiveX controls do not.

4. What are some advantages and disadvantages of specifying the server as the target scripting platform for a design-time control?

   One advantage is that the page will be cross-browser compatible. However, a disadvantage is that the code must execute only within the confines of an Active Server Page.

5. What are some advantages and disadvantages of specifying the client as the target?

   This depends on whether you have control over how the application will be viewed. For example, if you are developing an intranet application and you know which browser will be used, the fact that only a DHTML-capable browser (such as IE) can be used might not be a disadvantage. However, for an Internet application, this would probably represent a huge disadvantage to using the client target scripting platform.

6. Why don't you have to provide a runtime binary component for each design-time control used in your Web application if the design-time control is actually an ActiveX control itself?

A

Because the ActiveX component of the design-time control needs only to reside on the development workstation to provide the interface to the setting of the control's properties. At runtime, the control creates a script object (using the Scripting Object Model) that carries out the control's work. Therefore, the ActiveX part of the design-time control is seen only at design time (hence its name).

7. What advantage does using the Scripting Object Model give you over using HTML and Active Server Pages?

The Scripting Object Model was specifically designed to provide an object-oriented approach to Web page development by defining a set of objects whose properties, methods, and events can be used in script to build Web applications more quickly and easily.

8. What object is associated with a Recordset design-time control?

A data command.

9. In order to use data-bound controls (such as a Textbox or Checkbox), which control must you also use on the same page?

Data-bound controls are associated with a Recordset design-time control. Therefore, at least one Recordset control must be defined on the page.

10. Which design-time control enables the user to navigate through a resultset more easily?

The RecordsetNavBar design-time control.

Exercise

To solidify what you've learned in this hour, create an application that allows for the scrolling and modification of another table such as Employees.

This should be relatively easy if you use the things you've learned in this hour. However, if you do get stuck, just look back at the DTCExamples for help. This application is also available on the book's accompanying CD-ROM if you need additional help.

Hour 21

Quiz

1. What two Active Server Page Object Model objects contain cookie collections?

Request (to retrieve) and Response (to store).

2. Show the two ways to store a cookie value from script?

```
Response.Cookies(cookie)=value
Response.Cookies(cookie)(key)=value
```

3. Where must the script exist within an Active Server Page that stores or retrieves values from a cookie?

A script that accesses cookies must exist before any HTML-generating code in an Active Server Page.

4. Are keys that are stored in a cookie case sensitive?

Keys are stored in all uppercase letters and are therefore not case sensitive.

5. How is a cookie's expiration date set?

A cookie's expiration date is set via its Expires attribute.

6. How is a cookie programmatically deleted?

A cookie can be programmatically deleted by setting its Expires date to a date that's prior to the client workstation's current date.

7. What method is used to ensure session initialization?

Implementing the Session_OnStart method in the global.asa file will ensure that the initialization code for your Web site is called each time a user visits the site.

8. What Scripting Object Model collection is used to store environment variables?

The ServerVariables collection can be used to store session- or application-level variables for use across pages.

9. How are values set in the Session object?

```
Session("myVar") = value
```

10. How are objects stored and retrieved from a Session object when the scripting language being used is VBScript?

If VBScript is being used and you want to store an object in the Session object, you must use the VBScript Set command, as follows:

```
Set Session("myObject") = Server.CreateObject("myComponent.myClass")
```

Exercise

Create a main menu that points to several pages. Write the necessary code to redirect users to the main menu regardless of which page they surf to.

You're on your own for this one.

Hour 22

Quiz

1. What application is used to define users and groups in Windows NT?

   The Windows NT User Manager.

2. What part of Windows NT security is used to define how passwords are used by all user accounts?

   Account policy.

3. What are the three IIS authentication methods?

   Anonymous, Basic, and Windows NT Challenge/Response.

4. What is the IIS anonymous user account?

   The anonymous account (IUSR_*COMPUTERNAME*) is a user account created by IIS to allow a Web application to be used by users who are unknown to the underlying operating system.

5. What must you do to enable Anonymous Authentication?

   Specify the Allow Anonymous option from within IIS.

6. Why is the Basic Authentication method not considered to be a prudent security measure for a Web application?

   Because logon information is transmitted as clear text. Although this information is encoded, it is not encrypted and, therefore, can be read by unintended applications or people.

7. What is the main difference between how data is transmitted using the Basic Authentication method and using the Windows NT Challenge/Response Authentication method?

   The main difference is that unlike the Basic Authentication method, the Windows NT Challenge/Response Authentication method encrypts the logon information being sent from the client to the server.

8. What are the limitations of the Windows NT Challenge/Response Authentication method?

   It cannot be used through a firewall via a proxy and is not supported on all browsers.

9. What technology does SSL use to encrypt information and authenticate other machines?

   Public key cryptography.

10. Where can a digital certificate be obtained to participate in an SSL connection?

    www.thawte.com

    www.verisign.com

Hour 23

Quiz

1. What two main Visual InterDev files that you work with all the time are not a part of the master Web application?

   The Visual InterDev solution file (.sln) and project files (.vip) are not part of the master Web application file set.

2. What is the difference between the master working mode and the local working mode?

   With the master working mode, any modifications that are made to the local project are automatically replicated on the master Web application. With the local working mode, any changes made to the local project are not replicated on the master Web server until you explicitly specify to do that.

3. What is the biggest advantage of the local working mode as it pertains to testing?

   The local working mode's biggest advantage is that it enables developers to work in an isolated environment so that they can test and debug their projects before integrating them with the master Web application.

4. When would you use the offline working mode?

   The offline working mode is extremely useful when you're in a situation where you want to make changes to a project and you're not connected to the Web server.

5. What information constitutes a deployment target?

   The deployment target consists of the target Web server's HTTP address, its available deployment services, and the files that will be deployed to the server when you select the deploy option.

6. When would you use the Deployment Explorer as opposed to simply duplicating the application via the Copy Web Application feature?

   The Copy Web Application feature, although useful, basically lets you do nothing more than duplicate a Web application on another Web server. The Deployment Explorer, on the other hand, is meant for situations where you want more control over which projects and files are being deployed. The Deployment Explorer, therefore, is great for situations where you have a Web application that will span multiple Web servers.

A

7. What are deployment outputs?

   Development outputs are simply the files and projects that will be deployed using a deployment target.

8. What are the supported deployment services?

   Client-side content and server-side content.

9. What is needed on the target Web server to support the server-side content deployment service?

   You can deploy server-side content to a Web server only if it has the Microsoft Posting Acceptor installed.

10. How does Visual InterDev communicate any deployment errors back to you?

    Deployment errors are communicated to the developer via the Task List window.

Exercise

Now that you know about the Deployment Explorer, lay out the deployment strategy with regards to your own Web site.

This is more of a research exercise that involves your own particular needs. Therefore, there isn't a "correct" answer that I can provide. However, some ideas that I can add are that you might want to consider the impact that multiple servers would have on the overall performance of your Web site. Taking that into consideration, think about how you would partition the different parts of your Web application to these different servers and how the Deployment Explorer would help you to efficiently manage the code that is spread across the different servers.

Hour 24

Quiz

1. What is a link diagram?

   A graphical representation of the link structure of a Web site. Link diagrams use icons to represent the different items in a Web application, such as HTML pages and Active Server Pages and show (via lines) which items link to one another.

2. What are the different link diagram layouts?

   Horizontal and radial.

3. What are the two methods of visually managing the content of a large link diagram?

   The zoom feature and the filtering options.

4. What are in links?

   Links in which the current item is being linked to by another item.

5. What are out links?

   Links in which the current item is referencing other items.

6. What are the two ways to zoom a link diagram?

   Via the link diagram's context menu and the Site Designer toolbar.

7. What are the two ways of displaying broken links?

   Running the Broken Link Report or viewing a link diagram.

8. What feature does Visual InterDev supply to help prevent broken links?

   The Link Repair feature.

9. What are the three options for Link Repair?

   Allows Visual InterDev to automatically repair the link, specifies that Visual InterDev should not attempt to repair the link, and specifies that Visual InterDev should ask each time it thinks a link should be repaired.

10. What is the difference between an explicit link and a relative link?

    An explicit link specifies the complete URL. A relative link specifies the URL in terms that are relative to the current file.

Exercises

1. Open a complex Web site on the Internet (such as www.microsoft.com or www.SourceDNA.com) as a link diagram and see if you can spot any broken links.

   This is accomplished via the Tools, View Links on the WWW menu option. Remember that if the site is too large to view, you can always incorporate different filters and zoom the layout to your liking. This feature of Visual InterDev is a great way to see how other sites are organized and possibly get some good ideas for your own site.

2. See if you can view all the links from the home page of the popular Visual C++/MFC development site, www.CodeGuru.com.

   This is a bit tricky because at www.CodeGuru.com, we don't use standard naming conventions for the HTML pages. The extension of our pages is .shtml (simple HTML). Therefore, if you were to simply select the Tools, View Links on the WWW menu option and specify www.CodeGuru.com, you would only see about half the actual links from the home page. The trick is that when the View Links on WWW dialog appears, you must uncheck the Only Show Pages check box. That way, Visual InterDev will show *all* the links and not just the ones that reference .htm, .html, and .asp files.

APPENDIX **B**

Installing and Configuring SQL Server

All the database code in this book uses the SQL Server 7 databases, Pubs and Northwind. Therefore, this appendix covers the SQL Server installation procedure, the different editions of SQL Server, and the options you should consider if SQL Server is going to be the relational database management system (RDBMS) for your Web server.

The highlights of this appendix include

- Learning about the different editions of SQL Server 7
- Selecting the correct edition of SQL Server for your project
- Understanding the installation options for SQL Server
- Learning how to correctly install and configure SQL Server

The Different Flavors of SQL Server 7

SQL Server 7 is the most exciting product to come out of Redmond in a very long time. For the first time, developers have a true relational database management system that scales all the way from a laptop running Windows 95 to terabyte symmetric multiprocessor clusters running Windows NT Server Enterprise Edition. But here's the kicker. It does all this using the same code base.

This last fact results in a couple of huge advantages. First, it means that you can finally install and use a consistent RDMBS across all the machines in a given corporation regardless of the version of Windows being run on each individual box. Second, with the same code base being used, you can also feel safe in knowing that each of the databases (and code) is 100 percent compatible with the others.

In order to provide a version of SQL Server that is tailored for the different versions of Windows and user needs, Microsoft has simultaneously released four different versions of SQL Server. However, once again, keep in mind that each is built on the same code base thereby guaranteeing compatibility.

After you've looked over the specifications for each of these releases, you should easily be able to discern which is the correct version for a given project.

Desktop Edition

Although SQL Server Desktop is designed specifically to run on Windows 95, Windows 98, or Windows NT Workstation, it is a fully featured RDBMS and supports many of the same features of the higher-end SQL Server editions. The main difference between this version and the higher-end versions is the number of concurrent users that can be efficiently handled. Although there is no enforced maximum number of users or file size, this version was designed to accommodate a handful of users (less than 10).

Small Business Server Edition

As the name implies, this edition of SQL Server is meant for small companies or work-groups. Its limitations are that it will support a maximum of 4 processors, 50 users, and a database size of 10 gigabytes. As opposed to the Desktop Edition, SQL Server strictly enforces these restrictions.

Standard Edition

This is the edition that most people are referring to when they mention SQL Server without specifying an edition. Regarding functionality, this edition has everything that all but the largest companies would need. This includes, but is not limited to, support for 4 processors and 2 gigabytes of memory. As with SQL Server 6.x, this edition must be run on Windows NT Server 4 Standard Edition (or higher).

Enterprise Edition

The Enterprise Edition is meant for users who require the highest level of scalability and reliability. Enterprise Edition includes failover clustering, the ability to partition OLAP Services, and the capability to use up to 32 processors and 64 gigabytes of memory. Needless to say, most users do not need this version. Enterprise Edition must run on Windows NT Server 4 Enterprise Edition (or higher) with Service Pack 4 installed.

Some of the examples in this book were done using the Desktop Edition (on a computer running Windows 95) and some of the examples were done using Enterprise Edition. However, it should be noted that every example in this book could be duplicated with any of the aforementioned editions of SQL Server 7.

Purchasing SQL Server 7

SQL Server 7 (like many Microsoft products) is distributed in several ways. Aside from being available in stores and from the Microsoft Web site, it is also available as part of the MSDN (Microsoft Software Development Network) Universal Subscription.

Because there are just too many options relating to pricing and upgrading SQL Server, I would recommend visiting the following URL on the Microsoft Web site:

www.microsoft.com/sql/70/gen/pricing.htm

This Web page not only gives you all the pricing options available for SQL Server 7, but also painstakingly enumerates all applicable upgrade paths.

B

If you want to evaluate SQL Server 7 before making a purchasing decision, the full product can be downloaded for a 120-day trial at the following URL:

http://www.microsoft.com/sql/70/trial.htm

It should also be noted that SQL Server 6.5 is no longer a shipping product. However, you can still receive this older version by ordering SQL Server 7 and then ordering the SQL Server 6.5 media and documentation directly from Microsoft.

Running the SQL Server 7 Installation Application

If you have the SQL Server 7 CD-ROM and you are ready to start the installation process, simply place it in the CD-ROM drive at this time. The file named autorun.inf will automatically be executed, which will start the installation application.

> If you have an MSDN Universal subscription and downloaded SQL Server 7 from the Microsoft MSDN Subscriber's Download Web page, simply run the self-extracting compressed file and specify where you want the files to be located when decompressed. When you've done that, you will have an exact duplicate of the files that are shipped on the SQL Server CD-ROM. In order to start the installation application at this point, simply execute the autorun.exe file by browsing to it in an Explorer window and double-clicking it.

The Installation Main Menu

After you've started the installation application, the main menu shown in Figure B.1 will be displayed. As you can see from the menu, several options that to be selected in a specific sequence in order to correctly install SQL Server 7. As the mouse cursor is moved over the different options, a detailed description is displayed on the left side of the menu. At this point, move your mouse cursor over the different options to get a feel for the different things you are going to have to do to install SQL Server.

FIGURE B.1

The SQL Server 7 installation main menu.

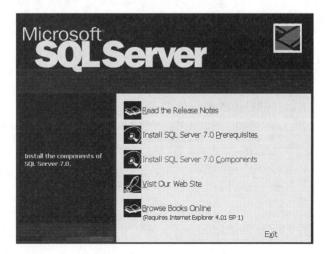

Late-Breaking News

As you can see on the main menu, the first option of the SQL Server 7 installation application is the Read The Release Notes option. Most software applications ship with a file called readme.txt. This file is used to provide information that became available after the software's documentation was finalized. In addition, this file also contains corrections to faulty documentation. As with any software installation application that provides this file, I would strongly urge you to read this file before proceeding with the installation process.

If you are installing SQL Server as you read through this appendix, click on this option to read any information that might be pertinent to your particular installation. When you are finished, return here to continue with the installation.

SQL Server 7 Prerequisites

The second menu option is for installing any prerequisite software upon which SQL Server relies in order to function correctly. These prerequisites are based on the operating system that SQL Server is being installed on.

You do not need to choose this option if you are running Windows 98 or Windows 2000. However, if you are running Windows 95, Windows NT Workstation 4, or Windows NT Server 4, you will need to choose this option. Doing so will result in the menu you see in Figure B.2.

FIGURE B.2

The SQL Server 7 Prerequisites screen.

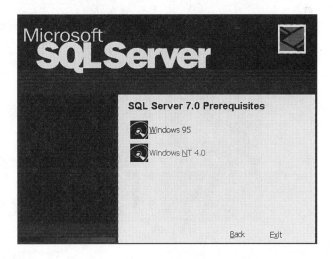

B

Don't become too alarmed if you're a Netscape user and you see that Internet Explorer 4.01 is a prerequisite for installing SQL Server. Internet Explorer is only needed for Books Online (the SQL Server documentation) and the SQL Server Enterprise Manager. However, you can install just enough of Internet Explorer so that the SQL Server installation runs successfully and SQL Server operates correctly without switching from your browser of choice.

Windows 95 Prerequisites

For Windows 95 installations (see Figure B.3), the prerequisites are as follows:

- Internet Explorer 4.01 SP1—Here you have the option of installing just enough of the Internet Explorer Service Pack 1 to make SQL Server function (Minimal Install option) or installing the entire package (Launch Install Wizard option). If you are using Internet Explorer as your default browser, I recommend choosing the Launch Install Wizard option. However, if you are using a competing browser (such as Netscape Navigator), you will probably want to choose the Minimal Install option.

- DCOM95—You only need to choose this option if you are not going to use Internet Explorer as your browser.

FIGURE B.3

Windows 95 prerequisites for installing SQL Server 7.

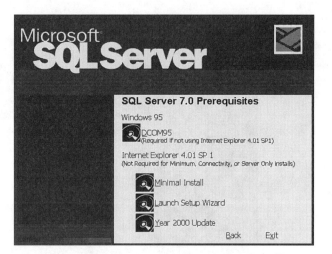

Windows NT (Workstation and Server) Prerequisites

For Windows NT installations (see Figure B.4), the prerequisites are as follows:

- Windows NT 4.0 SP4—This Service Pack was the latest one for Windows NT when SQL Server started shipping (SP5 is now the latest). You must install one of these two Service Packs in order to successfully complete the installation of SQL Server 7.

- Internet Explorer 4.01 SP1—Here you have the option of installing just enough of the Internet Explorer Service Pack 1 to make SQL Server work (Minimal Install option) or installing the entire package (Launch Install Wizard option). If you are using Internet Explorer as your default browser, I recommend choosing the Launch Install Wizard option. However, if you are using a competing browser (such as Netscape Navigator), you will probably want to choose the Minimal Install option.

FIGURE B.4

The Windows NT pre-requisites for installing SQL Server 7.

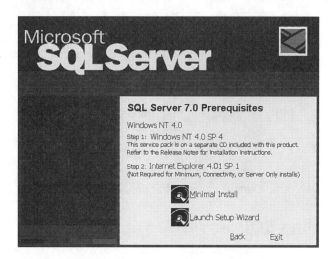

Selecting the Desired SQL Server Edition

After you have installed the necessary prerequisites, it is time to select which SQL Server edition and components you need on the target system. To do that, click on the Install SQL Server 7.0 Components option from the main menu. This will result in the menu you see in Figure B.5.

- Database Server Enterprise Edition—Select this option in order to install the full version of SQL Server 7.

- Database Server Desktop Edition—As you read earlier, this is a slightly scaled-down version of the full product and is meant to be used in conjunction with smaller companies or workgroups.

- SQL Server 7.0 OLAP Services—This option is used to install OLAP (Online Analytical Processing) functionality. OLAP is used to provide analysis of data stored in a database. OLAP tools enable users to analyze different dimensions of multidimensional data. For example, it can be used to provide time series and trend analysis views. Chances are that you will know if you need this (typically) very high-end functionality.

B

- English Query—This is a marvelous option. It allows you to install the tools necessary to create SQL Server applications that provide the user with a natural language interface to the data.

FIGURE B.5

The Components menu allows you to select the SQL Server edition and certain components.

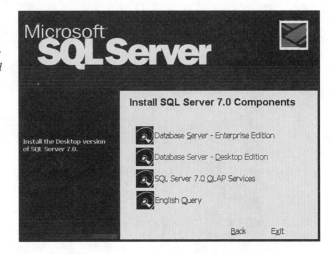

Installing SQL Server 7

At this point, it is time to decide which edition of SQL Server you will need to install and to finish the installation procedure. After you have clicked on either the Full Product or Desktop Edition options, you will be lead through an installation wizard in order to complete the installation of SQL Server 7.

One of the principal differences between the installation of the Desktop Edition and the Enterprise Edition of SQL Server deals with the fact that the Enterprise Edition supports clustering. However, this topic is not even covered by most beginner-level books that are dedicated to SQL Server. Therefore, it is well beyond the scope and purpose of this book. Unfortunately, not many books do cover this very powerful option to any degree. Therefore, if this is something you need or are interested in, I suggest either visiting the Microsoft Web site or reading about it in Books Online.

Follow these steps to begin the installation:

1. If you selected the Full Product option, you will see a dialog that allows you to specify whether you are installing SQL Server on the local computer or on a

remotely connected computer. In order to continue following along, you will need to select the option for a local installation. If you are installing the Desktop Edition, you will not see this dialog.

2. The second dialog for a Full Product installation (and the first for a Desktop Edition installation) appears to be nothing more than a Welcome dialog (see Figure B.6). However, I strongly urge you to read and follow the advice on this dialog very carefully. This dialog recommends that you close all currently active Windows applications before continuing with the installation. At this point, close the other applications and click the Next button.

FIGURE B.6

You will need to close all active Windows applications in order to successfully install SQL Server 7.

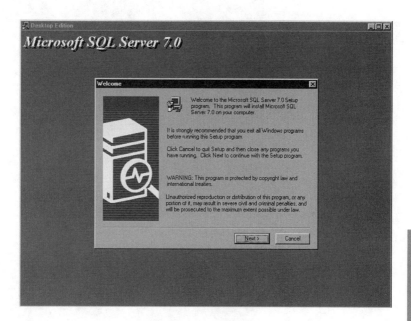

B

3. The next dialog that you will see is the EULA (End-User License Agreement) that Microsoft includes in all its installation applications (see Figure B.7). This simply explains the legal terms of using the product. Continuing with the installation at this point is tantamount to signing a contract with Microsoft agreeing to the terms specified in this dialog. Therefore, if after reading this information, you do not agree to those terms, you need to click the No button, which will abort the installation process. If you do agree with the terms of the agreement and want to continue with the installation, click the Yes button.

FIGURE B.7

Because the EULA represents a contract between you and Microsoft, you would be very wise to carefully read through it before continuing with the installation.

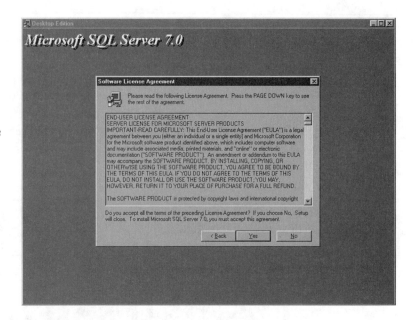

4. At this point (assuming you had no problems with the EULA), you will be presented with a dialog that allows you to specify your name and the name of the company that owns the license to this copy of SQL Server. Simply type those values in and click on the Next button when finished (see Figure B.8).

FIGURE B.8

This dialog allows SQL Server to personalize this installation.

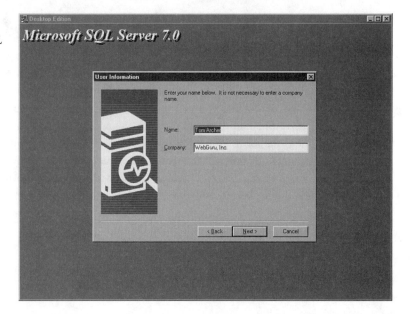

5. If you installed SQL Server from a CD-ROM (as opposed to downloading it to disk and installing it from there), you will see the CD Key Verification dialog. This dialog (not shown because I downloaded SQL Server as part of my MSDN Universal subscription) is used to ensure that you have a valid copy of the product because the CD key is usually located within the documentation for the product or on the CD sleeve. Needless to say, this doesn't stop anyone from copying the product and writing down the CD key, but having this dialog seems to make Microsoft happy.

> If you are installing SQL Server 7 over an installation of SQL Server 6.x, you will be presented with a dialog that gives you the option of upgrading any existing databases to the new format.
>
> You will not get this dialog if you do not have a current installation of SQL Server 6.x.

6. The next dialog that you will see is the Setup Type dialog (see Figure B.9). This dialog is used to specify the different SQL Server features that you want installed. Many users will simply want to click on the Typical radio button and then the Next button because this option causes the most common features to be installed. Selecting the Minimum option has the effect of selecting just enough features so that you can create an SQL Server database. However, it won't include any of the administrative tools that make this version of SQL Server so much easier to administrate than previous versions. For purposes of this appendix, I chose the Custom option.

B

FIGURE B.9

The Setup dialog allows you to specify which SQL Server features you want installed.

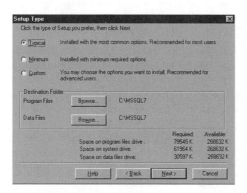

Custom Installation Options

If you chose the Custom option on the Setup dialog, the next dialog presented will be the Select Components dialog (see Figure B.10). This dialog displays the available SQL Server features that can be installed.

FIGURE B.10

The Server Components dialog includes the Replication Support option.

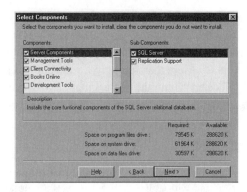

The Select Components dialog consists of two list boxes. The list box on the left contains the categories of features that are available for installation. When you click any of these items, the features that correspond to that category are listed in the list box on the right. At this point, take a look at the different categories and their associated features.

For purposes of this appendix, I chose to do a Desktop Edition installation. Therefore, if you chose the Full Product installation, the screen shots from this point will not match perfectly with what you see. However, each feature of each category will be described so that no matter which installation you are performing, you will have help in understanding what the feature provides for you so that you can make the decision on whether you want it based on your specific needs.

If for some reason, you do not know if you want to install a particular feature, you can return and install a feature at a later time. Say for example, that you want to install the core SQL Server engine, but haven't decided on whether you need replication support. You can simply check the SQL Server option and uncheck the Replication Support. Now if you decide later that you do want to use this feature of SQL Server, just run the installation application again. This time, however, you would uncheck SQL Server (because it's already installed) and check the Replication Support option.

Server Components

The first category is Server Components. You can choose the following features under Server Components:

- SQL Server—This option installs the SQL Server database engine. About the only thing you can do without choosing this option would be to install Books Online because without the engine, no other part of the SQL Server is going to function. However, as stated previously, if you are simply adding features to an existing installation (that included the installation of the engine), you do not need to select this feature.

- Upgrade Tools—This option (only available on Windows NT) installs the SQL Server Upgrade Wizard, which is used to upgrade SQL Server version 6.x databases to SQL Server version 7.

- Replication Support—Installs the scripts and binary files used for replication. See the following note for a description of replication.

- Full-Text Search—Installs the Microsoft full-text search engine (Microsoft Index Server), which allows for the creation of indexes on textual data so that the ability to search on character columns beyond the basic equality and LIKE operators. Unfortunately, this option is not available on the Desktop Edition of SQL Server.

> *Replication* is the process of creating and managing multiple copies of the same database. However, replication is much more than simply copying the database from one location to another. Replication actually allows for synchronization of a set of "replicas" so that when a change is made to one replica, those changes are reflected in all the others. The great thing about replication is that it enables multiple users to work with their own local copy of a database and then update the database as if they were working on a single, centralized database.

B

Management Tools

Management Tools is the next category of components that can be added. As you can see in Figure B.11, you have five features from which to choose:

- SQL Server Enterprise Manager—Used to perform server and enterprise administrative tasks via a graphical interface.

- SQL Server Profiler—Used to monitor, record, and support auditing of SQL Server database activity for the purpose of performance measurements. Using the Profiler, you can determine where your queries are taking too long to execute.

- SQL Server Query Analyzer—This option is used to interactively enter Transact-SQL (TSQL) statements and procedures. Typically only developers who are fairly proficient with TSQL will need to use this tool.

- MS DTC Client Support—MS DTC is used to extend database transactions across multiple physical machines by way of *two-phase commit*.
- Replication Conflict Resolver—This tool is used in conjunction with Replication Support option to view and resolve any database conflicts.

FIGURE B.11

Management Tools allow for the ability to profile queries and graphically resolve replication conflicts.

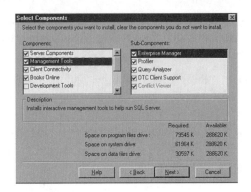

Client Connectivity

The Client Connectivity category is the only category without an associated feature list. This option is used to allow communication between clients and servers and includes the network libraries for ODBC, OLEDB, and SQL-DMO (SQL Distributed Management Objects), DB-Library, and the client-side network libraries (you will learn more about this shortly). If you don't select this option, your installation won't be able to do very much after you've completed the SQL Server installation. Therefore, you need to make sure that this option is selected.

Books Online

Another very simple category, Books Online, allows you to specify whether you want to copy the Books Online to your local system. In this day and age of incredibly cheap hard drives, I would recommend using some of that space with this very valuable information.

Development Tools

The Development Tools category is primarily aimed at C/C++ developers who want to write custom applications to control certain aspects of SQL Server (see Figure B.12). Here's a breakdown of each of the development tools and files you can choose to install:

- Headers and Libraries—This option installs the header (*.h) files and library (*.lib) files needed by C/C++ developers to create programs that use OLE DB, ODBC, DB-Library, Open Data Services, SQL-DMO, Embedded SQL for C, and MS DTC. These files will be installed to the \Mssql7\DevTools\Include and the

\Mssql7\DevTools\Lib folders by default. Because I am, by trade, a Visual C++ developer, I chose to install these tools. However, if you know that you will be developing your Web application without C or C++, I would recommend against installing these files.

- Backup/Restore API—Very handy if you are going to develop a backup and restore application. This option will not only copy the necessary header files and documentation for doing that, but it also includes a demo application that shows how this type of application is written.

- Debugger Interface—Installs an interface for stored procedure debugging from Visual Studio. Additionally installs the include (*.h) files and library (*.lib) files needed by C/C++ developers to create programs that use OLE DB, ODBC, DB-Library, Open Data Services, SQL-DMO, Embedded SQL for C, and MS DTC. Once again, these files are installed into the \Mssql7\DevTools\Include and the \Mssql7\DevTools\Lib folders by default and should only be of interest if you are planning on developing in C or C++.

FIGURE B.12

The Development Tools category enables you to install the files and tools necessary to perform such tasks as programmatically automating restores and backups.

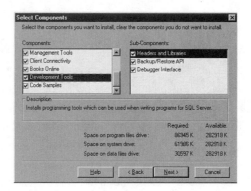

B

Code Samples

The Code Samples category allows you to copy examples of how to develop your own custom applications to control and manage certain aspects of SQL Server (see Figure B.13). The following is a brief description of each technology for which the sample is developed:

- ADO—ActiveX Data Objects is an object-based interface to OLEDB. OLEDB, in turn, is Microsoft's most recent attempt at providing a single interface to any data store regardless of the actual mechanism by which the data is being stored. For example, using OLEDB, you can access data stored in an SQL Server in the exact same manner as you would if the data was being housed in a Microsoft Exchange Server database.

- DBLIB—DB-Library was the native language used to program SQL Server in all releases prior to version 7. It still exists today in order to provide backwards-compatibility.

- DTS—Data Transformation Services is used to move data from one source to another.

- ESQLC—Embedded SQL for C is used in order to embed actual SQL code into a C/C++ source code module. An SQL precompiler is then run against the source, which results in another source file that contains the actual function calls that replace the original raw SQL code. This is used so that developers wanting the efficiency of embedded SQL can use the more traditional SQL instead of having to remember all the proprietary mechanisms for calling the SQL Server functions.

- MS DTC—The Microsoft Distributed Transaction Coordinator is a component that allows for transactions across disparate physical machines.

- ODBC—Open Database Connectivity was Microsoft's first attempt at providing a single (SQL) database interface to any database. Using ODBC, an Access database can be accessed with the same code base that is used to access an SQL Server database.

- OLEAut—OLE Automation allows for an application to be automated or controlled from another application.

- Repl—As mentioned previously, replication gives you the ability to work locally on a file (a replica) that will be synchronized with a central version of the file at a later time.

- SQL-DMO—The SQL Distributed Management Object is a collection of objects that encapsulate the SQL Server database and replication management.

- SQL-NS—The SQL Namespace is a set of COM interfaces that allow a Visual Basic or C++ application to invoke SQL Server Enterprise Manager components such as its wizards, property sheets, and dialogs.

FIGURE B.13

To someone not familiar with SQL Server, the number of advanced features that it exposes can be staggering.

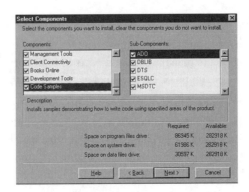

When you have made your decision on the features that you want installed, click the Next button to continue.

Character Set/Sort Order/Unicode Collation Settings

The Character Set/Sort Order/Unicode Collation dialog is used to decide which character set and sort order you will use with this installation of SQL Server. In addition, this dialog contains the options necessary to define several Unicode options.

By default, the installation application will use the settings of your operating system in order to set the defaults for this dialog.

> The issue of most importance here is that of Unicode. Traditionally, characters were stored (using a system called ASCII) in one byte or 8 bit chunks. However, the biggest problem with this is that there simply aren't enough values that can be represented by an 8 bit value ($8^2 = 256$) to encode all the languages and scientific symbols of the world. Therefore, Unicode was introduced as a standard for representing characters as integers. Because an integer is defined as 16 bits, this means that Unicode provides room to encode 16^2, or 65,535 possibilities.

When you have selected your options, click the Next button to continue to the last dialog of the installation application.

Network Libraries

The Network Libraries dialog is used to specify which communications libraries the clients of your SQL Server databases will use in order to communicate with those databases.

The important things to realize on this dialog are that Named Pipes must be used with Windows NT and that the TCP-IP port 1433 is used by default for SQL Server. Once again, the default settings for this dialog will suffice for most installations of SQL Server.

When finished, click the Next button to continue to the Start Copying Files dialog. This dialog is really nothing more than a confirmation dialog that gives you one last chance to click the Last button to go back and make any changes to your selected options before starting the actual copying of the files to install SQL Server. Therefore, unless you have any changes to make, simply click the Finish button when the Copying File dialog is displayed.

SQL Server Default Databases

When the SQL Server installation has completed, run the Enterprise Manager from the Microsoft SQL Server 7 program group (see Figure B.14). This allows you to view what has been created automatically on your behalf with regards to Login IDs and databases.

FIGURE B.14

The Enterprise Manager allows you to manage all your SQL Server databases from a single application.

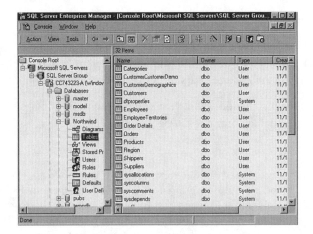

Using the Enterprise Manager, browse to the Databases folder for the machine onto which you installed SQL Server. At this point (as shown in Figure B.14), you will see that several databases have been created automatically for you. These databases include four system databases that cannot be removed (master, model, msdb, and tempdb) and two sample databases that are created to aid the new SQL Server user in learning (Northwind and pubs).

Throughout this book, you use the Northwind and pubs databases as you learn how to incorporate SQL Server databases into your Web applications.

Although the pubs database has always been automatically created during the installation process of previous versions of SQL Server as a learning tool, the Northwind database has also been supplied by Microsoft Access for the same purpose. With SQL Server now running on desktop operating systems such as Windows 95 and Windows 98, Microsoft realizes that many Microsoft Access users will be migrating to SQL Server 7. Therefore, in order to ease that transition, the Northwind database was also included in version 7 of SQL Server.

Summary

Congratulations! Certainly there are things that are a lot more fun to do in this life than installing a DBMS. However, you did accomplish some incredibly important things in this appendix. First, you learned about the features of SQL Server 7 and got an idea of the kinds of things you're going to be doing with it. Second, you installed this very powerful desktop/server DBMS so that you can continue on and start doing some of those fun things.

INDEX

results
   data commands, 326
   Query Designer,
      275-278
      clearing, 277-278
      printing, 276
**Results pane, Query
   Designer, 271**
resultsets
   columns, 274-275
   modifying data, Query
      Designer, 276
**retrieving code to differ-
   ent directory, 86-87**
**rights, Visual SourceSafe,
   76-77**
rows
   deleting, Delete query,
      281
   Query Designer, 277
   tables
      Insert Values query,
         280-281
      Make Table query,
         282
**running documents,
   debugging, 221-223**
**runtime, ActiveX control
   properties, 136-137**
runtime errors, 230

S

**schema, databases, alter-
   ing, 260-266**
SCRIPT tag, 94-95
scripting, 93-109
   benefits, 94
   HTML and, 94-95

languages, 96-100, 148,
   200
VBScript, 96
Scripting Object Model
   DTCs and, 333-334
   enabling, 202
scriptlets
   ActiveX controls com-
      parison, 169-170
   applets comparison,
      168-169
   component-based
      programming and,
      166-168
   containers, tests,
      172-173
   creating, 171-172
   defining to InterDev,
      172
   download time, 169
   events, 177-178
   HTMLT events, bub-
      bling, 177
   includes comparison,
      170
   learning curve, 169
   OBJECT element, 174
   overview, 166-168
   properties, 174-177
   security, 168
   writing, 165-178
scripts
   Active Server Pages,
      VBScript, 188, 190
   client
      debugging, 220-225
      document process-
         ing, 111-126
      form processing,
         111-126

Data Environment and,
   325-328
debugging, 217-234
document color,
   115-117
HTML pages, Active
   Server Pages and, 186
server
   cookies, 353-357
   debugging, 225-229
   SQL, 286-288
      creating from
         scratch, 286-287
      Database Designer
         and, 266
      templates, 287-288
   template, 286
search.htm file, 12, 16-17
searches
   criteria, 278-279
   text, 157-158
   version control, 87-88
security
   ActiveX controls, 131,
      169
   applets, 168
   data transmission, 367,
      374
   IIS, 372-374
   overview, 366-367
   scriptlets, 168
   user-defined, ActiveX
      controls, 129
   views, databases, 241
   Visual SourceSafe, 76
   Web applications,
      365-377
   Web sites, 365-377
**Select object, JavaScript,
   104**

X–Y–Z

Other Related Titles

Sams Teach Yourself Visual InterDev 6 in 21 Days
L. Michael Van Hoozer, Jr.
ISBN: 0-672-31251-4
$34.99 USA/$49.95 CAN

Sams Teach Yourself Active Server Pages in 24 Hours
Christoph Wille and Christian Kollier
ISBN: 0-672-31612-9
$19.99 USA/$29.95 CAN

Sams Teach Yourself HTML 4 in 24 Hours, Second Edition
Dick Oliver
ISBN: 1-57521-366-4
$19.99 USA/$28.95 CAN

Sams Teach Yourself SQL in 24 Hours
Ryan Stephens and Ronald R. Plew
ISBN: 0-672-31245-X
$24.99 USA/$35.95 CAN

Sams Teach Yourself Visual C++ 6 in 24 Hours
Mickey Williams
ISBN: 0-672-31303-0
$24.99 USA/$35.95 CAN

Sams Teach Yourself Visual Basic 6 in 24 Hours
Greg Perry and Sanjaya Hettihewa
ISBN: 0-672-31306-5
$19.99 USA/$28.95 CAN

www.samspublishing.com

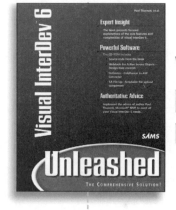

Visual InterDev 6 Unleashed
Paul Thurrott, et al.
ISBN: 0-672-31262-X
$49.99 USA/$74.95 CAN

Sams Teach Yourself MFC in 24 Hours
Michael Morrison
ISBN: 0-672-31553-X
$24.99 USA/$37.95 CAN

All prices are subject to change.

CD-ROM Installation Instructions

Windows 95/NT 4

1. Insert the CD-ROM into your CD-ROM drive. (See the Note following these steps.)

2. From the Windows desktop, double-click the My Computer icon.

3. Double-click the icon representing your CD-ROM drive.

4. Double-click the icon titled START.EXE to run the multimedia user interface.

 If Windows 95/NT 4 is installed on your computer and you have the AutoPlay feature enabled, the Start.exe program starts automatically whenever you insert the disc into your CD-ROM drive.

Read This Before Opening the Software

By opening this package, you are agreeing to be bound by the following agreement:

You may not copy or redistribute the entire CD-ROM as a whole. Copying and redistribution of individual software programs on the CD-ROM are governed by terms set by individual copyright holders.

The installer and code from the author(s) are copyrighted by the publisher and the author(s). Individual programs and other items on the CD-ROM are copyrighted or are under GNU license by their various authors or other copyright holders.

This software is sold as is without warranty of any kind, either expressed or implied, including but not limited to the implied warranties of merchantability and fitness for a particular purpose. Neither the publisher nor its dealers or distributors assume any liability for any alleged or actual damages arising from the use of this program. (Some states do not allow for the exclusion of implied warranties, so the exclusion may not apply to you.)

NOTE: This CD-ROM uses long and mixed-case filenames requiring the use of a protected-mode CD-ROM driver.